The Pet Shop Boys and the Political

The Pet Shop Boys and the Political

Queerness, Culture, Identity and Society

EDITED BY BODIE A. ASHTON

BLOOMSBURY ACADEMIC
LONDON • NEW YORK • OXFORD • NEW DELHI • SYDNEY

BLOOMSBURY ACADEMIC
Bloomsbury Publishing Plc
50 Bedford Square, London, WC1B 3DP, UK
1385 Broadway, New York, NY 10018, USA
29 Earlsfort Terrace, Dublin 2, Ireland

BLOOMSBURY, BLOOMSBURY ACADEMIC and the Diana logo are trademarks of
Bloomsbury Publishing Plc

First published in Great Britain 2024

Copyright © Bodie A. Ashton, 2024

Bodie A. Ashton has asserted his right under the Copyright, Designs and Patents Act, 1988, to be identified as Editor of this work.

For legal purposes the Acknowledgements on pp. x–xii constitute an extension of this copyright page.

Cover image: Neil Tennant and Chris Lowe of Pet Shop Boys perform live for fans at the Carriageworks on 6 June 2014 in Sydney, Australia. Photo by Mark Metcalfe/Getty Images.

All rights reserved. No part of this publication may be reproduced or transmitted in any form or by any means, electronic or mechanical, including photocopying, recording, or any information storage or retrieval system, without prior permission in writing from the publishers.

This book is an academic study which references the band and music of the Pet Shop Boys as a metaphor to explore the issues of queerness, culture and identity within society. Although this book references the band, it is in no way connected to or endorsed by them.

Bloomsbury Publishing Plc does not have any control over, or responsibility for, any third-party websites referred to or in this book. All internet addresses given in this book were correct at the time of going to press. The author and publisher regret any inconvenience caused if addresses have changed or sites have ceased to exist, but can accept no responsibility for any such changes.

A catalogue record for this book is available from the British Library.

A catalog record for this book is available from the Library of Congress.

ISBN: HB: 978-1-3503-3157-0
PB: 978-1-3503-3156-3
ePDF: 978-1-3503-3159-4
eBook: 978-1-3503-3158-7

Typeset by RefineCatch Limited, Bungay, Suffolk

To find out more about our authors and books visit www.bloomsbury.com and sign up for our newsletters.

For Kristian, Barry and Colin from revolution to revelation

CONTENTS

List of Figures ix
Acknowledgements x

Introduction: Hit Music, Disco Potential, Pop Kids *Bodie A. Ashton* 1

PART ONE It's All About Change, It's a Metamorphosis: The Personal-Political 15

1. Che Guevara and Debussy to a Disco Beat: Intellectualism and the Pet Shop Boys
   Antares Russell Leask 17

2. The End of the West: Community and Chorus in the Pet Shop Boys since 'Go West' *Adrian Daub* 35

3. He Dreamed of Machines: Queer Heritage and the Pet Shop Boys' 'Turing Test' *Bodie A. Ashton* 49

PART TWO Blaming the Colour TV: Neoliberal and Capitalist Critique 75

4. Buying and Selling your History: Navigating the Ruins of Neoliberalism with Tennant and Lowe
   Jonathan Dean 77

5. The Currency We Spent: The Pet Shop Boys and the Actualization of Thatcherite Economics
   Stephanie Polsky 95

6 Moscow or Manderley? Spectrality and Sovietism in the Pet Shop Boys' Oeuvre. *Carolin Isabel Steiner* 115

PART THREE We Came From Outer Space: Siting and Spatiality 139

7 'All That Swinging Sixties. It Didn't Do Anyone Any Good, Did It?' The Pet Shop Boys and the *Scandal* of the Profumo Affair *Christopher Spinks* 141

8 Go West, Young Band *Torsten Kathke* 165

PART FOUR We're the Pet Shop Boys: Metanarrativity and Manifestations 187

9 It's a Sin: Religious Imagery and Queer Identities in *It Couldn't Happen Here Lisa-Marie Pöhland* 189

10 What Have I Done to Deserve This? Personal, Professional and Political Representations in *Smash Hits* during the 'Imperial Phase' (1986–8) *Lexi Webster* 209

11 You've Been Around but You Don't Look Too Rough: *Dreamworld: The Greatest Hits Live* and the Pet Shop Boys as Legacy Artists *A. S. Waysdorf* 225

12 It's (Not) Obvious: Queerness and Queer Identities Pre- and Post-*Bilingual Bodie A. Ashton and Carolin Isabel Steiner* 245

Index 267

LIST OF FIGURES

0.1	The Pet Shop Boys (Chris Lowe and Neil Tennant) during a photo shoot coinciding with 1987's *Actually*.	6
3.1	Alan Turing, the computer scientist and mathematician to whom *A Man from the Future* is dedicated.	51
4.1	British Prime Minister Margaret Thatcher (1979–90), under whose government the United Kingdom entered a period loosely known as 'neoliberalism'.	84
5.1	The Brixton riots of 1981 underscored deep racialized and class tensions in the United Kingdom in the 1980s.	108
6.1	The architectural style of Brutalism is probably best exemplified by London's Barbican Estate.	122
6.2	The iconic Korg MS10 synth – typical of early Tennant/Lowe songs.	126
7.1	11 June 1963: Model and showgirl Christine Keeler with osteopath Stephen Ward. Sally Joan Norie is at the front.	143
8.1	Tennant and Lowe's costumes for 'Go West' (1993) – a distinct change from their previously dour, understated sartorial presentation.	167
11.1	The Pet Shop Boys' 2022–3 *Dreamworld: The Greatest Hits* tour.	227
11.2	Twitter thread reacting to the Glastonbury set in the *Dreamworld* tour.	237

ACKNOWLEDGEMENTS

We tend not to acknowledge when things don't go according to plan, so let me begin by stating that this book arose from an ambition going askew.

Back in 2020, I saw a call for papers for an edited collection that combined a number of my research and personal interests: history, spatiality, pop music. It was in the early days of the first lockdowns in Germany, I was nearing the end of my employment contract at my university, and in the dark and depressing atmosphere of those months I reached for one of my great loves – the Pet Shop Boys. I wrote an abstract and submitted it and, in relatively short order, I was informed that it hadn't been selected for the volume. It was disappointing, but as I reflected (okay, and sulked; I admit it) I began to wonder if there was more here than one short chapter could cover. So I began asking around: who else in my circles liked the Pet Shop Boys? Who might see some applicability to their research? Was there something deeper to say about them? The answer was a resounding yes.

And so here we are, and the first order of business must be to acknowledge all those who made this possible. The contributors to this volume – in alphabetical order: Adrian Daub, Jonathan Dean, Torsten Kathke, Antares Russell Leask, Lisa-Marie Pöhland, Stephanie Polsky, Christopher Spinks, Carolin Isabel Steiner, Abby S. Waysdorf and Lexi Webster – are among the brightest, most enthusiastic scholars it has been my pleasure to work with. In the course of this project, they have made my job as editor that much easier by approaching everything with verve, enjoyment, excitement and good faith. It was not uncommon to get an email well ahead of schedule from one or more of these authors, apologizing that they couldn't help but nerd out over their chapter, and therefore I was receiving their work early. Periodic emails from contributors sharing with me what album was playing while they were writing their conclusion, or letting me know that they'd just been to one of the Pet Shop Boys' most recent concerts, or that they'd just heard a song on the radio and thought I should know, brightened my days and reminded me once more that academia, for all its problems, can at its best be a wonderfully vibrant community. The success of this volume is down to these superstars; any errors are mine.

Maddie Holder at Bloomsbury has been enthusiastic about this work from the get-go. She, along with Meg Harris, has been patient and accommodating throughout the entire process, and I have always felt supported by them. I would also like to point to the beautiful cover design,

ACKNOWLEDGEMENTS

put together by Terry Woodley, introduced to me by email as 'our fabulous designer Terry'. I'm sure you can see precisely why he deserves that praise! Thanks as well to the production editor, Paige Harris, as well as Joe Kreuser and Wei Ming Kam, who are responsible for marketing. They have all contributed to making this project, above all, *fun*.

A special thank you must go to Wayne Studer. Many Pet Shop Boys fans will know Wayne from his website, *Commentary*, which contains an absolutely prodigious amount of information about every Pet Shop Boys song and album. Wayne was also extremely kind in making himself available to answer impromptu and sometimes arcane questions, and I know that it is not just me who has benefitted from his knowledge while putting this book together.

My love for the Pet Shop Boys springs chiefly from three people: my brother, Kristian Ashton, and my godparents, Barry Biddle and Colin Smith. I remember very fondly indeed the many, many house parties Barry and Colin would host at their home in Adelaide, when as a child I would sit outside under their trellises and *Very* or *Behaviour* would be blaring out of their verandah-mounted speakers. Barry's sound system and its attendant music library were like a wonderland for young me. As for Kristian, it is never easy for siblings with an age gap of nearly a decade and a half to get along, but something that never failed to bridge that gap was our mutual excitement for the Pet Shop Boys. Every Pet Shop Boys concert I have been to, from the Royal Albert Hall to Baden-Baden, I have been in Kristian's company. He was responsible for my first piece of Pet Shop Boys merchandise – a CD copy of *Bilingual* – and there are usually very good odds that, if there's a concert in Germany, he'll call me to tell me that he's also bought me a ticket. It goes without saying, then, that without Kristian, Barry and Colin, this volume would not exist.

Many thanks also must go to those who have given so much support, both material and moral, throughout this process (which has included not only the normal rigours of publishing and the uncertainties of working in academia in these difficult times, but also a global pandemic). Carolin Steiner's unstinting guidance and assistance has brought the joy back to writing and has been a firm reminder that this all works best when you're having fun. Esther Motavasseli, Enno Hulloch and Sascha Harnisch were kind enough to provide valuable feedback on working drafts, and the entire student cohort of my class 'Community, Identity, and Dissent in Modern Song' in the winter semester of 2022–3 at the University of Erfurt also gave fabulous input as I tested ideas on them. My colleagues at the University of Erfurt, particularly Sarah Frenking and Ned Richardson-Little, have not only been enthusiastic but also very understanding when my normally sporadic email responses dropped to virtually non-existent in the final phases of this project; thank you so much for your patience! And, of course, Sam Knapton and Bella Fuss were always available to offer a sympathetic ear (or shoulder) whenever it was needed.

My four-legged feline companions Cap and Bucky have been accompanying me on this journey since I wrote the call for proposals that lay the groundwork for this collection. During the final editing phases, they were joined by Amelia. I've discovered that they all have *excellent* taste in music. Any typographical errors are likely due to one of them – and therefore they're not so much 'errors' as 'editorial comment'.

Finally, of course, my enduring thanks to Neil Tennant and Chris Lowe, who met one day in a hi-fi shop on the King's Road in Chelsea and discovered that they had similar interests. The rest is history. So, it is fitting, then, that my contributors and I met because of our love of the Pet Shop Boys, and now we have the pleasure to write about that very history. But, as they say, that's the way life is.

Bodie A. Ashton
Erfurt, March 2023

Introduction

Hit Music, Disco Potential, Pop Kids

Bodie A. Ashton

'A basic principle of my lyric-writing and our songwriting is that we should try to bring ideas and concepts from outside pop into our songs,' Neil Tennant wrote in the introduction to his *One Hundred Lyrics and a Poem* in 2018.[1] As the more visible (and more vocal) half of the English pop group Pet Shop Boys, Tennant has now been writing lyrics and songs in a career spanning, at the time of writing, some five decades – beginning in the 1980s, through the 1990s and the 2000s and the 2010s, and continuing actively into the 2020s. In that time, Tennant and his bandmate, Chris Lowe, have amassed an impressive back catalogue that would make even the most successful industry veterans envious. At the time of writing, the group has released no fewer than fourteen studio albums, beginning with *Please* (1986) and concluding with *Hotspot* (2020). With those albums have come more than seventy singles, along with four remix albums – all named *Disco* – as well as four EPs and a number of compilations. The group's most recent collection, *Smash: The Singles, 1985–2020*, was released in 2023 and includes more than fifty tracks.

The reader might be forgiven for imagining *Smash* to be the group's swansong but, on the contrary, its publication would seem to cement a continuation of the Pet Shop Boys legacy; indeed, not only has the duo

---

[1] Neil Tennant, *One Hundred Lyrics and a Poem, 1979–2016* (London: Faber & Faber, 2018), xx.

released more music that, having come since 2020, will not appear on this Greatest Hits collection, but another studio album is in the works.[2] Beyond this already formidable discography, Tennant and Lowe have shaped the artistic landscape in other ways, too. In 1987 they starred in *It Couldn't Happen Here*, a surrealist film directed by Jack Bond and based around a soundtrack of the Pet Shop Boys' then-limited back catalogue. Two years later, they wrote 'Nothing Has Been Proved' for Dusty Springfield, which became the title track for the film *Scandal*. By 1993, they produced the soundtrack for the Academy Award-winning *The Crying Game*, with Tennant supporting Boy George with backing vocals for the title song. Other projects followed, demonstrating an increasingly ambitious drive: in 2001, in conjunction with Jonathan Harvey, they wrote and produced the musical *Closer to Heaven*, while in 2005 they collaborated with the Dresden Symphonic Orchestra to compose a new score for Sergei Eisenstein's legendary silent film, *Battleship Potemkin* (1925). The following decade, the duo wrote a score for the ballet *The Most Incredible Thing* (2011), along with music for a spinoff play to *Closer to Heaven*, entitled *Musik* (2019), and the soundtrack for a Leicester-based staging of Hanif Kureishi's *My Beautiful Laundrette* (2019). In between all of this, their music was celebrated at the BBC Proms in 2014 – an unprecedented honour for a pop group – and, in 2020, the *Guardian* named their debut single 'West End Girls' (1985) the greatest UK number one of all time.[3]

All this to say: the Pet Shop Boys have amassed a vast body of work, and that body is still growing. None of that, however, has happened within a social, political, economic or cultural vacuum. It is hardly groundbreaking to say that musicians, like authors or painters or other artists, are deeply influenced in what they create by the world around them and the lives they live. Indeed, Neil Tennant identifies this as the 'basic principle' by which he writes and records. For the Pet Shop Boys, the decades in which they have been active have seen extraordinary changes. They have witnessed – and produced songs about – the urban decay of Thatcher-era austerity; the crushing fear of being exposed as queer in Section 28-era Britain; the end of the Cold War and the collapse of European communism; the emergence of a hopeful movement of international queer pride that began to move LGBTQIA+ people and relationships into the mainstream; the horrors of terrorism and the excesses of the Western hegemony in the post-9/11 world; the advent of marriage equality for (some) queer couples in the United States, United Kingdom and many other parts of the world; Britain's entry into and exit from the European Union; and the rise of fascist-adjacent

---

[2]Alan York, 'Pet Shop Boys release "Lost" EP, their first new music in three years', *Dig!*, 17 April 2023, https://www.thisisdig.com/pet-shop-boys-lost-ep-new-music-three-years/.
[3]Laura Snapes, 'The 100 Greatest UK No 1s: No 1, Pet Shop Boys – West End Girls', *Guardian*, 5 June 2020, https://www.theguardian.com/music/2020/jun/05/the-100-greatest-uk-no-1s-no-1-pet-shop-boys-west-end-girls.

reactionary movements in countries once lauded as bastions of liberal democracy. At the same time, while these events and many others have affected the songs that Tennant and Lowe write, those songs have conversely also provided a soundtrack for those events.

The Pet Shop Boys and the Political seeks to glimpse both ways through this lens. This volume brings together scholars from a number of disciplines – history, English literature, German studies, media studies, political science and theory, among others – to cast fresh eyes (or perhaps, ears) on the Pet Shop Boys' oeuvre and the Pet Shop Boys themselves. In doing this, we ask elemental questions: what can we learn about the times in which Tennant and Lowe write and record? What can we learn about Tennant and Lowe? Are they simply mirrors of their eras? Or can we trace agency, action, a guiding hand through their works and acts? In other words: to what extent have the Pet Shop Boys not only reported on and reflected events, but fashioned them?

A single volume cannot hope to take into account all that there is to say; with *The Pet Shop Boys and the Political*, we aim to make a comprehensive, but by definition incomplete, foray. We hope that fans will find new ways to listen to Tennant and Lowe, that academics will recognize the potential importance of the Pet Shop Boys to our disciplines, and that newcomers might be as entranced as we are by the Pet Shop Boys' 'alchemy'. Their endurance, we argue, not only reflects their ability, as identified by the *Economist* in 2019, to 'transmute sadness into joy',[4] but rather a singular ability to bear witness to, reflect and also shape distinct moments in identity formation and politics. The Pet Shop Boys are not just a source through which history can be viewed. They themselves are history.

But if is wasn't and isn't were: reading the Pet Shop Boys academically

Neil Tennant and Chris Lowe began recording music together in the early 1980s, after a fateful meeting in a hi-fi store in Chelsea in 1981. Tennant, who had majored in history at a polytechnic, was a journalist and editor at the music magazine *Smash Hits*; Lowe, an architecture student at the University of Liverpool, was on placement in London. Their collaboration came at an auspicious moment, in which historical currents – artistic, political, social, economic – were busily converging over their heads and on the streets they walked. Disco, it appeared, was dead. Rock offered empty, unrelatable content, typified by 'big and pompous and ugly [. . .] dinosaur groups'.[5] Tennant and Lowe's mutual love for pop music, and their interest

---

[4]"Pet Shop Boys achieved a kind of alchemy that only pop music can', *Economist*, 23 June 2022, https://www.economist.com/culture/2022/06/23/pet-shop-boys-achieved-a-kind-of-alchemy-that-only-music-can.
[5]Chris Heath, *Pet Shop Boys, Literally* (London: William Heinemann, 2020), 181.

in the electronic-inspired styles of Depeche Mode, Soft Cell, Orchestral Manoeuvres in the Dark and Kraftwerk, merged into a palpable disenfranchisement and a complex relationship with the time and place in which they found themselves. After some initial demo recordings in Camden, Tennant was sent to New York to interview The Police; here, he took the opportunity to meet with legendary producer Bobby Orlando. Impressed with what he heard, Orlando produced Tennant and Lowe's very first singles: 'West End Girls', 'One More Chance' and 'Opportunities (Let's Make Lots of Money)'. None achieved commercial success, but the potential was obvious. In March 1985, they signed with EMI and began re-recording with Stephen Hague, with the aim of producing an album of ten songs.

Chris Heath, the music journalist who would become something of a chronicler of the group, would later recount the genesis of this album in his liner notes for its remastered edition in 2018:

> *Please* was recorded with Stephen Hague at Advision studios in London between November 1985 and January 1986, working from midday until midnight, breaking mid-evening to visit Efre's Turkish kebab house down the road. 'We would drink a bottle of retsina, if not two bottles, and come back half-drunk', says Neil. Occasionally they would take time off to perform 'West End Girls' on *Top Of The Pops* and *Wogan*, as it slowly rose to number one in the British chart. At one point during the recording, the studio manager said, 'So you're the singer, Neil? I thought you were the manager.'[6]

This experience typifies much of the Pet Shop Boys themselves: in many ways understated, sometimes overlooked but, ultimately, a big deal (how else would they appear on *Wogan* at the height of Terry Wogan's popularity?) They blended in, and in doing so could stand above and observe. They were queer-coded before the term existed, but they were so at the time of the Section 28 restrictions on the 'promotion of homosexuality' in neo-conservative, Thatcherite Britain. They toyed with the hallmarks of Britishness – sly references dot their work, many of which would be impenetrable to those not already familiar with Britain, and Tennant's exacting enunciation and his received pronunciation while performing became immediate hallmarks of their discography – even while offering a side-eye to an establishment they felt had clearly failed them. It was here that their reputation for irony was established, one that is at once both earned and unfair. Like all good artists, their work reflects the circumstances in which it was made, but as their careers now enter their fifth decade, they have assumed the type of timelessness that very few musical artists manage to achieve. What's old is

---

[6] Chris Heath, 'Pet Shop Boys 1984–1986', *Pet Shop Boys Please/Further Listening 1984–1986* liner notes (2018), i.

new again; is it any wonder that a group that produced songs about one deadly illness would, as the 2020 Covid pandemic struck, re-record their very first hit in a 'lockdown version'? As queer rights come under renewed assault in their native Britain, how fitting that 'It's a Sin', the quintessential song of the 1980s gay identity struggle, would lend its name to an acclaimed television production about that era, whose message seems as urgent today as it did back then? And what does it tell us when, as Britain withdrew from the European Union, a synthpop group that has been labelled throughout their careers as 'quintessentially English' recorded a brand-new album in Berlin and declared themselves to be 'so tired of my homeland'?

Songs, like all artistic media, are open to the interpretation of the listener. The death of the author – or singer, as the case might be here – can, however, clash with historical fact. No matter how much a source might *seem* to comment on an event, we must be careful not to give too much credit (or perhaps agency) and see the tiger in the shadows where there is none. In 2022 I taught an undergraduate course on the cultural histories of modern disasters, in which one of my examples was the 1987 King's Cross Underground Station fire in London. This fire, which killed thirty-one people, seemed in many ways to exemplify the malaise that had gripped late-1980s Britain: disorganization, moribund infrastructure and a peculiar lack of care and concern, as people who could see smoke and flames nevertheless made their way on to a burning wooden escalator and bustled past each other to queue in the ticket hall. As a cultural artefact I imagined 'King's Cross', the last song on the Pet Shop Boys' 1987 album *Actually*, because of how eloquently it spoke to the tragedy: 'Good luck, bad luck, waiting in a line', the allusions to the 'dead and wounded on either side', and 'murder' skulking in the shadows. The one problem with this, as I only realized well into my excitement, was that 'King's Cross' is not about the fire at all, for the simple reason that it couldn't be; the tragedy occurred on 18 November 1987, more than two months after *Actually* was released to the public. Crisis suitably averted, but a timely and object lesson in not reading more into the sources than they will actually allow.

Such critical reflection also came at the very beginning of this project, indeed at the very point of submitting the proposal to the commissioning editors at Bloomsbury. Putting together an edited collection is difficult for a number of reasons, but one of them is that, as the editor, you hope that the idea that you have had for the book, an idea that excites *you*, will translate into an equal excitement for others, who will believe in the project and who will devote time to writing for it. This volume is blessed with a number of outstanding scholars from a variety of fields, as I had hoped when I wrote the call for papers extolling the global influence and universality of the Pet Shop Boys. Yet, for a collection appealing to global applicability, it is remarkably constrained: as far east as Germany, as far west as California, and (if we're being generous) the equator as its southernmost extent. Initially, this surprised me. I know that the Pet Shop Boys have an extensive fanbase

FIGURE 0.1 *The Pet Shop Boys (Chris Lowe (left) and Neil Tennant) during a photo shoot coinciding with 1987's* Actually. *Getty Images, Mike Prior / Contributor.*

that extends far beyond Europe or the United States. Their very first tour, in 1989 (and suitably titled *MCMLXXXIX*), took them to Hong Kong and Japan. In 1994, the *Discovery* tour took them to Australia, Puerto Rico, Mexico, Columbia, Chile, Argentina and Brazil. The cover of the single 'Was it Worth it?' (1991) features two hand-crafted woollen dolls representing both Neil Tennant and Chris Lowe; these were sent to them by a Japanese fan. Fertile ground, I imagined, for some truly intersectional considerations that would engage closely with those voices all too often marginalized within the academy, defined here not only by nationality but also through gender, sexuality and disability.

This volume showcases the work of a number of authors at different career stages, ranging from professors to early career researchers. A variety of gender identities and sexualities are represented, as are neurodivergent scholars. This is heartening, and certainly what I had hoped we would accomplish when I originally mapped out this project. In one regard, however, this work fails to be representative, and that is with regards to the platforming of people of colour or from the Global South.

Why is this? A couple of reasons present themselves, and both require a bit of soul-searching. In the first instance, both academia and the publishing industry are in the process of a belated reckoning with themselves, the result of which is not yet clear. The treatment of scholars of colour, and particularly those hailing from the Global South, has long been a source of inequity within the academy, but in recent years this has been thrown into sharp relief. As many in academic circles are slowly waking up to the precarity faced by junior scholars, the urgent cries of colleagues from other marginalized communities have far too often been ignored.

Simply put, in pitching this volume as a work of scholarship through the conventional networks that I have become used to, it may well be that I have inadvertently excluded many who might otherwise have wished to participate. Alternatively, while the results of this work are exciting and innovative, and offer truly revolutionary ways to look at the Pet Shop Boys and pop music as historical artefacts, the genesis of the book comes via a well-trodden scholarly process that, as we are all too slowly acknowledging, contains built-in inequalities and reasons for underrepresented voices within academia to be suspicious. If this is the case, then I can only hope that this volume will encourage further scholarship that engages with the voices of racially- and geographically-marginalized writers and that, in turn, we may find ways to overcome the discriminatory inertia that characterizes our fields.

A second reason for this imbalance may also stem from a similar Eurocentric arrogance, this time squarely on my part. Having been aware of the Pet Shop Boys' international fanbase, and cognisant of the band's themes and messaging, I took it for granted that listeners in Rio or Osaka or San Juan would be drawing the same connections that I did, listening for the same lessons and allusions. But this is clearly not the case. There is certainly a universality to the Pet Shop Boys' work – of that I am more convinced than ever – but there is also significant particularism at play. *Actually* (1987) – argued by many to be the quintessential Pet Shop Boys album – could only have been recorded in the context of Thatcherism; *Fundamental* (2006) acts as a commentary on the War on Terror and the degeneration towards a Blairite surveillance state; *Hotspot* (2020) is a love letter to Europe from the perspective of the 'citizens of nowhere' of the Brexit generation. Many of the queer tropes that found such resonance in British nightclubs failed to do the same over the Atlantic, where the Pet Shop Boys were at various junctures either *too* gay or not gay *enough*. When *MCMLXXXIX* took Neil Tennant to Japan, he was astonished to find a fan magazine, *Out of Order*, in which two fans conducted an 'earnest debate round the relationship between love and materialism, ownership and security, food and love', framed via an attempt to find the 'true meaning' of the single 'Rent' (1987). The crucial issue, they argued, was the fact that a conjunction was missing in the chorus:

'I love you / You pay my rent', and the contention lay in whether Tennant meant to sing 'I love you *but* you pay my rent' or 'I love you *that* you pay my rent.' With bemusement, Tennant told Chris Heath that there was no need whatsoever for any insertion, as the two lines represented 'two separate functions: "I love you" and "you pay my rent"'.[7] That which seemed self-evident to Tennant was not necessarily so to his audience, especially an audience that shared neither his language nor his background. It is also not to be underestimated that a world still imprinted with the legacies of British imperialism may stand on unsteady ground when considering the Pet Shop Boys: a group that, on the one hand, has been outspoken in its criticism of the Royal Family – 'I think he should be garrotted,' Lowe once said (likely sardonically) of now-King Charles III[8] – but that, on the other hand, self-consciously reflects a quintessential Englishness, and that also toys playfully with the language and trappings of empire.[9]

The Pet Shop Boys do not speak to global or transracial experiences precisely because they cannot, and in some cases they seem to recognize this themselves. In this regard, it is perhaps of little surprise that this book reflects this situation. It is, however, our hope and intention that this volume might open up new avenues by which to consider Tennant and Lowe's decades-long careers, for which perspectives from outside a white, Global North baseline are not only welcome but, in our opinion, desired and overdue.

Bourgeois constructs

This collection is comprised of twelve chapters divided into four sections, each engaging with overarching themes within the Pet Shop Boys' oeuvre. The first focuses on what here is termed the 'personal-political', that is, the intersection between the artistic personae and political commentary. We open with Antares Russell Leask's 'Che Guevara and Debussy to a Disco Beat: Intellectualism and the Pet Shop Boys', which lays the programmatic foundations for this work. Leask argues for an intellectual rereading of the Pet Shop Boys, considered through the lens of a group too often dismissed as 'inauthentic pop'. In doing so, Leask reflects on the joy of being an academic and a Pet Shop Boys fan, and of combining the two.

Adrian Daub's 'The End of the West' reconsiders the use of chorus in Pet Shop Boys songs as a signifier of community and the struggles, both internal and external, engendered within that concept. While the Pet Shop Boys had occasionally used choral backing beforehand, most notably in 1990's 'My

---

[7]Heath, *Pet Shop Boys, Literally*, 191.
[8]Chris Heath, *Pet Shop Boys versus America* (London: William Heinemann, 2020), 14.
[9]Among other things, Neil Tennant famously invented the term 'imperial phase' to describe the period at which the Pet Shop Boys were at the zenith of their critical and commercial success.

October Symphony', with the advent of the disco-inspired *Very* (1993) the chorus became a vital element to the Pet Shop Boys' most explicitly queer works, typified by that album's famous cover of the Village People's 'Go West'. Daub orders the tonal experience of the chorus within the stories expressed in the songs, recognizing its use not only as a signifier of queer experience (indeed, consciously recalling the style of gay pioneer acts such as the Village People themselves) but also a means by which to express the cynical flipside of community. Thus, while the Pet Shop Boys often revel in gay existence, their compositions also reflect the realities of that existence, with harmonious voices often bringing to light doubt and conflict rather than unequivocal and naïve affirmation.

In 'He Dreamed of Machines: Queer Heritage and the Pet Shop Boys "Turing Test"', I turn my attention to the Pet Shop Boys' 2014 appearance at the BBC Proms, and the premiere of their operatic biography of the computer pioneer, mathematician and Second World War code-breaker Alan Turing, who was convicted in 1952 because of 'homosexual acts' and who ultimately took his own life. This was Tennant and Lowe's second intervention on behalf of Turing's legacy – in 2012, Tennant personally requested that the British government posthumously pardon Turing. However, I argue that both this appeal and the stage production, *A Man from the Future*, are not isolated incidents but rather logical culminations of consistent, decades-long activism and outreach that Tennant and Lowe have undertaken in the service of LGBTQIA+ rights.

The second section of this collection examines the Pet Shop Boys' relationship with the political-economic realities of the world in which they have performed (and upon which they have editorialized) since the 1980s. Having come to prominence in the mid-1980s, and being active ever since, the Pet Shop Boys' genesis was dominated by the Cold War, the supposed triumph of neoliberal capitalism over Soviet communism and ultimately the discrediting and crumbling of the neoliberal façade, leading inexorably to the seemingly contradictory but paradoxically symbiotic phenomena of hyper-capitalist consumption and the 'tightening of belts' of stark austerity politics. Jonathan Dean's 'Buying and Selling Your History' turns inwards, asking what the Pet Shop Boys understand neoliberalism to be. In doing so, Dean argues that the neoliberal critiques inherent in *Please* and *Actually* continue not only to permeate later Pet Shop Boys albums, singles and B-sides, but also to reflect that the damage wrought by Thatcher undergirds the key socio-economic difficulties faced by the United Kingdom to the present day. Thus, while Tennant and Lowe do not necessarily offer us blueprints to *overcome* the disasters of finance-at-all-costs, perhaps they *do* provide us with templates and patterns to recognize and to address as we continue to come to terms with a past that remains present (and threatens to endure). In 'The Currency We Spent: The Pet Shop Boys and the Actualization of Thatcherite Economics', Stephanie Polsky places the Pet Shop Boys' first two albums, *Please* (1986) and *Actually* (1987), within the context of the decaying economic power of the City of London and the shift of Margaret Thatcher's socio-economic policies towards those of punitive austerity and the extirpation of the urban working class. Polsky argues that the Pet Shop Boys' reputation for irony is a direct consequence of the transformation of London into a dystopia populated by 'skinheads' and 'ruthless City boys', and that the Pet Shop Boys' 'imperial phase' is intimately intertwined with the Thatcherite discrediting of the very idea of society.

If, then, neoliberal capitalism has failed, what is the alternative? In 'Moscow or Manderley? Spectrality and Sovietism in the Pet Shop Boys' Oeuvre', Carolin Isabel Steiner engages with two recurring motifs of the Pet Shop Boys' discography and performance: Soviet imagery and the haunting of ghosts. Through a hauntological analysis, Steiner argues that these motifs are connected to a wider malaise: a recognition that neoliberalism has deconstructed the ideals it claimed to represent, and a longing not for the long-discredited Soviet alternative but instead of what that alternative in its idealized form pretended to embody. Thus put, the 'ghosts of love' that haunt the Pet Shop Boys' music are not read only as romantic sorrow but also as a lamentation of a future that never was.

Part Three investigates the immediate spatiality of the Pet Shop Boys' work: what elements can tell us of their time and place. This section opens with Christopher Spinks, who returns to the infamous Profumo affair of 1963. This scandal saw the end of the career of the British Secretary of State for War, John Profumo, the suicide of prominent society osteopath Stephen Ward and ultimately the collapse of the Macmillan government. Spinks notes that Profumo, rather unexpectedly, appeared in song twice in 1989: Billy Joel's 'We Didn't Start the Fire' reduced the whole affair to 'British politician sex', while the Pet Shop Boys devoted a whole song, 'Nothing Has Been Proved', as a corrective to the treatment of Ward. Placing the song within the context of being recorded as a demo for the soundtrack of the film *Scandal*, Spinks relates that the recording of 'Nothing Has Been Proved' by Tennant and Lowe's collaborator Dusty Springfield provides its own level of meta-commentary. This suggests that the Pet Shop Boys sought not only to rehabilitate Ward by highlighting the prejudices ranged against him, but through this also aimed to facilitate the further rehabilitation of Springfield, whose career had foundered owing to the anti-queer press, only for it to begin to recover with the recording of 'What Have I Done to Deserve This?' in 1987.

This is followed by Torsten Kathke, whose 'Go West, Young Band' complements Adrian Daub's contribution by conducting a deep dive into the Pet Shop Boys' 1993 cover of the Village People's 'Go West'. In doing so, Kathke asks what the implications are for a minor hit by an American disco group in 1979 that was transplanted and overhauled in the 1990s by a British synthpop duo, and how, in turn, this affects the specifically American motifs employed in the song, ranging from nineteenth-century frontier expansionism to the immediate post-Cold War reality. Ultimately, the Pet Shop Boys' relationship with history is not only that of outside observers looking in, but also of actors within that history themselves.

The last section examines the metanarrativity of the Pet Shop Boys' texts – the occasions in which they provide commentary on themselves – and how these manifest. Tennant and Lowe's 1987 film *It Couldn't Happen Here* is the subject of Lisa-Marie Pöhland's chapter, as she analyses the religious motifs and imagery as it reflects on the Pet Shop Boys' own upbringings. Pöhland argues that the movie expresses the struggles of growing up queer under the influence of religious orthodoxy and thus also works as social criticism.

Continuing the theme of the Pet Shop Boys engaging with other forms of media, Lexi Webster's chapter, 'What Have I Done to Deserve This? Personal, Professional and Political Representations in *Smash Hits* during the "Imperial Phase" (1986–8)', explores the role played by the music magazine *Smash Hits* during the Pet Shop Boys' period of greatest success. Acknowledging that this 'imperial phase' directly followed Neil Tennant's tenure as an assistant editor at the magazine, Webster questions the relationship between the notoriously press-shy Tennant and Lowe and *Smash Hits* and, by analysing not only articles but also interviews, reviews and letters, she posits that *Smash Hits* played an integral (and perhaps contradictory) part in developing the image of the Pet Shop Boys that would endure until the present day.

Abby S. Waysdorf's chapter, 'You've Been Around but You Don't Look Too Rough: *Dreamworld: The Greatest Hits Live* and the Pet Shop Boys as Legacy Artists', poses the question of how musicians can shape *how* they are remembered, and what their legacy is and means. In order to do this, she examines the (at time of writing) most recent Pet Shop Boys tour, *Dreamworld*, billed as a 'greatest hits' tour, and thus postulates what 'greatest hits' means in the age of streaming, for whom it caters and how it can shape the public image of the band within the eyes of its fans and the public as a whole.

If legacy is important to the Pet Shop Boys, then it is clear that one of their most tangible legacies is that of their queerness. It is, indeed, through a queer lens that much of their work is understood. Yet to some extent this was never their intention; in fact, for the first decade of their careers, Tennant and Lowe studiously avoided making public comment on their sexualities – a policy that changed dramatically, albeit under some duress, when Tennant publicly came out in an interview in 1994. In 'It's (Not) Obvious: Queerness and Queer Identities Pre- and Post-*Bilingual*', Carolin Steiner and I return to this moment and postulate that it constitutes a vital pivot not only in the Pet Shop Boys' public personas, but also in their musical output. We argue that their work until 1994 was heavily queer-coded but for the most part avoided taking strong, explicit stances on queerness. After Tennant came out, however, the Pet Shop Boys embraced their newfound sexual openness, resulting in 1996's *Bilingual* – arguably their most gay album of all.

'Cause we love the pop hits and quoted the best bits

When I was growing up, my brother Kristian occupied a world that I, thirteen years younger, did not. In retrospect, it was surely not easy for him, going through the moody teenage years and all the trials of high school, to be saddled with an annoying kid brother, but to me, at the time, his invariably shut bedroom door at the end of the hallway was a rebuff, a distinct and sullen border drawn between the two of us.

There were a few exceptions to this rule, however. It was his most prized possessions, his ever-impressive stereo system and his seemingly uncontainable collection of cassette tapes, compact discs and VHS concert tapes, that would unite and bond us. Still very much in single digits, I didn't know anything about the clubs and parties he'd go to, where he'd hear the music that resonated so deeply with him – but I *did* know when he had something new to play, because then the amplifier would be turned up loud, the speakers would make the wooden floors vibrate and, even if his door was closed, I could still take up position outside, listening, learning. There is a reason why my own music collection is dominated by Elton John and Depeche Mode. And especially the Pet Shop Boys.

There is something a little ironic about this. The first song I remember learning by heart was 'Shopping', the third track on the Pet Shop Boys' second album, *Actually*. This should come as no surprise to anyone who knows my predilection for retail therapy – though of course I was too young to understand the critiques of neoliberalism wrapped up in the staccato 'S-H-O-P-P-I-N-G' chorus. As I developed a love for reading and writing, I'd also find ways to incorporate them into whatever I was doing; the first creative story I remember writing, perhaps at age five or so, included a section in which the main characters broke into an impromptu singalong of 'Domino Dancing', from 1988's *Introspective*.[10] Whatever plot I'd come up with escapes me now, but the inexplicable karaoke seems to have left an indelible memory. For Christmas 1996, my parents gifted me my own stereo, and Kristian gave me the latest Pet Shop Boys album, *Bilingual*, which would be played almost endlessly throughout the next year as I did my homework.

Simply put, the Pet Shop Boys were always there, providing the soundtrack as I worked out who I was and what I wanted to do with my life. I won't go so far as to claim that Neil Tennant and Chris Lowe turned me into a historian, but as I dutifully worked my way through their back

---

[10] This, it seems, is not something unique to me. More than one of the contributors to this volume, in our initial correspondences, told me that they often try to hide Pet Shop Boys lyrics in the titles, headings or body of their academic works, as a sort of in-joke for fellow fans.

catalogue, there were always tantalizing references to a history I didn't yet know, but which they made me want to find out. Who was Philby, who was 'in the desert, looking for a phone'? What happened in October, why would there be a symphony about it, and who wasn't saved? What history was being bought and sold? In the liner notes to *Alternative*, the two-disc collection of B-sides released in 1995, both Tennant and Lowe are interviewed by the journalist Jon Savage. Speaking about 'Don Juan', Tennant explained that the song was a metaphor for the political situation in the Balkans in the 1930s and the rise of Adolf Hitler in Germany, which apparently took Lowe by surprise. It isn't hard to imagine his cocked eyebrow as he asks his collaborator, 'Why isn't the song called "Hitler"?'[11] It may not have been my first introduction to historical allegory, but it remained in my head as an example of how music can comment on history, even if that history is abstracted by layers of artistic licence.

It would take a few years to grasp what Tennant and Lowe were trying to tell me; as a child, I knew very little of the HIV/AIDS epidemic and I understood 'Being Boring' only to be a very lovely song, bittersweet in ways I didn't yet quite have words for. 'Can You Forgive Her?' was a poppy break-up song (with a very snazzy swing version released on the single), but the queer subtext passed me by. It was clear that *Bilingual*'s 'Metamorphosis' was about sex (even going so far as to spell out 'the big S-E-X', which felt like some type of forbidden knowledge for a prepubescent listener), but it had only just been explained to me that my brother was gay, and what this meant – the awkwardly-phrased 'it means he enjoys the company of men', as though it was a type of country club or dinner party setting – and sexuality as a concept was still not on my radar.

Gradually, though, all these points would begin to converge. I would write essays while listening to *Bilingual*, *Actually*, *Please*, *Nightlife*, *Fundamental*, anything I could get my hands on. Echoes of the subject would be in the music that accompanied it. At the same time, as I slowly began to understand my own queerness, here were the Pet Shop Boys to help guide me through it. Fervent joy and unspeakable tragedy; the past, the present and the future: all these were wrapped up in the constant of Neil Tennant and Chris Lowe. And, as every new album was released, I'd comfort myself with their great familiarity, even as they experimented in different directions with their music. One of the most important lessons I learned while studying to become a historian is that, contrary to the old cliché, history does not repeat itself; in a similar fashion, a Pet Shop Boys record is unmistakably a Pet Shop Boys record, and yet not one of them is in the same mould of the one that comes before or after it.

---

[11]Chris Lowe and Neil Tennant, interview with Jon Savage, *Alternative Pet Shop Boys* liner notes (1995), 15.

Nothing is inevitable and everything is contingent; context is king. So here I might commit the cardinal sin for a historian and reach for inevitability: maybe it was preordained that I would at some point try to combine my love for the Pet Shop Boys with my love for history. As it turns out, I wasn't the only one who had made these connections. The result, which you are reading now, is a labour of serious scholarship, but also a labour of passion and love – and, indeed, sex, money, violence, religion, injustice and death. (If you, dear reader, did not hear the mournful refrain of 'Paninaro' while reading this, this book may not be for you.)

(On the other hand, maybe it is.)

Bibliography

Heath, Chris. 'Pet Shop Boys 1984–1986'. *Pet Shop Boys Please/Further Listening 1984–1986* liner notes (2018).

Heath, Chris. *Pet Shop Boys, Literally*. London: William Heinemann, 2020.

Heath, Chris. *Pet Shop Boys versus America*. London: William Heinemann, 2020.

'Pet Shop Boys achieved a kind of alchemy that only pop music can'. *Economist*, 23 June 2022, https://www.economist.com/culture/2022/06/23/pet-shop-boys-achieved-a-kind-of-alchemy-that-only-music-can.

Savage, Jon. *Alternative Pet Shop Boys* liner notes (1995).

Snapes, Laura. 'The 100 Greatest UK No 1s: No 1, Pet Shop Boys – West End Girls'. *Guardian*, 5 June 2020, https://www.theguardian.com/music/2020/jun/05/the-100-greatest-uk-no-1s-no-1-pet-shop-boys-west-end-girls.

Tennant, Neil. *One Hundred Lyrics and a Poem, 1979–2016*. London: Faber & Faber, 2018.

York, Alan. 'Pet Shop Boys release "Lost" EP, their first new music in three years'. *Dig!*, 17 April 2023, https://www.thisisdig.com/pet-shop-boys-lost-ep-new-music-three-years/.

PART ONE

It's All About Change, It's a Metamorphosis: The Personal-Political

CHAPTER ONE

Che Guevara and Debussy to a Disco Beat

Intellectualism and the Pet Shop Boys

Antares Russell Leask

I was singing, the words resonating through my body – ''Cause we were never being boring' – with tears streaming down my face, lost in this moment and this moment alone. It was my fifth Pet Shop Boys concert, but tonight, this song – 'We had too much time to find for ourselves' – just hit differently. My friends were somewhere behind me; I was standing on the lawn, having this moment entirely to myself: 'We dressed up and fought / then thought "make amends".'

Still sobbing, I turned back to my friends at the end of the song. They were unimpressed. One said, 'Well, that was certainly a boring way to end the concert.' I was confused. Don't they know the meaning behind that song? Don't they understand the importance of ending a concert with 'Being Boring', a song that Neil Tennant writes is 'infused with nostalgic sadness and anger'[1] about the AIDS crisis? That Tennant wrote the song in honour of a friend he had lost – and in honour of all the friends we have lost to AIDS? A song that on this 2022 tour was dedicated to those lost to Covid-19?

---

[1] Neil Tennant, *One Hundred Lyrics and a Poem: 1976–2016* (London: Faber & Faber, 2019), 11–12.

My confusion intensified when a friend of a friend wrote on Facebook, 'In what universe does New Order "warm up" for Pet Shop Boys?!??'[2] Yes, for the Unity Tour, the plan had been for the bands to alternate nights opening, and this had been two shows in a row that Pet Shop Boys had closed out the night. The New Order fans, who seemed to be the majority, were visibly bothered by the perceived slight. Don't they know about the cultural importance of the Pet Shop Boys?

Although it often feels like everyone around me misses the point and views the Pet Shop Boys as merely that 80s band who sang 'West End Girls', the duo has inspired a well-deserved following of die-hard fans, the sort of fans who know that the first version of 'West End Girls', which debuted on *Hits Des Clubs* in 1984, included the line, 'Who do you think you are, Joe Stalin?' and was 'influenced by the chattering voices in "The Wasteland"'.[3] Although devoted, these fans generally fall into two groups: those whose appreciation for PSB is limited to dancing to their catchy pop themes – what one columnist calls 'exhilarating, tastes-great-less-filling dance tunes injected with substantive lyrics'[4], and those who appreciate PSB on an intellectual level, for their thought-provoking and allusion-packed lyrics. The genius of Pet Shop Boys is that they acknowledge this duality and cater to each group without privileging one over the other.

Neil Tennant addresses the seeming dichotomy between dance music and intellectualism by telling biographer Chris Heath that the band 'genuinely love pop music'. First and foremost, their music is a self-conscious reflection of that love. But there's always something more going on beneath the surface of each song, if the listener wants there to be. Tennant goes on to explain:

> There's also a kind of assumption that if you're writing pop music it's not an important kind of music, whereas rock music [such as U2] is perceived as being an important kind of music [. . .] At the same time it doesn't mean that when you're writing a pop song it can't have some kind of serious meaning, and if people want to discover that for themselves that's great. At the same time if they don't want to . . . if they don't notice it . . . I think that's great as well, because they're just responding to pop music in different ways.[5]

But because of the honesty in their music and motivations, Pet Shop Boys expect other musicians to also present an honest view of the artist's role in society. Nearly thirty years after first contrasting their view of the power of pop with other bands such as U2, Tennant feels the same, writing in 2019

---

[2] Steve Kramer, 'In What Universe', Facebook, 21 September 2022, https://www.facebook.com/sheryl.stein.
[3] 'Back Story: Debussy to a Disco Beat', *Economist*, 25 June 2022, 86.
[4] Robert Seidenberg, 'Disco in the Time of AIDS', *Entertainment Weekly*, 8 October 1993, 52.
[5] Chris Heath, *Pet Shop Boys, Literally* (New York: Da Capo Press, 1992), 33.

that 'How Can You Expect to Be Taken Seriously' is 'A satire of late-eighties rock stars relentlessly saving the planet. I have always felt uneasy when the espousal of a cause becomes part of a celebrity's "brand". And I find it a bit depressing when pop stars announce that they now want to be "taken seriously" and are aiming for "longevity".'[6] Incidentally, and ironically, 'How Can You Expect to Be Taken Seriously' is the B-side of the twelve-inch version of PSB's cover of U2's 'Where the Streets Have No Name'.

Pet Shop Boys are the quintessential intelligent pop band, but they don't feel the need to be as pretentious as they view other bands to be. In fact, Tennant addresses the concept by saying 'Our idea in those days [the late 1980s] was to be slightly subversive, to say things without really following through [...] which I think is quite a good approach. We never wanted to preach or anything like that, because politics in pop music is a very tricky thing.' In the same article he states the belief that the only songs to successfully combine politics and pop are Elvis Costello's 'Shipbuilding' and the Specials' 'Ghost Town'.[7] Despite their professed disdain for mixing music and messages, Pet Shop Boys have used their celebrity for good on many occasions, such as advocating a royal pardon for Second World War codebreaker Alan Turing, convicted and chemically castrated for being a homosexual. The pardon was granted posthumously in 2013. They have also contributed money to several organizations working to make concerts safer and to support small music venues, but they have not heeded animal-rights group PETA's 2009 request that they change their name.[8]

The Pet Shop Boys frequently collaborate with other pop stars – the Robbie Williams song 'We're the Pet Shop Boys', a remake of a 2002 song by My Robot Friend, has an entire chorus of nothing but Williams reciting a list of Pet Shop Boys song titles while PSB sing backup. Williams seems like the logical next generation of Pet Shop Boys' disco-infused pop, but they have had an effect on much more different artists. Upon meeting the band during the 1991 American tour Chris Heath reports of Axl Rose: 'Then he tells me there's something in common between "My October Symphony" and this song he's struggling with in the studio at the moment, a song called "November Rain".'[9] However, the Pet Shop Boys still don't have positive opinions on many of their peers. Of their 2012 track 'Ego Music', Tennant writes that it is '[a] satire of the modern pop star in the narcissistic age of social media. Many of the lines are quotes from pop star interviews.'[10]

---

[6]Tennant, *One Hundred Lyrics and a Poem*, 67.
[7]Jude Rogers, 'Beyond the Suburbs to Utopia', *New Statesman*, 20 September 2013, 63.
[8]Rosie Swash, 'Pet Shop Boys Asked to Change Their Name by Peta', *Guardian*, 9 April 2009, https://www.theguardian.com/music/2009/apr/09/pet-shop-boys-peta.
[9]Chris Heath and Pennie Smith, *Pet Shop Boys Versus America* (Miami: Music Book Services Corp., 1996), 120.
[10]Tennant, *One Hundred Lyrics and a Poem*, 45.

While academics pore over the Pet Shop Boys' lyrics to find clues to deeper meanings, Neil Tennant confesses in *One Hundred Lyrics and a Poem* (2019) that '[e]very lyric-writer also has a guilty secret: the sound of the words is sometimes more important than the sense of them. We're writing songs to be sung.'[11] Sometimes practicality is the answer while trying to conflate pop music and intellectualism. Sometimes, there is no profound message – just an earworm that sticks.

Even those who know the words to a song or two from the early albums don't always realize the Pet Shop Boys are still playing music. When I talk about this project, I usually get responses like, 'The Pet Shop Boys! I loved them! Back then ... in the 80s ...' I gave a friend a copy of the greatest hits collection *Pop Art* and suggested she add some songs into the soundtrack for her dance class. She said, 'Of course I'll listen to it! I loved them in the 80s!' Someone asked me if I had gone to the 2016 reunion tour, and I had to think about the question, because there was no cause for reunion: PSB have never broken up. All this about a band, Neil Tennant and Chris Lowe, who, in 2007, for instance, released a CD, a DVD, toured, published a coffee-table book of their album covers and did a guest spot on *Dancing with the Stars*. All this about a band whose lead singer lamented, in 1989, regarding their record company, 'EMI-have-got-the-jitters-about-the-Pet-Shop-Boys feeling ... it was "They've been popular for too long. How long's it going to last?"'[12] And yet it did last, and has continued to last, mostly because of PSB's ability to be meaningful, authentic and so damn easy to dance to.

Danceability is a factor in any disco/pop band's career, and it is undoubtedly true, as Simon Watney writes of PSB and their various side projects, that '[t]o understand this music it is necessary to understand (and respect, and probably love) the sensation of being one among hundreds of others on a packed dance-floor, dancing because dancing is what we enjoy most, and because dance music (like sex) binds us intimately'.[13] This is a sentiment echoed by Jan Jagodzinski in his book *Music in Youth Culture: A Lacanian Approach*, describing techno and electronica as 'a "pure" dance style – unadulterated and unstained jouissance', before quoting Simon Reynolds' concept that this sort of music is 'between consciousness raising and consciousness razing'.[14] The Pet Shop Boys offer their audience the deliberate choice to think or to feel, or both, or neither.

In any case, PSB's intellectual side is not to be dismissed. Although pop music is considered by many to be 'low culture', good pop music contains

---

[11]Tennant, *One Hundred Lyrics and a Poem*, xxiii.
[12]Heath, *Pet Shop Boys, Literally*, 88.
[13]Simon Watney, 'How to Have Sax in an Epidemic (The Pet Shop Boys' Music for Gays and AIDS Sufferers)', *Artforum International* 32, no. 3 (November 1993).
[14]Jan Jagodzinski, *Music in Youth Culture: A Lacanian Approach* (New York: Palgrave Macmillan, 2008), 256.

the same elements as good literature. For Simon Frith, in *Performing Rites: On the Value of Popular Music*, PSB's appeal lies in:

> [. . .] their emotional fluency, it's as if the spaces they occupy are actually frozen moments in time, the moments just before and just after emotion (which is why this is disco music with an intensely intellectual appeal), the moments which the best pop music has always defined (nothing else can stop time like this). Listen to any Pet Shop Boys track and you know that they too have had their life reduced to a single catch in the voice, a single melodic phrase [. . .] that must be played again and again. They know that in this sort of music it is such surface noise that resonates most deeply in our lives.[15]

The Pet Shop Boys deserve just as much credit for their intellectual lyrics as they do for releasing one song, forty years ago, that everyone remembers. The general impression that 'West End Girls' is the only success that Pet Shop Boys has had is reductive in the face of a career that has spanned decades and featured several songs people know every word to without knowing which artists are behind them.

So, what is the purpose of a Pet Shop Boys song? Chris Heath, a friend of PSB who wrote a recollection of their first tour, *Pet Shop Boys, Literally*, as well as their first American tour, *Pet Shop Boys Versus America*, poses the question of their intent in his first book: '[A]re the Pet Shop Boys, as is often assumed, more often by critics who like them than by those who don't, just making pop music as some sort of superior, clever clever, ironic joke, forever secretively tapping their noses to those smart enough to be in the know?'[16] Simon Frith similarly comments that PSB's musicality and the effect of their lyrics means that

> [. . .] their music is always funny (a surprisingly unusual quality in pop) [. . .] but there's also a profoundly regretful undertow to the Pets' ironies, a regret permanently lodged in the rhythmic hesitations of Chris Lowe's keyboard lines, in Tennant's flat tones. This means that Pet songs, for all their simple pop forms, are run through with emotional tension.[17]

These songs can be considered intellectually elitist, or amusing, but they are full of the pathos of our lives. Chris Lowe explains the inspiration behind their music's combination of body and brain:

---

[15]Simon Frith, *Performing Rites: On the Value of Popular Music* (Oxford: Oxford University Press, 1996), 8.
[16]Heath, *Pet Shop Boys, Literally*, 33.
[17]Frith, *Performing Rites: On the Value of Popular Music*, 7.

One of the things I've never understood is that when I was at university and we all used to go out to nightclubs on Friday and Saturday nights, we used to have a really good time dancing to the dance music, but we'd go back to our rooms and listen to Genesis and Pink Floyd. I used to wonder 'why do we do this? Why can't we admit to liking the music we genuinely like?' We'd dance to it at night, then kind of pooh-pooh it the next day. It seemed very odd.[18]

Here Lowe examines the lived experience of being someone who can relate to the lyrics of 'Can You Forgive Her?': 'you dance to disco and you don't like rock'. He continues, 'I think a lot of people like music for the wrong reasons – for intellectual reasons or because of peer pressure or because they've read in a magazine that this group is really good, rather than admitting that they like *Saturday Night Fever*, which they genuinely did like and that most people did buy anyway.'[19] Many consider commercial success to be an indicator of societal trends and acceptance, ignoring the natural impulse to follow the crowd, which, by the mid-80s, had mostly drifted away from disco.

Critics also don't know what to do with the band, with academic Ian Balfour writing to the band about his 1991 article, 'Revolutions per Minute or The Pet Shop Boys Forever': 'I hope you won't find my piece on your work too academic or funereal – perhaps I should apologize for taking you too seriously. It may well come across as pretentious in some places – part of that is a deliberate strategy to level the differences between the ways people talk about high and pop culture respectively.'[20] While Balfour, other academics and critics defend the band's intellectual honour, even Neil Tennant still struggles with finding a balance: 'I just think there's a fundamental problem with pop music thinking about itself as art. This idea seems to ruin it [. . .] There's a different intellectual motive going on [. . .] When pop music gets weighed down with a load of theories which art seems to have written into it, it seems to destroy what it is that makes pop music.'[21] Many academics have fallen into the trap of no longer enjoying what they research, and it is kind of Tennant to warn us away from this path. Unlike his pop and rock star contemporaries, Tennant is fine with the audience just wanting to dance without considering the intricacies of the lyrics in relation to the AIDS crisis, Thatcherite economics or Donald Trump. Pet Shop Boys are willing to dance the line, literally, between pop music and academic topics without forcing their fans to choose one aspect of their music over the other.

---

[18]Heath and Smith, *Pet Shop Boys versus America*, 71.
[19]Heath and Smith, *Pet Shop Boys versus America*, 71.
[20]Heath and Smith, *Pet Shop Boys versus America*, 173.
[21]Philip Hoare and Chris Heath, *Pet Shop Boys, Catalogue* (London: Thames & Hudson, 2006), 9.

Even if he tries to protect us from an analysis of art, and even if he's comfortable with just writing a great dance track, Tennant makes sure the deeper meanings of some songs are perfectly clear. He never shies away from snarky commentary on politics and current events. He makes the intent of their 2006 album, and especially the song 'Luna Park' clear: 'The idea for our album Fundamental [. . .] was to put into music the domestic atmosphere of the "War on Terror".'[22] This particular song was Tennant conceiving of 'the "War on Terror" [. . .] as a ride in a funfair', with lyrics such as 'And when we're feeling scared / we're happy / With circuses and bread / we're happy.'[23] The Pet Shop Boys force their audience to face their own reactions and avoidance strategies when faced with a reality that is not what they envisioned. If an amusement park can be a thinly veiled reference to war, disco can be informative, timely and introspective (album-title pun intended) without becoming pedantic.

War is also the subject of their 2013 cover of Bruce Springsteen's 'Last to Die'. While Springsteen's 2007 song directly quotes John Kerry's Congressional testimony about Vietnam in 1971 – 'How do you ask a man to be the last man to die for a mistake' – Pet Shop Boys change the lyric. As Tennant explains, 'I changed "a mistake" to "our mistakes" [. . .] So then the song casts more blame on us, as individuals in a democratic society, and the responsibility that we have for what happens in our name.'[24] The dance floor is a community, as much as a nation is, and PSB want to make sure each listener evaluates how they impact and are impacted by their shared experiences.

Beyond politics and pure pop culture, Neil Tennant also uses his lifelong interest in literature and philosophy in his lyrics. Some of PSB's allusions are blatant. For example, in 'Left to My Own Devices', Tennant sings, 'I was faced with a choice, at a difficult age, / Should I write a book? Or would I take to the stage? / But at the back of my mind I heard distant feet, / Che Guevara and Debussy to a disco beat.' These lyrics have been interpreted so literally as to have dancers dressed up as Che Guevara and Claude Debussy during the 1991 *Performance* tour, and these are the lyrics academics and critics most often use when looking at the band through a scholarly lens. In a literary reference that was later dropped, PSB considered alluding to Oscar Wilde and calling their early 90s greatest hits album *The Importance of Being Pet Shop Boys*.[25] The work later became *Discography*, playing on both their disco focus and the literal definition of the word.

'Where angels fear to tread', the second half of Alexander Pope's admonition of where fools rush in, has featured prominently as a lyric in two separate PSB songs: 1996's 'Discoteca' and 2006's 'Sodom and

---

[22]Tennant, *One Hundred Lyrics and a Poem*, 79.
[23]Tennant, *One Hundred Lyrics and a Poem*, 117.
[24]Rogers, 'Beyond the Suburbs to Utopia', 65.
[25]Heath and Smith, *Pet Shop Boys versus America*, 63.

Gomorrah Show'. 'Discoteca', from the *Bilingual* album, tells the story of a traveller looking for the only place he knows he will be safe and accepted – no matter the language – a disco. Tennant sings of not understanding a word of a language he doesn't speak, the trepidation that 'where angels fear to tread / I've sometimes walked and tried to talk', before lamenting that he is lost. In the last lines of the verse, Tennant's narrator is resigned to his fate: 'I'm doing what I do to see me through / I'm going out, and carrying on as normal.' The reference is repeated in 'The Sodom and Gomorrah Show', in a somewhat different context: 'You've got to love / to learn to live / where angels fear to tread / I did it and I don't regret the day.' The song, obviously alluding to the biblical story of Sodom and Gomorrah, promises a show that has 'everything you need for your complete / entertainment and instruction / sun, sex, sin, divine intervention, death and destruction.' Writing in 2019, Tennant explains the story of the song:

> A quiet, bookish man is faced with the reality of the modern media in all its vulgar, phone-hacking, sex-obsessed, reality TV, celebrity tittle-tattle, economical-with-the-truth, 24-hours-a-day, rolling news frenzy. He comes away feeling surprisingly liberated, realising he shouldn't hide away from the world but should participate fully in it. It can also be read as being a story of a quiet, repressed man who is taken to a gay club for the first time and has a life-changing experience. And, as a metaphor of America, it was imagined in the era of George W. Bush but now seems to have anticipated Donald Trump.[26]

Who then are Alexander Pope's fools? Both songs read, on the surface, as an indictment of conservative religious condemnation of homosexuality and a celebration of those who can see beyond such arbitrary restrictions, yet, in Tennant's description, the lyrics of 'Sodom and Gomorrah' are left open to a positive or negative interpretation. Does each song celebrate the choice to express oneself however one chooses, or is it a warning about the superficiality of society? While Tennant's book of annotated lyrics clears up many issues of authorial intent, here he muddies the water intentionally – putting the onus of interpretation on the listener.

This is not Pet Shop Boys' first time writing prescient lyrics, and some lyrics, intended or unintended, have clear interpretations, even if PSB only realize them in hindsight. Of 'The Dictator Decides', Tennant remembers, 'When we toured North America in the autumn of 2016, before and after the American presidential election, the lines "My facts are invented / I sound quite demented / so deluded it beggars belief" seemed each night to conjure up the spectre of Donald Trump.'[27]

---

[26]Tennant, *One Hundred Lyrics and a Poem*, 183.
[27]Tennant, *One Hundred Lyrics and a Poem*, 167.

PSB have always confronted the politics of social issues in the moment, such as 1988's 'It's Alright', which begins with the lines, 'Dictation being forced in Afghanistan / Revolution in South Africa taking a stand / People in Eurasia on the brink of oppression', and ends with the promise that, 'I hope it's gonna be alright / 'Cause the music plays forever', but their political claws truly came out on 2006's album, *Fundamental*. The first single, 'I'm with Stupid', is an imagined ode from British Prime Minister Tony Blair to American President George W. Bush, both celebrating and lamenting their relationship. The song features lines such as 'No one understands me, where I'm coming from / Why would I be with someone who's obviously so dumb?' and 'Before we ever met I thought like everybody did / You were just a moron, a billion dollar kid.'

Although PSB were originally Blair supporters, this is not the only song to attack his leadership. For example, 'Integral' condemns the proposed British ID card system, a programme the song mockingly says is 'designed solely / to protect you', going on to explain, 'Everyone has their own number / in the system that we operate under. / We're moving to a situation / where your lives exist as information.' The most poignant lines, however, are found in the chorus: 'If you've done nothing wrong, you've got nothing to fear / If you've something to hide you shouldn't even be here.' The choice of the word 'mandate' in the following line – 'You've had your chance, now we've got the mandate / if you've changed your mind, I'm afraid it's too late' – is, of course, also a reference to George W. Bush's showboating after narrowly winning the 2004 American presidential election.

While they don't shy away from commenting on American politics, Pet Shop Boys have never quite known what to do with America, to the point that they released a memoir of their 1991 tour entitled *Pet Shop Boys versus America*, in which biographer Chris Heath laments, 'The Pet Shop Boys treat America with an uneasy mixture of priorities and prejudices. It is a country they face both with a sense of mission and with a sense of disdain. The same conundrum would restate itself time and again during the tour – what does it mean if they want success here but dislike so much of what modern America, and the modern American, is?' How could PSB win over American fans they don't like, and did they even seem to want to? Heath tries to answer that question:

> One solution – a rationalization that proud Englishmen abroad have used for generations – was to convince themselves that the Americans to whom the Pet Shop Boys appealed were somehow special. They were the disenchanted! The outcasts! The cheesed-off! In other words, they were precisely those Americans who saw in America from within the same faults the Pet Shop Boys saw from the outside.[28]

---

[28] Heath and Smith, *Pet Shop Boys versus America*, 1.

And yet, the band's commitment to conquering America has never been quite whole-hearted, as Heath expounds:

> Their feelings about this [their appeal in America] would swing from hour to hour, from being annoyed that the largest nation of pop listeners were stubbornly resisting them to being arrogantly dismissive of anyone silly enough not to like them, to having the detached pride of those whose creative accomplishments are sufficient satisfaction in themselves, to being studiously determined to woo new converts, to keenly wanting not to even be seen to be trying to be liked.[29]

Some of this wavering, reminiscent of playground strategies, relates back to Chris Lowe's views on musical integrity:

> You should always be honest with yourself as to the kind of music you genuinely do like [. . .] [Heath: discussing the undercurrent of sadness in seventies dance music, a facet he feels has escaped most contemporary revivalists] There was a real pathos in the music which was what I liked about it. I've always liked kind of *up* music with sad lyrics 'cause it just gives this tension and melancholy to the whole thing. I think the message of the Pet Shop Boys is that it's not going to be all right. You know it's not going to be all right.[30]

Of course, this quote from their 1991 American tour is in direct conflict with the summation of their 1988 remake of the Sterling Void, Marshall Jefferson and Paris Brightledge song 'It's Alright', which concludes with a celebration of the promise of music's healing power: 'I hope it's gonna be alright / 'Cause the music plays forever.' As critic Ian Balfour writes of the *Being Boring* video, while placing it in the context of 'It's Alright': 'For the music goes on and on forever – it has to go on and on – because in the logic of the Pet Shop Boys, silence equals death.'[31]

And the Pet Shop Boys have never chosen silence. The 1993 song, 'Dreaming of the Queen', is a vision of a nude Neil Tennant hosting Queen Elizabeth II and Princess Diana for tea. The title is an allusion to the book *Dreams of the Queen*, as Tennant elaborates: 'The most popular anxiety dream commoners have is of the Queen coming to tea and there isn't any, or the dog pees on the carpet. I combined it with that anxiety dream of finding yourself walking around with no clothes on.'[32] However, there is much more

---

[29]Heath and Smith, *Pet Shop Boys versus America*, 2.
[30]Heath and Smith, *Pet Shop Boys versus America*, 71.
[31]Ian Balfour, 'Revolutions per Minute or the Pet Shop Boys Forever', *Surfaces* 1 (1991), https://doi.org/10.7202/1065250ar.
[32]Seidenberg, 'Disco in the Time of AIDS', 52.

to the song than that. There are several aspects that require attention in order to fully grasp the intended meaning. The surface nightmare of standing naked before the Queen covers a more important significance for a man dreaming in the 90s, while also addressing the cultural impact of the British royal family. For example, when, during the 2006 *Fundamental* tour, the background video for 'Dreaming of the Queen' was of Princess Diana's funeral procession, true fans understood that the meaning of the song had been fundamentally changed – pun intended. In the 1993 song, written before Diana's 1997 death, the lyrics read, 'The Queen said, "I'm aghast. / Love never seems to last / However hard you try"', before Diana offered her own explanation: 'That there are no more lovers left alive / No one has survived / So there are no more lovers left alive / And that's why love has died.' The original song was a lamentation about the AIDS epidemic. Simon Watney writes that this refrain 'speaks far more about the effects of the epidemic in gay men's lives than about a famously unhappy royal marriage'.[33] Nevertheless, the song has bits of collective memories of both – true touchstones of the late 80s and early 90s. Scholar Wayne Studer quotes Jeffery Durst as having pointed out that

> [. . .] the famous line from the chorus 'There are no more lovers left alive' – may have been influenced by the 1964 novel *Only Lovers Left Alive* by Dave Wallis, or perhaps even more likely by the Wanderers' 1981 post-punk cult-classic album of the same name. After all, 1981 was the year in which Charles and Diana were married, not to mention when Neil and Chris met and when the first cases of AIDS were reported by the U.S. Center for Disease Control.[34]

With the added concert visual of Diana's final motorcade, the lyrics evolve into an ode to the Princess herself, and a condemnation of the Queen's alleged lack of understanding – of Diana as well as of the AIDS crisis. Diana's bodyguard, Ken Wharfe, reported that the Queen asked Diana in the 80s to 'get involved with something more pleasant'.[35] Through 'Dreaming of the Queen', the Pet Shop Boys, AIDS and Diana are forever intertwined, seeking emotional resonance in something decidedly not pleasant.

The AIDS epidemic has always been a major topic for the PSB. AIDS was the subject of not just 'Dreaming of the Queen' but also of 'Being Boring', which includes lyrics spotlighting the absence of many of 'the people

---

[33] Watney, 'How to Have Sax in an Epidemic'.
[34] Wayne Studer, 'Dreaming of the Queen', *Commentary: Interpretation and Analysis of Every Song by Pet Shop Boys*, 2022, http://www.geowayne.com/newDesign/very/dreaming.htm.
[35] Ryan Smith, 'Did Queen Elizabeth II Try to Stop Princess Diana's HIV/AIDS Work?', *Newsweek*, 9 September 2022, https://www.newsweek.com/did-queen-elizabeth-ii-try-stop-princess-dianas-hiv-aids-work-1741565.

I was kissing', or the bittersweet regret that 'I never dreamt that I would get to be / the creature that I always meant to be / but I thought in spite of dreams / You'd be sitting somewhere here with me.' Tennant has publicly commented that he wrote the song in honour of a friend who had died of AIDS, that it is 'about our lives when we [were] teenagers and how we moved to London, and I suppose me becoming successful and him becoming ill',[36] but the raw emotion speaks to all who have loved and lost.

Possibly the most well-documented PSB song about the effect of AIDS on gay culture is their 1993 cover of the Village People's 1979 hit 'Go West'. Scholar Simon Watney writes that 'the song embodies a sense of gay culture, and above all the club scene, as an almost utopian domain of consensual choice and pleasure – things that of course [were] anathema to the grim moralists of the '90s'. Watney continues, 'More than any song I know, "Go West" speaks profoundly of both our losses and our absolute determination to survive them, to come through all this, to go forward rather than backward, and to do so by insisting on the unbroken vitality of our culture.'[37] As they have done with so many remakes, the Pet Shop Boys do not just blithely re-record someone else's words. Critic Mark Butler analyses the additional bridge the Pet Shop Boys add to the song:

> Here the phrase 'we'll be what we want to be' (line 30) speaks of freedom to express personal identity, while line 31, 'now if we make a stand', implies political activism. The climactic reference to the 'promised land' in line 32 takes the song to a new level, invoking the weight of a familiar biblical image to suggest that the West is not just a nice area in which to live, but also a place where an oppressed group can be free.[38]

Tennant himself explained that 'the song is about the gay ideal of the late 70s, the idea of moving to San Francisco for a life in the sun, where you could be free, be yourself, do what you liked. And, of course, AIDS was about to change that ideal completely. So now the song has an elegiac kind of quality as well.'[39] Watney views the song more positively in the context of when it was released, writing upon the song's release that '"Go West" is the "I Will Survive" of our times.'[40] The Pet Shop Boys' remake of 'Go West' is an anthem for the LGBTQ+ community at a time when, as the band explains, '[AIDS] changed pop music completely, because pop music is

---

[36]Neil Tennant, 'The Pet Shop Boys Special', interviewed by Andi Peters, *O Zone*, BBC2, 1 October 1993, quoted in Marcin Wichary, 'Materials. interviews. Printed', *10 years of being boring*, 30 July 2003, https://10yearsofbeingboring.com/materials/interviews/printed.
[37]Watney, 'How to Have Sax'.
[38]Mark Butler, 'Taking It Seriously: Intertextuality and Authenticity in Two Covers by the Pet Shop Boys', *Popular Music* 22, no. 1 (January 2003): 8.
[39]Seidenberg, 'Disco in the Time of AIDS', 52.
[40]Watney, 'How to Have Sax'.

about sex and AIDS has changed sex [...] Disco was *sexual* – "love to love you baby", heavy breathing. Dance music now is heavy beats and you dance by yourself.'[41]

'Go West' also has another significance. *Billboard*'s 'Brits Around the World' reports that '"Go West" hit the mood and mentality of pro-American tendencies, appealing to the youth in both the West and the former East Germany. The tongue-in-cheek irony of the video being shot at Red Square was duly noted.'[42] The West, however, was not the ideal those without and those within thought it was and would be. Tennant wrote the 1996 song 'Up Against It' while he 'was thinking about how, through so much of the post-war period, people had been urged to tighten their belts and work hard to achieve a utopia which never quite emerged'.[43] The post-war reality didn't materialize the way many had expected it to, and the Pet Shop Boys found their inspiration and niche chronicling the reality of working-class life. Tennant explains their style: '[W]e are serious, comic, light-hearted, sentimental and brittle, all at the same time [...] We are of the middle class and, at the same time, we attack that kind of life. Just as we are of pop music and we attack it at the same time. There's a mocking edge to our music. We're mocking ourselves, as well as just about everybody else.'[44]

The Pet Shop Boys are in no way unique just because they write about the daily minutiae their audience faces. Yet while Jan Jagodzinski dismisses 'Sheryl Crow and Alanis Morisette [sic] [...] whose content dwells on the banality and trivia of everyday life, [as] paradigms of "reality singing" and best examined as part of the reality television phenomenon',[45] the Pet Shop Boys, who have appeared on reality TV, have the ability to make descriptions of day-to-day life meaningful rather than just platitudes. Simon Frith observes:

> It's as if the Pet Shop Boys are both quite detached from their music – one is aware of the sheer craftiness of their songs – and completely implicated by it: they suggest less that they have been touched by the banality of love than by the banality of love songs; they seem to understand the fear as well as the joy of sex (fear and joy which always lie in the *anticipation* of the physical moment); they capture the anxiety of fun.[46]

Neil Tennant writes of their first steps in this method, starting with 1984's 'Rent': 'We were gradually developing a technique for writing songs: take a brutal or crude or funny idea and romanticise it.'[47] While PSB titles can

---

[41] Heath and Smith, *Pet Shop Boys versus America*, 12–13.
[42] Steve McClure, 'Brits Around the World', *Billboard*, 12 February 1994, 48.
[43] Tennant, *One Hundred Lyrics and a Poem*, 213.
[44] Hoare and Heath, *Pet Shop Boys, Catalogue*, 9.
[45] Jagodzinski, *Music in Youth Culture: A Lacanian Approach*, 270.
[46] Frith, *Performing Rites*, 8.
[47] Tennant, *One Hundred Lyrics and a Poem*, 137.

combine to create the entire chorus of 'We're the Pet Shop Boys', it also adds to the relatability of the band. These huge British rock stars have the same good days and bad days and average days that we all do. Tennant elaborates: 'Common phrases of everyday speech have always been a rich sort of inspiration for songwriters, including me. "I made my excuses and left", "How can you expect to be taken seriously", "I wouldn't normally do this kind of thing", "Left to my own devices", "Do I have to?" – all very typical British phrases with a certain properness about them which can acquire pathos or humour in a musical setting.'[48]

One fan comments on the dichotomy within the lyrics, the delivery and the meaning that, 'They have a cold tone, but it makes you feel good,'[49] while another glorifies their brainy appeal: 'They're intelligent pop. They're geniuses.'[50] While fan praise can be hyperbolic, the significance is that their fans view them as intellectual geniuses, not just musical geniuses, and that they are able to successfully navigate both worlds. For Neil Tennant, this is another fine line to walk, as he wonders, 'Are such clichés [hearts being broken or dancing with danger] lazy or do they echo songs from the past and provide a link to the long continuum of popular music, which is itself an expression of the constant need for love and hope and freedom and fun and sex and dancing and remembering and sometimes forgetting?'[51]

Nowhere is this question more evident than in their detailed yet pedestrian song titles. In an interview with Tennant, columnist Alex Needham writes, 'He says he has the "slightly cold and dispassionate" ability to be having an argument with a lover and realise that an accusation like "You only tell me you love me when you're drunk" will make a good title for a song.'[52] The Pet Shop Boys put great thought into their album titles, as evidenced by the legend that their debut was called *Please*, so their fans would go to the record store and ask for 'the Pet Shop Boys album, please'. Sometimes this habit of using common phrases as album and song titles is both for Tennant's entertainment as well as the audience's enlightenment. He remembers, 'I have never thought that "Love is a bourgeois concept", but I liked the idea of bringing academic/Marxist language into a pop song, and then constructed a lyric which tells a story and gave me the excuse to use words like *Schadenfreude*.'[53] Unfortunately, the lofty philosophical concepts of the 2013 song do not bode well for its academic main character: 'The contrast between the notion of "love" and the language of "bourgeois construct"

---

[48]Tennant, *One Hundred Lyrics and a Poem*, xvii.
[49]Heath and Smith, *Pet Shop Boys versus America*, 63.
[50]Heath and Smith, *Pet Shop Boys versus America*, 97.
[51]Tennant, *One Hundred Lyrics and a Poem*, xxii.
[52]Alex Needham, 'Neil Tennant: "Sometimes I Think, Where's the Art, the Poetry in All This?"', *Guardian*, 21 October 2018, https://www.theguardian.com/music/2018/oct/21/neil-tennant-pet-shop-boys-collection-lyrics.
[53]Tennant, *One Hundred Lyrics and a Poem*, xx.

appealed to me and so it turned into a story about a hapless intellectual whose lover has deserted him.'[54] The leading man, a character in the 1988 novel *Nice Work* by David Lodge, is 'searching for the soul of England / Drinking tea like Tony Benn.' Tennant explains the allusion: 'He's reverting back to the extreme leftism of his university years and so we've mentioned one of the biggest figures of the Labour Party of his youth [. . .] I quite like doing things like that.'[55] Critic Lynsey Hanley writes of her youthful educational relationship with PSB, 'In interviews with *Smash Hits* they would refer casually to the existentialists and send me rushing to the nearest dictionary, which was more than could be said for my homework.'[56]

While their songs can introduce high-minded philosophical principles to their audience, Pet Shop Boys are just as comfortable facing the realities, however mundane, of the modern world, the realities, however mundane, of who they are, and who their fans are. The world has changed, and the Pet Shop Boys have adjusted, but haven't necessarily changed, which is part of their appeal. One fan seeing the band in Houston in 1991 explains, 'I like the fact that they've kept the same image. You don't see that too much. Most people change who they are, like Madonna, but they obviously liked who they were in the first place.'[57] Thirty years ago fans observed and appreciated the same aspect of the band current fans enjoy – they are comfortable with who they are and what they believe. While Madonna has just announced a fortieth-anniversary tour with a controversial *Vanity Fair* cover, the Pet Shop Boys don't need to showboat, to reinvent. Their strength lies in their authenticity and universality.

Much has been written about the Pet Shop Boys' 2005 score for the 1925 Soviet silent film *Battleship Potemkin*, and Neil Tennant's fascination with Russian history; as he explains, 'I have always been fascinated by the history and culture of Russia and the Soviet Union – the beauty and the cruelty, the ideologies and the reality – and this sometimes finds an expression in my lyrics and our songs (much to Chris's exasperation).'[58] Russia is not only an academic interest, but also a large part of their international fan base. In 1993, while doing publicity for *Very*, Tennant remembers that 'the Russian fans asked very formal questions like, "May I wish you the very best of health, Mr. Tennant?" They were really sweet. It was in the Moscow paper that it was my birthday, with a picture of me. I'm sure it wasn't in the London paper.'[59] Other followers are similarly appreciative. A Japanese fan interviewed in 1991 wanted to tell the band, 'your show have [sic] occupied

---

[54]Tennant, *One Hundred Lyrics and a Poem*, 112.
[55]Rogers, 'Beyond the Suburbs to Utopia', 63.
[56]Lynsey Hanley, 'Daydream Believers', *New Statesman*, 30 October 2006, 38.
[57]Heath and Smith, *Pet Shop Boys versus America*, 63.
[58]Tennant, *One Hundred Lyrics and a Poem*, xx.
[59]Kim Cunningham, 'Back in the (Former) U.S.S.R. (Music Group The Pet Shop Boys Describes the Experience of Touring in Russia)', *People Weekly*, 20 September 1993, 106.

a part of our mind for good. The meanings, the implications, the theme [sic] are too complicated to understand completely yet. But we never cease thinking about them.'[60] PSB weren't, and aren't, totally ignored in Britain, where Lynsey Hanley writes that '[e]verything that school doesn't teach you – about taking good pop culture as seriously as any good art, about the importance of living life on your own terms and pursuing your passion – they did, with the added bonus of songs so good, both musically and lyrically, that they remain imprinted on my mind 20 years after I first heard them.'[61] Whether the audience wants to have an intellectual discussion or just dance, the relevance of PSB's songs make them unforgettable.

Yet even though their songs have staying power, the interpretation often remains up to the individual. The band does not define a purpose to their work as a whole: '"No", [Neil] says, "I couldn't sum up a single message from our songs." Chris laughs. "I think we put out a complex set of messages, some of which are contradictory. It's how you don't have a single message, and how difficult it is to live life in a complex, difficult world."'[62] Yet the Pet Shop Boys have never abandoned us as we navigate our journey through this difficult world. One critic writes of the 2022 *Unity* tour – the one that found me sobbing during the encore – that '[t]hese hits teleport Pet Shop Boys older listeners to their youth, a thrill even if those years were hard. They capture the bygone mood of a gritty age. More than that, they let you smile at sorrow, at once echoing your woes and making you feel better. Doing either is an artistic achievement; doing both together is a feat that only words and music can perform, and only rarely. It will never get old.'[63]

The songs of PSB are their legacy and speak for themselves as well as the artists behind them. Their authenticity and honesty have empathized with and inspired generations of fans. Alex Needham interviewed Neil Tennant about his 2019 collection *One Hundred Lyrics and a Poem*, and relays Tennant's words that '[r]eally quite often, a publisher says, "Let's get Neil Tennant to write his autobiography" and it's quite nice that they do. [. . .] I'm not convinced my life's been interesting enough. *This* is my autobiography.'[64] Critic Richard Cromelin's 1991 words are as true today as they were when spoken: 'For all the knowing edges and satirical thrusts of their tart social commentaries about class, art, consumption, and sex, the Pet Shop Boys managed to generate a sympathy – not for themselves as stars, certainly, and not even as stage characters, but for the confusing, sad world whose poets they've become.'[65]

---

[60]Heath and Smith, *Pet Shop Boys versus America*, 11.
[61]Hanley, 'Daydream Believers', 38.
[62]Heath and Smith, *Pet Shop Boys versus America*, 217.
[63]'Back Story: Debussy to a Disco Beat', 86.
[64]Needham, 'Neil Tennant: "Sometimes I Think, Where's the Art, the Poetry in All This?"'.
[65]Richard Cromelin, 'Pop Music Review: Rock-Theater Revival: The Pet Shop Boys' Fans Finally Get to See the Band in the Flesh, in Its First U.S. Concert Tour since Its Ironic Records Hit the Charts', *Los Angeles Times*, 1 April 1991, https://www.latimes.com/archives/la-xpm-1991-04-01-ca-1160-story.html.

Neil Tennant and Chris Lowe, the Pet Shop Boys, are the bards leading us through our world. They catalogue the joys and pains of human existence. They make us laugh and cry; they make us dance. We can analyse deeper meanings, we can sob through concerts, but we will never experience the Pet Shop Boys without thinking or feeling something. They are never being boring.

Bibliography

'Back Story: Debussy to a Disco Beat'. *Economist*, 25 June 2022.

Balfour, Ian. 'Revolutions per Minute or the Pet Shop Boys Forever'. *Surfaces* 1 (1991), https://doi.org/10.7202/1065250ar.

Butler, Mark. 'Taking It Seriously: Intertextuality and Authenticity in Two Covers by the Pet Shop Boys'. *Popular Music* 22, no. 1 (January 2003): 1–17.

Cromelin, Richard. 'Pop Music Review: Rock-Theater Revival: The Pet Shop Boys' Fans Finally Get to See the Band in the Flesh, in Its First U.S. Concert Tour since Its Ironic Records Hit the Charts'. *Los Angeles Times*, 1 April 1991, https://www.latimes.com/archives/la-xpm-1991-04-01-ca-1160-story.html.

Cunningham, Kim. 'Back in the (Former) U.S.S.R. (Music Group The Pet Shop Boys Describes the Experience of Touring in Russia)'. *People Weekly*, 20 September 1993.

Frith, Simon. *Performing Rites: On the Value of Popular Music*. Oxford: Oxford University Press, 1996.

Hanley, Lynsey. 'Daydream Believers'. *New Statesman*, 30 October 2006.

Heath, Chris. *Pet Shop Boys, Literally*. New York: Da Capo Press, 1992.

Heath, Chris and Pennie Smith. *Pet Shop Boys versus America*. Miami: Music Book Services Corp., 1996.

Hoare, Philip and Chris Heath. *Pet Shop Boys, Catalogue*. London: Thames & Hudson, 2006.

Jagodzinski, Jan. *Music in Youth Culture: A Lacanian Approach*. New York: Palgrave Macmillan, 2008.

Kramer, Steve. 'In What Universe'. Facebook, 21 September 2022, https://www.facebook.com/sheryl.stein.

McClure, Steve. 'Brits Around the World', *Billboard*, 12 February 1994.

Needham, Alex. 'Neil Tennant: "Sometimes I Think, Where's the Art, the Poetry in All This?"' *Guardian*, 21 October 2018, https://www.theguardian.com/music/2018/oct/21/neil-tennant-pet-shop-boys-collection-lyrics.

Rogers, Jude. 'Beyond the Suburbs to Utopia'. *New Statesman*, 20 September 2013.

Seidenberg, Robert. 'Disco in the Time of AIDS'. *Entertainment Weekly*, 8 October 1993.

Smith, Ryan. 'Did Queen Elizabeth II Try to Stop Princess Diana's HIV/AIDS Work?' *Newsweek*, 9 September 2022, https://www.newsweek.com/did-queen-elizabeth-ii-try-stop-princess-dianas-hiv-aids-work-1741565.

Studer, Wayne. 'Dreaming of the Queen'. *Commentary: Interpretation and Analysis of Every Song by Pet Shop Boys*, 2022, http://www.geowayne.com/newDesign/very/dreaming.htm.

Swash, Rosie. 'Pet Shop Boys Asked to Change Their Name by Peta'. *Guardian*, 9 April 2009, https://www.theguardian.com/music/2009/apr/09/pet-shop-boys-peta.

Tennant, Neil. 'The Pet Shop Boys Special', interviewed by Andi Peters, *O Zone*, BBC2, 1 October 1993, quoted in Marcin Wichary, 'Materials. interviews. Printed', *10 years of being boring*, 30 July 2003, https://10yearsofbeingboring.com/materials/interviews/printed.

Tennant, Neil. *One Hundred Lyrics and a Poem: 1976–2016*. London: Faber & Faber, 2019.

Watney, Simon. 'How to Have Sax in an Epidemic (The Pet Shop Boys' Music for Gays and AIDS Sufferers)'. *Artforum International* 32, no. 3 (November 1993).

CHAPTER TWO

The End of the West

Community and Chorus in the Pet Shop Boys since 'Go West'

Adrian Daub

Introduction

This chapter explores a noticeable shift in the Pet Shop Boys' sound following their 1993 cover of the Village People hit 'Go West': textures got lusher, and above all back-up singers began entering the mix – often, it seems, when the group wanted to reflect on queerness, community and identity. This stylistic shift had a political valence, one that reflected on an earlier understanding of a 'gay community' and submitted it to an internal critique. Their songs celebrated that community but also questioned what it meant for a community to move to the same beat, aesthetically and politically. They acknowledged viciousness and internal tensions. And they asked what the role was for disco music in a community that they understood to be far more complex than the one the Village People had put on stage and celebrated.

PSB tended to use choruses and groups of back-up vocalists in a call-and-response pattern inherited from the Village People, one that was neither strictly dialogical nor a mere echo. In 'Go West' there are many lines following the pattern '(Together) we will work and strive', where the 'Together' thunders forth from a collective and the main line comes from a soloist. At others, however, there are a 'you' and a 'me' in the chorus and the solo voice, and the song seems to want to construct something like a dialogue between them. Both the question of whether there was such a dialogue, and if not, what relationship obtained between the different speaking positions in the song lyrics, cut to the heart of what kind of community was finding its voice through openly queer dance music.

But crucially, the answer to this question given by the Village People's version of the song was quite different from the one PSB would give fifteen years later. The give-and-take was different, the voices involved were markedly different, and the affective dimensions of their exchange are different. There is, simply put, a far more complex relationship between chorus and individual in PSB's post-'Go West' songs, one that seems to point to a more complex, articulated relationship between (queer) individual and (queer) community. With José Esteban Muñoz we could speak of a *dis*identificatory energy that obtains in PSB's arrangements. The Village People, for a variety of reasons, sought to put on stage a politics of joy that was to signify community in a straightforward way. By contrast, PSB's chorus emerges as a locus of dialogue, variation, ironization, friction.

From their first album opener ('You Got Me', *San Francisco* (1978)), the Village People's sound relied on the interplay between lead vocals (usually from Victor Willis) and a chorus of fairly anonymized background singers. Before Felipe Rose (the Native American), Alex Briley (the GI) or Mark Mussler (the construction worker) were cast (and eventually given their iconic outfits), these background singers were in fact interchangeable. They were, more to the point, for much of the Village People's history, identical with the lead vocals: in many of the classic tracks, the back-up voices largely consist of overdubbed samples of lead singer Victor Willis. On some of them, Phil Hurtt is credited as vocal arranger – Hurtt was known for providing background vocals on Philadelphia soul records, often without explicit credit, so there is a good chance we are hearing him too.

Vocal doubling or not, the multiplicity of voices seems essential both to the Village People's aesthetic impact and to their historic moment. There had been other queer anthems, of course, but they had – more often than not – been products of the attention economy characteristic of the diva. An attention economy, in other words, in which singer and audience member could build up a highly charged affective and identificatory bond, but in which singer and audience member were interpellated as single, often very lonely, individuals. Being a friend of Dorothy meant being familiar with her feelings of alienation.

The Village People, precisely because they were pure cheese, because they weren't actually very good, and, well, because there were six of them, were a participatory act. They were a community on stage, their wink-wink, nudge-nudge play with queer signifiers ensured that that community radiated outwards with every thudding beat and singalong-friendly lyric. And of course, the fact that Village People vocals tended to be choral was anything but accidental: the Stonewall Chorale was founded in New York City in 1977; gay men's choruses quickly became a central institution in the emerging community.[1] The idea that one of the ways in which 'the' LGBT community could be outspoken was by singing in unison likely shaped both the Village People's signature sound and the way it was received.[2]

But from the self-titled debut record to *Go West*, we are listening, more often than not, to a dialogue between two overdubs of the same voice – and even if we're not, we are listening to the dialogue between noticeably similar voices. From the beginning, then, the group's 'joyous – if oblique – celebrations of the then emergent gay subculture'[3] had a slightly ambivalent relationship to identity: the group's signature projective, joyful vocal sound was both an assertion of an identity that was still far too frequently muted or modulated in public and a celebration of a subculture, a community. But due to the commercial investments in the making and marketing of disco tracks in 1977, the joyous community belting out the sing-along hymns on 'Macho Man', 'Cruisin'' and 'Go West' was – as a rule – just a single cis man.

The aesthetic around which the Village People phenomenon was cast and promoted (the original ad calling for dancers specified that they 'must have mustaches') was deeply entwined with two things: homosexuality and a very specific way of living that homosexuality. For all the diversity in their individual signifiers, construction worker, native chief and cop were clones – Castro clones. Singing and dancing in a group celebrated community both as something inclusive and as something implicitly exclusive. While the songs never said so, the overall aesthetic of the group suggested that there were ways of being queer without belonging to this community.

But the odd dialogue between Willis and himself (while four bronzed bandmates gyrated to the music) of course had a generic dimension as well. Overdubbing was invented long before disco, but disco was always particularly comfortable with having been studio-created. The use of synthesizers and overdubbing constituted an unusually frank acknowledgement of the amount of manufacture involved in pop records, unusually frank when compared to most classic rock. The resistance to disco, the 'Disco Sucks' movement, decried 'glitter and gloss, without substance, subtlety or more than surface sexuality', as Robert Vare put it in his 1979 *New York Times* essay 'Discophobia'.[4] Recording technology and the willingness to deploy it affirmatively was clearly part of this charge of inauthenticity.

But of course, discophobes were reacting to something more than just technology. The homophobia of the 'Disco Sucks' backlash has been amply

---

[1] John Gill, *Queer Noises: Male and Female Homosexuality in Twentieth Century Music* (Minneapolis: University of Minneapolis Press, 1995).
[2] Karen Ahlquist, *Chorus and Community* (Urbana: University of Illinois Press, 2006).
[3] Richard Smith, *Seduced and Abandoned: Essays on Gay Men and Popular Music* (London: Bloomsbury, 2016), 20.
[4] Robert Vare, 'Discophobia', *New York Times*, 10 July 1979, 15.

documented. Nevertheless, the homophobic reaction to disco was not primarily about who danced to disco music or who made it (which would have been at any rate hard for mainstream audiences to intuit in 1979). It reacted to aesthetic considerations, among them the way disco deployed technology to reconfigure music's specific modes of community-making. As Gillian Frank has written, 'while rock music was a live medium with an emphasis on the relationship between performers and fans, disco was organized in terms of dancers and recorded music. In rock concerts the primary bodies that were on display were those of the performers.' Disco, by contrast, 'placed the bodies of its audience on display'.[5]

As Tavia Nyong'o has explored with respect to Donna Summer's uber-anthem 'I Feel Love', the flagrantly artificial layering of sonic elements in disco songs seemed to model moments at which an individual dissolved into a near-oceanic mass: what the vocal textures mimic in their relationship to beat and instrumentals seemed to allegorize the teeming, dissolving mass of bodies on the dancefloor. 'I Feel Love,' writes Nyong'o, 'is the quintessential recording of a modulated aim, layering the sonic emblem of the "disco diva" into a pulsating dance-floor scorcher built entirely out of the "artifice" of synthesize sounds, out of which the voice raises and back into which – courtesy of a judicious echo effect – it merges.'[6] Recording technology managed – even to the most insensate consumer of this music – to make a point about identity and its suspension, about togetherness and about intimacy.

It is my contention in what follows that in their dialogue with the Village People, and with disco more broadly, PSB seems to be grappling with these two facts: that Village People managed to celebrate queer community with hitherto unimaginable openness in the face of a brutal heteropatriarchal backlash; and that the community whose image they projected was necessarily partial and on some level implicitly exclusionary. PSB seems intent on expanding what counts as community and they draw on a queer lineage in music-making to ask that question. But a strange thing happens in this process, as considerations of queer community give way to a much broader question about what counts as a community and how it operates politically.

(Re)Covering disco

In the call-and-response structure that seems to dominate much of the Village People's initial output (the songs that made them household names),

---

[5] Gillian Frank, 'Discophobia: Antigay Prejudice and the 1979 Backlash against Disco', *Journal for the History of Sexuality* 16, no. 2 (2007): 291.
[6] Tavia Nyong'o, 'I Feel Love: Disco and its Discontents', *Criticism* 50, no. 1 (2008): 110.

three things come together: a celebration of a very specific masculinity (the titular macho man), its communal aspect (the navy, the YMCA, etc.), and the ostentatious artificiality of disco music, which the songs almost seem to think is of one piece with the artificiality of the Castro clone persona. When PSB covered the Village People's 'Go West' on 1993's *Very*, they retained this stylistic device – and they kept returning to it sporadically but consistently in their post-*Very* output. However, as I will try to show, they did so with radically different aims and with a cleverly updated set of enduring concerns.

At first, the sly, restrained androgyny of PSB would seem to make an odd fit for the boisterous, butch drag of the Village People. And PSB began to sound different after 'Go West' and the Village People arrived in the PSB catalogue. For one thing, *Very*, the album where one title is a straight Village People cover and another ('Liberation') nods in its title to another Village People hit, introduced backing vocals into the PSB discography. For much of the 80s, PSB's sound had been defined by the relative loneliness of the performers' voice (and in rare instances, voices): quivering and achingly sincere, it was often dwarfed by the massive arrangements and thudding beats.

Starting in 1993, the instrumentation gets heavier, but so does vocal backing. On *Very* alone, the songs 'Can you Forgive Her?', 'Liberation', 'The Theatre', 'One in a Million' and 'Go West' feature some kind of backing vocals. The album even acknowledges that some kind of transition has taken place: 'Go West' in the album version goes on for about three minutes after the song is over. After a long silence, an easter egg song plays – 'Postscript (I Believe in Ecstasy)', the rare PSB track sung by Lowe. Where 'Go West' is lush and expansive, 'Postscript' is extremely reduced both in instrumentation and vocal part. Backing vocals never really went away after *Very*. *Bilingual* features choruses singing in several languages. And 'Love etc.' off their 2009 album *Yes* returns almost exactly to the organizing principle established with 'Go West'. Can one read a politics into this kind of stylistic evolution?

Pet Shop Boys have, over time, become a historicist group. They have always been a fairly queer one. Judith Peraino has suggested that early synth pop engaged in something like queerbaiting: even when they were straight, performers flirted with queer subtexts.[7]

PSB's lyrics, their song covers, their collaborations suggested from the first a sensibility for a possible community of queer listeners (and perhaps, as in the case of Village People, queer bodies dancing). In his coming out interview in *Attitude* in August 1994, Neil Tennant said about PSB that 'I do think we have contributed to, through our music and through our videos, and the general way we've presented things, rather a lot to what you might

---

[7] Judith A. Peraino, 'Synthesizing Difference: The Queer Circuits of Early Synthpop', in Olivia Bloechl, Melanie Lowe and Jeffrey Kallberg (eds), *Rethinking Difference in Music Scholarship* (New York: Cambridge University Press, 2015), 288ff.

call "gay culture".' Coming out for PSB meant coming out as a part, and as a reflection, of 'gay culture'.[8]

But the same covers and collaborations have proven them students of what David Halperin has described as a 'distinctive way of feeling, and a unique way of relating to the world', through a practice of 'reappropriating bits of mainstream culture and remaking them into the vehicles of gay or queer meaning'.[9] PSB's appropriations frequently reiterate earlier, less commercial, more communal ones. Collaborating with Dusty Springfield, Liza Minnelli, Kylie Minogue, Soft Cell, Elton John and Rufus Wainwright, working with Diane Warren, or covering the Village People for that matter, is not a deliberate queering of mainstream culture so much as an attempt to honour the aesthetic alignments of earlier queer appropriations. The process is, in other words, about the gay community's historic relation to musical culture. PSB have not been content to play with LGBT signifiers; they seem eager to place themselves in a queer musical genealogy – of carrying on a specific queer tradition.

This is true even if, or perhaps especially if, this act of self-placement takes their music out of pop history to some extent: put bluntly, PSB are a group that always sounds like it's still 1983 in some part of their brains. The fact that the group in 2022 collaborated on a single with Soft Cell (it appeared in Soft Cell's new album *Happiness not Included) feels like a hat-tip to that fact: PSB's historicism and their queerness are never far apart, and collaborating with a band that had its heyday in the early 1980s, but acting on the energized dance track as though no time has passed since then, is part of what makes them queer. They may at times have what we could think of as a queer aesthetic; but even more often they have what, with Elizabeth Freeman, we could call a queer temporality: time doesn't pass as it 'should' – present and past commingle, all in the service of a kind of transhistoric community Heather Love describes as inhering in any mode of queer historical recovery.

As Halperin and others have argued, this kind of play with historical influences is never to be understood as a simple act of nostalgia. It is true that PSB have not followed mainstream pop trends. The act of recovery and of identifying with a specific queer history introduces, as Heather Love has argued, 'discontinuity into our very being'.[10] In the case of PSB, the turn towards implicitly queer canons is itself a way to unsettle and decentre mainstreamed pop aesthetics. It is a way of not moving on, not being done with, not disinvesting from. Aesthetically, then, PSB at times self-consciously take on the aesthetic struggles of yesteryear. Take a line from a song off

---

[8]Paul Burston, 'Honestly', Attitude 1, no. 4 (1994): 66.
[9]David Halperin, How to be Gay (Cambridge, MA: Harvard University Press, 2009), 44.
[10]Heather Love, Feeling Backward: Loss and the Politics of Queer History (Cambridge, MA: Harvard University Press, 2009), 44.

1993's *Very*, 'Can You Forgive Her?', which rehearses the politics of 'Disco Sucks' with a kind of anguish that might have made sense to muster in 1979, but that feels – at least on first glance – utterly out of step with the concerns of the year 1993: 'She's made you some kind of laughing stock / Because you dance to disco and you don't like rock. / She made fun of you and even in bed / Said she was gonna go and get herself a real man instead.'

Why rehash this tired disco-versus-rock juxtaposition fourteen years after Disco Demolition Night? Far from just an implicit and implicitly queer response to mainstream pop aesthetics, PSB's use of queer pop lineages suggests an engagement with who exactly the community is that is reflected, celebrated and called into being in and through pop culture. That is what the 'she' of 'Can You Forgive Her?' needs to be forgiven for: she has implicitly negated a kind of queer community formation, has turned a moment of 'dancing to disco' into a 'laughing stock'. But PSB's recuperation of these moments manages to never simply be affirmative: they understand disco, for instance, as both a moment where bodies got to move together in ways they'd never been allowed to before, but they are not blindly celebratory of the moment just for that. Their oeuvre can be read as an immanent critique of a particular construction of 'the gay community' – one that, for better or worse, the Village People may have embodied more clearly than most other acts.

Who, then, is the community? As noted, the visual presentation of the Village People constituted one answer to that question – the macho man, the Castro clone – though it should be noted that their genre – disco – tended to evoke a different one. But when Pet Shop Boys covered 'Go West', they brought to bear on the song a very different version of queerness, one that implied a different understanding of a queer community. PSB's vocals had always been one reason why they were understood as queer-coded well before Tennant came out. Their voices sounded untrained, their songs placed them in the upper registers, or in others ('What Have I Done to Deserve This?') mimed a dishy, chatty spoken voice. Their voices were naive, fey and a bit effete, but they were more than that – in the mode of several New Romantic acts, their vocals were unassertive, non-dominant. The instrumental arrangements had a tendency to overshadow them. When a voice like Tennant's intoned 'how am I gonna get through?', you really believed the anxiety of that question.

This is very different from the bellowing, assertive shout-along vocals the Village People were known for. In 'Go West', of course, they both coexist. It's true that Tennant dials down the vulnerabilities of his vocals. Nevertheless, the song derives its dynamism from Tennant's voice, naive and high pitched, juxtaposed with the background chorus, boisterous and self-assured where Tennant's voice has that slightly nasally scepticism, that slight irony that sneaks in whenever PSB hit the upper registers. The community of PSB's 'Go West' is an ironized community. It's not that the singer doesn't seem to believe his promises of a golden west. Rather, the link between an historically specific mode of vocality and the community, the ability to unproblematically sing that community into existence, seems to have come apart.

Shifting communities

The tracks gathered on *Bilingual*, *Very*'s 1996 follow-up record, continue the trend of having the lead vocals (usually by Tennant) play off against a backdrop of groups of voices. 'A Red Letter Day' featured three back-up singers and the Choral Academy of Moscow in a pseudo-religious background chorus. 'To Step Aside' features a strange Spanish-language chorus. The lyrics likewise continuously loop back to questions of togetherness, community, the possibilities and impossibilities of making an intersubjective connection. However, perhaps even more so than on *Very*, the songs work hard to ironize that sense of togetherness: only rarely is community straightforwardly celebrated. As in the line from the title track ('Single-Bilingual') 'they call this a community / I like to think of it as home', the invocation of community frequently seems accompanied by a kind of sneer. Part of the reason is that the 'community' of which *Bilingual* speaks (and sings) seems to be something slightly different from the one implicit in much of *Very*.

To be sure, there are plenty of songs in which the 'community' still is rather straightforwardly the gay community of *Very*: in 'Metamorphosis', for instance, a disco beat, a soulful brass section and 70s back-up vocals stage what is clearly a drama of queer self-discovery. Neil Tennant's vocals are essentially a *Sprechgesang*, as he slips into the role of a man who 'hoped my instincts / would do what they were told'. This single narrative voice is challenged by two sets of back-up vocals: the main speaker tells us that 'what I wanted to be was a family man / but nature had some alternative plans'. A funky, all-female back-up chorus chimes in to question this heteronormative life plan: 'I wanna know, yeah' and 'Why? Why? Why?' This same chorus, clearly an externalized version of the main speaker's inner voice, leads into the chorus: 'You grow up and experience this / A total metamorphosis'; at which point another set of voices (Neil Tennant and Chris Lowe in rare joint vocals) add what might well be the moral of the story: 'It's all about change / It's a metamorphosis.'

Queerness, queer experience, queer joy in 'Metamorphosis' are about change, and about exchange. The song's celebration of queer experience seems indissolubly bound to the dynamic call-and-response between three separate sets of voices – sets that are neither fully distinct nor simply identical, Village People-style. There is our speaker, lonely, sensible, awkward and a little unmusical; there is the funky disco-queen *jouissance* of the female back-up singers; and there is the amplified version of the first voice, the two members of Pet Shop Boys singing together. 'Metamorphosis' doesn't contain an individual and a community, at least not in a way that they could be easily played off against each other. To be a queer individual means to call forth a community, to be more-than-one, to admit multitudes. For all its dizzy raptures, however, 'Metamorphosis' is perhaps most remarkable in that brief Tennant/Lowe couplet: for this line suggests that the slightly square, slightly inhibited main speaker is not the butt of some kind of queer joke. If 'it's all about change', his position contains as much truth as all the others in the song. Community brings joy, but those joys ought to be regarded with a certain portion of irony, an instinct that other songs on *Bilingual* return to – often by putting a choir into the mix.

Between *Very*'s 1993 release and *Bilingual*'s 1996 debut falls the transition of the EEC, often simply called the 'European Community', to the EU. While *Bilingual* is not an EU record by any stretch, the big question seems to be about how to make community across linguistic and cultural barriers. And the album at times comes close to saying that you can't. The record opens with a portrait of what would come to be called a eurocrat, a 'player in the continental game / with unlimited expenses to reclaim'. The speaker is technologically connected, well versed in international corporate newspeak, itinerant. And though he claims of himself that 'In Brussels, Bonn or Barcelona /I'm in demand and quite at home there', he does seem to anticipate the kind of European that – in an infamous turn of phrase – a long-since forgotten UK prime minister would call a 'citizen of nowhere'. 'Single-Bilingual' uses bilingualism (parts of the song are in Spanish) as an indicator for deracination and – as the title indicates – as the opposite of a community: 'I'm single, bilingual, / single, bilingual.'

The speaker in 'Single-Bilingual' seems to be a businessman of some sort, but the song is explicit about the fact that pop music, and in particular dance music, are implicated in the same international circuits. The song, after all, closes on the Spanish phrase 'Hay una discoteca por aquí?' In 'Single-Bilingual', the kind of community promised by dance music is no different from the inorganic, transactional, superficial community described in the song. 'Single-Bilingual' does not have a strong backing chorus, but is rather dominated by an overweening percussion section (which likewise is the main visual motif of the song's music video). In another track from the same album, 'A Red Letter Day', a chorus that feels straight out of *Very* seems to enter the arrangement precisely to raise questions about togetherness: about its promises, about its pitfalls, about its politics – 'All I want is what you want / I'm always waiting for a red letter day.'

If *Very*, then, could be said to excavate the inherent queerness in the kind of togetherness PSB's music had long revelled in, *Bilingual* is about something else: about using a lens trained on the peculiar communities that obtain in discos, and in gay discos at that, on the idea of community more broadly. If *Very* was about the queerness of a specific mode of togetherness, *Bilingual* is about what a queer look at togetherness tells us about togetherness.

When the chorus reappears in the PSB canon after *Bilingual*, it frequently raises this heavily ironized, yes queered, sense of community. The songs off

1999's *Nightlife* seem largely to be about oddballs, individuals, washouts and their attempts to find their footing, to find some kind of community, in 'the community'. 'New York City Boy' features a disco beat and a butch choral anthem, and brass band touches that make the song a virtual Village People-pastiche, and tells the story of finding one's place in queer New York. 'Happiness is an Option' combines two solo voices (Neil Tennant and Sylvia Mason-James) in the song's chorus – in a way that it becomes increasingly unclear who is the back-up singer and who is the soloist.

'In Denial' plays off Tennant's voice at its most sincere and melodic, against a far more challenging call-out from Kylie Minogue, accompanied by far sparer electronic beats, who insists that 'this is a fantasy'. But if Minogue's voice (likely the main speaker's daughter) is supposed to represent something like a reality principle ('less drugs, less drinking'), the song's arrangement seems to side with the fantasy rather than her cold dose of reality: a lush orchestral track, almost treacly solo instruments and an utterly absurd angelic choir give the whole song the feel of a movie soundtrack. The song as song, in other words, casts its lot decisively with the beauty, the fantasy, the 'queens and fairies and Muscle Marys', 'the rough-trade boyfriends', and, yes, with denial. It hears Minogue out, but then delves headlong into Broadway textures, friendship with Dorothy, and on down the Yellow Brick Road.

On 2006's *Fundamental*, both the immanent exploration of queer communal life and the critique of broader social trends and developments by means of queer communal intuition return and essentially share the album. 'The Sodom and Gomorrah Show' presents another individual who finds himself absorbed by a queer community. Tennant (in perfect ingenue mode) opens the song with the following lines: 'I lived a quiet life / A stranger to champagne / I never dared to venture out / To cities of the plain.' His introduction to queerness is initially tinged with scepticism ('I heard about their way of life / Took it with a pinch of salt'). By the end of the song, however, the narrator looking back remembers (who has loved 'to learn to live / where angels fear to tread. / I did it and I don't regret the day / Even now') 'you' turning to him and beckoning him to the Sodom and Gomorrah Show. At this point, however, a choir begins to cheerily belt out the real content of that show ('Sun, sex, sin, death and destruction'), while Tennant's vocals step from the role of the ingenue into that of the seducer asking again the question that gives the song its chorus: 'Are you gonna go?' What this seems to suggest is that the individual can be either seducer or seduced, can wreck lives or change them forever; the group, the community, the Sodom and Gomorrah Show itself, speaks the perfect truth about itself. 'The Sodom and Gomorrah Show' is another one of PSB's sort-of celebration of queer community: it is deeply, affirmatively queer and open about the isolation of living a closeted life; but it is anything but naïve about being queer. Sure, the song makes queer life *sound* ravishing, but the lyrics return again and again to make matters more complex – to point to exploitation, superficiality, inequality. The kind of straightforward communal joy that characterized the Village People's fist-pumping anthems is something that PSB isn't interested in letting stand without further investigation.

On *Fundamental*, that sense of ambivalence becomes once again an overt politics well beyond the bounds of the queer community. 'Integral' isn't a particularly queer song, but it has an unsettling chorus with a massively overdubbed Tennant, sounding like a choir of multiple Tennants: 'Long live us / The persuaded we.' Playing Big Brother, the singer addresses a specific you as a panoptic kind of collective that treats the individual as 'not integral to the project': 'If you've done nothing wrong, you've got nothing to fear / If you've something to hide, you shouldn't even be here.'

The song's single featured a QR code on the cover, and makes none-too-subtle references to the UK's National Identity Register, which was established in 2006. Other songs off *Fundamental* – 'Indefinite Leave to Remain' with its clear allusions to UK immigration policy, the chorus of 'Luna Park' and the anti-George W. Bush-song 'I'm with Stupid' – explore the kinds of violence communities are capable of, the kinds of codes and double-speak that hide that violence from them. In promoting *Fundamental*, Tennant explained that he would cease supporting Tony Blair and the Labour Party – in the title of a song that PSB had covered in a duet with Elton John in 2002, he was 'Alone Again (Naturally)'.

The song 'Love etc.' (off the 2009 album *Yes*) features a call-and-response dynamic that at first glance appears to follow the mould established in 'Go West'. Tennant's solo voice in a high register plays off against a strongly masculinized back-up chorus. Even the distribution of roles seems to hew to pattern: there is something sneering in the back-up vocals. Like an inebriated pub singing about football coming home, there is something boisterous, sloppy and a little bit threatening about the way the chorus belts out line after line about how you don't have to live your life. The solo voice meanwhile inhabits a position of at times superhuman naiveté: 'I believe that we can achieve / the love that we need. / I believe, call me naïve / that love is for free', Tennant intones in a way that makes clear that love is, no matter what the singer may believe, very much not for free.

And yet, for the vast majority of 'Love etc.', the song's back-up singers and lead vocals actually have the exact opposite relationship. In the song's (long) chorus, the back-up vocals repeatedly insist on the simple life, while the trappings of 'power and wealth' the song hallucinates are entirely dreamed up by the lead vocals. In the following quotation the lead vocals are rendered in italics: 'Don't have to be *a big bucks Hollywood star* / Don't have to drive *a super car to get far* / Don't have to live *a life of power and wealth* / Don't have to be *beautiful but it helps*.' The chorus continues in this vein, at once dismissing but also introducing the allure of '*a house in Beverly Hills*' or '*your daddy paying the bills*', before once again returning – perhaps longingly – to the refrain: 'Don't have to live *a life of power and wealth* / Don't have to be *beautiful but it helps*.'

What are the respective roles of community and solo voice in this chorus? One thing that 'Love etc.' foregrounds that may have been inexplicit whenever PSB had previously played off choral textures against a solo voice: whatever their exchange is, it isn't a dialogue. There is reinforcement, duplication, ironization. But there is little give-and-take. In 'Love etc.' the polyvocality of the arrangement (the bilingualism?) renders the song's message deeply unclear. Do you or do you not have to buy a house in Beverly Hills? The chorus seems quite confident that the answer is no, but Tennant's solo vocals seem to undercut them at every turn. You don't have to be beautiful, the chorus insists, but the soloist is sure to insert 'but it's nice'. The song seems to imagine a community in which certain things are agreed upon, except that no one is sure they really agree. It's a community that isn't interested in the shallow pursuit of power, inherited wealth, beauty – except that, like Gatsby and Daisy Buchanan, it is borne back ceaselessly into all that it so explicitly disavows. The chorus may list all the things 'you' don't need, but an overdub of Tennant's voice repeatedly insists that 'you need more': Gerhard Richter paintings, 'a Gulfstream jet to fly you door to door'.

The 'Love' and the 'etc.' of the song's title at times are presented as antonyms – the 'etc.' the stuff that keeps us from what really matters, namely love – or, more troubling, as one and the same. It's perhaps not a profound point, as far as it goes. What renders it profound is the dialogue it carries out with its own medium: it was easy for a disco song, it still is easy for a dance track, to celebrate the selflessness and anti-materialism of a community united around nothing more than moving to the same beat. But better disco songs were always aware that this celebration was itself a put-on: that of course the dancefloor was a place of yawning social differences, racial microaggressions, music history pilfered and packaged. What seems remarkable about PSB's double-tongued celebration of community is that it thinks through the politics of community with the thudding, sweaty dancefloor of a late-70s discotheque in mind as its primal scene.

At least from *Very* onwards, PSB seem to have recognized two things: their music was part of a queer culture and needed to position itself as such; and one way to bring a queer community, its aesthetics and history, to life was to include groups of back-up vocals: doubled voices, multiple soloists, entire choruses, real or sampled. By 1993, the problematic side of the kind of gay community the Village People had simply affirmed and naively celebrated was readily apparent: the gay press had acknowledged that queer communities could be exclusive, could be classist, racist, ableist, lookist, shallow, abusive and so on. But by 1993 the queer community was in dire need of affirmation – and PSB felt they needed to oblige. 'Go West' was initially written for an AIDS fundraiser, organized by Derek Jarman: the song PSB wound up recording was born of a sense of obligation to stand with the community, and – in the case of Tennant – to do so publicly as a gay man.

This dual origin is inscribed in the sense of community evinced by PSB's neo-disco explorations throughout the next thirty years. Through the element of the chorus, PSB was able to both create ravishing, exuberant celebrations of queer community and explore the sense of scepticism about certain aspects of that community. What the Village People's pure affirmation-cheese had hidden, PSB wanted to explore. Tennant and Lowe, even when they return to the gay community and to gay disco as a place of affirmation, of home, sound literal notes of caution. Their queer community can be self-destructive, shallow, exploitative. They have made room for queer negativity. And they have exported that queer negativity into using their songs to think through political issues more immediately related to the LGBT community. Being a citizen of disco nation was, to them, an invitation to reflect critically on disco – but also on being citizens.

Bibliography

Ahlquist, Karen. *Chorus and Community*. Urbana: University of Illinois Press, 2006.

Frank, Gillian. 'Discophobia: Antigay Prejudice and the 1979 Backlash against Disco'. *Journal for the History of Sexuality* 16, no. 2 (2007): 276–306.

Gill, John. *Queer Noises: Male and Female Homosexuality in Twentieth Century Music*. Minneapolis: University of Minneapolis Press, 1995.

Halperin, David. *How to be Gay*. Cambridge, MA: Harvard University Press, 2009.

Love, Heather. *Feeling Backward: Loss and the Politics of Queer History*. Cambridge, MA: Harvard University Press, 2009.

Nyong'o, Tavia. 'I Feel Love: Disco and its Discontents'. *Criticism* 50, no. 1 (2008): 101–12.

Peraino, Judith A. 'Synthesizing Difference: The Queer Circuits of Early Synthpop'. In Olivia Bloechl, Melanie Lowe and Jeffrey Kallberg (eds), *Rethinking Difference in Music Scholarship*, 287–314. New York: Cambridge University Press, 2015.

Smith, Richard. *Seduced and Abandoned: Essays on Gay Men and Popular Music*. London: Bloomsbury, 2016.

Vare, Robert. 'Discophobia'. *New York Times*, 10 July 1979.

CHAPTER THREE

He Dreamed of Machines

Queer Heritage and the Pet Shop Boys' 'Turing Test'

Bodie A. Ashton

Introduction

The Closing Ceremony of the 2012 Olympic Games in London was designed to be a celebration of British ingenuity and creativity. The glittering extravaganza began with the arrival of newspaper taxis *à la* John Lennon, their payload being the Spice Girls. The reunion of the quintessential Britpop girl group of the 1990s set the tone for the evening; current acts, such as One Direction, were overshadowed by long-established names – a curious reflection, in an event ostensibly celebrating the global present and future of Britain, on the glories of the past, where George Michael and Madness and Fatboy Slim set the musical agenda. 'We were partying like it was 1999,' noted the *Guardian*'s Zoe Williams, before acerbically noting that the night could have been improved by Prince, except 'he's not British, of course'.[1]

One of the highlights of the night, however, was the surprising appearance of the Pet Shop Boys. Pulled by cyclists in blue pinstripe and oversized orange pointed hats, they arrived to the tune of 'West End Girls'. The appearance solidified Neil Tennant and Chris Lowe's reputation as the 'Best

---

[1] Zoe Williams, 'London 2012 Closing Ceremony: Unleashing a Musical Superpower', *Guardian*, 13 August 2012, https://www.theguardian.com/uk/2012/aug/13/london-2012-closing-ceremony-music.

of British', prompting a further invitation from Prime Minister David Cameron and the Mayor of London, Boris Johnson, to appear at the winners' parade for the British Olympic and Paralympic team the following month. Despite some reluctance on Tennant and Lowe's part – not least driven by the fact that they had a television engagement in Berlin on the same morning for the release of their new album *Elysium* – they went ahead with it outside Buckingham Palace, reprising their performance of 'West End Girls' from the Closing Ceremony, while also performing their newest single (the very fitting 'Winner'), as well as their old classic, 'Go West'. Afterwards, Tennant reflected, the decision to appear, in spite of the tight scheduling had been the right one, and he texted one of Cameron's advisers to thank the Prime Minister for the opportunity: 'Thanks for asking us – actually it was really worth doing.'[2] But Tennant had an ulterior motive, as he later relayed to the journalist Jude Rogers. 'It was a bit cheeky,' he explained, but he added a postscript to the text: 'Could you pass on to the prime minister that in Alan Turing's centenary year it would be an amazing inspirational thing to do to pardon him?'[3]

The following year, the British mathematician and computer scientist Alan Mathison Turing was issued a posthumous pardon for his historical convictions for homosexual behaviour. Turing, who had died in 1954 after being subjected to chemical castration rather than face imprisonment, had already become a well-known figure to the British and international public before this, but the pardon bolstered his reputation. One of his most famous interventions in the field of computation had been a hypothetical means of testing whether a computer could replicate the behaviours of a human such that it became indistinguishable from that human; known universally as the 'Turing test', this idea was referred to by Turing himself as an 'imitation game', a term that was then adopted in a highly successful (if historically contentious) 2014 Hollywood production of the same name, starring Benedict Cumberbatch as Turing. Turing's face now appears on the Bank of England's £50 note, and his reputation is such that, in 2019, BBC Two's *Icons* television show, polling audiences for the 'greatest person of the twentieth century', ranked Turing as the winner, above Nelson Mandela, Albert Einstein and Mahatma Gandhi.[4] Not incidentally to these developments, on 23 July 2014 the Pet Shop Boys debuted their

---

[2]Jude Rogers, 'The Pet Shop Boys on Texting Cameron and Russian Homophobia', *New Statesman*, 26 September 2013, https://www.newstatesman.com/culture/music-theatre/2013/09/beyond-suburbs-utopia.
[3]Jude Rogers, '"We Wrote it for Alan": Pet Shop Boys Take Their Turing Opera to the Proms', *Observer*, 20 July 2014, https://www.theguardian.com/music/2014/jul/20/pet-shop-boys-alan-turing-enigma-proms-tribute-interview.
[4]*Icons – The Greatest Person of the Twentieth Century*, episode 8, 'Live Final', directed by James Morgan, 5 February 2019, BBC Two, https://www.bbc.co.uk/programmes/m0002fl3.

FIGURE 3.1 *Alan Turing, the computer scientist and mathematician to whom* A Man from the Future *is dedicated.*

biographical work *A Man From the Future* at the BBC Proms, based on Turing's life.[5]

It is not the contention of this chapter that Neil Tennant's 'cheeky' message to David Cameron was the causative factor in rehabilitating Alan Turing, nor in sparking the remarkable resurgence in his public reputation and persona. (As Tennant himself notes, his text was sent in the context of having heard 'rumours' that Cameron's government was intending to pardon Turing.) However, Tennant and Lowe's advocacy of Turing must be seen in the context of their broader work. On the surface, the Pet Shop Boys' overt, decades-long criticism of celebrity activism, represented not only by their public statements but also by their oeuvre, stands at odds with Tennant's proactive intervention at the highest levels of government on behalf of righting a historical injustice. Certainly, throughout their careers the Pet Shop Boys have often been dismissed by critics for merely producing

---

[5]*Proms 2014*, 'Prom 8: The Pet Shop Boys', performed by Neil Tennant et al., 23 July 2014, BBC Three, https://www.bbc.co.uk/programmes/b04b2m2y.

'emotionally bankrupt dance music' with no broader significance than offering catchy pop beats and synth refrains, while Tennant himself once stated in an interview with Reuters, 'I don't want to talk about [politics]. We are musicians, not politicians.'[6]

However, I argue here that the 'calculated nonchalance' that has been cultivated by Tennant and Lowe since the 1980s masks a much deeper commitment to activism (or, perhaps more appropriately, restorative justice) than their oft-repeated criticisms of celebrity campaigning suggest. It is hardly revolutionary to point out that the Pet Shop Boys' discography contains political and social commentary; instead, this chapter posits that the public persona adopted by both Tennant and Lowe, in conjunction with their performance, is designed so as to make precise interventions in causes they deem to be particularly relevant to their identities as artists and, crucially, as *queer* artists. This form of 'quiet activism' has been a hallmark of their work since the 1980s, and their profound interest in Alan Turing – resulting not only in direct messaging to the British prime minister but also, indeed, an entire staged operatic biography dedicated to his life and legacy – serves as both the most visible example but also the logical culmination of these acts. In the final analysis, *A Man From the Future* is not an outlier in their back catalogue but emblematic of the 'unique contribution they make to music, art, and wider culture', as well as a salient reminder that 'if Neil and Chris didn't move to make an electronically-fuelled, modern musical biography in this style' – especially one designed as an act of restoration and of justice – then 'no one else really could'.[7]

Another major artist on a higher plane? Celebrity activism and the Pet Shop Boys

On the face of it, it seems to be quite some achievement to be responsible for uncounted high-energy dance tracks and to have personified so much of the tentatively-optimistic euphoria of 1990s queerness, and yet to continue to carry the label of 'the grumpiest men in pop'. Nevertheless, these two seemingly paradoxical positions are part and parcel of the Pet Shop Boys as a whole. There are many reasons why this reputation took hold. For one, as Adrian Daub notes, even the most exuberant of the Pet Shop Boys' output is

---

[6]Patricia Juliana Smith, '"Go West": The Pet Shop Boys' Allegories and Anthems of Postimperiality', *Genre* 34, no. 3–4 (2001): 308; Chris Heath, *Pet Shop Boys versus America* (London: William Heinemann, 2020), 241.
[7]Ben Kelly, 'Festival Review: Pet Shop Boys' "A Man from the Future"', *Attitude*, 7 September 2017, https://www.attitude.co.uk/culture/film-tv/festival-review-pet-shop-boys-a-man-from-the-future-281193/.

tinged with notes of sometimes-bitter caution.[8] For every moment of queer liberation, in other words, there is always a mitigating factor in the background, threatening to undermine it – jealousy, fear, uncertainty, ambition. Nor are these threats always external; all too often, argues Daub, the call is coming from inside the house. Such nuances contrast the work of the Pet Shop Boys with other, comparable groups, who embrace queer joy with enthusiasm. The darker subtext – effectively an asterisk after the most smile-inducing verses and choruses to remind the listener that happiness and love are conditional and that terms and conditions apply – characterizes much of the Pet Shop Boys' back catalogue, providing a significant lyrical foundation for their aura of grumpiness.

Another aspect of this 'grumpiness' concerns their public and, sometimes, performance personas. In 1991, on the eve of their first United States tour, they were labelled 'the world's most wilfully perverse pop stars' by the *Washington Post*, specifically because 'they refused to smile on album covers and videos and publicity photos', their love of disco, their having 'dug up de trop divas such as Liza Minelli [sic.] and Dusty Springfield', and because of their 'archly, outspokenly ambivalent' attitude towards rock.[9] Of particular note here is Chris Lowe, who in general remains less publicly active than his bandmate, and whose stage persona is often so static that, once more, American audiences wondered if he contributed anything.[10] Lowe also recalls that his subdued style came about as a reaction to the saturation of overly positive, energetic pop acts of the 1980s: 'Everyone was so *active*. It was a big party where everyone was having a great time and smiling at the camera. Thumbs aloft! We just didn't want to do that. So we ignored the cameras and the jollity of the situations.'[11] The sense of affected antipathy typifies Lowe's on-stage presence; famously, during the Pet Shop Boys' 1991 *Performance* tour, Lowe appeared on stage to provide the vocals for the B-side track 'We All Feel Better in the Dark', only to strip to his underwear and read *Playboy* magazines ('the crew used to sellotape in other pictures', Lowe assured the music journalist Jon Savage, 'so I never knew quite what was going to appear').[12] The sensation of the moment – 'one of the highlights of the second tour', according to Savage – was underscored by Lowe's

---

[8]Cf. Adrian Daub, 'The End of the West: Community and Chorus in the Pet Shop Boys since "Go West"', in this volume.
[9]Joe Brown, 'Pet Project Boys on Tour', *Washington Post*, 5 April 1991, https://www.washingtonpost.com/archive/lifestyle/1991/04/05/pet-project-boys-on-tour/9ca2aa22-b864-429b-a51a-17634471a3b8/. '[S]inger Tennant even yawned on the cover of their best-selling 1987 album *Actually*', Brown notes, scandalized, in what was apparently, for the late-1980s and early-1990s United States, a gesture that was beyond the pale.
[10]Brown, 'Pet Project Boys on Tour'.
[11]Andrew Harrison, 'Pop Kid – Chris Lowe of Pet Shop Boys Interviewed', *The Quietus*, 22 March 2016, https://thequietus.com/articles/19915-pet-shop-boys-chris-lowe-interview.
[12]Chris Lowe, interview with Jon Savage, *Alternative Pet Shop Boys* liner notes (1995), 19–20.

impassive mien as he removed his trousers. Even more emblematic was the interview Lowe gave to *Entertainment Tonight* in Los Angeles in 1986, in which he declared, 'I don't like country and western. I don't like rock music, I don't like rockabilly or rock and roll particularly. I don't like much, really, do I?' Rather than disavowing the sentiment, Tennant and Lowe took it to heart, sampling the interview audio to form the spoken-word bridge in their 1987 club hit 'Paninaro'.[13]

The Pet Shop Boys' apparent apathy towards the conventions of show business extend further than affect and dismissive interviews. On a more substantial level, their 'grumpiness' is underlined and typified exemplarily by what they have frequently painted as the empty, cynical 'activism' that they consider to be an expected part of the music business. Speaking to Chris Heath about the Irish rock group U2, Tennant infamously claimed:

> The fact of the matter is that the Pet Shop Boys stand against all of this [. . .] Because we hate everything that they [U2] are and stand for. We hate it because it's totally stultifying, it says nothing, it is big and pompous and ugly. We hate it for exactly the same reasons Johnny Rotten said he hated dinosaur groups in 1976. To me U2 are a total dinosaur group. They're saying nothing but they're pretending to be something. I think they're *fake*.[14]

Jan-Niklas Jäger has pointed to the specific reasons why U2 was a target for Tennant's ire. Firstly, Jäger notes, U2 had received significant praise for their 1983 single 'Sunday Bloody Sunday', referring to the 1972 massacre of fourteen unarmed Catholic protestors in Derry by British paratroopers. Though 'Sunday Bloody Sunday' has entered the public consciousness as a brave intervention in the Northern Irish conflict – among other accolades, it was named by *Time* magazine in 2010 as one of the ten greatest protests songs in popular music history[15] – this legacy ignores that U2 self-consciously shied away from making any political statement of any sort. Indeed, the band's drummer Larry Mullen explained at the time, 'Like you talk about Northern Ireland, "Sunday Bloody Sunday", people sort of think, "Oh, that time when 13 Catholics were shot by British soldiers"; that's not what the song is about [. . .] I don't care who's who – Catholics, Protestants, whatever.'[16] Such statements likely bolstered Tennant's belief that Bono,

---

[13]Chris Lowe and Neil Tennant, interview with Jon Savage, *Alternative Pet Shop Boys* liner notes (1995), 10–11.
[14]Chris Heath, *Pet Shop Boys, Literally* (London: William Heinemann, 2020), 181.
[15]Alexandra Silver, 'Top 10 Protest Songs: "Sunday Bloody Sunday"', *Time*, 3 May 2010, https://entertainment.time.com/2010/05/04/kent-state-40-years-later-top-10-protest-songs/slide/sunday-bloody-sunday-1983-u2/.
[16]Jan-Niklas Jäger, *Factually: Pet Shop Boys in Theorie und Praxis* (Mainz: Ventil Verlag, 2019), 32.

Mullen and their bandmates were dabbling in politics about which they were thoroughly ignorant, a position no doubt exacerbated by the prominent role U2 played in Bob Geldof's 1984 charity supergroup Band Aid, which produced the catchy yet tin-eared 'Do They Know It's Christmas?' How else to read Bono's exhortation to 'thank God it's them [i.e. those starving through the Ethiopian famine] instead of you', but with a cocked eyebrow and cynicism? And how else to understand the characterization of the famine as a product of disastrous but common climate conditions ('There won't be snow in Africa this Christmas time', 'Where nothing ever grows / No rain or rivers flow'), when 'the song never comes upon the idea that the poverty of the continent also could have something to do with the wealth of the industrial nations'?[17] With this in mind, it is little wonder that Tennant once told journalists that he did not like 'the idea of people projecting themselves as being important humanitarian figures, which is the tendency for rock personalities nowadays'.[18]

Hence, the animus against a band that 'says nothing' while being 'big and pompous and ugly'. Tennant and Lowe took up this criticism in 'How Can You Expect to Be Taken Seriously?', the third single to be released from 1990's *Behaviour*. In a song dripping with Pet Shop Boys' classic sarcasm, Tennant lampoons celebrities who claim to 'really hate publicity' yet 'live within the headlines so everyone can see' that they are 'supporting every new cause'. The credibility given these celebrities, Tennant reasons, comes down to their ability to 'live upon a stage', resulting in them being seen as 'the brightest hope by far' for causes they do not understand and to which they have nothing meaningful to contribute; the outcome, he notes with some irony (and in another thinly-veiled jab at U2), is the likelihood that 'they'll put you in the Rock and Roll Hall of Fame'.[19] In an effort to solidify the link between this sort of meaningless activism and the activities of the Irish band, the Pet Shop Boys released the song as a joint A-side with their own cover of U2's 'Where the Streets Have No Name', to which they added their own twist of irreverence by mashing it up with Frankie Valli's 1962 hit, 'Can't Take My Eyes Off You'.[20] Three years later, Tennant and Lowe would once more take aim at celebrity-for-the-sake-of-celebrity on 'Shameless', the

---

[17] Jäger, *Factually*, 33.
[18] Heath, *Pet Shop Boys, Literally*, 36.
[19] Pet Shop Boys, 'How Can You Expect to Be Taken Seriously?', Parlophone, 1990.
[20] The choice was quite deliberate, according to Tennant: 'It worked as a concept: one song is about rock stars so to have a U2 song with it serves as a further comment.' 'Where the streets have no name (I can't take my eyes off you). How can you expect to be taken seriously?', *PetShopBoys.co.uk*, https://www.petshopboys.co.uk/product/single/where-the-streets-have-no-name-i-cant-take-my-eyes-off-you-how-can-you-expect-to-be-taken-seriously. For their part, Bono et al. appear to have taken the 'feud' in good humour: not only did U2 authorize the rights for the cover recording, but they also released a simple public statement: 'What have we done to deserve this?' Brown, 'Pet Project Boys on Tour'.

B-side to 'Go West', in which Tennant satirizes public figures who are 'a slave to glamour, applause and clamour' and who are 'ready to crawl to obtain celebrity'.[21] Criticism of celebrity culture remains a staple of the Pet Shop Boys' output, as demonstrated by their 2019 EP *Agenda*, on which one of the four songs constitutes a critical engagement with and against Instagram influencers and Twitter trendsetters ('On Social Media'), while another castigates the wealthy for twisting the political agenda against the public interest and to their own ends ('What Are We Going To Do About The Rich?').

It is tempting to read in these a dismissal of politics as a whole, a declaration of principles that it is not the place of artists and musicians in particular to meddle in affairs that fall outside their ken; the Pet Shop Boys, as Tennant succinctly noted, are not politicians. Yet, as others emphasize, this would be a curious position for a group whose output is principally political in nature. The present volume alone demonstrates this through multiple avenues.[22] Beyond these, their engagement with politics has sometimes been more explicit than others. 'London' (2002) sought to engage with the problems faced by immigrants from the collapsed Soviet Union, seeking to find their place in the British capital in a capitalist system that demonized them and offered them only the dichotomous solutions of 'hard work or credit card fraud' in order to survive. 'I'm With Stupid', the lead single from 2006's *Fundamental*, was written in answer to Britain's 'special relationship' with the United States and, in particular, the invasion of Iraq in 2003. It portrays then-Prime Minister Tony Blair as a lovelorn sycophant, pandering to his 'moron, a billion-dollar kid', then-United States President George W. Bush. On the same album, Tennant continued his vitriol against Blair, in particular in relation to the attempt by Blair's Labour government to introduce compulsory identity cards – a proposed policy that caused Tennant to leave the Labour Party. The resulting song, 'Integral', borrows heavily from the themes of Yevgeny Zamyatin's dystopian novel *We* (1924), and in this way accuses Blair's New Labour project of the type of authoritarian overreach Zamyatin warned about through his construction of the totalitarian One State.[23] Uncountable examples abound; most recently, the 2020 album *Hotspot* acts as a long love letter to Berlin – Tennant and Lowe's adopted hometown – with its lead single 'Dreamland' acting as both an extolling of a (heavily idealized) Germany within a Europe in which 'you

---

[21] Pet Shop Boys, 'Shameless', Parlophone, 1993.
[22] Cf. Stephanie Polsky, 'The Currency We Spent: The Pet Shop Boys and the Actualization of Thatcherite Economics', and Jonathan Dean, 'Buying and Selling Your History: Navigating the Ruins of Neoliberalism with Tennant and Lowe', both in this volume.
[23] Amy L. Atchison and Shauna L. Shames, *Survive and Resist: The Definitive Guide to Dystopian Politics* (New York: Columbia University Press, 2019), 4.

don't need a visa / You can come and go and still be here', and by implication criticizing the reality of post-Brexit Britain.[24] *Agenda*'s lead track, 'Give Stupidity a Chance', explicitly criticized not only American President Donald J. Trump but also the UK's then-Education Secretary Michael Gove, whose infamous declaration that 'people have had enough of experts' prompted Tennant to muse 'Why face the facts when you can just feel the feelings?'[25]

Self-evidently, then, the exhortation that 'we're musicians, not politicians' does not preclude Tennant and Lowe from engaging in politics. Their criticism of political engagement by their fellow musicians has never rested on the fact of that engagement, rather the means by which that engagement is effected – the '*modus operandi* of these politically-motivated popstars'.[26] Their contempt and scorn stemmed not from the fact that Bono or Bob Geldof were wading into movements and events of great political importance – ongoing civil war and sectarian violence in Northern Ireland, or the endemic deaths of hundreds of thousands of people due to extreme poverty and malnutrition – but instead because these efforts seemed undergirded by a combination of naïveté and cynicism. On the one hand, the stars lacked any significant insight or knowledge concerning the cause they had adopted. Glib statements that Catholics and Protestants were united in their suffering sounded especially callous when applied to events in which the overwhelming force of the state had been applied with asymmetric brutality against unarmed civilian protestors, and the feelgood vibes of 'Do They Know It's Christmas?' not only conflated Ethiopia with the entire African continent but also obfuscated the complex local and transnational influences that had resulted in extreme hunger. Needless to say, knowing whether or not it was Christmas could not have been further from the minds of those the song purportedly represented, a fact both painfully obvious at the time but also pointedly elided by the enduring image of megastars coming together for a good cause and a chart-topper. On the other hand, it is this latter point – commercial and reputational success – that seemed to provide much of the motivation. The tendency of pop- and rockstars to hop from cause to cause,

---

[24]In discussing the lack of need for visas, Tennant repeats the critique that he levelled at Blair and Labour during the identity card debate: 'I hate the whole idea of, "Your papers please." We do not and should not have that in this country.' Somewhat paradoxically, Germany, portrayed in 'Dreamland' as a 'free land', has similar identity card laws to those proposed by Blair's government (albeit without a duty to carry, merely to possess). Carter F. Hanson, 'Pop Goes Utopia: An Examination of Utopianism in Recent Electronic Dance Pop', *Utopian Studies* 25, no. 2 (2014): 403.
[25]Ben Beaumont-Thomas, 'Pet Shop Boys lampoon Donald Trump and Michael Gove on new song', *Guardian*, 5 February 2019, https://www.theguardian.com/music/2019/feb/05/pet-shop-boys-donald-trump-michael-gove-give-stupidity-a-chance.
[26]Jäger, *Factually*, 33.

earning them plaudits for their social consciousness, characterized the 'fakeness' of the 'plastic posers' Tennant in particular had 'come to despise'.[27]

What of the alternative? The Pet Shop Boys' own long-running engagement with socio-political issues points not to a hypocrisy but instead underscores their critique of celebrity activism. Indeed, if the fatal flaws of the 'dinosaur groups' was that their background on the issues they preached about was superficial at best, and that they wielded activism as an instrument of their own commercial ambitions, then the antidotes are, logically, a genuine commitment to a cause and the uncoupling of it from the group's commercial success. The latter, at least, the Pet Shop Boys have always eschewed. 'We were always anxious to come over as not really proper pop groups,' Tennant said. 'We don't want to be the biggest group in the world.'[28] As to genuine commitment to a cause, another interview conducted by Tennant in 2013 offers further insight. Speaking of the band's success and appreciation, Tennant argued: '[W]e always have a tendency to feel oppositional. That's really inherent in what we do.'[29] While he was referring to their musical tendencies ('In the middle of Britpop, we're doing a Latin record, *Bilingual*'), Tennant could well have been providing commentary on how the group understands its role in public discourse: to represent those left behind by the establishment, to advocate for change and to provide meaningful input to debate.

When Lowe gave his interview with *Entertainment Tonight* in 1986, the enduring message was that he, and by extension the Pet Shop Boys as a whole, were apathetic, joyless, disdainful. But Lowe's emphasis, repeated in the sampling of the interview for 'Paninaro', was not on those things that he did not like or care about – country and western, rock, rockabilly, rock and roll – and much more on his concluding sentence: 'But what I do like, I love passionately.' If the Pet Shop Boys can be said to have engaged with anything consistently, critically and *passionately* over their careers, it is above all their advocacy for queerness and queer rights. In this context, and given their predilection for historical analogy, the text message to David Cameron's advisor and the biographical performance that would follow at the Proms demonstrate precisely the decades-long engagement with queer activism and the desire to say *something* as opposed to nothing, and it is to this engagement that we now turn.

---

[27] Pet Shop Boys, 'Shameless'.
[28] Bob Stanley, *Yeah Yeah Yeah: The Story of Modern Pop* (London: Faber & Faber, 2013), 458.
[29] Ian Harrison, '"We Prefer Not to Be Fake . . ." Neil Tennant of the Pet Shop Boys Interviewed', *MOJO* (2013), https://www.mojo4music.com/articles/stories/we-prefer-not-to-be-fake-pet-shop-boys-interviewed/.

I hope it's going to be alright: history and queer heritage from Section 28 to Pussy Riot

On 5 June 1988, the Piccadilly Theatre in London hosted *Before the Act*, a variety show-turned-theatrical production spearheaded by the actors Michael Cashman and Ian McKellen, the composer Stephen Oliver and the American screenwriter Martin Sherman. The event, an extravaganza featuring a variety of contemporary stars of stage, cinema, comedy and music, was conceived as a protest against the Thatcher government's imposition of Section 28 of the Local Government Act 1988 (more commonly known simply as 'Section 28' or, occasionally, 'Clause 28'), which stipulated that 'A local authority shall not [. . .] intentionally promote homosexuality or publish material with the intention of promoting homosexuality', nor that it should 'promote the teaching in any maintained school of the acceptability of homosexuality as a pretended family relationship'.[30] In essence, while homosexuality had been (partially) decriminalized since 1967, its practice had retained regulation that distinguished it from heterosexuality and marked it as less desirable behaviour in the eyes of the state; in 1988, the Conservative government sought to further marginalize gay people by stipulating that 'local authorities' could not treat homosexuality as a legitimate or acceptable 'lifestyle'.[31] *Before the Act*, billed as 'a celebration to counter the effects of Section 28', served partially as a protest against the imposition of the law, as well as a fundraising drive for the Organisation for Lesbian and Gay Action, a grassroots advocacy group devoted to 'bring[ing] together a wide range of all the different sections of lesbian and gay society and through which our many different voices could be heard', thereby spearheading direct political action against Section 28.[32]

As a display of solidarity on behalf of 'the happiness and dignity of every lesbian and gay man in the country', the show was a tremendous success. McKellen, in particular, rallied some 320 cast and crew across sixty acts for the evening, including Patrick Stewart, Jane Asher, Judi Dench and Stephen Fry (who himself had only recently publicly come out).[33] The opening act for the second half of the gala, in their first live performance since bursting into the charts with 'West End Girls' in 1985, was the Pet Shop Boys.[34]

---

[30] Local Government Act 1986, c.28.
[31] Paul Baker, *Outrageous! The Story of Section 28 and Britain's Battle for LGBT Education* (London: Reaktion, 2022), 11–12.
[32] Jennie Wilson, Kris Black and Phil King, 'Dear Friends', in *Before the Act: A Celebration to Counter the Effects of Section 28*, theatre programme (1988), 1.
[33] Darryl W. Bullock, *Pride, Pop and Politics: Music, Theatre and LGBT Activism, 1970–2021* (London: Omnibus, 2021), 272.
[34] Presumably unhappily, given their antipathy towards rock and rock artists, one journalist covering the event referred to Tennant and Lowe as '[r]ock stars The Pet Shop Boys'. Graham McKerrow, *Capital Gay*, 10 June 1988.

Lending their support to *Before the Act* was not a given. Indeed, as Michael Cashman notes, appearing at the event would tie performers' reputations to their relationship to the queer community, which would risk not only serious discrimination but also 'the synonymy with AIDS'. As a result, a number of potential contributors refused the invitation: despite Sherman's best efforts, only Sandy Wilson represented musical theatre, while Stephen Sondheim refused to allow a live performance of 'Somewhere' from *West Side Story* (although Leonard Bernstein, citing his own bisexuality, had given his blessing). 'A raft of "known-to-be-gay" performers', presumably fearing that appearing at the Piccadilly would effectively 'out' them in public, declared themselves 'unavailable' or heading 'out of town' for the weekend.[35] Given these circumstances, it is even more extraordinary that Tennant and Lowe gave their unconditional support to the cause.[36] Their two-song set was led by 'It's a Sin', which ultimately would not only become one of the group's most enduring megahits but also stands as arguably one of Tennant's most personal reflections on his own homosexuality and the reconciliation (or lack thereof) of this aspect of his being with his Catholic upbringing. While others might have been afraid that lending support to *Before the Act* might too closely tie them to public LGBTQIA+ identification, Tennant's appearance on stage coupled with his declaration that he '[t]urned over a new leaf / Then tore right through it' was a hardly subtle identification not only with the cause of opposing Section 28, but also with the very queer community that Section 28 threatened.[37]

---

[35] Michael Cashman, *One of Them* (London: Bloomsbury, 2020), 243–4.
[36] A common fallacy is that this was the Pet Shop Boys' first live performance. This is not true; Darryl Bullock states that it was their fifth live performance, and their first live show was a set performed at the Fridge Nightclub in Brixton on 24 September 1984. The confusion may come via two avenues. Firstly, Wayne Studer suggests that this would have been the first live performance since 'West End Girls' and 'Opportunities (Let's Make Lots of Money)' hit the charts in their re-recorded (and far more commercially successful) forms in 1985 and 1986, thus making this their first performance *since becoming famous*. Over the years, this caveat seems to have been forgotten. Neil Tennant himself stoked this mistaken belief as well: in February 1988, Pet Shop Boys appeared on stage at the BPI Awards, and mimed 'What Have I Done to Deserve This?' Afterwards, Tennant declared, 'I quite like proving that we can't cut it live. We're a pop group, not a rock 'n' roll group.' This may have solidified the impression that the Pet Shop Boys considered live performance to be a hallmark of rock musicians and, since they rejected rock, that they had therefore no intention of performing live before asked to do so by Ian McKellen. Bullock, *Pride, Pop and Politics*, 272; Wayne Studer, private correspondence with the author, 10 March 2023; 'History (1988)', *PetShopBoys.co.uk*, https://www.petshopboys.co.uk/history/1988.
[37] The messaging of the song, though obvious to queer listeners, somehow passed many others by; at the time, and perhaps led astray by the *Confiteor* spoken by Tennant at the end of the track, the Salvation Army's *War Cry* newsletter praised Tennant and Lowe for taking the concept of sin seriously. Arwa Haider, 'It's a Sin – Pure pop provocation from the Pet Shop Boys', *Financial Times*, 11 October 2021, https://ig.ft.com/life-of-a-song/its-a-sin.html.

Throughout the 1980s and 1990s, as the Pet Shop Boys more and more overtly embraced queerness, so too did their social commentary on queer life deepen. As early as 1987's *Actually*, Tennant and Lowe had tackled the effects of social censure ('It's a Sin') and the disastrous consequences of the HIV/AIDS pandemic ravaging international queer communities ('It Couldn't Happen Here').[38] Four months after taking to the stage at the Piccadilly, they released their third studio album, *Introspective*, whose rainbow cover resembled, while not actually replicating, Gilbert Baker's iconic Pride flag.[39] With the release of *Behaviour* in 1990, the Pet Shop Boys also released arguably their most influential AIDS-related song, 'Being Boring', lamenting the crumbling of queer hopes and dreams in the face of a virus and a public health catastrophe that robbed so many, as Tennant's haunting lyrics remind us, of the chance that 'you'd be sitting somewhere here with me'.[40]

Indeed, many of the Pet Shop Boys' songs have concerned the HIV/AIDS epidemic and its lasting effects on the queer community, events and issues that by their very nature were and are intrinsically political in nature. '[P]op music is about sex,' Tennant told Chris Heath, but such narratives could not help but engage in the politics of the body because 'AIDS has changed sex'.[41] By this reckoning, Tennant's mourning in 'Being Boring' is not merely the hopeless lamentation of a gay man who has lost friends and lovers, but a bittersweet protest that not more was done to save them. Its provocative accompanying video, showing naked men and two men kissing, was not only revolutionary for a pop music video, but also an oblique attack on the newly-tabled Criminal Justice Act 1991, according to which, 'Two men kissing, or simply holding hands, in the street would now be committing a serious sexual offence.'[42] 'It Couldn't Happen Here' sailed even closer to the wind.

---

[38]'It Couldn't Happen Here' is, in fact, listed on the official programme for *Before the Act*, which may suggest that it was the Pet Shop Boys' initial intention to perform this, rather than 'It's a Sin' and/or 'One More Chance'. Alternatively, given that both of these songs make up part of the soundtrack of the Jack Bond-directed film *It Couldn't Happen Here*, the billing on the programme may have been acknowledging Tennant and Lowe's writing credits for the film, rather than the songs. If so, it was premature, as *It Couldn't Happen Here* would not be released until the next month. *Before the Act*, /; see also Lisa-Marie Pöhland, 'It's a Sin: Religious Imageries and Queer Identities in *It Couldn't Happen Here*', in this volume.

[39]Wayne Studer, whose extraordinary website must be considered the first port of call for any Pet Shop Boys trivia, argues that this was likely by coincidence more than design, and resulted from graphic designer Mark Farrow emulating a page in a book of colour swatches. If this is the case, then the accident was remarkably fitting, given the six tracks of extended queer-coded dance music, the title recalling inward-looking self-reflection, and the cover emulating the most visible symbol of gay community. Wayne Studer, 'Introspective', *Commentary: Interpretation and Analysis of Every Song by Pet Shop Boys*, 7 March 2023, http://www.geowayne.com/newDesign/introspective/introspective.htm.

[40]Pet Shop Boys, 'Being Boring', Parlophone, 1990.

[41]Heath, *Pet Shop Boys versus America*, 14–15.

[42]Bullock, *Pride, Pop and Politics*, 291.

The title reflects not only Sinclair Lewis's 1935 dystopian novel *It Can't Happen Here*, in which the United States falls into the grips of xenophobic fascism, but also the cult 1966 independent film *It Happened Here*, which presents an alternate history in which the United Kingdom fell to the Nazis and the resulting occupation was propped up not with the overwhelming force of the foreign invaders but instead opportunistic collaborators. In this way, the destruction of an exuberant gay community 'in six inch heels, quoting magazines' is intertwined with the acts of an implicitly fascistic authority, taking advantage of the occasion of a deadly contagion to purge itself of social 'undesirables'. By 1993 and the more overtly camp *Very*, Tennant enmeshes the AIDS crisis with the very highest offices of the British establishment, using the analogy of meeting Queen Elizabeth II and Diana, Princess of Wales for tea to narrate the horror of there being 'no more lovers left alive'.[43] In the *New York Times*' review of 'the Pet Shop Boys' superb new album', critic Stephen Holden noted that, 'Without specifically mentioning AIDS, the crises involving the royal family or tabloid journalism, "Dreaming of the Queen," [sic.] paints a picture of a society being slowly torn at the seams by a malaise of which these things are all symptoms.'[44]

In this regard, *Bilingual* (1996) ostensibly appears to have jettisoned much of the dark pessimism of the state's relationship to queerness, in favour of the boppy exuberance of 'a brand new day' and throwing 'skeletons out of your closet' of 'Se a Vida É', or the celebration of the gay person who was 'once a caterpillar, now a butterfly' in 'Metamorphosis'.[45] One explanation for this apparently sunnier outlook is that *Bilingual* was not only the first album recorded since Neil Tennant 'officially' came out in 1994, but also that it was the first recorded since John Major's government had announced a reduction of the age of consent for male–male sexual relations to eighteen, down from the twenty-one that it had previously been. This was a major step towards repudiating some of the inequalities that had still been built into the law after the partial decriminalization of homosexuality in 1967.[46] Yet – as also noted by Daub – even the more optimistic notes of *Bilingual* were tempered with caution, and Tennant's 'waiting' and 'hoping' for a 'red letter day' spoke to the incomplete journey to equality (indeed, it would not be until 2001 that the age of consent for homosexual relationships was equalized with that for heterosexual relationships, at sixteen, while Section 28 remained in force until repealed by Blair in 2003).[47] Moreover, the funeral procession at the

---

[43]Pet Shop Boys, 'Dreaming of the Queen', Parlophone, 1993.
[44]Stephen Holden, 'Recording Views: Wry Musings on a Queen', *New York Times*, 21 November 1993, 42.
[45]Pet Shop Boys, 'Se a Vida É', Parlophone, 1996; Pet Shop Boys, 'Metamorphosis', Parlophone, 1996.
[46]'Everyone forgets it was [John Major] that started things off', Tennant said in an interview in 2014. Jude Rogers, '"We Wrote it For Alan"'.
[47]Cf. Daub, 'The End of the West'; Pet Shop Boys, 'A Red Letter Day', Parlophone, 1996.

heart of 'The Survivors' speaks to the lingering desolation of the AIDS crisis, while the album's lead single, the upbeat and dancy 'Before', reminds listeners of 'the man who loved too much' and who 'ended up inside a prison cell' – the 'suspicious hell' that had awaited queer people until the recent past.[48]

Tennant and Lowe did not limit themselves to the caprices of lyrical interpretation, however; nor was *Before the Act* the only time that they would explicitly campaign for queer rights and support queer causes. In 1997, coinciding both with the release of *Bilingual* in the previous year and the fall of the Conservative government in Britain, they headlined the Gay Pride music festival in London, which until this point was the largest Pride event in British history. Here, in addition to the obligatory 'It's a Sin' and 'Go West', they also played 'Somewhere' – the same show tune that Stephen Sondheim had refused permission to be performed a decade earlier. In October of the same year, they also played the Equality Show at the Royal Albert Hall, organized by the LGBTQIA+ charity and advocacy group Stonewall.[49] This was, in fact, the second time the Pet Shop Boys had played the Stonewall Equality Show. The first, in 1993 at the London Palladium, was at the direct invitation, once more, of Ian McKellen, with the explicit goal of campaigning for the equalization of the age of consent.[50] Prior to this, they had already played an AIDS benefit show in New York. At the end of the decade, Tennant and Lowe also announced *Wotapalava*, billed as the 'first openly gay pop music festival to tour the United States' and featuring the Pet Shop Boys alongside Sinéad O'Connor, Soft Cell and Rufus Wainwright; the festival, however, fell through after O'Connor pulled out.[51]

Whatever the form of their commentary, what is clear from this trajectory is that the Pet Shop Boys have actively involved themselves in queer causes, effectively since the onset of their careers. At times, this activism was viewed in cynical terms, especially among gay critics. In 1991, for example, one American gay magazine presented Tennant and Lowe's lack of public statements about their sexuality as an example of cynical appropriation of gay culture without giving adequate recompense. 'The Pet Shop Boys owe a lot to gay men,' one editorial argued. 'We gave them their material. We are their audience *and* their brothers. We made them stars, yet they stay in the

---

[48]Pet Shop Boys, 'The Survivors', Parlophone, 1996; Pet Shop Boys, 'Before', Parlophone, 1996.
[49]'History (1997)', *PetShopBoys.co.uk*, https://www.petshopboys.co.uk/history/1997.
[50]'History (1993)', *PetShopBoys.co.uk*, https://www.petshopboys.co.uk/history/1993. Sir Ian McKellen, answering fan mail, recalled asking them to play the Equality Show, but mistakenly placed the year at 1992. Ian McKellen to Lee Richards, in 'E-Post: Correspondence with Ian McKellen. Bits and Bobs', *Ian McKellen Official Home Page*, https://www.mckellen.com/epost/m001003.htm.
[51]'O'Connor causes Palava for Pet Shop Boys', *NME*, 31 May 2001, https://www.nme.com/news/music/osinead-connor-4-1386970. From 2018 until her death in 2023, O'Connor changed her name to Shuhada' Sadaqat. While recording and publishing, however, she still used the name Sinéad O'Connor, and it is for this reason that this work will refer to her as O'Connor rather than Sadaqat.

closet. It's time they paid that bill.'[52] Yet it is hard to reconcile this with the reality of the Pet Shop Boys' long-standing and targeted activism in support of queer causes. Indeed, the very same American gay critics condemning Tennant and Lowe for not publicly coming out, in spite of the fact that 'every nuance of their music, lyrics, personal style and sensibility *screams* it', also cried plaintively for people to 'get your butts out in the streets with us and protest AIDS and gay issues'. This very pattern of action would be a hallmark of the Pet Shop Boys' political engagement, beginning at the Piccadilly and continuing – but by no means ending – over a quarter-century later in the Royal Albert Hall, in celebration of Alan Turing.

One could conform, rebel, or withdraw: Turing and the culmination of queer activism

And so here, at last, we return to Turing. The reader may be forgiven for thinking this a late juncture to address the subject of this chapter. In many ways, however, Turing is not central to the story being told here. Rather, he provided an *occasion*, an exemplary opportunity, to place the Pet Shop Boys' activism into sharp relief. He is, in other words, and with the full awareness of the irony of describing a man famous for his code-breaking as such, a *cipher*: a vehicle to illustrate Tennant and Lowe's grasp of queer history and its application to the present.

Turing is by no stretch of the imagination the first historical queer person to figure in a Pet Shop Boys work. 'Jack the Lad', the B-side of the 1987 single 'Suburbia', not only invokes the figure of T. E. Lawrence (better known as 'Lawrence of Arabia'), whose sexuality has long been disputed, but also borrows a line from Oscar Wilde, whose trial for gross indecency in 1895 remains a touchstone of British queer history and a parallel example of homophobic injustice similar to that which would befall Turing six decades later.[53] Wilde would once more be referenced in the 1991 single 'DJ

---

[52]Joe Clark, 'In and Out with the Pet Shop Boys', *OutWeek* 97 (May 1991): 53. The magazine had a special opprobrium for Tennant and Lowe; in the preceding issue, its journalists declared the Pet Shop Boys to be 'terminally bored shopping monsters', 'self-indulgent' and 'cold', while the very next issue viciously declared that they lacked queer solidarity and were 'two big, greedy, creepy, hopeless pieces of shit'. Liz Tracey and Sydney Pokorny, 'Out on the Town with Liz & Sydney', *OutWeek* 96 (May 1991): 57; Michelangelo Signorile, 'Gossip Watch', *OutWeek* 98 (May 1991): 48.

[53]Also mentioned in the lyrics is the figure of 'Philby'. Kim Philby, the infamous Soviet double-agent, was known to be a philanderer and there was scandal surrounding the homosexual proclivities of the so-called 'Cambridge Five'; in the event, though, only two of them – Guy Burgess and Donald MacLean – were gay. Neil Tennant has also stated in interviews that Philby, in this case, not only refers to Kim, but also to his father, St John Philby, a noted British Arabist. Neil Tennant, interview with Jon Savage, *Alternative Pet Shop Boys* liner notes (1995), 21; Bullock, *Pride, Pop and Politics*, 14.

Culture', through a close paraphrasing of his retort having been sentenced at his trial: 'And I, my Lord – may I say nothing?'[54] Stephen Ward, the society osteopath whose role in the Profumo sex scandal in the 1960s led to his evisceration in the media and ultimately his suicide, is both eulogized and defended in 1989's 'Nothing Has Been Proved', which the Pet Shop Boys wrote and demoed for Dusty Springfield. Ward, whose sexuality was ambiguous, was assumed in more than one quarter to be 'a homo [...] struggling wildly to be let out', frustrated by 'latent homosexuality or impotence', which may in turn have influenced the hostility towards him.[55]

However, though these figures have made appearances in Pet Shop Boys works, it is Turing, rather than Ward or Wilde, who inspired – or perhaps necessitated – a full biographical treatment, rather than a single song or recurring mention. In part, this may be attributed to Tennant's long-term interest in Turing as a subject. In the 1980s he had seen the play *Breaking the Code*, in which Turing is the protagonist: an 'extraordinary quirky genius' with 'this incredible vision of the Universal Machine, and going round telling people he was homosexual'.[56] By his own admission, however, Tennant's conception of Turing did not exceed this image of an eccentric but brilliant man, who seemed not to recognize that publicly declaring his homosexuality in the pre-Wolfenden era could be dangerous. Given the time at which Tennant became aware of Turing, this was understandable. Turing's specialization in computing had little resonance in a decade in which the personal computer was still the purview of science fiction. Moreover, with the advent of Section 28 and the AIDS crisis, the queer community faced clear and present existential threats, in which politicians and journalists alike openly engaged in queerphobic genocidal rhetoric. In such a climate, Tennant and Lowe's willingness to publicly declare their support of LGBTQIA+ causes such as *Before the Act* already placed them at the vanguard of contemporary artist-activists and, while not irrelevant to the moment, the injustice suffered by Turing in the 1950s was understandably not an immediate priority. Indeed, it would take more than two decades before Tennant, watching a documentary on Channel 4, remembered Turing and began to research him further. After reading Andrew Hodges' biography of Turing (the same work, as it happens, that provided the basis for *The Imitation Game*), Tennant and Lowe began work on what would become *A Man from the Future*.[57]

---

[54]Pet Shop Boys, 'DJ Culture', Parlophone, 1991.
[55]Cited in Richard Davenport-Hines, *An English Affair: Sex, Class and Power in the Age of Profumo* (London: William Collins, 2013), 100. See also Christopher Spinks, '"All that Swinging Sixties. It Never Did Anyone Any Good, Did It?" The Pet Shop Boys and the Scandal of the Profumo Affair', in this volume.
[56]Rogers, '"We Wrote it for Alan"'.
[57]Rogers, '"We Wrote it for Alan"'.

Comprising eight movements and narrated through both spoken word and choral interventions, *A Man from the Future* tells the abridged story of Turing's life, beginning as 'a child of the British Empire' at 'Sherbourne, a moderately distinguished public school'.[58] The gift of a children's textbook – Edwin Tenney Brewster's *Natural Wonders Every Child Should Know* (1912) – is here interpolated by Tennant and Lowe not just as the origin point for Turing's fascination with science, but also his investigations into his own sexuality. The intertwined nature of these two strands of Turing's being provide a cohesion to the work, a constant narrative thread. Turing's early scientific curiosity also opened avenues to understand himself; it had, according to Juliet Stevenson's narration,

> [. . .] opened his eyes to science, but more than that, it opened the book of life, attempting to answer the question: what have I in common with other living things? And how do I differ from them? And by what process of becoming did I, myself, finally appear in this world? It was an introduction to science and sex, and conveyed the idea that there had to be a reason for the way things were, and the reason came not from God, but from science . . . because the body, of course, is a machine.[59]

Here, Turing's sexuality – 'for although he had surely learned by now about the birds and the bees, his heart was to be elsewhere' – is presented as an immutable (indeed, a natural) fact, no different from 'why the sky is blue / and grass is green', and intrinsically connected to the scientific genius that originally manifested itself in 'chemistry experiments and inventing things'. Indeed, Turing's first love, a fellow schoolboy at Sherbourne named Christopher Morcom, is also passionate about science, and his death from tuberculosis spurs Turing to 'put as much energy, if not as much interest, into my work as if he were alive'.[60] Emerging from this, the libretto demonstrates, Turing's unique faculties unfolded, in which '[t]hinking and doing, the logical and the physical' were intricately connected. The lack of differentiation between the personal and the professional, or the scientific and the sexual, results in the libretto flowing seamlessly between the two. By the sixth movement ('The Trial'), Turing's intellectual struggles with 'the problem of his theory' is juxtaposed with his first meeting with Arnold Murray in 1951, the relationship that would end with Turing's arrest on charges of gross indecency. Moreover, once arrested, Turing recognizes not

---

[58] Pet Shop Boys, 'Natural Wonders Every Child Should Know', *A Man from the Future*, at *Proms 2014*, 'Prom 8: The Pet Shop Boys'.
[59] Pet Shop Boys, 'Natural Wonders Every Child Should Know'.
[60] Pet Shop Boys, 'Natural Wonders Every Child Should Know'; Andrew Hodges, *Alan Turing – The Enigma* (Princeton, NJ, and Oxford: Princeton University Press, 2014), 61.

only the devastating consequences to his person and reputation but also to his work; belatedly he realizes that, now that he has been identified as a homosexual, the great accomplishments of his life will be discredited. This is expressed through a bitter syllogism: 'Turing believes machines think. Turing lies with men. Therefore machines do not think.'[61]

In presenting Turing in this fashion, Tennant and Lowe seek to undercut one of the key contentions facing Turing's pardon. In 2009, then-Prime Minister Gordon Brown, crediting 'a coalition of computer scientists, historians and LGBT (lesbian, gay, bisexual and transgender) activists', issued an apology for Turing's punishment and eventual suicide. This stopped short of a pardon for, while Brown recognized that 'his treatment was of course utterly unfair', he conceded that 'Turing was dealt with under the law of the time.' The apology, however, focused extensively on Turing's achievements as a mathematician, a computer scientist and a code-breaker during the war. Indeed, the apology seemed more predicated on the fact that 'Turing was a quite brilliant mathematician, most famous for his work on the German Enigma codes', without whom 'the history of the Second World War could have been very different', and that because of this 'it [is] all the more horrifying, therefore, that he was treated so inhumanely'.[62] Such a focus has the effect, intentional or otherwise, of affirming the lawfulness of the persecution of Turing *as a gay man*, but problematizes it only in relation to his status as an exceptional figure and, arguably, a war hero. This tension is explicitly referenced in the narration of the final movement, 'A Man from the Future': as the choir recites the text of the official pardon posthumously issued to Turing by the Queen on 'the twenty-fourth day of December 2013, in the sixty-second year of Our Reign', Stevenson reminds us that '[a]n exception was made' and that '[t]he convictions for gross indecency of tens of thousands of other men, dead and alive, remain unpardoned'. Thus, while Turing's pardon came because he was, as the performance insists, a 'man from the future', that future was not simply based on his breakthroughs in computer science, nor in mathematics, nor even in that his work during the Second World War proved important to the reliable gathering of German signals intelligence. Instead, Turing's innovation was that he 'had imagined a world with intelligent computers [and] where homosexual life is normal'.[63] Neither of these should be viewed in isolation from the other – in fact, Tennant and

---

[61]Pet Shop Boys, 'The Trial', *A Man from the Future*, at *Proms 2014*, 'Prom 8: The Pet Shop Boys'.
[62]Caroline Davies, 'PM's apology to codebreaker Alan Turing: We were inhumane', *Guardian*, 11 September 2009, https://www.theguardian.com/world/2009/sep/11/pm-apology-to-alan-turing.
[63]Pet Shop Boys, 'A Man from the Future', *A Man from the Future*, at *Proms 2014*, 'Prom 8: The Pet Shop Boys'.

Lowe's libretto, narrated with gravitas by Stevenson, makes it clear that they *cannot* be separated one from the other.

A Man from the Future therefore occupies a complex and, at first, seemingly paradoxical position within the Pet Shop Boys' pattern of activism and restorative justice. On its surface level, its objectives are limited to the rehabilitation of Alan Turing, in much the same way that Tennant's text message to a Downing Street staffer after the Olympics winners' parade called for Turing's pardon on the occasion of his centenary year. The work does much to remind its listeners of Turing's brilliance in his fields. In particular, the second movement, 'He Dreamed of Machines', places special emphasis on the revolutionary idea of the 'Universal Machine', which (with some poetic licence) Turing conceived while '[a]t Grantchester, lying in a meadow'.[64] Over the course of the piece's forty-eight minutes, there is no doubt that Turing was an exceptional figure. Yet, in the last moments of the final movement, the audience is reminded that Turing's treatment at the hands of the state he had faithfully served was not exceptional, but rather the rule, and that his fate was shared by thousands of other gay men who lacked the cultural capital and historical import to be considered for a prime minister's apology or, indeed, a Royal Pardon. Tennant and Lowe make clear that Turing's obsession with machines and computation were bound to his efforts to understand his own body, mind and sexuality. His genius, therefore, cannot be understood without engaging with his queerness. As a result, while both the apology and the pardon seemed to cite Turing's brilliance as the deciding factor, the Pet Shop Boys insist that it was not the computer scientist who required pardoning, but the gay man – and if this was the case, then there could be *no* exception made, because no historical conviction under gross indecency laws was just. To that end, while Turing's example provides an exemplar, the conception of *A Man from the Future* emphasizes that 'homosexual life is normal' and, in doing so, brings together the many strands of Pet Shop Boys' queer activism that began in the Piccadilly Theatre in 1988 and continued, via AIDS benefits and Stonewall shows and Pride parades, to this crowning moment in the Royal Albert Hall.

Conclusion: ranting and raving and bitching 'bout Putin

The Pet Shop Boys' activist work and political engagement did not begin with Alan Turing, nor has it ended with him. Though *A Man from the Future* was a celebration of Turing's life, and the reciting of the Royal Pardon was

---

[64] Pet Shop Boys, 'He Dreamed of Machines', *A Man from the Future*, at *Proms 2014*, 'Prom 8: The Pet Shop Boys'.

accompanied by a triumphant crescendo, the concluding reminder of the many thousands of historic convictions visited upon gay men serves to demonstrate not only that past injustices cannot simply be undone, but that there remains significant work to be done in the present and future. That much has been made clear by Tennant himself. In 2017, for the first time since headlining Pride on Clapham Common in London twenty years earlier, the Pet Shop Boys played at the Tel Aviv Pride in Israel. Speaking a few weeks after the event, Tennant was asked, given the then-recent lurch to the right in the United States under the Trump presidency and its attacks on the LGBTQIA+ and, particularly, trans community, 'if there will be an extra sense of defiance and expression from the gay community at Prides across the world?' Tennant's response was unequivocal: 'Violent homophobia is still practised and even encouraged around much of the world – nothing can be taken for granted.'[65]

Tennant's words reflect not only the determination of an old hand who has campaigned for queer rights much of his professional life, but also someone keenly aware of the contingent nature of those rights. Certainly, while the Trump administration's myriad queerphobic initiatives made headlines, and have had significant consequences, they did not spring from nothing; speaking to *Vanity Fair*'s Marc Spitz in 2012, Tennant noted the curious dichotomy of the 'extremes living side by side' in the United States, such that 'America is quite homophobic, but it's also totally gay. It's really weird.'[66] In 2014, in response to homophobia closer to home, Tennant and Lowe sampled a speech by the Irish drag queen Panti Bliss, releasing it on their website as a ten-minute-long single entitled 'The Best Gay Possible'.[67] Such works recognize that, though the days of artists fearing being associated with queer causes might be over, homo- and queerphobia remain oppressive social constants to be called out and combatted.

But, of course, it is also not true to say that those days *are* over. Since the beginning of the 2010s, amid significant crackdowns against LGBTQIA+ rights in Russia, Tennant and Lowe have emerged as outspoken critics of the regime of Vladimir Putin.[68] Initially, this came in the form of signing an open

---

[65] Edwin Gilson, 'Pride headliners Pet Shop Boys: "Nothing can be taken for granted"', *The Argus*, 4 August 2017, https://www.theargus.co.uk/leisure/music/15453763.pride-headliners-pet-shop-boys-nothing-can-be-taken-for-granted/.
[66] Marc Spitz, 'Pet Shop Boys' Neil Tennant Talks About American Homophobia', *Vanity Fair*, 29 August 2012, https://www.vanityfair.com/culture/2012/08/pet-shop-boys-neil-tennant-olympic-closing-ceremonies-performance.
[67] 'Pet Shop Boys use Panti Bliss speech in new track', *Irish Examiner*, 10 March 2014, https://www.irishexaminer.com/lifestyle/arid-30624713.html.
[68] One *Moscow Times* article painted Putin as the occasion by which the Pet Shop Boys 'get political', suggesting that this was the first occasion in which they had made any political statement. As this chapter has (hopefully) demonstrated, this can only be understood as a dramatic misreading of Tennant and Lowe's careers, both in music and elsewhere. Simone Peer, 'Pet Shop Boys Get Political', *Moscow Times*, 5 June 2013, https://www.themoscowtimes.com/2013/06/05/privatization-alternatives-from-the-baltics-part-2-a34526.

letter calling for the release of the queer feminist punk band Pussy Riot from prison, after their well-publicized 'punk prayer' criticizing Putin in the Cathedral of Christ the Saviour in Moscow in 2012. Over time, however, Tennant in particular has taken a firmer hand. 'Shame on Putin!' he posted to the Pet Shop Boys website in August 2012, after the prison sentence was handed down, noting that this also coincided with the banning of Gay Pride in Moscow.[69] In 2013, after Putin enforced so-called 'anti-gay propaganda laws', Tennant drew the parallel with Thatcher's Section 28, thus placing the band's opposition to Putin within the context of the very issue that began their public activism in the first place.[70] Putin's anti-queer authoritarianism has also been immortalized at least twice in the Pet Shop Boys' discography. The first explicit mention of him, in the bonus track 'Hell' (2012), imagines eternal damnation for those who 'love death, not life'. In this pantheon of evil (which, borrowing from Hannah Arendt's conception of the 'banality of evil', is referred to here as a 'bore with a big idea'), Putin shares space with Benito Mussolini, Adolf Hitler, Osama bin Laden and the serial killer Fred West.[71] Most recently, in 2023, the duo released via YouTube a 'home demo' of 'Living in the Past', with melancholy piano accompanying the narration of Putin's inner monologue as he strives to emulate Joseph Stalin. In the context of the 2022 invasion of Ukraine by Russia, the song ties the dictator's megalomania with toxic-masculine and queerphobic rhetoric.[72] Tennant emulates Putin's many wartime speeches by insisting that '[t]he West is effete / and they're begging for more' (perhaps unconsciously mirroring the Pet Shop Boys' previous lines in the guise of Donald Trump: 'Chicks are always up for it / You've got to grab whatever you can').[73] With characteristic irony, Tennant-*cum*-Putin declares, 'I'm the living embodiment / of a heart of stone; / A human monument / to testosterone.'[74]

Vladimir Putin's 'evil', as recognized by Tennant and Lowe, is planted firmly in his warmongering totalitarianism. An integral aspect of this is his queerphobic bigotry. Much as Alan Turing could not be understood as a computer genius without also taking into account his homosexuality, neither, the Pet Shop Boys argue, can Putin's desire for 'men to die / with my name on their lips' be separated from his hatred for men's lips to meet other men's

---

[69] Neil Tennant, 'Pet-Texts: Pussy Riot', *PetShopBoys.co.uk*, https://www.petshopboys.co.uk/pet-texts/2012-08-17/pussy-riot.
[70] Rogers, 'The Pet Shop Boys on Texting Cameron and Russian Homophobia'.
[71] Pet Shop Boys, 'Hell', Parlophone, 2012. Perhaps significantly, Putin is only one of two (then-) living denizens of Hell, the other being the Zimbabwean dictator Robert Mugabe.
[72] Among other statements by the group in support of Ukraine and against Russian aggression, as of the time of writing, navigating to the Pet Shop Boys website directs visitors to a landing page depicting the Ukrainian flag.
[73] Pet Shop Boys, 'Living in the Past', x2, 2023; Pet Shop Boys, 'Give Stupidity a Chance', x2, 2019.
[74] Pet Shop Boys, 'Living in the Past'. For further on this song, see Torsten Kathke, 'Go West, Young Band', in this volume.

lips.[75] This said, the Pet Shop Boys' agitation against Putin continues their long tradition of political activism: one based on those things that they, in Lowe's words, 'love passionately'. In their own estimation, this places them in direct contrast with rock bands such as U2, whose activism (in Tennant's more caustic analysis) has never extended beyond surface-level platitudes. In one respect, *A Man from the Future* can be seen as a culmination of decades of action for queer rights, a logical end-point that began with fighting for the right to acknowledge queerness as legitimate in its own right in spite of Section 28 and AIDS, continued to showcase queer pride within the public consciousness and ultimately sought at last to allow us, as a society, to reflect upon the wrongs that were inflicted in the past. Yet, in another respect, it demonstrates once more the Pet Shop Boys' mastery of ironic juxtaposition. The future Alan Turing was imagined having come from – that of computers and everyday queerness – has only partially come to pass. The future that we have *actually* arrived at is far more contingent. Far from entering a state of general acceptance and normalization, LGBTQIA+ existences remain subject to the whims of powers that may turn on them, and indeed have in many examples, the most emblematic of which (in the Pet Shop Boys' eyes, at least) is the regime of Vladimir Putin. But, as Tennant also argues, rights reversals in places that have previously, and through rose-tinted glasses, been considered bastions of queerness – in particular the United States and the United Kingdom, and explicitly with reference to the transgender community – mean that 'nothing can be taken for granted'. If Turing's future was the ideal, then it is clear that ours has fallen short. In this case, one wonders if the next stage is to take the Pet Shop Boys' own advice: 'Let's tear the whole bloody lot down / And start all over again.'[76]

Bibliography

Atchison, Amy L. and Shauna L. Shames. *Survive and Resist: The Definitive Guide to Dystopian Politics*. New York: Columbia University Press, 2019.

Baker, Paul. *Outrageous! The Story of Section 28 and Britain's Battle for LGBT Education*. London: Reaktion, 2022.

Beaumont-Thomas, Ben. 'Pet Shop Boys lampoon Donald Trump and Michael Gove on new song'. *Guardian*, 5 February 2019, https://www.theguardian.com/music/2019/feb/05/pet-shop-boys-donald-trump-michael-gove-give-stupidity-a-chance.

Brown, Joe. 'Pet Project Boys on Tour'. *Washington Post*, 5 April 1991, https://www.washingtonpost.com/archive/lifestyle/1991/04/05/pet-project-boys-on-tour/9ca2aa22-b864-429b-a51a-17634471a3b8/.

---

[75]Pet Shop Boys, 'Living in the Past'.
[76]Pet Shop Boys (featuring Phil Oakey), 'This Used to Be the Future', Parlophone, 2009.

Bullock, Darryl W. *Pride, Pop and Politics: Music, Theatre and LGBT Activism, 1970–2021*. London: Omnibus, 2021.
Cashman, Michael. *One of Them*. London: Bloomsbury, 2020.
Clark, Joe. 'In and Out with the Pet Shop Boys'. *OutWeek* 97 (May 1991).
Davenport-Hines, Richard. *An English Affair: Sex, Class and Power in the Age of Profumo*. London: William Collins, 2013.
Davies, Caroline. 'PM's apology to codebreaker Alan Turing: We were inhumane'. *Guardian*, 11 September 2009, https://www.theguardian.com/world/2009/sep/11/pm-apology-to-alan-turing.
Gilson, Edwin. 'Pride headliners Pet Shop Boys: "Nothing can be taken for granted"'. *The Argus*, 4 August 2017, https://www.theargus.co.uk/leisure/music/15453763.pride-headliners-pet-shop-boys-nothing-can-be-taken-for-granted/.
Haider, Arwa. 'It's a Sin – Pure pop provocation from the Pet Shop Boys'. *Financial Times*, 11 October 2021, https://ig.ft.com/life-of-a-song/its-a-sin.html.
Hanson, Carter F. 'Pop Goes Utopia: An Examination of Utopianism in Recent Electronic Dance Pop'. *Utopian Studies* 25, no. 2 (2014): 384–413.
Harrison, Andrew. 'Pop Kid – Chris Lowe of Pet Shop Boys Interviewed'. *The Quietus*, 22 March 2016, https://thequietus.com/articles/19915-pet-shop-boys-chris-lowe-interview.
Harrison, Ian. '"We Prefer Not to Be Fake . . ." Neil Tennant of the Pet Shop Boys Interviewed'. *MOJO* (2013), https://www.mojo4music.com/articles/stories/we-prefer-not-to-be-fake-pet-shop-boys-interviewed/.
Heath, Chris. *Pet Shop Boys, Literally*. London: William Heinemann, 2020.
Heath, Chris. *Pet Shop Boys versus America*. London: William Heinemann, 2020.
'History (1988)'. *PetShopBoys.co.uk*, https://www.petshopboys.co.uk/history/1988.
'History (1993)'. *PetShopBoys.co.uk*, https://www.petshopboys.co.uk/history/1993.
'History (1997)'. *PetShopBoys.co.uk*, https://www.petshopboys.co.uk/history/1997.
Hodges, Andrew. *Alan Turing – The Enigma*. Princeton, NJ, and Oxford: Princeton University Press, 2014.
Holden, Stephen. 'Recording Views: Wry Musings on a Queen'. *New York Times*, 21 November 1993.
Icons – The Greatest Person of the Twentieth Century, episode 8, 'Live Final', directed by James Morgan, 5 February 2019, BBC Two, https://www.bbc.co.uk/programmes/m0002fl3.
Jäger, Jan-Niklas. *Factually: Pet Shop Boys in Theorie und Praxis*. Mainz: Ventil Verlag, 2019.
Kelly, Ben. 'Festival Review: Pet Shop Boys' "A Man from the Future"'. *Attitude*, 7 September 2017, https://www.attitude.co.uk/culture/film-tv/festival-review-pet-shop-boys-a-man-from-the-future-281193/.
McKellen, Ian to Lee Richards, in 'E-Post: Correspondence with Ian McKellen. Bits and Bobs'. *Ian McKellen Official Home Page*, https://www.mckellen.com/epost/m001003.htm.
McKerrow, Graham. *Capital Gay*, 10 June 1988.
'O'Connor causes Palava for Pet Shop Boys'. *NME*, 31 May 2001, https://www.nme.com/news/music/osinead-connor-4-1386970.
Peer, Simone. 'Pet Shop Boys Get Political'. *Moscow Times*, 5 June 2013, https://www.themoscowtimes.com/2013/06/05/privatization-alternatives-from-the-baltics-part-2-a34526.

'Pet Shop Boys use Panti Bliss speech in new track'. *Irish Examiner*, 10 March 2014, https://www.irishexaminer.com/lifestyle/arid-30624713.html.

Proms 2014, 'Prom 8: The Pet Shop Boys', performed by Neil Tennant et al., 23 July 2014, BBC Three, https://www.bbc.co.uk/programmes/b04b2m2y.

Rogers, Jude. 'The Pet Shop Boys on Texting Cameron and Russian Homophobia'. *New Statesman*, 26 September 2013, https://www.newstatesman.com/culture/music-theatre/2013/09/beyond-suburbs-utopia.

Rogers, Jude. '"We Wrote it for Alan": Pet Shop Boys Take Their Turing Opera to the Proms'. *Observer*, 20 July 2014, https://www.theguardian.com/music/2014/jul/20/pet-shop-boys-alan-turing-enigma-proms-tribute-interview.

Savage, Jon. *Alternative Pet Shop Boys* liner notes (1995).

Signorile, Michelangelo. 'Gossip Watch'. *OutWeek* 98 (May 1991).

Silver, Alexandra. 'Top 10 Protest Songs: "Sunday Bloody Sunday"'. *Time*, 3 May 2010, https://entertainment.time.com/2010/05/04/kent-state-40-years-later-top-10-protest-songs/slide/sunday-bloody-sunday-1983-u2/.

Smith, Patricia Juliana. '"Go West": The Pet Shop Boys' Allegories and Anthems of Postimperiality'. *Genre* 34, no. 3–4 (2001): 307–37.

Spitz, Marc. 'Pet Shop Boys' Neil Tennant Talks About American Homophobia'. *Vanity Fair*, 29 August 2012, https://www.vanityfair.com/culture/2012/08/pet-shop-boys-neil-tennant-olympic-closing-ceremonies-performance.

Stanley, Bob. *Yeah Yeah Yeah: The Story of Modern Pop*. London: Faber & Faber, 2013.

Studer, Wayne. 'Introspective'. *Commentary: Interpretation and Analysis of Every Song by Pet Shop Boys*, 7 March 2023, http://www.geowayne.com/newDesign/introspective/introspective.htm.

Tennant, Neil. 'Pet-Texts: Pussy Riot'. *PetShopBoys.co.uk*, https://www.petshopboys.co.uk/pet-texts/2012-08-17/pussy-riot.

Tracey, Liz and Sydney Pokorny. 'Out on the Town with Liz & Sydney'. *OutWeek* 96 (May 1991).

'Where the streets have no name (I can't take my eyes off you). How can you expect to be taken seriously?' *PetShopBoys.co.uk*, https://www.petshopboys.co.uk/product/single/where-the-streets-have-no-name-i-cant-take-my-eyes-off-you-how-can-you-expect-to-be-taken-seriously.

Williams, Zoe. 'London 2012 Closing Ceremony: Unleashing a Musical Superpower'. *Guardian*, 13 August 2012, https://www.theguardian.com/uk/2012/aug/13/london-2012-closing-ceremony-music.

Wilson, Jennie, Kris Black and Phil King. 'Dear Friends'. In *Before the Act: A Celebration to Counter the Effects of Section 28*, theatre programme (1988).

PART TWO

Blaming the Colour TV: Neoliberal and Capitalist Critique

CHAPTER FOUR

Buying and Selling your History

Navigating the Ruins of Neoliberalism with Tennant and Lowe

Jonathan Dean

Introduction

The relationship between politics and popular music has always been fraught. In the popular imagination – and particularly in these resolutely 'anti-political' times – politics is seen as the preserve of a small professional elite, cut off both spatially and ideologically from the mass of ordinary people. Pop music, by contrast, is something we consume for pleasure, and is, for many of us, a familiar ingredient of our everyday lived experience. But the connections between politics and pop music are, in fact, far more intimate than they may at first appear. And few artists demonstrate the closeness of this connection more vividly than the Pet Shop Boys.

At times, this has taken the form of expressing overt political stances, such as the frequent condemnations of the Russian invasion of Ukraine on their social media channels. More usually, however, the Pet Shop Boys' politics is more subtle: indeed, part of their enduring appeal is their unrivalled capacity to range seamlessly between the personal and the political, or even to break down the very distinction between the personal and the political. Consider, for example, their examinations of the personal and political aspects of queer life in well-known early hit singles such as 'It's a Sin' (1987) and 'Being Boring' (1990), which offer highly affecting accounts of, respectively, navigating institutionalized homophobia at school, and the losses arising from the AIDS crisis. The personal and the socio-political are also bridged – often to humorous effect – in several songs about fame and celebrity, such as 'How Can You Expect to be Taken Seriously?' (1990), 'Shameless' (1993), 'Flamboyant' (2003) and 'On Social Media' (2019). A further particularly vivid but lesser-known song that fits a similar mould is 'Indefinite Leave to Remain' from 2006, in which a story of a turbulent relationship functions as a metaphor for precarious immigration status.

Against this backdrop, I want, in this chapter, to tease out some of the connections between the personal and the political in the Pet Shop Boys' work, by focusing on their treatment of neoliberalism. Not only is a concern with neoliberalism a central theme in their work, but in exploring their critical engagements with neoliberalism, we can garner a fuller appreciation of the richness, subtlety and power of Tennant and Lowe's political engagements. By neoliberalism, I mean the dominant mode of politics, culture and economics in the UK since the late 1970s. Neoliberalism designates a set of policies, practices and ideologies that valorize the free market, capital accumulation, competition and entrepreneurship. Neoliberalism is, of course, not a word that crops up in any Pet Shop Boys lyric, and one suspects that Lowe in particular would likely react with sneering derision at the suggestion that the Pet Shop Boys can tell us something interesting about the subject.

Mindful of these concerns, I want nonetheless to suggest that a consideration of neoliberalism is important in two ways. First, it brings to light a distinctive and important aspect of the Pet Shop Boys' contribution to popular music and, second, it shows how Tennant and Lowe can in fact help us analyse and critique key aspects of contemporary cultural and political life. Such an argument is not as controversial as it may at first appear: few would dispute that the Pet Shop Boys are astute socio-political commentators, and neoliberalism has formed the dominant horizon of our culture and politics over the course of their career. As such, it is hardly surprising that many Pet Shop Boys songs comment on, analyse, critique and poke fun at various aspects of the neoliberal condition. Granted, Tennant and Lowe do not offer explicit sloganeering critiques of neoliberalism, and nor should we expect them to. But they do offer a series of illuminating reflections, by turns entertaining and affecting, on the absurdities and contradictions of everyday life in neoliberal times.

To substantiate this argument, I begin with a short overview of academic debates about neoliberalism. I draw in particular on a 2016 article in the *New Left Review* by the political economist William Davies. Davies' article suggests that neoliberalism has undergone several significant transformations during its period of dominance, distinguishing between three distinct phases: combative neoliberalism (1979–89), normative neoliberalism (1989–2008) and punitive neoliberalism (2008–present). Using Davies' periodization, I highlight three songs in particular that correspond to each of the three stages described by Davies. 'Shopping' (1987) pokes fun at combative neoliberalism;

'Single-Bilingual' (1996) reflects the dominant sensibilities of normative neoliberalism; and, finally, 'Twenty-Something' (2016) offers an moving account of everyday life for young people in an age of punitive neoliberalism.

The American political theorist Wendy Brown has persuasively argued in a recent book entitled *In the Ruins of Neoliberalism* that the rise of various forms of reactionary politics (including, but not limited to, Trump and Brexit) must be understood in the context of the ruinous effects neoliberalism has wrought in our politics, culture and everyday life over the past forty years. While we cannot turn to Tennant and Lowe to lead us out of those ruins, their music – and these three songs in particular – can help us to better understand and navigate the precise contours of a cultural and political landscape scarred by more than four decades of neoliberalism.

Neoliberalism and the Pet Shop Boys

Neoliberalism matters simply because, as feminist political scientist Elizabeth Evans puts it, it is 'the dominant economic, political, and cultural ideology of [the] late twentieth century and early twenty-first century'.[1] As such, neoliberalism has had a profound, albeit contested, impact on the wider contours of recent British history. And, as Stuart Hall puts it, 'naming neoliberalism is politically necessary to give the resistance to its onward march content, focus and a cutting edge'.[2] Consequently, it is important to talk explicitly about neoliberalism if we want to understand the ways in which dominant power relations infuse a wide variety of ostensibly different domains, such as the financial sector, electoral politics and popular culture. As with any 'big' concept, one always runs the risk of conceptual overstretching. However, this risk is counterbalanced by the necessity of understanding neoliberalism as something which accurately identifies the wider terrain of British cultural and political life during the period in which the Pet Shop Boys have been making music.

But what, precisely, is neoliberalism? Simplifying somewhat, scholarly research on neoliberalism tends to bifurcate into Marxist-inspired approaches and those inspired by Michel Foucault, with Gramscian approaches perhaps sitting somewhere in between.[3] Marxist accounts of

---

[1] Elizabeth Evans, *The Politics of Third-Wave Feminisms: Neoliberalism, Intersectionality, and the State in Britain and the US* (Basingstoke: Palgrave MacMillan, 2015), 41.
[2] Stuart Hall, 'The Neo-Liberal Revolution', *Cultural Studies* 25, no. 6 (2011): 705–28, esp. 706.
[3] For useful overviews, see Simon Choat, 'The Iron Cage of Enterprise or the Restoration of Class Power? Approaches to Understanding Neoliberalism', *Political Studies Review* 17, no. 4 (2014): 416–27, and Galen Watts, 'Are you a neoliberal subject? On the uses and abuses of a concept', *European Journal of Social Theory* (2021), doi:10.1177/13684310211037205.

neoliberalism – of which David Harvey's is arguably the best known[4] – typically emphasize its character as a project of economic restructuring. Neoliberalism, Marxists argue, names the project, enacted from the mid-70s onwards, of undoing the post-war social democratic settlement, and reasserting the power of capital over labour. Although different authors emphasize different aspects, as an economic project, neoliberalism entails some or all of the following: privatization of goods and services hitherto publicly-owned; removal of barriers to free trade and the cross-border movement of people, goods and services; a weakening of trade unions and organized labour; increased 'flexibility' and precarity in the labour market; reduced and increasingly punitive welfare provision; and increased dependence on the financial sector.[5] Taken together, neoliberalism has thus engendered a wholesale reconfiguration of British – and, to some extent, global – capitalism, largely at the expense of labour.

Approaches that draw on the work of the Italian Marxist thinker Antonio Gramsci – of which Stuart Hall's essay 'The Neo-Liberal Revolution' is perhaps the most famous example – adopt the Marxist emphasis on the restructuring of capitalism but also emphasize how this is also a hegemonic project, that is, one aimed at restructuring wider ideological and discursive horizons of intelligibility.[6] A central element of Hall's analysis is to stress neoliberalism's contradictory character: it is a curious amalgamation of conservative and liberal discursive formations. For instance, in its initial Thatcherite iterations, neoliberalism was linked to a 'strong', heavily militarized state, as well as a traditional morality in relation to the family, race and sexuality. These elements of neoliberal discourse existed uneasily alongside its valorization of conspicuous consumption, self-promotion and individual freedom: the 'loadsamoney' money-grabbing city boy that has come, in the popular imagination, to epitomize the neoliberal 80s was in many ways at odds with traditional conservatism. And yet, says Hall, despite these tensions, and despite neoliberalism's failure to win broad popular support, it is nonetheless hegemonic. It has become hegemonic, Hall argues, in 'its ambition, depth, degree of break with the past, variety of sites being colonized, impact on common-sense and everyday behaviour [and] restructuring of the social architecture'.[7] Hall suggests that neoliberalism infuses a wide variety of different kinds of action and thinking, and has become the default mode of operation, rendering alternatives to neoliberalism difficult to imagine, let alone implement.

---

[4]David Harvey, *A Short History of Neoliberalism* (Oxford: Oxford University Press, 2005).
[5]See Harvey, *A Short History of Neoliberalism*; Andrew Glyn (ed.), *Social Democracy in Neoliberal Times: The Left and Economic Policy since 1980* (Oxford: Oxford University Press, 2001).
[6]Hall, 'The Neoliberal Revolution'.
[7]Hall, 'The Neo-Liberal Revolution', 728.

This emphasis on the infusion of neoliberalism into our everyday assumptions and practices is even more prominent in the recent turn to the work of French philosopher Michel Foucault. The past ten years have seen a substantial engagement with Foucault's writings on neoliberalism, following the 2008 publication of *The Birth of Biopolitics*, which contains English translations of his 1979 lectures on the topic. For Foucault, neoliberalism is less a restructuring of class relations and more a mode of governmentality, or a governing rationality, which shapes, moulds and conditions the everyday practices of people and institutions.[8] Such an account differs from Marxist accounts insofar as neoliberalism is not cast as an economic logic (i.e. one concerned with forms of production, distribution and exchange). Rather, neoliberalism refers to a remaking of human conduct and subjectivity, which in turn infuses almost all domains of everyday life. More specifically, neoliberalism refers to an *economization* and *marketization* of everyday life.[9] As Wendy Brown puts it in *Undoing the Demos*, under neoliberalism

> [...] both persons and states are construed on the model of the contemporary firm, both persons and states are expected to comport themselves in ways that maximize their capital value in the present and enhance their future value, and both persons and states do so through practices of entrepreneurialism, self-investment, and/or attracting investors.[10]

Brown's Foucauldian understanding of neoliberalism thus refers to the promulgation and dissemination of an entrepreneurial mode of conduct and subjectivity throughout a whole variety of social, cultural and political spheres.[11] To some extent, then, Foucauldian approaches could be considered even more pessimistic than Marxist or Gramscian approaches, given the difficulty, or even the impossibility, of carving out a space of resistance beyond the reach of neoliberal rationality. Neoliberalism, Brown suggests, is not simply an external environment that individuals have to negotiate. Rather, it serves to remake the individual. Indeed, Brown goes so far as to suggest that neoliberalism entails a remaking of the soul.[12]

---

[8] Michel Foucault, *The Birth of Biopolitics: Lectures at the College de France, 1977–78* (Basingstoke: Palgrave, 2008); Wendy Brown, *Undoing the Demos: Neoliberalism's Stealth Revolution* (New York: Zone Books, 2015).
[9] Choat, 'The Iron Cage of Enterprise or the Restoration of Class Power?', 418.
[10] Brown, *Undoing the Demos*, 22.
[11] See Christina Scharff, 'The Psychic Life of Neoliberalism: Mapping the Contours of Entrepreneurial Subjectivity', *Theory, Culture and Society* 33, no. 6 (2016): 329–48.
[12] Brown, *Undoing the Demos*, 22.

My own position sits somewhere between the more Gramscian-inflected take of Stuart Hall and the Foucault-inspired analysis offered by Wendy Brown. While the former emphasizes the consolidation of neoliberalism at the level of wider political discourse and structural power relations, the latter stresses the embeddedness of neoliberal habits and practices in our everyday lives. Consider, for example, the fact that even ostensibly anti-neoliberal left-wing academics like myself nonetheless replicate neoliberal modes of conduct in our everyday working life through, for example, our active complicity in fostering competition between universities, departments and individual academics, and trying to 'optimize' our performance in terms of publications, leadership, social media profile and research funding. The appeal of the Brown/Foucault account thus arises in part from its attentiveness to the fact that neoliberalism – as a set of everyday practices – endures despite the crisis of legitimacy it has undergone in the aftermath of the 2008 crash, and despite relatively few people being ideologically committed to it.

But this provisional account of neoliberalism begs the question of, how, precisely, it features in the Pet Shop Boys' oeuvre. As indicated, 'neoliberalism' is not explicitly *named* in the Pet Shop Boys' lyrics; what is more, if Stuart Hall is correct about the importance of naming neoliberalism, then one might reasonably cast doubt on the potency and relevance of their political engagements with the subject. However, I want to suggest that if one takes their back catalogue as a whole, one can find a broad range of insightful reflections on, and critical engagements with, key elements of the neoliberal condition. These function at different levels. Some, such as 'What are We Going to do About the Rich' (2019) and 'Integral' (2006), are explicit political critiques of key foundational principles of neoliberalism, namely wealth inequality and citizen surveillance respectively. Others, such as 'Opportunities (Let's Make Lots of Money)' (1986) and 'Single' (1996) – discussed in more detail below – are more parodic rather than overtly critical. That is to say, in both songs Tennant inhabits a character who typifies certain aspects of the neoliberal condition – respectively, a desire to become wealthy, and the romanticization of a transnational business elite – whilst offering, with varying degrees of subtlety, a critique of the absurdities and hypocrisies of the neoliberal archetypes the songs depict.

Furthermore, the vividness of Tennant and Lowe's depictions of the neoliberal condition, coupled with their longevity, mean that their work gives us a rich sense of the ways in which neoliberalism has changed significantly since its initial consolidation around the time of Thatcher's ascent to power. Indeed, as mentioned above, William Davies has provided a helpful periodization charting three distinct phases of neoliberalism's dominance, which he terms combative, normative and punitive.[13] Davies' tripartite distinction is helpful in part because it helps trace some of the

---

[13] William Davies, 'The New Neoliberalism', *New Left Review* 101 (2016): 121–34.

changing ways in which neoliberalism has unfolded in recent decades. Furthermore, while this subject has, as I shall make clear, been a consistent theme in their work, Tennant and Lowe's most striking and powerful critiques of neoliberalism work because they dissect key features of the changing neoliberal landscape, at specific historical moments that broadly align with Davies's periodization. The following sections explain each of these phases in more detail, illustrated and discussed in relation to specific examples from the Pet Shop Boys' back catalogue.

Combative neoliberalism: 'I heard it in the House of Commons, everything's for sale'

In Davies' article, he coins the term 'combative neoliberalism' to refer to the period broadly coinciding with the Thatcher years in the UK and concluding with the end of the Cold War in 1989. During this period, neoliberalism was 'combative' insofar as it was engaged in a bitter struggle against its antagonists. Rhetorically, this entailed assertive declarations of the primacy of the free market and of the virtues of individual freedom. Neoliberalism's enemies – which included the 'inefficient' public sector and the trade union movement at home, and the state socialist regimes abroad – were vociferously denounced. Economically, combative neoliberalism emphasized, among other things, the transfer of state assets into private hands and aggressive use of monetary policy to combat inflation. Politically, it was an attempt at extinguishing any and all challenges to the Thatcherite vision of free market dominance.

A number of early Pet Shop Boys songs offer commentaries on the neoliberal culture and politics that characterized the Thatcher era. 'West End Girls', the Pet Shop Boys' first and arguably still their best-known hit single, can plausibly be read as a tale of the confusion and disorientation that mark the neoliberal condition ('faces on posters and too many choices'). A more explicit example is the 1986 single 'Opportunities (Let's Make Lots of Money)', in which Tennant plays the role of an archetypal 'new Thatcherite' trying to exploit new business opportunities. But even more relevant to this discussion is the song 'Shopping' from the second Pet Shop Boys album, *Actually*, released in 1987. Although not released as a single, it has become a well-known song within the Pet Shop Boys' back catalogue, and has been performed live regularly. Although at face value it is a simple catchy pop ditty, the song presents a searing critique of the politics and economics of Thatcherism. In so doing, it offers a paradigmatic statement of the key features of combative neoliberalism.

Musically, 'Shopping' is uncomplicated. It is structured around a prominent six-note bassline and follows a simple verse/chorus structure with relatively few affectations, barring a synth melody towards the end of

FIGURE 4.1 *British Prime Minister Margaret Thatcher (1979–90), under whose government the United Kingdom entered a period loosely known as 'neoliberalism'. Courtesy of the Library of Congress.*

the song that bears more than a passing sonic resemblance to the work of (now ex-) New Order bassist Peter Hook. The chorus does nothing more than spell out the title of the song: 'we're S-H-O-P-P-I-N-G, we're shopping'. It is knowingly simple, banal even. And its political allegiances are unambiguous: indeed, it is the most explicitly political of the three songs discussed in this chapter, taking aim at the asset stripping and privatization pursued by the Thatcher government.

In the song, Tennant plays the role of a successful businessman who stands to gain from the Thatcher government's privatization programme, playing up to the stereotype of the crass, greedy city boy. 'We're buying and selling your history, how we go about it is no mystery,' announces Tennant in the first line: the listener is left in little doubt that the song's protagonist – in keeping with combative neoliberalism as a whole – is shameless, unapologetic and combative. More than that, the second verse suggests that the success enjoyed by the song's protagonist has been generated nefariously, benefiting from collusion between financial and political elites: 'it's easy when you've got all the information, inside help, no investigation' sings Tennant, before noting 'there's a big bang in the city, we're all on the make'.

Towards the end of the song the chorus is briefly interrupted by a short spoken-word section in which Tennant declares: 'Our gain is your loss / that's the price you pay. / I heard it in the House of Commons: / everything's for sale.' 'Shopping' presents us with a simple yet powerful narration of the politics of Thatcherism, the latter cast as an unapologetic valorization of competition and inequality amidst a convergence between political and business elites. The song's simple, driving and repetitive character might also be read as a reflection of the determination and sense of inevitability with which the Thatcherite project was carried through.

And yet the song itself contains no explicit critique of the practices being narrated. Instead, it uses a narrative technique common in Pet Shop Boys songs, whereby Tennant assumes the role of a character who embodies, in a slightly exaggerated form, certain unappealing archetypes associated with the song's topic: in this case, a brash, unapologetic, morally bankrupt businessman. Interestingly, in the liner notes for a reissue of *Actually*, Tennant is very explicit about this matter:

> 'Shopping' is also the other song, along with 'Opportunities', which created the myth that the Pet Shop Boys were ironic. Songs where you take the character of someone you hate. *Shopping* takes the character of this hideous city type in Fulham or somewhere, and the idea that, in the same way you might go shopping for a Hermes scarf, they'll go shopping for essential services and nationalised industries.[14]

The song's critique of Thatcherism works primarily through the laughter or disgust that the listener feels towards the character concocted by Tennant. And yet, thirty-five years on, that critique – and the listener's laughter – feels rather hollow. As Davies points out, although the age of combative neoliberalism did not – contrary to popular stereotypes – result in reduced spending on social security as a percentage of GDP, it nonetheless succeeded in its 'diffuse ethical agenda, of anchoring political hopes and identities in non-socialist economic forms'.[15] In that sense, the parodic thrust of 'Shopping' was, ultimately, a decidedly ineffective tool against the might of the assembled forces of combative neoliberalism. But the song still works as a catchy critical distillation of the bombastic 'loadsamoney' zeitgeist of the mid- to late Thatcher years.

Normative neoliberalism: 'I'm a player in the continental game'

William Davies suggests the post-Thatcher years (i.e., from 1989 to 2008) were marked by what he calls 'normative neoliberalism'. During this period, centrist politicians – including, but not limited to, Clinton in the US, Blair in the UK, and Schröder in Germany – broadly accepted the terms of combative neoliberalism's ideological victory. However, they presented it in

---

[14] Neil Tennant, interview with Chris Heath, 'Pet Shop Boys 1987–1988', *Pet Shop Boys Actually/Further Listening 1987–1988* liner notes (2018), 6.
[15] Davies, 'The New Neoliberalism', 127.

a technocratic, 'post-political' light, downplaying its antagonistic character and, in some cases, deploying various policy instruments to rein in the worst of neoliberalism's more socially destructive consequences. As a result, by the mid-90s, the divisiveness and antagonism of the era of combative neoliberalism had largely given way to a depoliticized landscape in which neoliberalism's hegemony went largely unchallenged.

The cultural and political contours of the era of 'normative neoliberalism' are vividly narrated across much of Tennant and Lowe's output during this era, particularly in the lead-up to the 2008 crash, where several Pet Shop Boys songs document emerging cracks in neoliberalism's moral and political authority. The popular 1996 B-side 'Delusions of Grandeur' is ostensibly about a fascist dictator, but also reads as an allegory of neoliberal celebrity culture. Several songs from 2002's *Release* album also speak to these themes: 'London' references immigration from the post-socialist and newly neoliberal states of East/Central Europe, whilst 'I Get Along' is famous for its documenting of the faltering career of Peter Mandelson, a key architect of the New Labour project. The 2006 follow-up, *Fundamental*, contains 'I'm With Stupid' – which takes aim at the "special relationship" between Blair and Bush around the time of the Iraq War – as well as closing track 'Integral', which offers a searing critique of the creeping authoritarianism in the later years of the New Labour government.

For me, however, the Pet Shop Boys' richest engagement with normative neoliberalism can be found in the opening medley of the 1996 album, *Bilingual*. The opening track, entitled 'Discoteca', is rhythmic but fairly slow, underpinned by a feeling of melancholy generated by minor chords, a mournful atmospheric synth lead and liberal use of the Pet Shop Boys' signature strings pad sound. The lyrics are a little opaque, with Tennant – singing at his most plaintive– invoking inchoate feelings of loss and disorientation as he tries to navigate an unfamiliar place: 'I don't speak the language, I don't understand a word' he says. This vague feeling of loss and frustration is further compounded when Tennant segues into Spanish: 'Te quiero, entiende usted? / Digame: cuanto tiempo tengo que esperar?'[16]

The song is punctuated by Tennant rhythmically and repeatedly asking 'hay una discoteca por aqui?',[17] suggesting that finding a club/discotheque holds out the possibility of refuge from his disorientation. It's a slightly strange narrative, but there's something quintessentially Pet Shop Boys about the casting of a 'discotheque' as the ultimate place of safety, given the centrality that dance music culture occupies within their work, both sonically and lyrically (see, for instance, 'Vocal' which closes the 2013 *Electric* album and is a particularly compelling paean to dance music culture).

In the second verse of 'Discoteca', after further unspecified expressions of fear and regret, Tennant tells the listener that he is 'going out, and carrying

---

[16]This broadly translates as 'I want you, do you understand? Tell me: how long must I wait?'
[17]'Is there a discotheque near here?' (author's translation).

on as normal'. The Spanish lyrics quoted above are then briefly reprised, before 'Discoteca' morphs into the album's second track, entitled simply 'Single' on the album, but later released as a single under the name 'Single-Bilingual'. As 'Discoteca' gives way to 'Single', the tempo picks up, the percussion intensifies (thanks to the involvement of Glasgow-based drumming collective SheBoom), and the entire feel of the song shifts away from melancholic disorientation towards a more upbeat, forward-moving pop sensibility.

'Single-Bilingual' is in many ways similar to 'Shopping'. Tennant plays the role of a successful businessman who embodies the zeitgeist of the historical moment in which the song appears. However, their personalities are slightly different: the protagonist of 'Shopping' is crude and brash, whereas the 'single' businessman of 'Single-Bilingual' fancies himself as sophisticated, cosmopolitan and outward looking: 'I come to the community / From U.K. p.l.c. / Arriving at my hotel, there are faxes greeting me / Staying in a junior suite, so there's room to meet and greet.'

The businessman of 'Single-Bilingual' is single in the literal sense of having no apparent ties to family or place; he moves effortlessly across borders and seeks to strengthen links between British business and the EU (or 'the community' as it is rendered in the song). In this sense, he is the embodiment of 'normative neoliberalism': he epitomizes a sensibility in which ideological antagonisms are – after the 'end of history' – passé and unfashionable. What matters, instead, is free trade, flexibility and responsiveness to the shifting demands of the 'knowledge economy'. He is after all, a 'player in the continental game' and is 'in demand' and 'quite at home' in 'Brussels, Bonn or Barcelona'. He is, one could say, the archetypal 'citizen of nowhere', the antithesis of everything Brexit is claimed by some to represent.

And yet, for all the self-congratulation offered up by the protagonist of 'Single-Bilingual', there is a sense that all is not well. The song is preceded (in 'Discoteca') by the claim that he is 'going out and carrying on as normal' despite the narrator's palpable existential disorientation. This in turn suggests that the breezy nonchalance assumed by the narrator of 'Single-Bilingual' is possible only through disavowing the unease and disorientation he evokes in 'Discoteca'. This interpretation is given further credence by the song's promotional video, in which Tennant's upbeat narration of his character's antics jars with the cold, grey, impersonal environment he navigates (whilst Lowe makes an amusing appearance as a S&M-inflected airport security guard). The video also features a scene in which Tennant utters the words 'perdoneme me llamo Neil'[18] as he attempts to hit on an attractive blonde woman in a hotel bar, who disdainfully rolls her eyes. The scene is played for comic effect, the absurdity and humour of the situation

---

[18] 'Excuse me, my name is Neil' (author's translation).

relying on the audience's prior knowledge of Tennant's sexuality (Tennant had officially 'come out' in an interview with *Attitude* magazine two years earlier). But this merely compounds the feeling that the character portrayed in 'Single-Bilingual' is simply a front, sustained only by the disavowal of his angst, unease and, perhaps, his queerness.

It seems clear, therefore, that 'Discoteca' and 'Single' each represent slightly different inflections of the same character: the angst and disorientation narrated in 'Discoteca' needs to be repressed for the narrator of 'Single' to successfully adhere to the aesthetic, sexual and cultural norms of the transnational business elite of which he purports to be a member. Indeed, as the medley finishes, the mask slips: a synth strings minor chord comes in, affording a slight air of menace to the hitherto upbeat major key vibe of 'Single', just as Tennant again poses the question 'hay una discoteca por aqui?', no longer able to sustain the illusion of control. The sound of a police siren at the song's close merely compounds the unease.

'Discoteca' and 'Single' – along with the *Bilingual* album more broadly – are probably not usually considered among the Pet Shop Boys' best work, but they evince a subtlety and a depth in capturing the contradictions of the historical moment in which they were made. The 'Discoteca/Single' medley suggests that despite the triumphalism that accompanied the 'end of history' and the rise of the 'knowledge economy', the age of 'normative neoliberalism' was in fact one of profound angst, disorientation and injustice. Given the continued tendency among some liberal commentators to look back at the mid- to late 1990s with misty-eyed nostalgia for a supposedly more 'grown-up' politics, the Pet Shop Boys' work cautions against the temptation to regard 90s-style 'Third Way' politics as a viable model for progressive political change in the present. Although – as 'Discoteca/Single' clearly convey – normative neoliberalism saw itself as more sophisticated, progressive and urbane in its outward appearance than its predecessors, Tennant and Lowe show us – with their characteristic wit – that this was largely illusory. The positive veneer afforded to neoliberal culture and politics in the 90s and 2000s did not, in any meaningful sense, serve to displace either the structural logics of exploitation or the anxiety, alienation and insecurity that constitute neoliberal societies. During the era of normative neoliberalism, these feelings of anxiety and alienation were bubbling under, palpable yet largely hidden. After the 2008 crash, however, Tennant and Lowe were quick to notice that a culturally pervasive sense of anxiety and insecurity were becoming impossible to ignore.

Punitive neoliberalism: 'Sometimes it's hard, day to day, to pay your way'

Neoliberalism endured a significant blow to its legitimacy in the aftermath of the 2008 financial crash. At the time, there were triumphalist claims from some on the left about the imminent demise of neoliberal capitalism. But, despite a resurgence of anti-neoliberal politics in many parts of the world, neoliberalism has not only survived but has arguably been rejuvenated in the years since the crash. And yet, as Davies points out, this is a rather different neoliberalism to that which prevailed prior to 2008. Punitive neoliberalism – as Davies terms it – is marked by an emphasis on vengeance and punishment: neoliberal austerity was justified as a collective punishment for the supposed indulgences of the boom years ('not fixing the roof while the sun was shining'), whilst individuals frequently find themselves subjected to myriad arcane mechanisms of control, audit and regulation (backed up by the threat of punishment) from the state and from employers, often without any obvious rationale. Under punitive neoliberalism, younger workers in particular are forced to navigate a harsh and unforgiving job market in which precarity, low wages, indebtedness and poor career prospects are the norm for most. Taken together, the landscape of punitive neoliberalism is marked by a 'prevalent psychology of melancholia, whereby debt exacerbates a sense of self-recrimination and the expectation of further punishment'.[19] In this bleak terrain, stress, anxiety and poor mental health become normalized: neoliberalism dominates not because it is able to canvas widespread popular support – even its most ardent supporters now avoid tubthumping endorsements of free-market capitalism – but because many of its would-be opponents are too poor, stressed, indebted or disenfranchised to muster the energy necessary to challenge its dominance.

This upsetting state of affairs has not escaped Tennant and Lowe's attention. The much celebrated 'Love is a Bourgeois Construct' of 2013 – a song whose lyrical richness could command a whole chapter unto itself – is sung from the point of view of someone unable or unwilling to muster the productivity and resourcefulness neoliberalism demands of them. Meanwhile, several of the injustices of punitive neoliberalism are tackled in a very direct manner in the duo's 2019 *Agenda* EP, a quartet of songs each of which tackles a topical theme: 'Give Stupidity a Chance' is an anti-Trump anthem; the themes of 'On Social Media' and 'What are we Going to do About the Rich?' are self-explanatory; and the EP finishes with 'The Forgotten Child', a mournful song about the plight of child refugees. 'What are we Going to do About the Rich?' is particularly pertinent to our discussion of neoliberalism: it is an upbeat pop tune with a 6/8 rhythm which charts several of the ills of contemporary capitalism. The titular rich are accused of destroying 'the very notion and feeling of community' while 'poisoning the public discourse hour by hour', while zero-hour contracts, tax avoidance, the collapse of the welfare state and the acquisition of football clubs by wealthy individuals also receive an honourable mention. Thematically, the *Agenda* EP could scarcely be any closer to the topic of this

---

[19]Davies, 'The New Neoliberalism', 130.

chapter. And yet, the EP's impact is limited by it being too literal: the subtlety and ambiguity of the Pet Shop Boys' best politically charged work is jettisoned in favour of explicit political claims that leave little to the listener's imagination. Precisely for this reason, the EP received lukewarm reviews from fans and critics alike.

A much more effective and affecting rumination on the ravages of punitive neoliberalism can be found on 2016's 'Twenty-Something', a single from the underrated *Super* album. 'Twenty Something' is a haunting and heartfelt account of the difficulties faced by young people in an increasingly harsh neoliberal landscape, and is – in my judgement at least – one of the band's best singles of the twenty-first century. It is a fast up-tempo number, with a distinctive double snare clap on the offbeat, giving it an almost reggaeton-style rhythm. It does not, strictly speaking, have a chorus: rather, it offers a catchy staccato synth melody in lieu of a sung chorus.[20] And, again very much in keeping with the band's distinctive sonic palette, the song's danceable, high-tempo quality is offset by a distinctly mournful chord progression, enhanced by periodic use of a sad, glistening arpeggio. Combined with Tennant's downbeat lyrics, it is – for me anyway – a very sad song beset by a sense of despair and hopelessness.

Lyrically, the song describes the activities and experiences of a young person in a big city (presumably London), trying to succeed personally and professionally. The lyrics – underpinned by the sadness of the musical accompaniment and Tennant's sparse, mournful delivery – leave the listener in little doubt about the frustrations and difficulties endured by the titular 'twenty-something'. They must 'join the queue', despite the fact that they have 'got a few' expectations. The song's subject has, Tennant says, 'got a start-up, good to go, when the money starts to flow': they clearly aspire to the entrepreneurial spirit of the neoliberal age, but the opportunity to do so has not yet arisen and, one suspects, never will. Tennant continues: 'That's how you are, or have to be / In a decadent city, at a time of greed / You can make believe, that it's all you need / Sometimes it's hard, day to day, to pay your way.'

While the lyrics are simple, they nonetheless powerfully convey several of the indignities endured by young people navigating a neoliberal terrain: the injunction to be 'how you are' colliding with intense pressure to meet very particular expectations; the disjuncture between the poverty endured by the young precariat, and the wealth enjoyed by the super-rich; and the sheer difficulty of everyday living. A later section of the song develops these themes further: 'Twenty-something, hard to beat / Check your reflection, walking

---

[20]Although this is not a song structure the Pet Shop Boys frequently use, it is a well-worn musical trope within the synth pop genre. Perhaps the best-known exponents are Orchestral Manoeuvres in the Dark (OMD), whose early singles 'Electricity' and 'Enola Gay' are notable for their use of a catchy synth melody rather than a sung chorus.

down the street / Thirty's calling, round the bend / Will your ideas, ever trend? / Oh, Twenty-something, feel the heat.'

Again, we are offered a powerful invocation of a young person's everyday life. They 'check their reflection' in a window: the listener wonders whether this is done out of narcissism, or anxiety about their appearance, or both? As several feminist scholars have pointed out, 'self-monitoring' is central to neoliberal culture,[21] as the subject of 'Twenty-Something' well knows. Furthermore, the person described in the song has endured these anxieties and insecurities for a long time: they are approaching thirty, and yet their hopes that their 'ideas will trend' remain unfulfilled. It is not surprising that they are 'feeling the heat'. Ultimately, the end of the verse implores: 'Find an issue, get ahead / Got it sorted, like you said / You're twenty-something, and so to bed' – with bed offering the only respite from their unsuccessful attempts at 'getting ahead'.

The character conjured up in Tennant's lyrics is familiar and believable. They have taken on the neoliberal rhetoric of entrepreneurship, opportunity and hard work, but find themselves thwarted by precarity, anxiety and insecurity – both financial and psychological. The character in the song could, frankly, be one of my undergraduate students: well educated, well networked, brimming with 'cultural capital', but cast out into an unforgiving landscape marked by a cruel housing market, poor employment prospects and little by way of a financial safety net. In this sense, the character of 'Twenty-Something' is paying the price for the ruinous injustices and inequalities perpetuated by the protagonists of 'Shopping' and 'Single-Bilingual'.

Despite persistent stereotypes of young people being weak snowflakes who squander their income on overpriced sandwiches, the UK is marked by profound and worsening intergenerational inequality, particularly in relation to housing and employment.[22] And yet, when this is raised in public discourse, it often provokes a defensive reaction from so called 'boomers', that is, the generation who enjoyed unusual levels of affluence and job security prior to the ravages of neoliberalism being inflicted. The power of 'Twenty-Something' partly arises from the highly refreshing and sincere expression of cross-generational solidarity that Tennant offers. Despite being almost forty years older than the song's character, Tennant evinces a level of empathy and understanding for young adults which many of his contemporaries would do well to heed. Despite their reputation for irony, many Pet Shop Boys songs are in fact deeply sincere and heartfelt, with no trace of irony at all. 'Twenty-Something' is one such example, and it is all the better for it.

---

[21] Ana Sofia Elias and Rosalind Gill, 'Beauty surveillance: The digital self-monitoring cultures of neoliberalism', *European Journal of Cultural Studies* 21, no. 1 (2018): 59–77.
[22] Keir Milburn, *Generation Left* (Cambridge: Polity Press, 2019).

Conclusion: 'Now I'm digging through my student paperbacks, flicking through Karl Marx again'

Despite decades of scholarly research on popular music, the belief that pop music is unworthy of political or scholarly consideration has proved infuriatingly resilient. Indeed, audits of scholarly practice in my own academic field – political science – have revealed that teaching and research remains skewed towards traditional understandings of politics, in which the latter is equated with the exercise of formal state power.[23] This means that students who wish to explore more dynamic conceptions of politics – for instance through considering the ways in which popular culture functions as a site in which political processes are constituted and contested – often find their interests thwarted. As such, any scholarly attempt at taking seriously the politics of popular music, or indeed popular culture more generally, will often find itself confronted by a stifling array of cultural norms and institutional structures.

Against this backdrop, I want to make it clear that my argument about the ways in which Pet Shop Boys' back catalogue offers us a vivid cultural history of neoliberalism is entirely serious: it is not intended as a frivolous or whimsical aside. So, while I concede that readers may or may not agree with the specific interpretation of the songs I have offered, there are two more general issues which my discussion gives rise to, and which deserve serious scholarly consideration.

The first concerns the precise nature of Tennant and Lowe's engagement with neoliberalism. One of the reasons why the Pet Shop Boys' critical dissections of the neoliberal condition are so effective is because of their emphasis on ambiguity and entanglement. More precisely, the Pet Shop Boys' most powerful broadsides against neoliberalism do not come from a place unambiguously 'outside', or in opposition to, neoliberal imperatives. Rather, in songs such as 'Shopping' and 'Single', Tennant *inhabits* the space of certain neoliberal archetypes, parodying and deconstructing them from within. Indeed, this is a narrative strategy the Pet Shop Boys have frequently used: take, for example, 'This Must be the Place' on 1990's *Behaviour* album. Although very clearly a critique of the brutalities of the English public school system, Tennant sings from a place which acknowledges that he is, in fact, conditioned and shaped by the very structures of power that 'he has waited years to leave'. Similarly, when it comes to neoliberalism,

---

[23]Emma Foster, Peter Kerr, Anthony Hopkins, Christopher Byrne and Linda Ahall, 'The Personal is not Political: At Least not in the UK's Top Politics and IR Departments', *British Journal of Politics and International Relations* 15, no. 4 (2013): 566–85.

Tennant depicts himself not as someone heroically combating neoliberalism from outside; rather, he acknowledges complicity and entanglement within neoliberal power relations, whilst seeking nonetheless to parody, subvert and critique the absurdities and injustices they engender. One could even say that this logic of immanent critique – a position that is 'in and against' neoliberalism – is central to the Pet Shop Boys' entire image and presentation. Consider, for instance, how Tennant and Lowe have bequeathed to us several songs (such as 'Shameless' and 'Flamboyant') which parody and critique neoliberal celebrity culture, despite the fact that they themselves inhabit this landscape and, in their public image and stage performances, exhibit a certain kind of consumerism and flamboyance. But far from being evidence of hypocrisy on Tennant and Lowe's part, this inhabiting of a space 'in and against' neoliberalism offers an honest and engaging account of the complexities and tensions that we are all compelled to navigate; even those of us who oppose neoliberalism politically still, inevitably, find ourselves shaped by its rationalities. We may even derive a certain pleasure from our immersion in various elements of neoliberal culture. In doing so, Tennant and Lowe offer a rich account of complicity and critique which is in many ways more sophisticated than much academic and activist discourse about neoliberalism, the latter often marked by a rather tiresome purism premised upon the disavowal of complicity with neoliberalism.[24] Tennant and Lowe's engaging tales are, therefore, a salutary reminder of the challenges, pleasures and complexities that confront anyone seeking to loosen neoliberalism's grasp.

The second general issue raised by my discussion is that, beyond the specific question of neoliberalism, the analysis offered here has implications for how we think about the relationship between popular music and the academic study of cultural and political history. While I am mindful of the fact that pop music – and pop musicians – cannot be said to be representative of the wider societies from which they are drawn in any straightforward way, pop music almost by definition can serve to distil and make visible distinctive features of the culture and politics of specific historical moments. Granted, not all popular music contains cultural commentary as incisive as that offered by Tennant and Lowe, but that does not preclude pop music being used as a window through which to discern broader cultural, historical and political trends. The only reason that pop music is relatively infrequently analysed in these terms (at least in academic settings) is because of a lingering squeamishness about taking popular music seriously as an object of academic study. If Tennant and Lowe teach us anything, it is that it is high time we jettisoned that squeamishness once and for all.

---

[24] For an engaging dissection of these dynamics, see Akane Kanai, 'Between the perfect and the problematic: everyday femininities, popular feminism, and the negotiation of intersectionality', *Cultural Studies* 34, no. 1 (2020): 25–48.

Bibliography

Brown, Wendy. *Undoing the Demos: Neoliberalism's Stealth Revolution*. New York: Zone Books, 2015.

Brown Wendy. *In the Ruins of Neoliberalism*. New York: Columbia University Press, 2019.

Choat, Simon. 'The Iron Cage of Enterprise or the Restoration of Class Power? Approaches to Understanding Neoliberalism'. *Political Studies Review* 17, no. 4 (2019): 416–27

Davies, William. 'The New Neoliberalism'. *New Left Review* 101 (2016): 121–34.

Elias, Ana Sofia and Rosalind Gill. 'Beauty surveillance: The digital self-monitoring cultures of neoliberalism'. *European Journal of Cultural Studies* 21, no. 1 (2017): 59–77.

Evans, Elizabeth. *The Politics of Third-Wave Feminisms*. Basingstoke: Palgrave MacMillan, 2015.

Foster, Emma, Peter Kerr, Anthony Hopkins, Christopher Byrne and Linda Ahall. 'The Personal is not Political: At Least not in the UK's Top Politics and IR Departments'. *British Journal of Politics and International Relations* 15, no. 4 (2013): 566–85.

Foucault, Michel. *The Birth of Biopolitics: Lectures at the College de France, 1977–78*. Basingstoke: Palgrave MacMillan, 2008.

Glyn, Andrew (ed.). *Social Democracy in Neoliberal Times: The Left and Economic Policy since 1980*. Oxford: Oxford University Press, 2001.

Hall, Stuart. 'The Neoliberal Revolution'. *Cultural Studies* 25, no. 6 (2011): 705–28.

Harvey, David. *A Short History of Neoliberalism*. Oxford: Oxford University Press, 2005.

Kanai, Akane 'Between the perfect and the problematic: everyday femininities, popular feminism, and the negotiation of intersectionality'. *Cultural Studies* 34, no. 1 (2020): 25–48

Milburn, Keir. *Generation Left*. Cambridge: Polity Press, 2019.

Scharff, Christina 'The Psychic Life of Neoliberalism: Mapping the Contours of Entrepreneurial Subjectivity'. *Theory, Culture and Society* 33, no. 6 (2016): 329–48.

Watts, Galen. 'Are you a neoliberal subject? On the uses and abuses of a concept'. *European Journal of Social Theory* 25, no. 3 (2022): 458–76.

CHAPTER FIVE

The Currency We Spent

The Pet Shop Boys and the Actualization of Thatcherite Economics

Stephanie Polsky

Introduction

The rise of the Pet Shop Boys as a cultural force on both sides of the Atlantic at the beginning of the 1980s reflects the emphasis placed on personal financial gain during the Thatcher and Reagan years. The dissolution of Britain's formal empire profoundly informed Margaret Thatcher's strategy to transition its international reputation into one synonymous with finance and service sectors. This approach radically exacerbated gaps in wealth between Britain's classes, concentrating its least vulnerable members within the finance sector and its most within the service sector. Thatcher's economic policies were indeed groundbreaking, providing 'the first example of a global neoliberal economic movement that reshaped the world economy in the 1980s', presenting a 'model for other neoliberal governments to implement market reforms such as Ronald Reagan in the United States and Deng Xiaoping in China'.[1] Thatcher's greatest contribution was to move

---

[1] Bradley W. Bateman, 'There Are Many Alternatives: Margaret Thatcher in the History of Economic Thought', *Journal of the History of Economic Thought* 24, no. 3 (2002): 309.

the economics of the City of London onwards from a colonial model concentrated on banking and insurance to a globalist model driven by products and markets. This shift, which led to a transformation of the financial sector, was superficially fuelled by a combination of economic liberalization and financial market deregulation. At a much deeper level, the financialization of the British economy was an ideological project that retooled techniques of colonial governance to bear on metropolitan trade.

As the 1980s wore on it became clear that Britain's outsized contribution to a rapidly increasing globalization, financialization and deregulation of the world economy could only be sustained through a paired service economy reliant on an influx of immigrants, refugees and casual workers. While the rich were incentivized to reposition themselves around the UK's burgeoning 'financial centres, glistening high-tech enclaves, and quirky high-culture districts', the poor were hindered in their progress by their coerced 'displacement' from public housing that led to 'the rapid increase in slums and homelessness'.[2] Real estate became not a place for individuals to dwell within, but an asset class for interests to exploit. The division between these two concerns fell along highly racialized lines that abstractly coded wealth as white and poverty as Black, making the urban landscape a free-market zone of self-reinforcing segregation. Within this environment, it is 'capital' that 'produces race as a socio-political category of distinction and discrimination'.[3] As a consequence, the free-market principle that supported Britain's former colonial empire was transferred wholesale into neoliberal ideological modes of urban governance allowing for 'practices of urban planning, slum administration, and law-and-order policing' to become prime elements within its initial ventures into the new world of global capitalism.[4]

The period between 1978 and 1979 can be viewed as a contest between 'emboldened socialists and free-market capitalists' to remake the conditions of post-colonial Britain in their image.[5] It was not immediately obvious that Thatcher would be successful in her bid to establish Britain as a nation remade to conform to a free-market orthodoxy. It 'was only in 1980–1 that she purged her cabinet of "wets" and promoted key allies', whose loyalty would allow her to continue her progress, despite the rise of mass unemployment and the intensification of trade union strikes.[6] Both of these had to be bitterly endured and ultimately exhausted for Thatcherism to

---

[2] Ida Danewid, 'The Fire This Time: Grenfell, Racial Capitalism and the Urbanisation of Empire', *European Journal of International Relations* 26, no. 1 (March 2020): 294.
[3] Danewid, 'The Fire This Time', 296.
[4] Danewid, 'The Fire This Time', 297.
[5] Phil Tinline, 'Back to the Future: What the Turmoil of the 1970s Can Teach Us Today', *New Statesman*, 8 May 2019, https://www.newstatesman.com/politics/uk/2019/05/back-future-what-turmoil-1970s-can-teach-us-today.
[6] Tinline, 'Back to the Future'.

emerge as an outcome of what was previously considered unthinkable. It was Thatcher's use of anti-immigrant rhetoric that ultimately dried tensions amongst white Britain's warring classes and focused their attention on it as the cause of the emergency, rather than the fact that the country's post-war economic model was stalling because it had largely failed to consider that it's model of socialism only worked in the context of massive imperial revenues coming in to sustain it. Without this revenue, Britain would have had to cede its place as an advanced industrial nation. Instead, it found a way to transform itself into an international financial services broker in an effort to offset the reality of its diminished geopolitical position in the world.

At this time the British Empire was morphing into what would become 'the modern offshore system' we recognize today.[7] Its third empire emerged from a network of jurisdictions that remained either under British colonial rule or recently became independent colonies or held the status of British Overseas Territories and Crown Dependencies. Places such as Hong Kong, Singapore, the Bahamas, Cyprus, Bahrain, Dubai, the Cayman Islands, Bermuda, the British Virgin Islands, Turks and Caicos, Gibraltar, Jersey, Guernsey, and the Isle of Man all became tax havens for an affluent white settler class now in the process of formally retreating from empire. The City of London emerged as the core of this new empire, with these financial-colonial outposts functioning as its colonies.

Left behind was the special status afforded to Britain's imperial metropoles of London, Manchester, Liverpool and Sheffield as national tax rates rose to objectionable levels, targeting, in particular, wealthy earners whose revenues were used to finance Britain's welfare state and to effect wealth redistribution across the nation in the immediate decades following the Second World War. Those metropolitan centres had increasingly come to resemble Britain's former colonies through a principle of racialized, urban segregation that created a new version of the colonial world, complete with a national programme to facilitate white tax avoidance to deprive these populations of state revenues. At the same time, British elites had effectively evolved the empire so that it remained a place where the sun never sets and where they could continue to grow rich from the former empire's remnant properties in the Caribbean, Asia and the Pacific. These small island nations would now be used to help launder money before it got back to the City of London and was distributed to other large finance centres. 'For the City, it was a beautiful self-reinforcing dynamic: The more that countries opened their financial systems, the more business would float around internationally, ready to be caught in the nearby nodes of the British offshore spiderweb and then sent up to be serviced by the City and its allies on Wall Street.'[8]

---

[7]Nicholas Shaxson, *Treasure Islands: Uncovering the Damage of Offshore Banking and Tax Havens* (New York: St. Martin's Publishing Group, 2011), 8.
[8]Shaxson, *Treasure Islands*, 85.

The Pet Shop Boys uniquely occupy a position between these worlds through their music, whose lyrics make continuous the urban and ex-urban landscape of de-industrialization and finance capitalism with the emergence of hip hop, techno and house music, situating them at the very centre of the seismic social changes that reshaped the 1980s. These musical genres had their beginnings in the protest movements of the late 1970s, before finding their way into abandoned warehouses that were themselves artefacts of the cooling-off period of post-war industrialization when acts of final refuse were spilling onto the dance floor through acts of chaotic release. The emerging club scene that followed was not a space of political rebellion but of social withdrawal that signalled the rise of a post-industrial nomadism reflective of the dystopian elements of urban sprawl. It was a scene that promoted a stylish vision of a near future replete with aesthetic references to robots, virtual reality, video games and electronic music. It was also a scene that promoted the riotous expression of subcultural identities including homosexuality and Blackness, albeit much of it contained within a predominantly white, heterosexual, socially-mobile space. There was also a darker side to this scene, having to do with the enforcement of public order through divided communities and suppression of certain bodies through socio-economic hardship, police brutality and political disillusionment.

One a larger scale, neoliberalism's economic experiment offered queer people access to a unique political assemblage, where several elements of their identity could be addressed, but ultimately its influence on space remained limited in terms of its market philosophy. The designs it had on gay clubs and venues would engender material and technological conditions that structured the landscape in which an ordered vision of queerness emerged, which coalesced as a culture identity, celebrity, wealth and exclusivity through several iterations of melding the margin into mainstream, the colony into the metropole, thereby exerting greater authority over it. The nascent neoliberal (albeit ambivalent) appreciation of queerness that was emerging throughout the 1980s related to the way that persona perpetuated itself through code-switch and self-translation in a way that led materially and fluently to a new order of capital. Although this new order remained steeped in heterosexual and patriarchal expression, it nevertheless allowed those classed as Other to capitalize themselves through its projection of a one-world inclusivity. Thus, against the real threats of violence that persist within categorical difference, this new order of capital pitches a superficial culture and defence of these communities through the currency of speculative interest.

Dead end worlds

The story of the Pet Shop Boys' success does not begin in London, but rather in New York. Their first single, 'West End Girls', released in April of 1984, was envisioned and received as a New York dance record. From there it became a club hit in Los Angeles and San Francisco. Despite this success, it was only available in the United Kingdom as a 12" import. The city at night they were imagining at the time was the Big Apple, and their lyrics were directed at New York's local versions of London's West End girls (Manhattanites) and East End boys (Outer Boroughs), cruising for one another, seeking illicit sorts of pleasure at night in the heart of the city. In London in the early 1980s, the dominant pop acts of the time were Culture Club, Frankie Goes to Hollywood, Spandau Ballet and Duran Duran. In many ways the Pet Shop Boys were ahead of their musical peers in predicting that dance music would overtake pop as the decade progressed. In making that crucial calculation they were importing New York's decadent aesthetics into London. What The Pet Shop did in their first iteration as a duo in the United States was to bring the politically wry and sub-culturally stylized lyricism of American hip hop to bear on the rhythmic and up-tempo qualities typical of English pop music. What appears universally relatable is the emergence of a social inequality that had seemingly spread to 'every city, in every nation', as a consequence of the sharp rise of rational economic models in late 1970s, thus making self-interest the evidential element of participation in a postmodern world.

Certain lyrics in 'West End Girls' seem to reflect an aimlessness and lack of identity commonly associated with the American concept of a protean self ('We've got no future, we've got no past'). It was a sentiment increasingly felt by Brits themselves, with the dissolution of empire being the defining characteristic of a national identity. Indeed, for a generation coming of age in the 1980s, little meaning could be attached to the notion of a contemporary British identity apart from the imperative to acquire and maintain wealth and status. Rich and poor, upper class and lower classes were united through this new cultural preoccupation with the limits of social mobility amidst a geography of class that seemed to be turning on its axis. Similarly, the drug culture of the streets was making itself felt in the club culture of the boardroom, and every young person appeared to be chasing after the dream of escaping the dullness of the conditions to which they were born in favour a fantasy of radical transmutability within the individual themselves. This is born out in the popular novels and films on both sides of the Atlantic portraying this era, including *Wall Street, American Psycho, St. Elmo's Fire, Less than Zero, A View to a Kill* and *My Beautiful Laundrette*.

The Pet Shop Boys' first hit single reflects this desire to experiment at all levels with class, with sexuality, with the edges of a perceivably dead-end world where it didn't matter who you screwed, because it the end we all were screwed and trying to temporarily escape the consequence of such a conclusion about neoliberal reality. The West End is as dirty as the East End, as corrupt and perverse, and this had long been understood by a knowing public who illicitly sought out their visceral entertainments amidst such an atmosphere of mutual assured exploitation. The Pet Shop Boys would make of themselves just one of the dubiously imported substances amongst many enjoyed on a Friday by the ordinary punter.

Along these same lines, this was to be an era of 'stylistic conservatism', where Young Fogeys and Sloane Rangers formed their own colonies in places like Sloane Square, Chelsea, Mayfair and Fitzrovia.[9] This new generation of youth drawn from the English upper-middle-class and upper-class elites devised their own discreet set of fashions. They departed from exclusivity by incorporating the various social rituals and etiquettes of past British elites, but also a queering of the conservative and historical imaginary, therefore positioning them as the vanguard of British culture. This was happening at a time when both Reagan and Thatcher were touting the re-emergence of a conservative lifestyle and way of thinking, after a long ideological period of liberal egalitarianism.

Rave culture was in many ways a product of 1980s Thatcherism, situated in abandoned warehouses and the open spaces surrounding them, and perpetuated through the landscapes generated by deindustrialization. Organizers, many of whom were young Conservatives, made commercial use of these newly disused spaces once occupied by heavy industry, situated at the edges of the inner city and at a crossroads of the divergent economic fortunes of Britain's post-colonial, post-industrial worlds, north and south. These young entrepreneurs were taking advantage of other young people's disposable incomes to charge not-taxable cash in hand entrance fees, proceeds that would normally have gone to the traditional nightclub trade. They paired their operations with organized criminal gangs who furnished their illegal gatherings with fashionable class A drugs.

It was an irony of history that the sexually ambiguous duo Pet Shop Boys captured the attention of this new, more conservative generation bent on devising a different sort of packaging of imperialism than their parent's generation. Their indictment of them had to do with their fascination for preserving the traditions and heritage of British culture, while simultaneously failing to appreciate and exploit their commercial potential. If the lyrics of 'West End Girls' were, as Tennant says, actually 'about rough boys getting a bit of posh', equally they were about posh girls getting a bit of rough, and ultimately this was a song about eroticized transactions and their routings within London's inner-city.[10] Tennant later said that some listeners thought the song was about prostitutes, but not again of the sort that one would imagine; who was for hire in this new atmosphere of wealth was a very different sort of trade actor. 'West End Girls' would end up being re-recorded

---

[9] Kari Kallioniemi, 'New Romantic Queering Tactics of English Pop in Early Thatcherite Britain and the Second British Invasion', *Radical Musicology* 7 (2019), pars. 1–30.
[10] 'The Story of ... "West End Girls" by Pet Shop Boys', Smooth Radio, 12 October 2018, https://www.smoothradio.com/features/pet-shop-boys-west-end-girls-lyrics-meaning-video/.

after the duo signed with EMI, and the track formed part of their first studio album in 1986, entitled *Please*.

On the surface, this album was a call to arms for a new conservative generation of youth who were convinced that looking 'for a partner' in both a financial and sexual sense was the gateway to opportunities squandered by their liberal-leaning, complacent parents who had failed to make the most of their imperially-sponsored opportunities. Instead, as the music video for *Please*'s second single, 'Opportunities (Let's Make Lots of Money)' appears to imply, they had let others – specifically the Americans – take advantage of them. By contrast, this new generation was far cannier about how brains and looks could be manipulated for financial gain, and, perhaps as significantly, how aggression was a necessary evil for getting ahead. These young people were also aware that Britain's class economy and economic stagnation had frustrated social mobility, as metaphorically evidenced by the line in 'Opportunities', 'My car is parked outside, I'm afraid it doesn't work / I'm looking for a partner, someone who gets things fixed', followed by the bold rejoinder, 'Ask yourself this question, do you want to be rich?' This question becomes the formulation for a generation's collective ambition on both sides of the Atlantic: 'Let's make lots of money.'

The currency to do so is not so much measured in education, but the cultural capital Oxbridge offers for entrance into the establishment, an establishment that had for centuries been based on hereditary wealth and private schooling. In 1980, the Conservative government introduced the Assisted Places Scheme to allow academically able children from modest-income families to gain entrance to private schools. Such 'opportunities' were promoted as being based on merit rather than class status alone, providing a pathway to privilege previously reserved solely for Britain's class elites. The main criteria for acceptance 'other than passing the school's entrance examination' was financial need, which in reality 'meant the policy was significantly "colonised" by parents who might have been suffering short-term financial hardship (often because of divorce), but who were in many ways quite culturally and economically advantaged'. Hence their children would by any other measure have been described as middle class, demonstrating once again functional discrepancies within these domains of access.[11] The lyrics of 'Opportunities' read like the script of an informal interview, only available to those having the right sorts of class connections: 'You can tell I'm educated, I studied at the Sorbonne, doctored in mathematics, I could have been a don.' All of these could have described the attributes of social privilege in any generation, but one: 'I can program a computer.' The digital knowledge economy was just transforming channels

---

[11] Sally Power, 'The state has helped poor pupils into private schools before – did it work?' *The Conversation*, 9 December 2016, https://theconversation.com/the-state-has-helped-poor-pupils-into-private-schools-before-did-it-work-70222.

of class ascension, and in this way transgressing the known order of how such transactions worked, thus posing the somewhat dubious prospect of technology as a potential leveller of the class playing field. Institutional reputation, was therefore, becoming less of a socially viable attribute and more of a way into, as it were, the class system. Those already on the inside were in a position to 'choose the perfect time' for this infiltration of class outsiders to penetrate the highest echelons of power, but only if they've 'got the inclination'; then their class superiors are there to furnish 'the crime', meaning that these outliers are there to do the dirty work involved in producing new forms of capital, whilst the others are there to be the brains behind that operation.

The candidate for the job explains to his more inexperienced partner, '[O]h, there's a lot of opportunities, if you know when to take them, you know there's a lot of opportunities, if there aren't, you can make them (make or break them).' The rules here don't apply to those well versed in settling the odds in their favour, nor to those who are there to provide the brawn needed to force past boundaries 'regardless of expense'. This is definitely a proposition, but the deal is that the naïve partner has to get over their feelings of hesitation and alter their moral sensibilities, in order to make a killing here. The transatlantic affective economy here is being turned inside out, causing this relationship to falter along lines of emotional sublimation. It is now tilted in favour of immediate material gratification, and most of all the question of who will ultimately take care of us, when it becomes common knowledge that we screwed everyone else over: 'all the love that we had, and the love that we hide, who will bury us, when we die?' speaks to the faltering of a system of patrilinear wealth in favour of the hypocritical affectations of new money. This question foreshadows another: what will happen when this new liberal economy does away altogether with material labour, replacing it with a system of rentier capitalism? This question is bracketed by the nature of this arrangement being one implicated as homosocial in nature and queered in proportion. In this scenario, Neil Tennant fits into the mould described by Kari Kallioniemi:

> [T]he stylistic notion of the white British soul boy was originally constructed by David Bowie in his album *Young Americans* (1975), the record seeming to work as the blueprint for the whole genre at the same time paraphrasing Colin MacInnes's utopian promise of young England being half English and the other half being young American, 'stylised, slick, expensive and fake, simultaneously nostalgic and forward looking' – much like the cultural ethos of the Thatcherite 1980s.[12]

---

[12]Kallioniemi, 'New Romantic Queering Tactics', par. 4.

In many ways at the start the Pet Shop Boys could have become an America act. What distinguished them was the way they consciously synthesized a Thatcherite version of an imaginary British affluency achieved through Tennant's vocal affectation of received pronunciation with lyrics that suggested an assimilation of an American preoccupation with escapism, in particular of its own dark colonial legacy born out through the compulsive appropriation of Black music. The romanticism of British pop in the New Romantic movement is here overtaken by the aftermath of liberalism, much as the success of post-war British popular music culture and its world-conquering style succumbs to an acknowledgement of materialism as something essentially vulgar and bastardized. During the years 1983 and 1984 Pet Shop Boys recorded twelve songs with the American producer Bobby Orlando at Unique Studios in New York. Amongst the tracks that would go on to become transatlantic hits were 'West End Girls', 'Opportunities (Let's Make Lots of Money)', 'Rent' and 'It's a Sin'. In retrospect, it borders on the absurd to contemplate how Orlando could envision the Pet Shop Boys as a white 'rap duo' whose commercial selling point would be Tennant's posh British accent, rather than capitalize on the suggestive queerness of their dual self-making, but this was entirely in keeping with an era in popular culture that made any public acknowledgement of gayness something akin to a criminal offence. Tragically, this was materially borne out in 1988, during Thatcher's third and final government, with the enactment of Section 28 of the Local Government Act, which forbade the promotion of gay politics by local authorities and the teaching in schools of the acceptability of homosexuality.

When the duo eventually broke with Orlando in 1985 and returned to Britain to sign up with EMI, it was under the proviso that these singles be totally re-engineered as synth-pop to emulate the success of the style-conscious acts from the New Romantic movement in the US. The visual iconography of the videos produced for the album *Please* ambiguously unites the two cultures in terms of a sense of urban decay contrasted with concentrations of power. The Pet Shop Boys' new formulaic style was highly successful on the US dance charts, as were their videos produced specifically for MTV that showed London, like New York, as a place of an exuberant club culture during a time when there wasn't much to celebrate in the socially regressive Reagan/Thatcher eras. Both cities are figured as places of fantasy and escape from the culturally repressive nature of life everywhere else, especially for those who identified as gay. As such, there is an affinity between Neil Tennant's queered social choreography of London packaged for American export and the promiscuous behaviour of global capitalism.

A hard or soft option

In 1987 the Pet Shop Boys released their follow up album to *Please*, entitled *Actually*. Its cynical lyrics acknowledge that at every level there was no going back; time was money moving from the periphery to the metropole. Now capital was something administered to the metropolitan inhabitant by ruthless City boys high on a potent mix of plentiful cocaine and lucrative expropriation. Nowhere was this more excoriatingly expressed than in the album's third track, 'Shopping'. Shopping, here, takes on a whole other level of meaning by being transposed from a civic activity to a criminal occupation. When Neil Tennant refers to the buying and selling of history, he is referring directly to Thatcher's sale of state assets on one level, but equally the concept that this has gone far beyond the reach of national jurisdiction into a territory of lawless speculation on a fundamental scale. Now you, the city trader, 'want some more', and that more involves 'all the information' and being able to crack the code, hence, 'we're S-H-O-P-P-I-N-G'. Tennant acknowledges explicitly the 'big bang in the city' that allows politicians to be 'on the make' and make gains out of society's losses, to the extent that there is eventually no such thing as society. The price of this is passed onto those on the outside looking in – those who don't have a channel into the chambers of power where their futures are being cryptically sold out: 'we're S-H-O-P-P-I-N-G' meaning not only are we shopping but, in the process, we're also being shopped.

The flip side of such illicit shopping is peonage and this is everywhere borne out in the lyrics to 'Rent'. When there is nothing left to own, then your only recourse is to rent. Here Tennant refers to the basics – clothing, food, attention – that are now distorted into categories of transaction borrowing. Each individual now must be able to act accordingly and symbiotically within a system of commerce that demands that it be loved in exchange for 'being in sympathy, with everything we see'. Desire is the casualty of such an economy – 'I never want anything, it's easy' – that is, if you don't want to suffer. 'You buy whatever I need / But look at my hopes, look at my dreams', they are as much spent as anything else in the arduous arrangement of cost to need. Progress even here is only allowed to travel in one direction: 'You phoned me in the evening on hearsay / And bought me caviar / You took me to a restaurant off Broadway / To tell me who you are / We never, ever argue, we never calculate' – but only because there is nothing like a partnership demanded here, only that you appreciate me for what I am to you: nothing. This, then, is 'the currency we've spent': the currency of voidance and oblivion, the place love becomes ecstatic to the extent that it overwhelms and ultimately evacuates its value, 'words mean so little and money less when you're lying next to me'. What is left behind is a counterfeit ease, without the true promise of comfort. Without this capacity, however, for trade of one's self, the alternative very bleak, evidenced by the lyrics which imagine the station not only where the North meets the capital, but where bodies deemed useless to conspicuous consumption become little more than distasteful waste. The London of the 1980s is a place of endemic poverty and domestic violence. The connection between the two reflects how Thatcherite geographies converge with another zone of crisis: that of AIDS, which takes over the country as a collective panic. King's Cross here represents the convergence of gay nightlife and life-and-death activism; departing from the static nihilism of the early 80s, this convergence emphasized that the former industrial zones around London's West End had now become synonymous with exposure and contagion.

To the degree that the 'hard option', as Tennant first referred to it in 'West End Girls', is gendered, those in the dole queue face an immediate future of emasculation at the hands of a government headed by a cruel maternal figure in Thatcher. In *Actually*'s concluding track, 'King's Cross', Tennant sings of the man at the back of the queue, who was meant 'to feel the smack of firm government'. However, it's not just this man but everyone around him that is subject to this merciless beating that is all too relatable to the song's contemporary audience: '[I]t's the same story every night / I've been hurt and we've been had.' The poor advice about self-reliance in the face of such abuse comes to the fore: 'you leave home, and you don't go back'. Where exactly to place yourself is anyone's guess and nobody's business. You are to rely on your patience for a way forward to materialize: 'Someone told me Monday, someone told me Saturday / Wait until tomorrow and there's still no way.' No one in government is listening anymore to the grievances of the people – people who are told 'to read it in a book or write it in a letter / Wake up in the morning and there's still no guarantee' of anything changing. North of London and South of the City presents a no man's land in terms of opportunities, and nothing points in the direction of a livelihood in any traditional sense of trade. Ben Campkin refers to the scenario as a 'nightmare' that 'evokes the social anxiety and the sense of political impotence among the disaffected in Thatcher's Britain'.[13] In a later interpretation of the lyrics, Tennant explained how the area was an emblem of downbeat London, of a city and country in crisis, the city's north-east corner standing as a metaphor for the profound lack of opportunity in the Northeast of England, where he was originally from.

As a duo, the Pet Shop Boys' 'particular evocations of England in the 1980s and 1990s depend on a repression that is part of the residue of English nationalism's effect on the body'.[14] John Gill criticizes their failure to embrace the term gay as evidence of the way they 'fit the bourgeois English tradition of discreet perversion and collusion with the establishment'.[15] Perhaps their involvement with the rave culture has something to do with their resistance to be identified as queer rather than gay and their opposition to classification for the sake of racial or sexual formers of community identity, making it appear that they are the camp of One Nation Tories. Yet

---

[13] Ben Campkin, *Remaking London: Decline and Regeneration in Urban Culture* (London: I.B. Tauris, 2013), 5.
[14] Nabeel Zuberi, *Sounds English: Transnational Popular Music* (Urbana-Champaign: University of Illinois Press, 2001), 86.
[15] Zuberi, *Sounds English*, 85.

at another level, they fully admit that there is no dignity in passing as straight in a city where AIDS is becoming epidemic with 'murder walking round the block, ending up in King's Cross', leaving everyone waiting, as 'it takes more than the matter of time' to right this situation.

There is a sense of a sort of imperial hangover dogging this whole new project of capital. Tennant sings in the single 'It Couldn't Happen Here' that 'now it almost seems incredible, we've laughed too loud, and woke up everyone', in which 'everyone' may be the last few countries finally waking up to the implications of centuries of British exploitation at the pleasure of Her Majesty's Government. This situation had been coming home to roost for some time and here it is presented in stereotypical British understatement: 'I may be wrong / But I thought we said it couldn't happen here.' The loss of empire had put Britain in a place that 'almost seems impossible, we've found ourselves back where we started from', contemplating the spectre of a Little England.

The early AIDS discourse of the late 1970s and early 1980s in Britain and the United States drew on enduring stereotypes of native Africans as a primitive race living in isolated tribes cut off from civilization. It assumed that Africa, as a 'dark continent', harbored unique diseases which differed in kind to the rest of the world. It perpetuated the old belief that Africans were closely related to monkeys, having potentially interbred with them for centuries, or at the very least involved them in their sexual customs. Thus, they were more vulnerable to their diseases as compared to other human populations. The disease itself was deemed to be out of control in Africa because it primarily affected the majority heterosexual population, as opposed to the West where it was believed to be largely confined to a minority homosexual population. Presumably, these homosexual men acquired it through sexual tourism in Africa in the early to mid-1970s.[16]

Those types of 'illicit encounters' were not to be brought home like 'some deadly cargo' from Africa, threatening to bring down the institution of the British family by infecting it with some exotic disease.[17] As Simon Watney observed in 1987, AIDS was treated as a reminder 'that negritude has always, for whites, been a sign of sexual excess and death'.[18] In this way the homosexual himself had no place within Britain and needed to be isolated, registered and expelled so that the nation as a whole could be protected from this outside invasion. Watney commented that the spectacle of AIDS was thus always modified by the fear of being 'too shocking' for its domestic audience, while at the same time amplifying and magnifying the collective '"wisdom" of familialism':[19]

---

[16]Rosalind J. Harrison-Chirimuuta and Richard C. Chirimuuta, 'AIDS from Africa: A Case of Racism Vs. Science?', in George Clement Bond, John Kreniske, Ida Susser and Joan Vincent (eds), *AIDS in Africa and the Caribbean* (London: Routledge, 2019): 165–80.
[17]Simon Watney, 'The Spectacle of AIDS', *October* 43 (1987): 74, doi: 10.2307/3397565.
[18]Watney, 'The Spectacle of AIDS', 74.
[19]Watney, 'The Spectacle of AIDS', 82.

[T]he spectacle of AIDS is thus placed in the service of the strongly felt need for constant domestic surveillance and the strict regulation of identity through the intimate mechanism of sexual guilt, sibling rivalries, parental favoritism, embarrassment, hysterical modesty, house-pride, 'keeping-up-with-the-Joneses', hobbies, diet, exercise, personal hygiene and the general husbandry of the home. These are concrete practices that authorize consent to 'political' authority, and it is in relation to them that the entire spectacle of AIDS is choreographed, with its studied emphasis on 'dirt', 'depravity', 'license' and above all 'promiscuity.'[20]

This attitude is also referred to implicitly in the lyrics of 'Suburbia', where, as Tennant reminds us acerbically, 'the suburbs met utopia', and in doing so created a new form of dystopia no one had quite imagined – a place where the project of post-war racial and class containment has led to a generation of roaming suburban white boys who have nothing to do with themselves but look for trouble – 'in the distance a police car to break the suburban spell' – and get involved in petty crime as they '[b]reak the window by the town hall', presuming to bring down with them 'all the suburban dreams' of their parents' generation, ordinary tedium begetting gratuitous violence. What goes around comes around, from being a dream to becoming a nightmare, and looking all the while for someone to blame for how it all was turning out. The precarity surrounding Britishness (or, rather, British whiteness) is apparent in the speculation that these new towns had the potential to become the slums of the future, by which time its current residents would have presumably moved on to either more lucrative developments – or more serious crime. The destination of choice for those at the periphery is London, a city that on the whole was becoming indistinguishable from the financial arrangement at its core. The single 'Suburbia' was partly inspired by the Brixton and Toxteth riots of 1981 and explores the rise of racialized violence in what were euphemistically referred to as once-prosperous urban areas.

Jacquelin A. Burgess argues that the 'meanings given to the concept of the inner city in the press reports of the disturbances [in] Brixton, Toxteth and Moss Side fulfil an ideological role in which a myth is being perpetuated of *The Inner City* as an alien place, separate and isolated, located outside white, middle-class values and environments'.[21] Conservative '[p]apers such as the *Daily Mail*, *Daily Star*, *Daily and Sunday Telegraph* came down firmly on issues of law and order, immigration policies, criminality, lack of parental control and the need to equip the police', whereas, 'the more "liberal" press, such as the *Guardian*, *Daily Mirror*, *Observer and Sunday Times* were much

---

[20] Watney, 'The Spectacle of AIDS', 82–3.
[21] Jacquelin A. Burgess, 'News from Nowhere: The Press, the Riots and the Myth of the Inner City', in Jacquelin A. Burgess and John R. Gold (eds), *Geography, the Media and Popular Culture* (London: Routledge, 2015), 192–228.

FIGURE 5.1 *The Brixton riots of 1981 underscored deep racialized and class tensions in the United Kingdom in the 1980s.*

more concerned with the "deprivation" thesis and its associations with government policies'.[22] During the major disruptions in July 1981, the latter newspapers devoted more attention to a discussion of underlying causes, which included unemployment levels, urban deprivation, race and policing issues, rather than 'the much more explosive issues of racism and policing practices' that 'were marginalised' discursively at this time in favour of a narrative of economic, social and environmental decay.[23]

In an interview about 'Suburbia', Neil Tennant has stated:

> I thought it was a great idea to write a song about suburbia and how it's really violent and decaying and a mess. It's quite a theme in English art, literature and music, like in Graham Greene or Paul Theroux – that the suburbs are really nasty, that behind lace curtains everyone is an alcoholic or a spanker or a mass murderer. Also, this was the era of the riots in Toxteth and Brixton. I remember some friends of mine having to drive through the riots in Brixton to visit me in Chelsea, and being scared. Brixton was a prosperous Victorian suburb, and eighty years later it had become this decaying inner city.[24]

---

[22]Burgess, 'News from Nowhere', 203–4.
[23]Burgess, 'News from Nowhere', 205–6.
[24]Rupa Huq, *Making Sense of Suburbia Through Popular Culture* (London: Bloomsbury Academic, 2013), 7.

The implication here is that Brixton had moved from being a prosperous white suburb to being a decaying Black inner city. Much of the image of dystopia that Thatcher was peddling to both her party loyalists and the greater population of voters was racially coded. In her 1978 Conservative conference speech, she invoked 'inner-city' as culpable in the advent of a time 'when the rule of law breaks down' and 'fear takes over'. Thatcher further warned:

> There is no security in the streets, families feel unsafe even in their own homes, children are at risk, criminals prosper, the men of violence flourish, the nightmare world of *A Clockwork Orange* becomes a reality. Here in Britain in the last few years that world has become visibly nearer.[25]

The film *A Clockwork Orange* (1971) is very much a critique of socialist Britain as a place of moral depravity that is drifting ever closer to totalitarianism. Set in a Britain of the near future, its main protagonist, Alex, is an ultra-violent and psychopathic delinquent, leading a group of other white youth on a spree of robbery, rape and murder. These acts escalate until he is eventually apprehended by the police, and through a new experimental psychological technique stripped of his natural proclivity towards violence. When he is released, he realizes he is defenceless in a world riven by violence. The film portrays in salacious detail the criminal exploits of Alex and his gang, the *Droogs*. After its UK release, it was cited as having inspired copycat acts of violence, and the film was withdrawn from British cinemas at the behest of its director, Stanley Kubrick. What is striking about *A Clockwork Orange* is how jarringly white a world it portrays, exemplified by the exploits of its young white male gang who spend their time performing terrifying acts of violence for pleasure. The juvenile delinquency the film portrays acknowledges the escalating tensions with immigrant Black communities in the decades following the Second World War, that had by the early 1970s coalesced around the rise of white racist skinheads. Although in reality, they were often the more frightening presence on the streets, the uptick in urban crime was portrayed in the media as the effect of a 'blackening' of Britain.

Sally Davison and George Shire observe that in Britain, both 'references to race and immigration have been a consistent part of the mobilizing repertoire of the authoritarian aspect of neoliberalism since the 1970s' and that 'race was at the heart of political battles during the transition to Thatcherism'.[26] They argue that the project of racist populism on the right

---

[25]Tinline, 'Back to the Future'.
[26]Sally Davison and George Shire, 'Race, Migration and Neoliberalism', *Soundings* 59 (2015): 86–7.

began with Enoch Powell and, indeed, that Thatcherism would have been impossible without his ability 'to establish [itself] between the themes of race and immigration control and the images of the nation' as something essentially white; i.e. the British people themselves.[27] As a consequence, it is possible to construe popular racism as the foundation upon which the neoliberal project rests both economically and politically. Through this lens, it is possible to distinguish mugging as an *opportunistic* act, one that sets the stage for the arrival of the black(ened) body into Britain as something both unplanned and invasive. If the 1960s mark the end of empire, then the 1970s conversely mark the beginning of a reconceptualization of a Britain that was never willingly touched by it, that never saw its place as one of conscious opportunism, but rather of unconscious entitlement.

If we take seriously her assertion, we can surmise that when Thatcher dispatched her Environment Secretary Michael Heseltine to the deepest recesses of inner-city Liverpool in 1981, she did so with the supposition that these white working-class populations were categorically endangered. Burgess maintains that,

> [...] this political manoeuvre by the Conservative government effectively shifted attention back into the well-worn, familiar debate about relative deprivation. For a crucial period, the presence of Heseltine in Liverpool for three weeks allowed journalists to make the most of their long-standing fascination with the city and much good copy was generated by the contrast between the affluence of 'the menswear ad' Minister and the poverty of the local people.[28]

Heseltine had long been known to his Conservative colleagues by the nickname 'Tarzan', but this was enthusiastically picked up by locals at this time, partly due to his enviable mane of blond hair but also because of his appearance as a white man of privilege going native in the urban jungle, reflecting his fascination with the environment. After the arrival of Heseltine and his ministerial team, they quickly came to the consensus that 'the decivilising conditions of urban life' in places like Toxteth make 'violence, individual and collective, inevitable'.[29] This is so because the economies of colonial yesteryear no longer sustain them through active trade. By 1988, the Conservative government's contribution to the decline of the inner cities was evident through 'its abandonment of automatic investment grants for firms locating in depressed regions [and] its recent overhaul of the welfare system [...] [that] has left millions of the poorest inner city residents

---

[27]Davison and Shire, 'Race, Migration and Neoliberalism', 86.
[28]Burgess, 'News from Nowhere', 206.
[29]Burgess, 'News from Nowhere', 212–13.

worse off'.[30] However, Michael Jacobs identifies something of far greater consequence happening throughout the 1980s. Within this decade, Thatcher's government had begun to tactically promote inequality through its huge defence programme, which directed government contracts 'almost exclusively to firms in the south-east; particularly west of London', making it inevitable 'that the rest of the high technology' sector would follow suit.[31] This initiative reveals a significant connection between the Conservatives' newly revised plans for exterior defence and interior settlement and the rapid financialization of Britain's economy following on from 1986's 'Big Bang'. This move, coupled with the 'further relaxing of housing controls in the "Green Belt" around the capital, suggests that there was a coordinated strategy of racial segregation taking place to politically and economically re-engineer these local geographies'.[32] Thanks to new information technologies, post-colonial Britain's economies of retailing, banking and insurance have been able to decamp from cities altogether, relocating their businesses in suburban and rural areas that require not hard labour, but rather the soft skills associated with light assembly. Computers have made work clean and the enterprise around it green. The appearance of dereliction associated with past labour is now left far out of sight, and with it the requirement to reckon with imperial losses.

Jacobs gives the example of the Conservative inner London borough of Westminster, that had been 'literally "deporting"' its residents to specially-built estates outside of London in order to sell their (refurbished) flats to wealthier people'.[33] Jacobs makes no explicit mention of race in his observations, but it is implied that the process of what he calls 'deliberate gentrification', which has the desired effect of what Thatcher called 'winning the inner cities back to our cause' by defeating the claims of an intergenerational right to residence for migrant communities predominantly of colour.[34] The neoliberal elements of the campaign of dispossession were evident in the description of such practices as matters 'of efficiency'.[35]

They say the past is a foreign country and so it is for the Pet Shop Boys, who referred implicitly to the 'terrifying' aspects of North London in the 1980s in their lyrics.[36] Tennant recalls that, 'London back at the start of the

---

[30]Michael Jacobs, 'Margaret Thatcher and the Inner Cities', *Economic and Political Weekly* 23, no. 38 (1988): 1944.
[31]Jacobs, 'Margaret Thatcher and the Inner Cities', 1944.
[32]Jacobs, 'Margaret Thatcher and the Inner Cities', 1944.
[33]Jacobs, 'Margaret Thatcher and the Inner Cities', 1944.
[34]Jacobs, 'Margaret Thatcher and the Inner Cities', 1944.
[35]Jacobs, 'Margaret Thatcher and the Inner Cities', 1944.
[36]Teddy Jamieson, 'I prefer to be Neil Tennant, man of mystery', *The Herald*, 25 January 2020, https://www.heraldscotland.com/life_style/arts_ents/18184913.prefer-neil-tennant-man-mystery/.

1980s could be frightening [. . .] you were always scared on the way back that you were going to get beaten up by a skinhead.'[37] Prior to that, he 'grew up in Newcastle in the seventies. Newcastle was pretty bad. So, you grew up in a very different culture which made you a very different person [. . .] I think we just grew up in a more violent time.'[38] The Pet Shop Boys' depiction of London in the 1980s is that of an apocalyptic city where dreadful skinheads operate in close proximity to ruthless City boys. It exists as a space where deprivation mixes promiscuously with privatization, where space is bought and sold as a commodity, where historical time is implicated in value and where lives are now actually lived within the horrific thrall of calculations and transactions. Tennant's warm, pleading tone is set against a degenerating social order that threatens to consume all.

Banging on and on

In an interview with the magazine *Women's Own* on 23 September 1987, Prime Minister Margaret Thatcher famously declared that 'there is no such thing as society'.[39] Conversely, the thing that can be said to exist for Thatcher is a 'living tapestry of men and women and people', each of which is 'prepared to take responsibility for themselves'.[40] For Thatcher, 'there is nothing wrong with doing that' or for money to act as 'the great driving engine, the driving force of life'.[41] Thatcher's comments were made nearly one year after the London Stock Exchange's sudden deregulation of financial markets on 27 October 1986, an event thereafter referred to as 'the Big Bang'. The Big Bang ushered in an economic *terra nullius*, in which the City of London was able to effectively dominate financial markets through the deformation of individuals and institutions and the spread of financial risk around the world. Thirty-six years later, while British government ideology continues to emphasize and privilege a baseline white citizenry and encourages these citizens to strive towards limited opportunities afforded them by state neoliberalism, that very neoliberalism is incapable of offering any guarantee of protection, surety or prosperity.

In the Pet Shop Boys' hit single duet with Dusty Springfield, 'What Have I Done to Deserve This?', Springfield sings, '[Y]ou always wanted a lover', to

---

[37]Jamieson, 'I prefer to be Neil Tennant, man of mystery'.
[38]Jamieson, 'I prefer to be Neil Tennant, man of mystery'.
[39]Douglas Keay, 'Margaret Thatcher Interview for "Woman's Own" ("No Such Thing as Society")', *Margaret Thatcher Foundation*, 23 September 1987, 30.
[40]Keay, 'Margaret Thatcher Interview', 31.
[41]Keay, 'Margaret Thatcher Interview', 29.

which Tennant sighs in reply, 'I only wanted a job.' The coy re-engineering of that track reflects nothing so much as the emphasis placed on personal financial gain during the Thatcher and Reagan years, and the futility of caring within such an era. Perhaps without irony, the Black Monday stock market crash of 1987, itself a consequence of Britain's imperial hangover, bookends what is now commonly referred to as Pet Shop Boys' 'imperial era'.

Bibliography

Bateman, Bradley W. 'There Are Many Alternatives: Margaret Thatcher in the History of Economic Thought'. *Journal of the History of Economic Thought* 24, no. 3 (2002): 307–11, https://doi.org/10.1080/104277102200004758.

Burgess, Jacquelin A. 'News from nowhere: The press, the riots and the myth of the inner city'. In Jacquelin A. Burgess and John R. Gold (eds), *Geography, the Media and Popular Culture*, 192–228. London: Routledge, 2015.

Campkin, Ben. *Remaking London: Decline and Regeneration in Urban Culture*. London: I.B. Tauris, 2013.

Danewid, Ida. 'The Fire This Time: Grenfell, Racial Capitalism and the Urbanisation of Empire'. *European Journal of International Relations* 26, no. 1 (March 2020): 289–313, https://doi.org/10.1177/1354066119858388.

Davison, Sally and George Shire. 'Race, migration and neoliberalism'. *Soundings* 59, no. 59 (2015): 81–95, muse.jhu.edu/article/590756.

Harrison-Chirimuuta Rosalind J. and Richard C. Chirimuuta. 'AIDS from Africa: A Case of Racism Vs. Science?'. In George Clement Bond, John Kreniske, Ida Susser and Joan Vincent (eds), *AIDS in Africa and the Caribbean*, 165–80. London: Routledge, 2019.

Huq, Rupa. *Making Sense of Suburbia Through Popular Culture*. London: Bloomsbury Academic, 2013.

Jacobs, Michael. 'Margaret Thatcher and the Inner Cities'. *Economic and Political Weekly* 23, no. 38 (1988): 1942–4.

Jamieson, Teddy. 'I prefer to be Neil Tennant, man of mystery'. *The Herald*, 25 January 2020, https://www.heraldscotland.com/life_style/arts_ents/18184913.prefer-neil-tennant-man-mystery/.

Kallioniemi, Kari. 'New Romantic Queering Tactics of English Pop in Early Thatcherite Britain and the Second British Invasion'. *Radical Musicology* 7 (2019).

Keay, Douglas. 'Margaret Thatcher Interview for "Woman's Own" ("No Such Thing as Society")', *Margaret Thatcher Foundation*, 23 September 1987.

Power, Sally'. 'The state has helped poor pupils into private schools before – did it work?' *The Conversation*, 9 December 2016, https://theconversation.com/the-state-has-helped-poor-pupils-into-private-schools-before-did-it-work-70222.

Shaxson, Nicholas. *Treasure Islands: Uncovering the Damage of Offshore Banking and Tax Havens*. New York: St. Martin's Publishing Group, 2011.

'The Story of . . . "West End Girls" by Pet Shop Boys', Smooth Radio, 12 October 2018, https://www.smoothradio.com/features/pet-shop-boys-west-end-girls-lyrics-meaning-video/.

Tinline, Phil. 'Back to the Future: What the Turmoil of the 1970s Can Teach Us Today'. *New Statesman*, 8 May 2019, https://www.newstatesman.com/politics/uk/2019/05/back-future-what-turmoil-1970s-can-teach-us-today.

Watney, Simon. 'The Spectacle of AIDS'. *October* 43 (1987): 71–86 (74), https://doi.org/10.2307/3397565.

Zuberi, Nabeel. *Sounds English: Transnational Popular Music*. Urbana-Champaign: University of Illinois Press, 2001.

CHAPTER SIX

Moscow or Manderley?

Spectrality and Sovietism in the Pet Shop Boys' Oeuvre

Carolin Isabel Steiner

'Pop music is about sex,' Neil Tennant told an interviewer in 1991, as the Pet Shop Boys prepared for their first tour of the United States.[1] This may have come as a surprise to his long-time collaborator, Chris Lowe, who in a much later interview with Chris Heath extolled the virtues of the 1986 song 'Later Tonight', from their first album, *Please*. 'It's all about turning off the lights and it all getting a bit steamy,' he explained, before reflecting: 'Our records aren't sexy enough now. It's all bloody politics and the intricacies of Russian history. No one wants to hear about that, do they?'[2]

While Lowe might have been (characteristically) grumbly about the duo's lack of output focusing on sex and relationships in favour of Soviet allusions and references to Russian literature, this should be taken with a note of scepticism. Indeed, in the same interview in 1991, Tennant explained to the reporter on the other end of the telephone line that he recognizes a nexus between sex, relationships and politics:

> AIDS has changed sex. Night-clubbing has become more about dancing and getting out of your head than a courtship ritual, and so dance music

---

[1] Chris Heath, *Pet Shop Boys versus America* (London: William Heinemann, 2020), 15.
[2] Chris Lowe, interview with Chris Heath, 'Pet Shop Boys 1984–1986', *Pet Shop Boys Please/Further Listening 1984–1986* liner notes (2018), 23.

has become more pure. Disco was *sexual* – 'love to love you baby', heavy breathing. Dance music is now heavy beats and you dance by yourself. These two things – that and the death of communism – have changed society entirely, and I think that it's difficult to know what to do or think in the aftermath.[3]

Far from an either/or proposition, then, Tennant recognized that the music he and Lowe produced would be indelibly influenced, and in turn reflect, the great catastrophes of their moment in history. If songs were about sex, then they must inevitably consider AIDS and the great swathes of devastation it wrought; if their songs were about politics, then the collapse of the Eastern Bloc meant not only the final submission to Western neoliberal capitalism that had 'won' by default, but also the necessity to come to terms with the loss of an alternative, and the dispelling of the dreams of a different future that that engendered. In a sense, therefore, the Pet Shop Boys' work is always haunted – both by the things that have shaped their lived experience in the past, as well as the future possibilities that never materialized.

This chapter proposes a hauntological reading of losses and absences in the Pet Shop Boys' body of work. I will use selected songs as case studies, though I argue that much of their oeuvre can be read as a literary (and sonic) representation of futures that never were. I will engage with the ways in which spectres interact with cultural artefacts and can function as representants of repressed pasts and their future implication, before illustrating how neoliberalism quashed modern dreams of postmodern futures, and where the Pet Shop Boys are temporally located in this process. It is imperative here to emphasize that the terms 'haunting', 'ghosts' and 'spectres' '[do] not involve the conviction that ghosts exist or that the past (and maybe the future they [the spectres] offer to prophesy) is still very much alive and at work within the living present'.[4] Rather, '[t]o haunt does not mean to be present, and it is necessary to introduce haunting into the very construction of a concept. Of every concept, beginning with the concepts of being and time. That is what we would be calling here a hauntology.'[5]

Lastly, I will engage with the lyrics of selected songs to demonstrate how both (micro-)historical losses and transhistorical absences serve as means of literary representation of failed futures and therefore constitute an important aspect of memory work, which conjures spectres rather than exorcizing them.

---

[3]Heath, *Pet Shop Boys versus America*, 15.
[4]Frederic Jameson, 'Marx's Purloined Letter', in Michael Sprinker (ed.), *Ghostly Demarcations: A Symposium on Jacques Derrida's Specters of Marx* (London and New York: Verso, 2008), 38.
[5]Jacques Derrida, *Specters of Marx: The State of the Debt, the Work of Mourning and the New International*, trans. Peggy Kamuf (London: Routledge, 2011), 161.

Ghosts of myself: spectres, hauntings and disjointed time

Hauntology is a concept that originated in the work of French philosopher Jacques Derrida. The term itself is a pun on the words *ontology* and *haunting* and describes a spectral state of being, which is both *revenant*, invoking what was, and *arrivant*, announcing what will come. This means that the spectre operates on several temporal planes, most crucially the future and its possible interactions with the present and the past. Derrida avers with respect to the temporality of the spectre:

> But if the commodity-form is not, presently, use-value, and even if it is not actually present, it affects in advance the use-value of the wooden table. It affects and bereaves it in advance, like the ghost it will become, but this is precisely where haunting begins. And its time, and the untimeliness of its present, of its being 'out of joint.' To haunt does not mean to be present, and it is necessary to introduce haunting into the very construction of a concept. Of every concept, beginning with the concepts of being and time. That is what we would be calling here a hauntology. Ontology opposes it only in a movement of exorcism. Ontology is a conjuration.[6]

Hauntology arose in the context of Derrida's engagement with Marxism, and specifically his response to the collapse of the Soviet Union and the supposed 'end of history' propagated by neoconservative thinkers like Fukuyama, who saw history as a war of competing ideologies, which ended with the Soviet Union's dissolution. Derrida argued that the collapse of socialist regimes did not mean the end of communism, but rather the emergence of a spectral state of being that was neither entirely past nor entirely present nor entirely future. In other words, the spectre of communism continued to haunt the present, even as it seemed to have been consigned to the dustbin of history.[7] At its very core, Derrida critiques scholarship for its compulsion to ontologize and limit itself to the realm of the rational, while at the same time disregarding everything non-ontologizable. As Elisabeth Roberts avers, he therefore 'argues that scholars are not in a position to speak with spectres or let them speak because they draw sharp distinctions between the real and unreal, the living and the non-living, the being and non-being. Haunting brings this either/or logic into question.'[8] It is, however, fundamental to distinguish between Derridean ghosts and the supernatural:

---

[6] Derrida, *Specters of Marx*, 201–2.
[7] John A. Riley, 'Hauntology, Ruins, and the Failure of the Future in Andrei Tarkovsky's Stalker', *Journal of Film and Video* 69, no. 1 (2017): 18, https://doi.org/10.5406/jfilmvideo.69.1.0018.
[8] Elisabeth Roberts, 'Geography and the Visual Image: A Hauntological Approach', *Progress in Human Geography* 37, no. 3 (June 2013): 161, https://doi.org/10.1177/0309132512460902.

save for the imagery, hauntological spectrality is intrinsically worldly. The spectres are composed of cultural content, inscribed deeply into collective memories, which scaffold the perception of temporal spaces, and whose conjuring can 'evoke an affective sense of temporal disjuncture'.[9] One example of such conjuring can be found around the output of Ghostbox. The British record label's artists emphasize the sound of bygone eras (such as typewriter noises) and invoke a distinctly creepy atmosphere through the use of, for instance, recording noises. Jamie Sexton refers to this as the 'technological uncanny', in which 'being itself is haunted, constituted from a number of hidden traces whose presence is felt but often unacknowledged'.[10] This process, described as *visible remediation* by Bolter and Grusin, creates a reimagined form of art, where contemporary media and settings are combined with historical cultural artefacts to form a 'mosaic', in which the individual artefacts are distinct and noticeable, but the audience too notices their out-of-placeness in the new, contemporary setting.[11] This act of creative reproduction of cultural artefacts is one of the two approaches Peter Schofield outlines with respect to how hauntology manifests in media: *mimesis* and *appropriation*. Mimesis creates contemporary art that, in an act of pastiche or faithful recreation, or anything in between, mimics 'fondly remembered cultural artefacts', while appropriation merely synthesizes new media out of authentic old media.[12] At the core of hauntology lies the question of how, if something belonging to the past continues to affect presence and future, it can be ontologically confined to a singular temporal state? Martin Hägglund elaborates on the spectre:

---

[9] Lisa Perrott, 'Time Is out of Joint: The Transmedial Hauntology of David Bowie', *Celebrity Studies* 10, no. 1 (2 January 2019): 2, https://doi.org/10.1080/19392397.2018.1559125.
[10] Jamie Sexton, 'Weird Britain in Exile: Ghost Box, Hauntology, and Alternative Heritage', *Popular Music and Society* 35, no. 4 (October 2012): 562, https://doi.org/10.1080/03007766.2011.608905.
[11] J. David Bolter and Richard A. Grusin, *Remediation: Understanding New Media* (Cambridge, MA: MIT Press, 1999), 47.
[12] Michael Peter Schofield, 'Re-Animating Ghosts: Materiality and Memory in Hauntological Appropriation', *International Journal of Film and Media Arts* 4, no. 2 (31 December 2019): 26, https://doi.org/10.24140/ijfma.v4n2.02. Schofield further argues that mimesis is 'the less hauntological of the two approaches', and while I disagree with the premise of quantifying a degree of hauntedness in the first place, I would also like to point towards the concept of traumatic repetition, in which traumatic events might be compulsively revisited in a reinterpretative, recreative process (cf. Michelle Balaev, 'Trends in Literary Trauma Theory', *Mosaic: An Interdisciplinary Critical Journal* 41, no. 2 (2008): 149–66). While trauma studies and hauntology are distinct approaches, there are a multitude of overlapping ideas (as outlined in Maria del Pilar Blanco and Esther Peeren, 'The Spectral Turn', in Maria del Pilar Blanco and Esther Peeren (eds), *The Spectralities Reader: Ghosts and Haunting in Contemporary Cultural Theory* (New York: Bloomsbury, 2013), 31–6), but when following Dominick LaCapra's distinction between loss and absence and subsequent acceptance of the multi-directed temporality of trauma, it would appear to be shortsighted not to consider mimesis as more meaningful than a mere parody of the past (cf. Dominick LaCapra, 'Trauma, Absence, Loss', *Critical Inquiry* 25, no. 4 (1999): 696–727).

What is important about the figure of the spectre, then, is that it cannot be fully present: it has no being in itself but marks a relation to what is no longer or not yet. And since time – the disjointure between past and future – is a condition even for the slightest moment, spectrality is at work in everything that happens. An identity or community can never escape the machinery of exclusion, can never fail to engender ghosts, since it must demarcate itself against a past that cannot be encompassed and a future that cannot be anticipated. Inversely, it will always be threatened by what it cannot integrate in itself – haunted by the negated, the neglected, and the unforeseeable.[13]

In this, the spectre in itself becomes a haunting realization: its temporal transcendence negates the impermeability of time and threatens the stability of what is perceived as the ontological reference frame for the self: the safety of knowing what is real remaining stable and untouched.[14] As Jameson puts it: '[A]ll [the spectre] says, if it can be thought to speak, is that the living present is scarcely as self-sufficient as it claims to be; that we would do well not to count on its density and solidity, which might under exceptional circumstances betray us.'[15]

As this conceptualization has mostly concerned itself with the past as a *spectre revenant*, that is, the spectre that invokes what has been, it is worth emphasizing the multi-directionality of haunting. As previously established, Derrida's ghosts are always *spectres arrivants* as well, announcing or foreshadowing what is yet to come, and therefore (re-)constructing time not as a linear, progressive line that moves inexorably forward, but as a complex, multidimensional entity that is constantly in flux. It is for this very reason that Mark Fisher avers that 'the future is always experienced as a haunting': the construction of what can be expected of the future collectively impacts the creative cultural outputs.[16] Demonstrating that hauntology has long left the realm of Marxism, he exemplifies this by pointing towards the case of electronic music: he argues that post-2005, the sound of electronic music was no longer futuristic. Though it had previously made use of novel

---

[13] Martin Hägglund, *Radical Atheism: Derrida and the Time of Life* (Stanford, CA: Stanford University Press, 2008), 82.
[14] Though Lewis argues that it represents 'more than the instability of the real; it also represents the ghostly embodiment of a fear and panic provoked by intimations of an impossible state of being. Recognition of the flawed or incomplete nature of being, Derrida suggests, can trigger emotional reactions aimed at denying or exorcizing such a recognition.' Cf. Tom Lewis, 'The Politics of "Hauntology" in Derrida's Specters of Marx', in Michael Sprinker (ed.), *Ghostly Demarcations: A Symposium on Jacques Derrida's Specters of Marx* (London and New York: Verso, 2008), 140.
[15] Jameson, 'Marx's Purloined Letter', 39.
[16] Mark Fisher, 'What is Hauntology?', *Film Quarterly* 66, no. 1 (1 September 2012): 16, https://doi.org/10.1525/fq.2012.66.1.16.

technology and was frequently used in art whenever the future was to be invoked, it had lost that capacity and merely referred to an established catalogue of sonic expression, which had become anything but novel. Fisher conceptualizes this stasis as 'digital cul-de-sacs': 'Twenty-first-century electronic music had failed to progress beyond what had been recorded in the twentieth century: practically anything produced in the 2000s could have been recorded in the 1990s. Electronic music had succumbed to its own inertia and retrospection.'[17] In a future that had failed to materialize, the signifiers for what was deemed to be futuristic in the twenty-first century lost their *signifié*, and it is precisely this untethering that cultivates media as a site of haunting for both the revenant and the arrivant, as Fisher elaborates:

> What haunts the digital cul-de-sacs of the twenty-first century is not so much the past as all the lost futures that the twentieth century taught us to anticipate. The futures that have been lost were more than a matter of musical style. More broadly, and more troublingly, the disappearance of the future meant the deterioration of a whole mode of social imagination: the capacity to conceive of a world radically different from the one in which we currently live. It meant the acceptance of a situation in which culture would continue without really changing, and where politics was reduced to the administration of an already established (capitalist) system.[18]

Those failed futures, as Riley points out, not only – naturally – encompass the glaring absence of the gleaming Soviet future lost with the collapse of the Soviet Union, but just as much the capitalist progress, which, in the twenty-first century, seems to have ground to a halt by dint of repeating cycles of once-in-a-lifetime financial crises, climate threats and global political instability.[19] It is not only the absence of these futures, but the final annihilation of any imaginable scenario in which the twentieth-century futures could still manifest. It is precisely here that the spectre implodes temporality in both repressed pasts and failed future, this 'deliberate indeterminacy, enforced hesitancy or uncertainty over presupposed givens and operations involving visibility and invisibility that constitute our reality' that 'rudely erupt everywhere into Modernity's linear narratives, cities and technologies [. . .] as uneasy presences reminding us of social injustices, or as animating forces intruding into the present'.[20] As Derrida frames it while quoting Hamlet ad nauseam: 'the time is out of joint', 'suggesting provocatively that this disjointed time is the political situation that must be

---

[17]Fisher, 'What is Hauntology', 16.
[18]Fisher, 'What is Hauntology', 16.
[19]Riley, 'Hauntology, Ruins, and the Failure of the Future in Andrei Tarkovsky's Stalker', 19.
[20]Roberts, 'Geography and the Visual Image', 392–3.

set right, the debt that we must settle'.[21] This, too, is where the haunting resists compartmentalization: it might first occur as a grim presence hovering over humanity's every move, so does it also hold a tremendous empowering potential; an impetus to reconfigure the certainties of neoliberal bleakness, a push to imagine futures beyond realist-capitalist imagination. Or, in the words of Derrida himself, 'Altogether other. Staging for the end of history. Let us call it a hauntology.'[22]

Putting the 'post' in post-punk: from settled dust to technocratic soundscapes

To read Tennant and Lowe's work in a context of spectrality, an attempt at localizing it in the flux and flow of British post-war temporality is inevitable. As Great Britain emerged victoriously out of the Second World War, the empire seemed to have got a second wind, another attempt at 'Rule Britannia'. As in much of the Western world, there was a distinct sense of optimism about the future: the atom promised a nuclear revolution (previous annihilations notwithstanding), liberal democracy had prevailed over fascism, and Britain was indulging in a 'spirit of technocratic utopianism [...] from the misunderstood Brutalist school in architecture (they meant well, really they did) to the democratization of learning undertaken by the Open University'.[23] In the same sense, polytechnical schools and libraries became a symbol for modernist ideas of intellectual progress, sites for an emancipative (re-)distribution of knowledge representing a broader 'longing for self-overcoming' emerging out of the democratic culture, whose 'aspirations were not confined to a hope that social democracy would simply continue'.[24] Coming as no surprise to the attentive reader, these aspirations did not, in fact, materialize.

With the Wind of Change in 1960 at the latest, but possibly as early as the Suez crisis, Britain's descent into post-imperiality was clearly, undeniability happening. The empire shrank, and much like it fell off the world's stage, so did Britain's political credibility abroad and at home. From John Profumo's unfortunate choice of sharing a lover with a Soviet naval attaché and the subsequent scandal it caused, to Britons dealing with electricity rationing while their Soviet and American contemporaries got to watch their respective space race contenders launch, to the Winter of

---

[21]Cf. Derrida, *Specters of Marx*; Riley, 'Hauntology, Ruins, and the Failure of the Future in Andrei Tarkovsky's Stalker', 19.
[22]Derrida, *Specters of Marx*, 10.
[23]Simon Reynolds, 'Haunted Audio', *The Wire*, 2006, 29.
[24]Fisher, 'What is Hauntology?', 18.

FIGURE 6.1 *The architectural style of Brutalism is probably best exemplified by London's Barbican Estate. The Barbican, 2014.*

Discontent in the late 70s: gradually it became clear that the shining futures post-war modernism had promised were becoming less and less likely to materialize. Unfortunately, 1981 also saw the first reported death in the UK of AIDS-related complications, foreshadowing an increase in AIDS-related deaths well into the 90s.[25] With British dreams of postmodernism shattered at the very latest with Thatcher's rise to power in the early 80s and the subsequent hegemony of neoliberalism and neoconservatism, Britons so

---

[25]Cf. R. M. Du Bois et al., 'Primary Pneumocystis Carinii and Cytomegalovirus Infections', *The Lancet* 318, no. 8259 (1981): 1339, https://doi.org/10.1016/S0140-6736(81)91353-2; '30 Years on: People Living with HIV in the UK about to Reach 100,000', *Health Protection Report* 5, no. 22 (2011), https://webarchive.nationalarchives.gov.uk/ukgwa/20140714095642/http://www.hpa.org.uk/hpr/archives/2011/news2211.htm.

inclined could still look to the Soviet Union to imagine an alternative, communist future. However, it was not to be:

> By 1990, the Soviet Union, the 'Evil Empire' that Ronald Reagan and Margaret Thatcher decried, was in the final stages of disintegration – not so much conquered by its enemies, but rather collapsing under its own weight when its center would not hold in the wake of economic crises and a prolonged war of imperialist misadventure in Afghanistan. By this time, too, the Thatcher era had ended with almost equal alacrity, the 'Iron Lady' having been unceremoniously dumped by her own party, in great part because her unshakeable nationalism would not allow Britain to form economically beneficial ties with the European Union. Even before Mrs. Thatcher was permanently dispatched to that political living death, the House of Lords, Reagan, the other great anachronism of the right wing, had retired into an Alzheimer's twilight. Thus, the Cold War, which for half a century threatened to annihilate the entire planet, was suddenly gone – with various whimpers instead of the big bang long anticipated.[26]

With the dissolution of the Soviet Union, neoliberalist futures were all that remained, and what eventually would become the 'haunt[ing ...] digital cul-de-sacs of the twenty-first century': 'not so much the past as all the lost futures that the twentieth century taught us to anticipate'.[27]

Neil Tennant broke onto the musical scene amid the rude awakening from these postmodern dreams. He first auditioned with music publishers in 1973 (after a brief stint with a short-lived folk-rock group called Dust), while a student at the Polytechnic of North London. His aspirations would not lead to anything until he met Chris Lowe almost a decade later, when his focus had shifted from earlier folk sounds to a taste for electronic music. He places a significant weight on the Buzzcocks' Pete Shelley and his single 'Homosapien', with its combination of synths and acoustic guitars, as an inspiration for the Pet Shop Boys' first, unproductive dabbles.[28] Biographic trivia aside, this places the emergence of what would be the Pet Shop Boys in the sociocultural context of punk and later post-punk, a musical scene arising out of the disenfranchisement caused by interchanging Labour and Conservative governments, which still peaked in the Winter of Discontent – the party, which was supposed to be a workers' party, turned out not to be a

---

[26]Patricia Juliana Smith, '"Go West": The Pet Shop Boys' Allegories and Anthems of Postimperiality', *Genre* 34, no. 3–4 (1 September 2001): 321, https://doi.org/10.1215/00166928-34-3-4-307.

[27]Fisher, 'What is Hauntology?', 16.

[28]Neil Tennant, *One Hundred Lyrics and a Poem: 1979–2016* (London: Faber & Faber, 2018), xi–xvii.

meaningful intervention in the progression of conservatism. Instead, both the Conservatives and the Labour Party failed to materialize the better futures promised after the war and, in a de facto two-party system, voters had run out of options.[29] Culturally and musically, punk rebelled against the polished productions of their rock predecessors, the glam rock of the 70s, in favour of dissonant, abrasive soundscapes. With the rapidly progressing commercialization and hyper-commodification of rock after the war, many punks felt that the formerly rebellious rock stars had sold out and cosied up with the mainstream, while enjoying their personal neoliberal success by dint of newly acquired wealth.[30] Punk picked up where its recently commodified predecessors had left and proceeded to 'throw acid at rock & roll and construct a genre out of what was left'.[31] Described as having 'had a uniquely therapeutic nature as a subculture for a generation of unemployed people [. . . providing] them with a reason to get up in the morning', punk was very much a product of political post-war flux and flow.[32] With unemployment numbers at an all-time high and the economy in deep recession, punk emerged as a cultural representation of the discontent and disenfranchisement felt by British youths.[33] At the epicentre of this tumultuous scene-genre-movement-hybrid lay the very city Neil Tennant stepped foot into right around the time punk took off: London. From Poly Styrene's first stage experiences singing to stray cats in Brixton bomb sites and Covent Garden's short-lived Roxy club organizing the first the Clash gigs, to Kensington's Rough Trade record shop and its classifieds connecting musicians (and inspiring Kurt Cobain some two decades later), British punk history is inextricably interwoven with the city.[34]

Whether Tennant and Lowe ever hung out with the punk crowds does not matter as much as punk being the music that, one way or another, gave birth to post-punk and paved the way for much of the Pet Shop Boys' work (though they do invoke punk in some of their songs, such as 'Requiem in Denim and

---

[29]Cf. Matthew Worley, *No Future: Punk, Politics and British Youth Culture, 1976–1984* (Cambridge: Cambridge University Press, 2017).
[30]Cf. Dylan Clark, 'The Death and Life of Punk, the Last Subculture', in David Muggleton and Rupert Weinzierl (eds), *The Post-Subcultures Reader* (Oxford: Berg Publishers, 2003), 223–36; Jesse Prinz, 'The Aesthetics of Punk Rock', *Philosophy Compass* 9, no. 9 (2014): 583–93, https://doi.org/10.1111/phc3.12145.
[31]Carola Dibbell, 'Inside Was Us: Women and Punk', in Barbara O'Dair (ed.), *Trouble Girls: The Rolling Stone Book of Women in Rock* (New York: Random House, 1997), 280.
[32]Helen Reddington, *The Lost Women of Rock Music: Female Musicians of the Punk Era* (Sheffield and Bristol, CT: Equinox, 2012), 7; Worley, *No Future*, 140.
[33]Cf. Jon Savage, *England's Dreaming: Anarchy, Sex Pistols, Punk Rock, and Beyond* (New York: St. Martin's Press, 1992).
[34]Cf. Celeste Bell and Zoë Howe, *Dayglo: The Poly Styrene Story* (London: Omnibus Press, 2019); Vincent Dowd, 'Julien Temple on The Clash: "The Energy of Punk Is Really Needed Now"', *BBC News* (1 January 2015), https://www.bbc.com/news/entertainment-arts-30641500; Jenn Pelly, *The Raincoats* (New York: Bloomsbury Academic, 2017).

Leopardskin').³⁵ Simon Reynolds avers that 'the entire postpunk period looks like an attempt to replay virtually every major modernist theme and technique via the medium of pop music', and it is worth reframing the Pet Shop Boys in this precise angle as well.³⁶ At the risk of upsetting both Tennant and Lowe as well as the Manchester purists, I argue that both sonically and thematically Pet Shop Boys can be read as a post-punk pastiche of pop rather than the (for them often derogatory) genre label of pop. While Tennant and Lowe span an extraordinary breadth of sonic influences and fusion sounds, their use of, for instance, an early Korg-MS10 synth or the then still new gated reverbs, mirrors the logical next step after the electronic guitar sound rock had pioneered and punk had arguably perfected. Seifert argues that 'genres like post punk but also neoclassicism and post dubstep orient themselves exclusively temporally and along the lines of (pop) music development, but say precious little about their musical appearance', a fact that the Pet Shop Boys' work takes advantage of in their wide sonic portfolio. As Karpe argues, while the *post* in post-punk recalls the spectres of earlier punk works, technological advancements and changes to songwriting conventions place post-punk as a distinctly autonomous genre with a more avant-gardist sound.³⁷ While punk had emphasized rage and anti-establishmentarianism, post-punk prioritized melancholia, loss and grief: 'Punk enabled you to say "fuck you", but it couldn't go any further. It was a single, venomous, two-syllable phrase of anger. Sooner or later, someone was going to say more; someone was going to want to say "I'm fucked".'³⁸ Post-punk, in itself, is therefore intrinsically hauntological: it is, after all, mimicry of the very thing punk was, and yet fundamentally different – an act of mourning rather than an act of raging.

Mourning is a fundamental part of human existence. It, too, is at the core of the Pet Shop Boys' discography: sometimes sonically, sometimes lyrically, sometimes shrouded in nostalgia, sometimes hidden in upbeat pop melodies, but always omnipresent. With their career falling right onto the intersection of failing futures and the onset of the AIDS epidemic, while being queer, this

---

[35] Chris Lowe himself positions their coming of age and musical identities as influenced by punk. 'I was at university during the whole punk thing. Groups of our era were still very punk in our attitudes, as opposed to musicians today who have a completely different attitude to the industry' (Chris Lowe, interview with Chris Heath, 'Pet Shop Boys 1984–1986', *Pet Shop Boys Please/Further Listening 1984–1986* liner notes (2018), 9). References to this crop up throughout their career, e.g., when talking about their song 'Positive Role Model', Lowe remarks they 'wanted to do punk disco' (Chris Lowe, interview with Chris Heath, 'Pet Shop Boys 1996–2000', *Pet Shop Boys Nightlife* liner notes (2018), 33).
[36] Simon Reynolds, *Rip It Up and Start Again: Postpunk 1978–1984* (New York: Penguin Books, 2006), 2.
[37] Cf. Jenny Karpe, 'Ian Curtis Mentale Gesundheit und die Popularität von Joy Division. Diskursanalyse im Spannungsfeld von Songpoesie, Medien und Fachliteratur' (MA diss., Universität Paderborn, 2021), https://www.grin.com/document/1267753.
[38] Wilson cited in Ben Hewitt, 'Joy Division: 10 of the Best', *Guardian*, 15 July 2015, https://www.theguardian.com/music/2015/jul/15/joy-division-10-of-the-best.

FIGURE 6.2 *The iconic Korg MS10 synth – typical of early Tennant/Lowe songs.*

should come as no surprise – there is plenty of grief to be found in merely existing amongst a dying world, as millions of Millennials and Gen Zs suffering from climate-induced anxiety and what has been liberally coined pre-trauma can attest to.[39] As Teittinen argues, the media plays a vital role in this as well:

> [Grusin's] primary claim concerns the way in which the new media has increasingly taken on 'a prophetic or predictive role of reporting on what *might* happen,' in contrast to what has already happened. [. . .] This development itself predates 9/11 by more than a decade, relating in Grusin's words to 'a shift in news reporting from historically oriented technologies like print, photography, and film to such real-time technologies as video and the Internet,' [. . .] but it markedly intensified after the attack (and seems not to have waned by 2019). The fall of the Twin Towers, Grusin claims, 'produced the desire or determination never to experience anything that has not already been premediated' [. . .]. To translate this into Derrida's terms, there is an increased fear of *l'avenir*, and an increased desire to see the future through the anticipatory mode of the future anterior.[40]

---

[39] Cf. Stef Craps, 'Climate Trauma', in Colin Davis and Hanna Meretoja (eds), *The Routledge Companion to Literature and Trauma* (London: Routledge, 2020), 275–84; Gabriele Schwab, 'Transgenerational Nuclear Trauma', in Colin Davis and Hanna Meretoja (eds), *The Routledge Companion to Literature and Trauma* (London: Routledge, 2020), 438–51.
[40] Jouni Teittinen, 'Post-Apocalyptic Fiction and the Future Anterior', in Colin Davis and Hanna Meretoja (eds), *The Routledge Companion to Literature and Trauma* (London: Routledge, 2020), 352. Emphases by Teittinen, who extensively cites Richard Grusin, 'Premediation', *Criticism* 46, no. 1 (2004): 23–5.

Much as 9/11 had an impact on media coverage, it also had, and continues to have to this day, an impact on creative media, like music, just as previous watershed moments had similar impacts.[41] It is here that I'd like to differentiate between two types of 'watershed moment': those, which are – like 9/11 – precisely locatable in the temporal space, that is, historical moments; and those moments which resist a precise temporal pinpointing, that is, transhistorical moments. In the context of trauma studies, Dominick LaCapra argues that the concepts of loss and absence need to be carefully considered as distinct: losses, whether personal or collective, are located on a historical level. Absences, however, are transhistorical:

> The affirmation of absence as absence rather than as loss [. . .] opens up different possibilities and requires different modes of coming to terms with problems. It allows for better determination of historical losses or lacks that do not entail the obliteration of the past [. . .]. Historical losses or lacks can be dealt with in ways that may significantly improve conditions – indeed effect [sic] basic structural transformation – without promising secular salvation or a sociopolitical return to a putatively lost (or lacking) unity or community. Paradise absent is different from paradise lost: it may not be seen as annihilated only to be regained in some hoped-for, apocalyptic future or sublimely blank utopia that, through a kind of creation ex nihilo, will bring total renewal, salvation, or redemption. It is not there, and one must therefore turn to other, nonredemptive options in personal, social, and political life – options other than an evacuated past and a vacuous or blank, yet somehow redemptive future.[42]

Losses and absences are, as LaCapra emphasizes, not binaries but merely varying degrees of salience. Yet, their conflation 'may create a state of disorientation, agitation, or even confusion and may induce a gripping response whose power and force of attraction can be compelling. The very conflation attests to the way one remains possessed or haunted by the past, whose ghosts and shrouds resist distinctions (such as that between absence and loss).'[43] Reframing losses from an absence-based perspective emphasizes their 'inherently ambivalent' mode as something anxiety-inducing, which is also a potential powerful impetus for future structural changes – something

---

[41]While 9/11 is often credited to have sparked the second/third wave of emo core, it continues to have lasting impacts, such as on My Chemical Romance's 2022 release 'Foundations of Decay': 'He was there the day the towers fell / And so he wandered down the road / And we would all build towers of our own / Only to watch the roots corrode' (My Chemical Romance, 'Foundations of Decay', Reprise, 2022).
[42]LaCapra, 'Trauma, Absence, Loss', 706.
[43]LaCapra, 'Trauma, Absence, Loss', 699.

that is 'ambivalent [also] in its relation to presence, which is never full or lost in its plenitude but in a complex, mutually marking interplay with absence'.[44]

Paradise lost is crowded with lovers

While the Pet Shop Boys' discography is, above all, always a celebration of love (and, at times, its devastating, destructive potential), it is, primarily, also a gallery of mourning. What makes them so extraordinary, Simon Frith argues, 'is their sense of musical space. Using what is, in fact, a rather limited repertory of sounds (a thin lead voice; the most superficial resources of the digital synthesizer – supporting noise tends to be buried deep in the mix), the Pets conjure up a remarkable variety of soundscapes – the dance floor obviously, but also shops and cars and flats and dreams.'[45] Questionable comments about Tennant's timbre notwithstanding, what Frith illustrates here is the exact liminality, the dichotomy-defying lyricism that the Pet Shop Boys apply so masterfully: 'spaces [. . . that] are actually frozen moments in time, the moments just before and just after emotion [. . .]. Listen to any Pet Shop Boys track and you know that they too have had their life reduced to a single catch in the voice, a single melodic phrase [. . .] that must be played again and again.'[46] These sonic spaces, I argue, become the sites of many different hauntings, ghosts of losses and absences who manifest themselves in mimicry and appropriation, in an act of memory work that does not exorcize, but rather conjures the spectres asking us to settle their debts.

It is often the loss of love, the loss of lovers that haunts Tennant's lyrics. 'King of Rome' (2009) is a song narrated by and focalized through a narrator inspired by Napoléon's only child, Napoléon François Joseph Charles Bonaparte, who subsequently died at the age of only twenty-one, while in exile.[47] The song experiences a twofold haunting: an earlier version, written about the King of Pop Michael Jackson rather than the aforementioned heir, and which by dint of Tennant's own commentary ('Somehow the ghost of Michael Jackson haunts this song') has slipped through the cracks;[48] and the lover, whom the narrator begs to come back. The song disassembles chronology by placing the exiled king in the age of intercontinental air travel, as he watches hours slip away in crossing date lines ('Across the sky

---

[44]LaCapra, 'Trauma, Absence, Loss', 707.
[45]Simon Frith, *Performing Rites: On the Value of Popular Music* (Cambridge, MA: Harvard University Press, 1996), 6.
[46]Frith, *Performing Rites*, 8.
[47]Christopher Meinhardt and Genevieve Pocius (trans.), 'To François-Charles-Joseph Napoleon, Born at the Chateau Des Tuileries March 20th, 1811' (Chicago: De Paul University), https://via.library.depaul.edu/cgi/viewcontent.cgi?article=1008&context=napoleon.
[48]Tennant, *One Hundred Lyrics and a Poem*, 97.

/ a change of time / Last night I lost day').[49] At the same time, a line later, the narrator places himself in 1930s Cornwall: we have a striking reference to Daphne du Maurier's *Rebecca*, which alludes to an uprooting from Manderley, the estate of the erstwhile Maxim de Winter, which he leaves to escape the ghost of his deceased wife, the titular Rebecca ('I'm here and there / or anywhere / away from Manderley'), but to which he remains drawn (and eventually returns with the unnamed narrator). Moving on, in conjunction with the third verse, the song conjures the exoticism and longing for times past of Rudyard Kipling's 1890 poem *Mandalay*. The narrator in 'King of Rome' cannot escape the absence-presence of the lover lost, 'roaming' an endless, exotic, beautiful world, without being able to return to the single place they wish to return to: their lover. In that sense, the narrator themself is haunted, but also becomes a haunting entity: they have been locked out by their lover, and the language in this lyric very much invokes a politicized notion of exile as a wrong to be righted. The exiled King of Rome, sent away and left powerless and dependent, despite 'being aware of his heritage', is denied what he feels he is owed, and instead loses himself in loneliness.[50] The narrator, in much the same way, is condemned to 'roam / so far from home / in search of my lost magic', a nod to the loss of a lover, who continues to haunt him, but just as much to the struggle for reconceptualization of the self in light of this loss.

Similar motifs are found throughout the Pet Shop Boys' works. In 'Domino Dancing', for instance, the narrator mourns the loss of love rather than the loss of a lover, who they are still very much with. The narrator chronicles the relationship falling apart ('I thought I loved you, but I'm not sure now / I've seen you look at strangers too many times'), while mourning the lost love, all while reflecting on the anticipation of loss ('Remember when we felt the sun? / A love like paradise, how hot it burned / A threat of distant thunder, the sky was red').[51] As far back as 1971, Neil Tennant recorded what he regards as his 'first "proper" song', a piece for BBC Newcastle called 'Can You Hear The Dawn Break?' with his then-band Dust, a song which engages with the loss of a love: 'Baby, can you hear the dawn break? / Can you see the sun shake? / You've come and I'm gone / Can you hear it break?'[52]

In 'Dreaming of the Queen', the narrator has an anxiety dream about having tea with the Queen and about the AIDS epidemic ('So there were no more lovers left alive / and that's why love had died / Yes, it's true / Look, it's happened to me and you').[53] The narrator is haunted in their dreams by the

---

[49] Pet Shop Boys, 'King of Rome', Parlophone, 2009.
[50] Tennant, *One Hundred Lyrics and a Poem*, 97.
[51] Pet Shop Boys, 'Domino Dancing', Parlophone, 1988.
[52] Tennant, *One Hundred Lyrics and a Poem*, xi.
[53] Pet Shop Boys, 'Dreaming of the Queen', Parlophone, 1993.

anxiety of being exposed, quite literally ('Diana dried her eyes / And looked surprised / For I was in the nude / The old Queen disapproved'), a lyric that is inevitably tied to the AIDS-epidemic.[54] It is here that the songwriting demonstrates the intersection of LaCapra's absences and losses – the narrator mourns the loss of someone close to him ('Look, it's happened to me and you'), while at the same time coming to terms with the absence of the emancipated future that the AIDS epidemic and its subsequent stigmatization of especially male homosexuality has robbed him of. Patricia Smith sees the nod to a pre-epidemic past-future not just as a nod to the AIDS epidemic but a reference to Dave Wallis's 1964 novel *Only Lovers Left Alive* and the 'Summer of Love':[55]

> Only the pop culture cognoscenti, however, would connect the line 'There are no more lovers left alive' with Dave Wallis's now forgotten 1960s pulp fiction *Only Lovers Left Alive*, which speculated about the ultimate teenage fantasy, a world in which all adults have been eliminated by an epidemic of suicide and enjoyed a considerable if short-lived vogue during the 'Summer of Love'. For those who do read beneath the surface, then, the message is as devastating as it is perilous: Love and lovers are things of the past, having died with the Permissive Society of 1960s Britain, a concept much derided by the governments of Margaret Thatcher and her successor John Major, who did all in their power to reverse its lingering heritage. So complete is this death of love, then, that no one, regardless of one's privilege, is exempt. [. . .] If love existed in the 1960s (so often a Pet Shop Boys referential landmark), which succeeded the conservative and backwards-looking imperialist 1950s, then it could conceivably live again in the aftermath of neo-imperialist Thatcherism – or at least it is pretty to think so.[56]

Smith foregrounds the fact that Thatcher blamed the 1960s' 'permissiveness' for a perceived decline in 'British social values'. 'Between the lines of this moralistic resurgence, redolent of the Puritanism that has long informed certain aspects of "Britishness", was an outrage against the cultural diversity that had increasingly become a part of British postimperial life, including the cultural influence of non-white Britishers and homosexuals.'[57] Thatcher's agenda not only led to policies discriminating against marginalized people, but also to a 'ruthlessly materialistic form of laissez-faire capitalism', that

---

[54]The song ends on a chorus, but before that, Tennant sings 'I woke up in a sweat / desolate', a line that is ambiguous in whether it is referring to the anxiety of being exposed in his dream, or whether the narrator himself wakes up into a reality where he has AIDS, as sweating is a symptom during the early onset of an HIV infection.
[55]Cf. Dave Wallis, *Only Lovers Left Alive* (Richmond, VA: Valancourt Books, 2015 [1964]).
[56]Smith, '"Go West"', 308–9.
[57]Smith, '"Go West"', 317.

would reverse the post-war rise of modernist structures, which had functioned as a source of civil empowerment.[58] In this sense, Tennant's writing about personal losses, the loss of love, becomes something more than a literary representation of 'moments frozen in time' – a metonymous image of human existence failing to mediate the increasing demands of hyper-capitalism, with the neoconservative Puritanism now marginalizing those deemed undesirable. Tennant and Lowe's narrators' despair for love lost, the begging narrators haunted by the relationships they were not able to maintain, which all cumulates in a *pars pro toto* representation of the spectres of neoliberalism, and a longing to dare to reimagine love in post-neoliberal worlds.

There are no communist composers in paradise absent

If the personal is political, so are the personal losses of the narrators inhabiting Tennant and Lowe's work. In much the same way that they give neoliberal salience to the space in which their words of loss move, their discography engages in mourning not only over losses but also over 'paradise absent': both sonically and lyrically, the Pet Shop Boys sketch out absences of *could be-futures* that turned out as *wouldn't-be futures*. Over the years, PSB have continuously engaged with imagery pertaining to the Soviet Union and especially the communist revolution.[59] While some might argue that using such reference imagery in the context of what is, essentially, hyper-commodified pop music leads to a depoliticization of any inscribed meaning, I argue that a reframed reading from a post-punk perspective of politicized mourning effectively counters any notion of apoliticality. Instead, cultural artefacts of an empire long past its glory days are reappropriated in the context of PSB's body of work and subsequently become sites of haunting: the implosion of temporality manifests itself in a reappropriation of the spectres of a never-materialized future positing an alternative to neoliberalism.

'West End Girls', written between 1982 and 1983, engages with the concept of existentialism in the neoliberal cityscape. Tennant intended the song to mirror a 'film noir journey through the West End of London on a busy night with random voices overheard', a concept that was inspired by the multifocality of T. S. Eliot's poem *The Waste Land*.[60] The crushing pressure

---

[58]Smith, '"Go West"', 317.
[59]D. Scott, 'Intertextuality as "Resonance": Masculinity and Anticapitalism in Pet Shop Boys' Score for Battleship Potemkin', *Music, Sound, and the Moving Image* 7 (1 April 2013): 72, https://doi.org/10.3828/msmi.2013.3; Smith, '"Go West"', 320.
[60]Tennant, *One Hundred Lyrics and a Poem*, 215.

of capitalist ideals of success are evident throughout the song: 'Too many shadows, whispering voices / faces on posters, too many choices / If? When? Why? What? / How much have you got? / Have you got it? Do you get it?'[61] At the same time, it chronicles the effects of this permanent state of being overwhelmed in the first verse, narrating a suicidal man's attempt to cause havoc in a dive bar. At the same time, there is a persistent sense of disorientation and disjointedness – in the third verse, the narrator speaks (presumably) to a lover: 'Just you wait 'til I get you home / We've got no future, we've got no past / Here today, built to last.' Being aware of the inalterability of their life in this capitalist reality, the narrator seeks to escape by blurring out the revenants and arrivants with casual sex. The impermeability of neoliberalism is cemented in the following lines: 'In every city, in every nation / from Lake Geneva to the Finland station / How far have you been?', which references Lenin's return from exile and which eventually played a decisive role in the Russian Revolution of 1917.[62] The narrator acknowledges that not even a similar return from exile could shake the foundations of the current system, that there will be no *spectres arrivants* foreshadowing a different future, while still carefully wondering how far the lines' addressee, presumably still the lover, has intellectually strayed from the prevailing ideology. It is therefore the final realization that a postmodern future has become indefinitely unattainable, a fact the narrator self-medicates with cheap thrills.

The sister piece of 'West End Girls', written almost a decade later, is – undoubtedly – 'My October Symphony' (1990). The song opens with a choir singing 'Oktjabrja' – 'October' in Russian – taken from Shostakovich's Symphony No. 2, Op. 14. The narrator, a disillusioned communist composer, is attempting to come to terms with the fact that their gleaming communist future has also failed to materialize. The narrator expresses the anxiety they perceive with respect to the uncertain future: 'Shall we remember / December instead? / Or worry about February?'[63] Here, December refers to the Decembrist revolt of 1825, which was quashed by Tsar Nicholas I, whereas February references the February Revolution of 1917, which led to the installation of a short-lived bourgeois democracy.[64] When Smith refers to Tennant's reading of Ian Macdonald's *The New Shostakovich* while writing 'My October Symphony', she poignantly declares that Shostakovich 'might well be regarded as one of the Pet Shop Boys' ghosts in the synthesizer (if not in the machine)'.[65] Indeed, the experience of listening to Shostakovich's 'To

---

[61]Pet Shop Boys, 'West End Girls', Bobcat Records, 1984.
[62]Tennant himself points out that, fittingly, *To the Finland Station* is also the title of Edmund Wilson's history of democratic socialism. Tennant, *One Hundred Lyrics and a Poem*, 215.
[63]Pet Shop Boys, 'My October Symphony', Parlophone, 1990.
[64]Tennant, *One Hundred Lyrics and a Poem*, 125.
[65]Smith, '"Go West"', 322. Smith, however, writes that Tennant was reading Shostakovich's memoirs, while Tennant claims it was *The New Shostakovich*. Tennant, *One Hundred Lyrics and a Poem*, 125.

October' is unsettling at best, anxiety-inducing at worst. At times regarded as one of the foundations of today's industrial genre, the short symphony received mixed reviews from critics upon its release, with criticism directed especially at its dissonances, use of industrial equipment, and abrasive sound.[66] Tennant mirrors this anxiety in the narrator's anticipation of a dark future, set against a soundscape that feels almost ironically smooth – it is easy to imagine Tennant and Lowe's instrumental as a muzak track on the elevator ride down into bourgeois hell, which sets in just seconds after Shostakovich's choir fervently shouting for October. 'My October Symphony' is an attempt to place the self in a fundamentally changed world, one charged with the revenants and arrivants of injustices past and futures denied, one charged with the revelation that previous revolutions were not able to deliver on their promises, and the resignation that future revolutions will fail to do so as well ('How October's let us down / Then and now'). Smith concludes:

> The ultimate irony, moreover, is not on the artists' part here, but rather on the part of history: not only did the Soviet Union fail to live up to its 'power to the people' promise, its demise was the result of an imperialism it claimed to eschew. Thus the Soviet Union becomes postimperial Russia, and, as the British have experienced, postimperiality breeds social and cultural confusion. But in 1990, one could only pose questions about what a postimperial Russia might be; answers would, for the moment, have to be deferred.[67]

Lastly, 'This Used To Be The Future' (2009) becomes the quintessential twenty-first-century anthem, a concerted eulogy to Paradise Absent.[68] Calling for the

---

[66] While Western criticism was harsh, some critics were quite taken by Shostakovich's work. Bill Zakariasen commented in the *New York Daily News* that '"October" seems a parody of Shostakovich's "public" image – noisy, banal, fundamentally insincere – but it takes such a great composer to write such enjoyable trash' (Bill Zakariasen, 'Opposites Attract', *New York Daily News*, 17 October 1988).
[67] Smith, '"Go West"', 323.
[68] The Pet Shop Boys have, of course, devised a broad portfolio of songs and/or videos engaging with Soviet imagery, most notably 'Go West', as further examined in Torsten Kathke's chapter in this volume. Moreover, Smith delivers an in-depth analysis of the video in the context of post-imperiality, while Padva, closely relying on Smith's text with a surprising lack of credit, examines queerness and the totalitarian ideals of male physique (cf. Smith, '"Go West"'; Gilad Padva, 'The Counterculture Industry: Queering the Totalitarian Male Physique in the Pet Shop Boys' Go West and Lady Gaga's Alejandro', in Uwe H. Bittlingmayer, Alex Demirović, and Tatjana Freytag (eds), *Handbuch Kritische Theorie* (Wiesbaden: Springer VS, 2019), 1285–1300). Moreover, Wayne Studer has compiled an impressive list of all Pet Shop Boys songs referencing Russia or the Soviet Union (Wayne Studer, 'PSB Songs with "Russian Connections"', *Commentary – Interpretation and Analysis of every Song by the Pet Shop Boys*, http://www.geowayne.com/newDesign/lists/russian.htm).

same kind of *ex nihilo* do-over that LaCapra attempts to discredit as a prerequisite for change, the narrator seeks to materialize the absence of the promised future into a personal loss of the presence to start with a blank slate, a thought process that in itself is, of course, as utopian as the failed futures turned out to be in the first place. While, on the surface, the song appears to be an attempt to exorcize the ghosts of the past ('Why don't we tear the whole bloody lot down / And make a new start all over again?'), it is primarily a mourning for the lost possibilities of better futures ('I can recall utopian thinking / Bold mission statements and tightening of belts').[69] At the same time, the narrator acknowledges the grim persistence of the only arrivants shaping the now: 'Now all we have to look forward to / Is a sort of suicide pact.' The song recalls modernist post-war, pre-neoliberalist ideas of progress, of overcoming prejudices and the seemingly endless possibilities brought forth by technological advancement; in the same breath, the song defies any attempts at *ex nihilo* transformation by arriving at the conclusion that the utopian future that is being mourned is the same future that has led to the grim present that the narrator now faces ('Was it the dear old future / That created the problems we face? / How do we deal with the fallout / Of the age we used to call space?'). Once the futuristic soundscape of the song draws to a close, the only thing we're left with is the glaring absence of a future many of us were not even raised to anticipate anymore.

Conclusion: sitting with ghosts

'The urge to seek out the ghosts of places,' Tim Edensor writes, 'is bound up with the politics of remembering the past.'[70] Pet Shop Boys have succeeded in creating a haunted space, liminally sonic and yet undeniably perceivable, which affords room to the revenants and arrivants. From references to Anna Akhmatova's poem *July 1914* in 'Silver Age', over the friends lost to the AIDS epidemic and the subsequent attempt to progress with life in 'Discoteca', to a communist composer grieving for a future that never was in 'My October Symphony', Tennant and Lowe's words are uneasy bedfellows with the deep-seated anxiety induced by the price humanity paid for capitalist progress: a 'suicide-pact' future that, while appearing indestructible, sparks flickers of resistance. Pet Shop Boys, throughout their career and throughout their work conjure up the ghosts of a past repressed and a future undelivered through their use of images of lost love and the

---

[69] Pet Shop Boys, 'This Used To Be The Future', Parlophone, 2009.
[70] Tim Edensor, 'The Ghosts of Industrial Ruins: Ordering and Disordering Memory in Excessive Space', *Environment and Planning D: Society and Space* 23, no. 6 (December 2005): 829.

Soviet Union. Listening to their work is an act of sitting with these ghosts, much like Tennant and Lowe have done during the creation of their oeuvre. And while hauntology is in part the work of memory and heritage – of sitting with ghosts, being attentive to them, even listening to them – it is also the work of mourning. Mourning here, however, does not simply denote the observation of sorrow, for its de facto deconstructive logic entails a coming back to, 'a structural openness or address directed towards the living by the voices of the past or the not yet formulated possibilities of the future'.[71]

Tennant and Lowe have engaged extensively in memory work, and evidently invite their listeners to follow suit. They have created an opus that does not seek to exorcize the ghosts, but rather to embrace them and immortalize them both in language and sound.[72] 'Because of imperatives to bury the past too swiftly in search of the new, modernity is haunted in a particularly urgent fashion by that which has been consigned to irrelevance but which demands recognition of its historical impact': while there is no resolution to the failed futures, a concerted engagement with the spectres of the past might help to draw out their impetuses for change, even if that change is just the imaginability of a different future than the one we are facing at present.[73]

As Chantelle Gray points out, the value of a spectography is 'not the revelation of a new "truth"'. Instead, it is an opportunity to re-examine the existing notions with which absences are connoted.[74] In the context of an increasing prevalence of these 'hauntings from the future', hauntological readings of cultural artefacts have become a tool for sense-making, a vehicle for decoding the overwhelming world we are faced with. Gabriele Schwab, who coined the term 'hauntings from the future', coincidentally invokes Tennant, Lowe and 'This Used To Be The Future' in the last paragraph of her work on transgenerational nuclear trauma, when she cites Walter Benjamin: 'The storm irresistibly propels him into the future to which his back is turned, while the pile of debris before him grows skyward. This storm is what we call progress.'[75]

---

[71] Colin Davis, 'Hauntology, Spectres and Phantoms', *French Studies* 59, no. 3 (2005): 379.
[72] There is much to be said about the Pet Shop Boys' sound if read from a hauntological perspective, especially the harsh industrial sounds in the *Battleship Potemkin* score, as well as the frequently used chorals all throughout their discography.
[73] Edensor, 'The Ghosts of Industrial Ruins', 829.
[74] Chantelle Gray, 'A Hauntology of Clandestine Transmissions: Spectres of Gender and Race in Electronic Music', *Indian Journal of Gender Studies* 29, no. 3 (2022): 330. In her work on electronic music, Gray explicitly (and importantly) refers to 'gendered and racialized erasure' in this paragraph.
[75] Benjamin cited in Schwab, 'Transgenerational Nuclear Trauma', 249.

Bibliography

'30 Years on: People Living with HIV in the UK about to Reach 100,000'. *Health Protection Report* 5, no. 22 (2011), https://webarchive.nationalarchives.gov.uk/ukgwa/20140714095642/http://www.hpa.org.uk/hpr/archives/2011/news2211.htm.

Balaev, Michelle. 'Trends in Literary Trauma Theory'. *Mosaic: An Interdisciplinary Critical Journal* 41, no. 2 (2008): 149–66.

Bell, Celeste and Zoë Howe. *Dayglo: The Poly Styrene Story*. London: Omnibus Press, 2019.

Blanco, Maria del Pilar and Esther Peeren. 'The Spectral Turn'. In Maria del Pilar Blanco and Esther Peeren (eds), *The Spectralities Reader: Ghosts and Haunting in Contemporary Cultural Theory*, 31–6. New York: Bloomsbury, 2013.

Bois, R. M. Du, M.A. Branthwaite, J. R. Mikhail and J. C. Batten. 'Primary Pneumocystis Carinii and Cytomegalovirus Infections'. *The Lancet* 318, no. 8259 (1981): 1339, https://doi.org/10.1016/S0140-6736(81)91353-2.

Bolter, J. David and Richard A. Grusin. *Remediation: Understanding New Media*. Cambridge, MA: MIT Press, 1999.

Clark, Dylan. 'The Death and Life of Punk, the Last Subculture'. In David Muggleton and Rupert Weinzierl (eds), *The Post-Subcultures Reader*, 223–36. Oxford: Berg Publishers, 2003.

Craps, Stef. 'Climate Trauma'. In Colin Davis and Hanna Meretoja (eds), *The Routledge Companion to Literature and Trauma*, 275–84. Routledge Companions to Literature Series. London and New York: Routledge, 2020.

Davis, Colin. 'Hauntology, Spectres and Phantoms'. *French Studies* 59, no. 3 (1 July 2005): 373–9, https://doi.org/10.1093/fs/kni143.

Derrida, Jacques. *Specters of Marx: The State of the Debt, the Work of Mourning and the New International*. Translated by Peggy Kamuf. Repr. Routledge Classics. London: Routledge, 2011.

Dibbell, Carola. 'Inside Was Us: Women and Punk'. In Barbara O'Dair (ed.), *Trouble Girls: The Rolling Stone Book of Women in Rock*, 277–92. New York: Random House, 1997.

Dowd, Vincent. 'Julien Temple on The Clash: "The Energy of Punk Is Really Needed Now.";' *BBC News*, January 1, 2015, sec. Entertainment & Arts. https://www.bbc.com/news/entertainment-arts-30641500.

Edensor, Tim. 'The Ghosts of Industrial Ruins: Ordering and Disordering Memory in Excessive Space'. *Environment and Planning D: Society and Space* 23, no. 6 (December 2005): 829–49, https://doi.org/10.1068/d58j.

Fisher, Mark. 'What Is Hauntology?' *Film Quarterly* 66, no. 1 (1 September 2012): 16–24, https://doi.org/10.1525/fq.2012.66.1.16.

Frith, Simon. *Performing Rites: On the Value of Popular Music*. Cambridge, MA: Harvard University Press, 1996.

Gray, Chantelle. 'A Hauntology of Clandestine Transmissions: Spectres of Gender and Race in Electronic Music'. *Indian Journal of Gender Studies* 29, no. 3 (1 October 2022): 319–34, https://doi.org/10.1177/09715215221111136.

Grusin, Richard. 'Premediation'. *Criticism* 46, no. 1 (2004): 17–39.

Hägglund, Martin. *Radical Atheism: Derrida and the Time of Life*. Meridian: Crossing Aesthetics. Stanford, CA: Stanford University Press, 2008.

Heath, Chris. *Pet Shop Boys versus America*. London: William Heinemann, 2020.

Hewitt, Ben. 'Joy Division: 10 of the Best'. *Guardian*, 15 July 2015, https://www.theguardian.com/music/2015/jul/15/joy-division-10-of-the-best.

Jameson, Frederic. 'Marx's Purloined Letter'. In Michael Sprinker (ed.), *Ghostly Demarcations: A Symposium on Jacques Derrida's Specters of Marx*, 26–67. Radical Thinkers 33. London and New York: Verso, 2008.

Karpe, Jenny. 'Ian Curtis Mentale Gesundheit und die Popularität von Joy Division. Diskursanalyse im Spannungsfeld von Songpoesie, Medien und Fachliteratur'. Universität Paderborn, 2021, https://www.grin.com/document/1267753.

LaCapra, Dominick. 'Trauma, Absence, Loss'. *Critical Inquiry* 25, no. 4 (1999): 696–727.

Lewis, Tom. 'The Politics of "Hauntology" in Derrida's Specters of Marx'. In Michael Sprinker (ed.), *Ghostly Demarcations: A Symposium on Jacques Derrida's Specters of Marx*, 134–67, Radical Thinkers 33. London; New York: Verso, 2008.

Lowe, Chris, interview with Chris Heath, 'Pet Shop Boys 1984–1986'. Pet Shop Boys, *Please/Further Listening 1984–1986* liner notes (2018).

Lowe, Chris. 'Pet Shop Boys 1996–2000'. *Pet Shop Boys Nightlife* liner notes (2018).

Meinhardt, Christopher and Genevieve Pocius (trans.). 'To François-Charles-Joseph Napoleon, Born at the Chateau Des Tuileries March 20th, 1811'. Chicago: De Paul University, https://via.library.depaul.edu/cgi/viewcontent.cgi?article=1008&context=napoleon.

My Chemical Romance. 'Foundations of Decay'. Reprise, 2022.

Padva, Gilad. 'The Counterculture Industry: Queering the Totalitarian Male Physique in the Pet Shop Boys' Go West and Lady Gaga's Alejandro'. In Uwe H. Bittlingmayer, Alex Demirović and Tatjana Freytag (eds), *Handbuch Kritische Theorie*, 1285–1300. Wiesbaden: Springer VS, 2019.

Pelly, Jenn. *The Raincoats*. London: Bloomsbury Academic, 2017.

Perrott, Lisa. 'Time is out of Joint: The Transmedial Hauntology of David Bowie'. *Celebrity Studies* 10, no. 1 (2 January 2019): 119–39, https://doi.org/10.1080/19392397.2018.1559125.

Prinz, Jesse. 'The Aesthetics of Punk Rock'. *Philosophy Compass* 9, no. 9 (2014): 583–93, https://doi.org/10.1111/phc3.12145.

Reddington, Helen. *The Lost Women of Rock Music: Female Musicians of the Punk Era*. 2nd edn. Studies in Popular Music. Sheffield and Bristol, CT: Equinox, 2012.

Reynolds, Simon. 'Haunted Audio'. *The Wire*, 2006, 26–33.

Reynolds, Simon. *Rip It Up and Start Again: Postpunk 1978–1984*. New York: Penguin Books, 2006.

Riley, John A. 'Hauntology, Ruins, and the Failure of the Future in Andrei Tarkovsky's Stalker'. *Journal of Film and Video* 69, no. 1 (2017): 18–26, https://doi.org/10.5406/jfilmvideo.69.1.0018.

Roberts, Elisabeth. 'Geography and the Visual Image: A Hauntological Approach'. *Progress in Human Geography* 37, no. 3 (June 2013): 386–402, https://doi.org/10.1177/0309132512460902.

Savage, Jon. *England's Dreaming: Anarchy, Sex Pistols, Punk Rock, and Beyond*. New York: St. Martin's Press, 1992.

Schofield, Michael Peter. 'Re-Animating Ghosts: Materiality and Memory in Hauntological Appropriation'. *International Journal of Film and Media Arts* 4, no. 2 (31 December 2019): 24–37, https://doi.org/10.24140/ijfma.v4.n2.02.

Schwab, Gabriele. 'Transgenerational Nuclear Trauma'. In Colin Davis and Hanna Meretoja (eds), *The Routledge Companion to Literature and Trauma*, 438–51. Routledge Companions to Literature Series. London and New York: Routledge, 2020.

Scott, D. 'Intertextuality as "Resonance": Masculinity and Anticapitalism in Pet Shop Boys' Score for Battleship Potemkin'. *Music, Sound, and the Moving Image* 7 (1 April 2013): 53–82, https://doi.org/10.3828/msmi.2013.3.

Seifert, Robert. *Popmusik in Zeiten der Digitalisierung: veränderte Aneignung – veränderte Wertigkeit*. Studien zur Popularmusik. Bielefeld: transcript, 2018.

Sexton, Jamie. 'Weird Britain in Exile: Ghost Box, Hauntology, and Alternative Heritage'. *Popular Music and Society* 35, no. 4 (October 2012): 561–84, https://doi.org/10.1080/03007766.2011.608905.

Smith, Patricia Juliana. '"Go West": The Pet Shop Boys' Allegories and Anthems of Postimperiality'. *Genre* 34, no. 3–4 (1 September 2001): 307–37, https://doi.org/10.1215/00166928-34-3-4-307.

Studer, Wayne. 'PSB Songs with "Russian Connections"'. *Commentary – Interpretation and Analysis of Every Song by the Pet Shop Boys*, http://www.geowayne.com/newDesign/lists/russian.htm.

Teittinen, Jouni. 'Post-Apocalyptic Fiction and the Future Anterior'. In Colin Davis and Hanna Meretoja (eds), *The Routledge Companion to Literature and Trauma*, 349–59. Routledge Companions to Literature Series. London and New York: Routledge, 2020.

Tennant, Neil. *One Hundred Lyrics and a Poem: 1979–2016*. London: Faber & Faber, 2018.

Wallis, Dave. *Only Lovers Left Alive*. Richmond, VA: Valancourt Books, 2015.

Worley, Matthew. *No Future: Punk, Politics and British Youth Culture, 1976–1984*. Cambridge: Cambridge University Press, 2017.

Zakariasen, Bill. 'Opposites Attract'. *New York Daily News*, 17 October 1988.

PART THREE

We Came From Outer Space: Siting and Spatiality

CHAPTER SEVEN

'All That Swinging Sixties. It Didn't Do Anyone Any Good, Did It?'

The Pet Shop Boys and the *Scandal* of the Profumo Affair

Christopher Spinks

Introduction

In 1989, a British political scandal that had unfolded more than two and a half decades earlier perhaps surprisingly re-entered the public domain by way of two pop songs. The first, Billy Joel's 'We Didn't Start the Fire', referred to it merely as 'British politician sex'. The other, performed by Dusty Springfield but written and produced by Neil Tennant and Chris Lowe, delved far deeper into the issues; 'Nothing Has Been Proved' is a song entirely about that which Joel had dismissed in three words.

The fact that these two songs referred to this scandal gives us an interesting opportunity not only to examine how songs can engage with history, but what messages can be conveyed in that engagement. Joel's 'laundry list' removes both the historicity but also the broader meaning of the scandal – the infamous Profumo affair – by simply listing it alongside (and presumably with equal billing with) another 117 people and events of varying importance in the twentieth century (the bankruptcy of Studebaker, the baseball career of Joe Di Maggio, the assassination of John F. Kennedy), all of which Joel equates to an ever-burning fire that led to the continuing crisis the world found itself within in 1989.[1] By contrast, the Pet Shop Boys place Profumo within its historical context ('*Please Please Me*'s number one'), with the whole song being devoted to a single event of (presumably) important proportions. In the process, it is the Pet Shop Boys rather than Joel who draw attention not only to the events of the history itself but invite implicit comparisons with the contemporary era.

An intriguing web of politics, spies and sex, the long-running saga from the summer of 1963 resulting from parliamentary questions on the activities of War Minister John Profumo, and his relationship with Christine Keeler, Mandy Rice-Davies, Stephen Ward and Russian spy Yevgeny Ivanov have fascinated political, social and cultural historians and commentators of the 1960s. It has become the benchmark by which future political scandals are judged, and made household names of its main protagonists. A baby-boomer, Neil Tennant's formative years were spent growing up during the 1960s, a period of progressive sexual liberation, and he has regularly indicated his interest in people (Dusty Springfield, Joe Orton) and events (Stephen Ward's trial) from this era. Through consideration of the Pet Shop Boys' involvement with the film *Scandal*, we can relate their relationship with the 1960s, particularly the events of the long hot steamy summer of 1963. Moreover, the relevance of their association with Dusty Springfield, the resurgence of her career and an analysis of the songs 'What Have I Done to Deserve This' and 'Nothing Has Been Proved' reveal the underlying sympathetic messages of support for the scandalous treatment of Dusty's sexuality by the media. Additionally, the appropriateness of the allocation and situation of these songs to 1960s soul singer and gay icon Dusty Springfield is examined.

Furthermore, this chapter supports the contemporary argument that modern historians and scholars can access a wealth of historical information from analysing the lyrics of post-war social and political songs. Observation of popular music through an analytical lens enables a comprehension of how the period is musically portrayed, specifically aimed at a record-buying public constituted mainly of teenagers. It suggests the possibility that public interpretations of these events may be heard outside of the typical academic channels because it views them through a cultural lens. Importantly, it argues

---

[1] According to Alex Forbes, 'laundry-list songs' are songs that give a continuous list of things, usually with the chorus, hook or title delivering the point of truth that the items in the list add up to. Joel's 'We Didn't Start the Fire' borrows stylistically and lyrically from Reunion's 1974 hit song 'Life Is a Rock (But the Radio Rolled Me)'. Only the chorus breaks up the fast-paced list of disc jockeys, artists, songwriters, record labels, song titles and lyrics from the 1950s, 1960s and 1970s. 'We Didn't Start the Fire' characterizes this stylization with its listing of post-war individuals and events, with their newsworthiness as the underlying theme. Alex Forbes, *Songlab: A Songwriting Playbook for Teens* (Ashland, OR: AudioGO/Blackstone, 2013).

ALL THAT SWINGING SIXTIES

FIGURE 7.1 *11 June 1963: Model and showgirl Christine Keeler (right) with osteopath Stephen Ward. Sally Joan Norie is at the front. Photo by Express/Express/Getty Images.*

that this research can add to the ongoing debate among popular music commentators regarding the social and political significance of popular music performers and tracks that have enjoyed popular commercial success. Questions about the connection between lived experiences and the different kinds of history that are created are raised by the history of retracing the past in order to inform the present.[2] With the post-war expansion of popular

---

[2] See Lucy Robinson, 'How hard is it to remember Bananarama? The perennial forgetting of girls in music', *Popular Music History* 12, no. 2 (2020): 152–73.

music and its greater accessibility to a teenage audience through the use of mass media such as radio and television, popular songwriters and musicians increasingly used this platform as a means to convey political messages and portray historical events. Joel and the Pet Shop Boys offer two different viewpoints on a period of social, political and cultural transformation. Observing them outside the viewpoint that they are simply musical time-pieces allows further investigation into the circumstances surrounding their composition whilst offering a rich and fascinating look at the musical performers and their individual narratives contained within the lyrics.

To contribute to our understanding of class history through popular music, this chapter offers an intertextual and historically-embedded interpretation. Instead of viewing these songs as a symbol or example of populist criticism, this chapter considers them as narratives of the subjects being discussed. I assert that these songs, which were written employing anthemic criticism, journalism and personal experience, offer a persuasive argument in favour of a critical evaluation and reflection of the post-war period. Unfolding within their lyrical content, an authentic picture is formed within the listener's mind of the events at hand. This interpretation is enhanced through the utilization of the music video. Critical analysis of the usage of historical references within the music video format reinforces the presentation of the artists' viewpoint, whilst still adhering to the primary aesthetic of delivering a platform for the music to be seen and heard. Understanding wider social gestures in videos and popular music in general still depends on stylistic elements. In analyses of the works of prominent popular musical artists, such as Joel and the Pet Shop Boys, dissecting these gestures for their political implications has evolved into the primary critical strategy. Moreover, this analysis also challenges the comparison of both songs to other historical song narratives from the Cold War period.

Nothing has been proved

Written by Neil Tennant and Chris Lowe as part of the soundtrack for the 1989 film *Scandal*, 'Nothing Has Been Proved' sung by Dusty Springfield reached number 16 in the UK Top 40. The song is heard throughout the film's closing credits. Film producer Stephen Woolley asked the band to submit a song for the soundtrack. Recalling a song he had written previously, Tennant and Lowe wrote new music for it and, with Woolley's permission, they asked Dusty Springfield to perform it. Penny Valentine comments that 'It would, of course, be the perfect match: Dusty the sixties icon singing about a sixties scandal that had rocked the British government at the time.'[3]

---

[3]Penny Valentine and Vicki Wickham, *Dancing with Demons: The Authorised Biography of Dusty Springfield* (New York: St Martin's Press, 2014), 188.

Tennant claims that Woolley liked the idea of having the song performed by a particular celebrity who had been well known during the Profumo scandal in 1963. The film had an exclusive 1950s and 1960s soundtrack. According to Steve Woolley, film and era purists felt that the inclusion of the Pet Shop Boys over the final credits 'bastardised' the movie, taking it out of context, but the producer believed that his marketable audience size would increase if he could persuade all of the Pet Shop Boys' fanbase to take the movie seriously.[4] This began a productive relationship between producer and artists; the Pet Shop Boys would work for Woolley once more in 1992, producing three tracks on the soundtrack for the film *The Crying Game*.

The original demo version of 'Nothing Has Been Proved', featuring Neil Tennant on lead vocals, was included in the expanded reissue of the Pet Shop Boys' 1988 album *Introspective* in 2001. Lyrically similar, it had a much different melody. Neil – long interested in the Profumo affair – wrote the original version of this song by drawing upon his reading of Ludovic Kennedy's 1964 book *The Trial of Steven Ward*. Kennedy acknowledged that his original intent in documenting the Profumo affair's sequence of events was to preserve a record of the scandal's final public act: the persecution and injustice delivered to Stephen Ward. He added that he hadn't expected to see the scale of injustice dealt to Ward and expressed regret if at times his recollections of the scandal had come out more forcefully than he had intended.[5] Tennant, sympathetic to Ward for the treatment he received and the public defamation of his character, resurrected the song from his original demo for Dusty and *Scandal*, albeit with a new melody. The original beguilingly differs from Dusty's version, which features Tennant and Lowe as support vocalists, intoning the lines 'It's a scandal ... such a scandal' during the bridge as well as repeating her lead during lines quoted (or at least paraphrased) from Ward's suicide note: 'Sorry about the mess ...'.

With the revised melody written to complement Dusty's vocal range, retrospectively listening to Tennant's demo it sounds strained. It can be contended that 'Nothing Has Been Proved' follows the original intention of 'What Have I Done to Deserve This?'; though written and initially recorded by the Pet Shop Boys as a demo, its true impact in the public domain came via another artist.[6] The original demo was sung by co-writer Alta Sherral 'Allee' Willis who had also been co-writer for Earth, Wind & Fire's classic disco hits 'September' and 'Boogie Wonderland'. Tennant recalled in January 2020 that when they wrote and planned their 'collaborations, we judged

---

[4]Interview with Steve Woolley, London, 7 November 1988, in Duncan J. Petrie, *Creativity and Constraint in the British Film Industry* (New York: Palgrave Macmillan, 1991), 129.
[5]Ludovic Kennedy, *The Trial of Stephen Ward* (London: Victor Gollancz, 1964), preface.
[6]'What Have I Done to Deserve This' appeared on the original demo cassette tape from the Pet Shop Boys from the early 1980s.

them very carefully'.[7] Their record label EMI had originally offered Tina Turner and Barbra Streisand, but Tennant recalls that he and Lowe vociferously demanded that 'we wanted Dusty' to record the song.[8] In 1990, Dusty released *Reputation*, which featured both 'Nothing Has Been Proved' and 'In Private', on the second side of the vinyl LP, produced by Tennant and Lowe.

It may be too much to expect the Pet Shop Boys to continue to define any era as definitively as they did the 1980s. They are the northerners who provided music for a decadent and disoriented London in the 1980s and early 1990s. Tennant coined the phrase 'imperial phase' to describe this period in his band's career, when the commercial success of their four singles from the album *Actually* from 1987 gave them pretty much free reign to do whatever they wanted. Following-on from their association with Springfield, their reputation and songwriting gave them the opportunity to collaborate through recording and producing with a number of musical divas, including Liza Minnelli, Kylie Minogue, Tina Turner, Shirley Bassey and Lady Gaga. The song selection, appearance and diva attitude link these artists despite their musical alignment to distinct genres. Several of the recordings came from prior songs that the group had produced demos for but which were awaiting the correct performer through whom they would ultimately release the track to the popular music listening public.

Vicki Wickham claims that Dusty's previous attempts to make a return to the British charts had been futile. 'West End Girls' and the sophisticated theatrical sensibility that it embodies played a key role in her decision to record with Tennant and Lowe. Legend has it that when Dusty first heard the song, it nearly caused her to crash her car.[9] Wickham recalls how she persuaded Dusty to consider recording with Tennant and Lowe:

> 'Who are they?' asked Dusty. 'You know,' I said, 'West End Girls'. Oh yes, said Dusty, recollecting who the Pet Shop Boys were and remembering that she really liked that record. 'They're two lads, I think they're gay and you know Allee writes a great song and she's lovely, so why don't you just listen to it and see what you think?' Vicki said. 'Dusty was very good, she listened to it directly it arrived and said yes straight away.[10]

---

[7]Alexis Petridis, 'Pet Shop Boys: "The acoustic guitar should be banned"', *Guardian*, 24 January 2020, https://www.theguardian.com/music/2020/jan/24/pet-shop-boys-the-acoustic-guitar-should-be-banned.
[8]Petridis, 'Pet Shop Boys'.
[9]Laura Snapes, 'The 100 greatest UK No 1s: No 1, Pet Shop Boys – West End Girls', *Guardian*, 5 June 2020, https://www.theguardian.com/music/2020/jun/05/the-100-greatest-uk-no-1s-no-1-pet-shop-boys-west-end-girls.
[10]Valentine and Wickham, *Dancing with Demons*, 186.

Dusty and the Pet Shop Boys share a link to style and elegance through their pioneering campness. Tennant and Lowe from the 1980s, as well as Dusty from the 1960s, provide an example of a persistent, unmistakably camp trend in British music that demands serious historical investigation.

The importance of the music video

Like many of the successful films of the 1980s, the soundtrack of *Scandal* was released as an album collection; the song 'Nothing Has Been Proved' was used to promote the film and released as the 'theme' single from the movie.[11] The imagery from the music video, produced by Lowe, Tennant and Julian Mendelsohn, is pivotal in relaying the song's lyrical message to the audience. Set in a typical 1960s London cabaret club, like Murray's, where Keeler and Rice-Davies met, Dusty assumes the role of a cabaret singer. To complement the stylized 1960s look, Dusty's scenes are shot in monochrome, apart from her purple dress. Further supporting the historical aspect of the plot is a complex mash-up of three separate sources: old newsreel footage from the time of the four key protagonists (Profumo, Keeler, Rice-Davies and Ward); movie snippets from the film *Scandal* complementing the original footage; and Dusty lip-synching the song with the stage behind her occupied by a Keeler look-alike being photographed and interviewed by Tennant and Lowe dressed as 1960s hacks. Breaking at 3 minutes 35 seconds, the video switches to Ward's televised statement of 23 March 1963 supporting Profumo's speech in the House of Commons of 22 March 1963 in which he stated that he 'last saw Christine Keeler in December 1961'.[12] Ward challenges the 'entirely baseless rumours and insinuations that had been started by the press'.[13] Our understanding and attentiveness to the historical messages being presented by the Pet Shop Boys and Dusty are reinforced through the content of the supporting music video to 'Nothing Has Been Proved'.

---

[11]In the 1980s, the value of movie themes for advertising purposes soared. It became clear that big-budget movies and well-known hit songs have an unbreakable symbiotic relationship. Blockbuster movies had chart-topping songs that made the musicians famous while simultaneously effectively promoting the film through the use of MTV-targeted music videos that frequently featured clips from the source material. Well-known examples being *Back to the Future* (Huey Lewis and the News, 'The Power of Love'), *The Jewel in the Nile* (Billy Ocean, 'When the Going Gets Tough') and *Dirty Dancing* (Bill Medley and Jennifer Warnes, 'I've had the Time of my Life').
[12]Hansard, Personal Statement from The Secretary of State for War (Mr. John Profumo), HC Deb 22 March 1963, vol. 674, cc809–10, https://api.parliament.uk/historic-hansard/commons/1963/mar/22/personal-statement.
[13]Chatham43, *Profumo Affair Dr Stephen Ward statement 22/03/63*, 28 July 2009, https://www.youtube.com/watch?v=6dcIxHW7_yE.

In contrast, the portrayal of historical events in Billy Joel's music video for 'We Didn't Start the Fire' is arbitrary and perplexing. It is 'tailor-made for Music Television', according to Steve Ettinger, with its 'information overload' and presumption that the spectator is aware of the historical references.[14] Commencing with a typical American white middle-class newlywed couple walking into their kitchen and culminating with the death of the father, the apartment is the focal point for the social and cultural changes that occur over the forty years detailed within the song's verses. Joel tubthumps the song's chorus, extolling his generation's attempts to fight the fire lit by others. This is delivered over a flaming backdrop depicting a series of dramatic and disturbing images from the twentieth century. These include the public execution of Viet Cong captain Nguyễn Văn Lém in 1968, the shooting of Lee Harvey Oswald by nightclub owner Jack Ruby in 1963 and the portrait of Colonel Oliver North, a National Security Council staff member during the Iran–Contra affair. One image is out of kilter with the song's designated time period, that of the lynching of Robert 'Bootjack' McDaniels, on 13 April 1937 in Duck Hill, Mississippi, but it is likely that this image was used because it was part of a feature in *Life* magazine in 1955.[15] Whilst none of these events are directly mentioned in the song, for the viewer, they serve to collapse both past and present. Atrocity imagery is pervasive: the form of these texts demonstrates the emotional impact that viewing this horror has upon the viewer. It 'is visceral, and its physical intensity calls upon us to feel sympathy', with or alongside another person's suffering.[16] Joel confusingly delivers a linear narrative centred on the nuclear family which does not relate to the lyrics, whilst offering the viewer an apologetic message in the chorus.

Scandal

For some, like the author and poet Philip Larkin, the sexual revolution of the Swinging Sixties was bookended by the obscenity trial of D. H. Lawrence's *Lady Chatterley's Lover* and the release of *Please Please Me*, the first long-playing album by the Beatles – the period between November 1960 and

---

[14]Steven Ettinger, *Torah 24/7: A Timely Guide for the Modern Spirit* (Jerusalem and New York: Devorah Publishing, 2003), 2.
[15]*Life* magazine had originally published the photograph in 1937 and then again in 1955. Entitled 'Death Slump at Mississippi Lynching', the picture was part of over 500 photographs that were the subject of a photographic exhibition entitled *The Family of Man*, first shown at the Museum of Modern Art in New York in 1955; Amy Louise Wood, '"Somebody do Something!": Lynching Photographs, Historical Memory, and the Possibility of Sympathetic Spectatorship', *European Journal of American Studies* 14, no. 4 (2019), https://doi.org/10.4000/ejas.15512.
[16]Wood, '"Somebody do Something!"'.

March 1963.[17] During this phase, Harold Macmillan's premiership had been rocked by a series of spy trials including MI6's George Blake (1961) and civil servant John Vassall (1962), who had been blackmailed by the Russians on account of his homosexuality. Moreover, Macmillan was living his own double life. The long-standing sexual relationship between his wife Dorothy Macmillan and Tory backbencher Robert Boothby was widely known to the press and in political circles. Due to his quiet and insecure demeanour, which showed his dislike for dealing with delicate personal situations, Macmillan hid behind his public character. The most significant human interaction in Macmillan's life was changed from a private haven to a public spectacle. He was unable to secure a divorce, which very likely would have put a stop to his political career, and so was forced to remain a cuckold in a marriage in which his wife remained unfaithful up until her death in 1966. For most commentators, the overriding moment within Larkin's period of sexual awakening is the sexual soap opera centred on Profumo, Keeler and Ward. Macmillan's No. 10 was mired in the salaciousness of the 1960s and, after a prolonged period of progressive sexual change and a liberal acceptance of personal sexual choices, Thatcher's decade-long premiership saw a determined drive to root it out of society at large. According to Anthony Aldgate and Jeffrey Richards, the 1960s' connotation and mythos as a 'permissive' or 'liberalising' decade had become problematic within British political discourse by the late 1980s.[18]

The 1980s saw the arrival onto the British pop scene of a succession of chart-topping pop duos: the Pet Shop Boys, Erasure, the Communards and Soft Cell. All these artists challenged the shackles that were being put on Britain's homosexual community through Draconian legislation by a Conservative government that was striving to maintain traditional family values. Thatcher remarked that 'Children who need to be taught to respect traditional moral values are being taught that they have an inalienable right to be gay.'[19] Section 28 was a collection of laws across Britain that prohibited local authorities from promoting homosexuality. It was implemented by Margaret Thatcher's Conservative administration in response to the Labour

---

[17]Larkin's famous poem *Annus Mirabilis* begins (with dates input for the events mentioned): 'Sexual intercourse began / In nineteen sixty-three / (Which was rather late for me) / Between the end of the Chatterley ban (2 November 1960) / And the Beatles' first LP (22 March 1963).' At the end of the poem, Larkin amends the first two lines to read: 'So life was never better than / In nineteen sixty-three.' Written in 1967 but published in his 1974 collection *High Windows*, the poem is a reflection from Larkin of the sexual revolution, pinpointing 1963 as the pivotal moment for this cultural development and sexual freedom. Phillip Larkin, *Annus Mirabilis (Poem 19)*, in *High Windows* (London: Faber and Faber, 1974), 30.

[18]Anthony Aldgate and Jeffrey Richards, *Best of British: Cinema and Society from 1930 to the Present* (London: I.B. Tauris, 2002), 219–31.

[19]Margaret Thatcher, 'Speech to Conservative Party conference', 9 October 1987, www.margaretthatcher.org/speeches/displaydocument.asp?docid=106941.

Party's support for LGBT education during their 1987 general election campaign.[20] It was a decade that saw increased discrimination politically and through the mass media. Misinformation and hysteria intensified with the emergence, spread and devastating effect of HIV (human immunodeficiency virus) and its degenerative disease AIDS (acquired immunodeficiency syndrome), with the male gay community regularly challenged because of their sexual liberation and targeted particularly after the death of Hollywood actor Rock Hudson in 1985.[21] With a perceived sexual scandal unfolding with the increase of reportable cases of AIDS, it was apt that Pet Shop Boys, at the time an assumed gay pop group (Tennant did not come out until 1994), should be chosen alongside the gay icon Dusty Springfield to record the title track to the forthcoming docudrama film *Scandal*.

The 1989 movie *Scandal* portrays the Profumo affair, an infamous British political humiliation that shook and severely undermined confidence in the ruling Conservative government in 1963. Filmmaker Michael Caton-Jones' debut movie sparked new discourse about 'tabloid hypocrisy' and 'chequebook journalism' and reignited old arguments over several contentious issues.[22] Duncan Petrie argues that with a focus on the lives of specific 'deviant' characters who pose a challenge to prevailing social mores and standards, often with some resonance today, biopics examine some of the more contentious episodes of recent British history and enjoyed a high profile during the 1980s.[23]

The controversy surrounding the production of *Scandal* serves as proof of this. The succession of events surrounding Profumo's actions, and the subsequent impact upon Macmillan's Conservative government, created a popular myth that still prevails well into the twenty-first century. There was something for everyone in the Profumo scandal, which included sex, politics, spies, country residences, court cases, incarceration and death.

Australian screenwriters Michael Thomas and Joe Boyd had suggested turning the Profumo affair into a movie throughout the 1980s and had approached both the BBC and Channel 4 with a view to the production of a mini-series recalling these events from 1963. Roy Jenkins of the SDP appeared on Radio 4 and vigorously opposed such a programme, convincing the BBC and eventually Channel 4 to withdraw their interest in the project.

---

[20]'When gay became a four-letter word', *BBC*, 20 January 2000, http://news.bbc.co.uk/1/hi/scotland/611704.stm.

[21]Both of the UK's highest circulation daily tabloid newspapers, the *Sun* and the *Daily Star*, had reported on Rock Hudson's illness during 1985 and, on 3 October 1985, they carried the news of his death as the front-page cover article.

[22]Richard Luck, 'Christine Keeler, Harvey Weinstein, and a very scandalous film', *New European*, 4 May 2019, https://www.theneweuropean.co.uk/brexit-news-profumo-affair-movie-remake-story-behind-original-45176/.

[23]Duncan J. Petrie, *Creativity and Constraint in the British Film Industry* (New York: Palgrave Macmillan, 1991), 142.

The Independent Broadcasting Authority, which regulates British commercial television, deemed the narrative to be 'unsavoury'.[24]

Additionally, Jenkins with Lords Hailsham, Drogheda, Carrington, Goodman and Weinstock, as well as MP James Prior, co-signed a letter to *The Times* in 1987 in which they expressed their 'admiration' of Mr and Mrs John Profumo and their family, highlighting their 'dignity and courage' throughout the past quarter-century on the matter of the political scandal.[25] Moreover, for the signatories, the letter reinforced the establishment viewpoint that 'it is now appropriate to consign the episode to history'.[26] To avoid the governmental influence over television, screenwriters Thomas and Boyd now began to consider transferring their idea to the big screen and enlisted the aid of Palace Pictures' co-founders Stephen Woolley and Nik Powell as well as other financiers to fund the production budget.[27]

Ultimately, the financial support that ensured that the film went into production came from Miramax by the late 1980s. In 1979, brothers Harvey and Robert (Bob) Weinstein had established the film production and distribution company Miramax in Buffalo, in upstate New York. They became well known for adopting exploitation marketing techniques to promote their movies. A $25 million debt/equity investment from Midland Montague Ventures, a branch of the London-based Midland Bank, in 1988 helped persuade the brothers to shift their focus from buying and distributing movies to producing them. Their first in-house production would be *Scandal*.[28] In an interview for BBC's *Moving Pictures*, the now-disgraced billionaire Harvey Weinstein stated that he had been certain the project would succeed from the beginning: '*Scandal* was an obvious choice – the subject matter of sex and politics was incredibly provocative.'[29]

Miramax gained a reputation for using exploitation-based marketing techniques and public relations gimmicks to promote their films,[30] and since

---

[24] Richard Farmer, 'The Profumo affair in popular culture: *The Keeler Affair* (1963) and "the commercial exploitation of a public scandal"', *Contemporary British History* 31, no. 3 (2016): 465.
[25] James Fox, 'Poor Stephen', *London Review of Books* 9, no. 14 (1987), https://www.lrb.co.uk/the-paper/v09/n14.
[26] In 2019, BBC One broadcast the six-part docudrama *The Trial of Christine Keeler*, directed by Leanne Welham and starring Ben Miles as Profumo, James Norton as Ward, Sophie Cookson as Keeler, Ellie Bamber as Rice-Davies, and Ben Miles as Profumo. Thirty years later, this risk aversion appears to have vanished at the BBC. Fox, 'Poor Stephen'.
[27] Wickham and Mettler argue that *Scandal* is a high point for Palace Pictures, a high-budget movie that had a good shoot and garnered favourable reviews in the US and the UK. The company's greatest competitive advantage throughout the 1980s was its distribution division, which managed key cultural movies that would come to define the decade in both British and international cinema. The film cost £3 million to produce, while worldwide receipts totalled over £30 million. Phil Wickham and Erinna Mettler, *Back to the Future: The Fall and Rise of the British Film Industry in the 1980s* (London: BFI, 2005).
[28] Alisa Perren, 'Sex, Lies and Marketing: Miramax and the Development of the Quality Indie Blockbuster', *Film Quarterly* 55, no. 2 (2001): 32.
[29] Luck, 'Christine Keeler'.
[30] Perren, 'Sex, Lies and Marketing', 31.

Lewis Morley's portrayal of Keeler had come to so vividly embody the Profumo scandal, it was the logical image to use when it came time to advertise the film. Joanne Whalley-Kilmer impersonated Keeler on posters for *Scandal* in a manner similar to how Yvonne Buckingham had impersonated Keeler to imitate Morley's photographic portraits for the 1963 film *The Keeler Affair*. The billboard artwork for *Scandal* portrays Whalley-Kilmer immodestly naked, mirroring Christine Keeler's iconic and decade-defining portrait of May 1963.[31] It is a hybrid pin-up and symbol that suggests both sexual independence and the detrimental implications of sexual exploitation in a morally ambiguous environment. The picture still seems to represent the public's fascination with shifting sexual morals throughout that time. When one of these prints was stolen from Morley's studio on Greek Street, above the Establishment Club, and published in the *Sunday Mirror*, Keeler's notoriety soared even further.

The image of a naked Keeler was replicated by Morley on numerous occasions: his portrait of author Joe Orton from 1965 was chosen by Neil Tennant as his favourite picture. Two years later, to promote the US production of *Entertaining Mr. Sloane*, Morley took a picture of Joe Orton, turning his well-known, heterosexual depiction of Keeler into a clear-cut homosexual affirmation. Orton puts himself forward to challenge Britain's legal position at a time when homosexuality was still illegal. Morley claims Orton wanted to be known as 'the fittest, best-built writer in the western hemisphere', while Tennant remarks that Orton's hidden image is both 'provocative and humorous', resulting in 'an engrossing portrayal of the time'.[32]

The twenty-first century has seen an apotheosis of Keeler to cultural respectability. Morley's portrait commands an enlightening position within the Profumo scandal that shows a reverence for Keeler and her role. The 'iconic' portrait, an enduring image of the Swinging Sixties, is displayed in the National Portrait Gallery in London. In 2002, another 'icon' from the portraiture, the curved back chair on which Keeler posed, went on view at the *Seeing Things: Photographing Objects, 1850–2001* exhibition at the Victoria & Albert Museum in London. Morley's portrait hung above 'The Keeler Chair', which he had previously donated to the museum's furniture collection.[33] The chair,

---

[31]National Portrait Gallery, *Christine Keeler*, portrait – npg p512(13), https://www.npg.org.uk/collections/search/portrait/mw08741.

[32]Neil Tennant, 'My Favourite Portrait', *Face to Face* (The Gallery Supporters' Magazine) 19 (2006), https://www.npg.org.uk/support/individual/face-to-face/my-favourite-portrait/my-favourite-portrait-by-neil-tennant.

[33]As *That Was The Week That Was*'s official photographer, Morley also used it to take pictures of David Frost and other celebrities. An iconographic image, many people have subsequently copied both the chair and the pose, using them to advertise luxury residences, alcoholic beverages and even Homer Simpson the animated character. The chair's alluring contours together with the naked and seductive legs-akimbo posture have left a lasting effect on the mind. Tasmin Blanchard, 'The photo that launched a thousand poses: photographing Christine Keeler', *Observer*, 10 February 2002, https://www.theguardian.com/theobserver/2002/feb/10/features.magazine57.

often confused as an original by Danish artist Arne Jacobsen (it was in fact a reproduction), like Morley's portrait is yet another cultural symbol of Keeler's position in the Profumo scandal. Moreover, following Keeler's death in 2017, Fionn Wilson's art exhibition *Dear Christine: A Tribute to Christine Keeler* made its debut in 2019.[34] Throughout the exhibition's national tour, influential feminist speakers Caroline Coon, Claudia Clare, Sadie Hennessy, Helen Billinghurst and Cathy Lomax revealed how Keeler's humanity took her beyond the stereotypical image of a political sex figure and 1960s icon.[35]

Dusty Springfield

Dusty Springfield had been the main vocalist of the folk group the Springfields, which included her brother Tom, who announced their disbandment on the popular television programme *Sunday Night at the Palladium* in October 1963. Her solo career was launched in November 1963 with the single 'I Only Want to Be With You', just before Keeler was imprisoned for nine months, having been found guilty of perjury in the Aloysius 'Lucky' Gordon trial. Between 1963 and 1969, Springfield achieved unwavering popular chart success within both the UK and the US, often with releases that were not simultaneous in each country. Her 'eyes sooty with mascara', she created a visual image that resonated with girls from the mod subculture.[36] In reinventing the Spector/Brill Building-moulded US girl-group sound of the Ronettes and Shangri-Las alongside that of Martha Reeves and the Vandellas and numerous other Motown ensembles, Bob Stanley argues that she paved the way for girl singers from 'Bradford, Bellshill and Bournemouth' to recreate an American pop/soul sound for the UK record market.[37] The year 1968 saw the release of *Dusty in Memphis*, an album that despite its poor sales performance on release has grown in stature to become an essential part of any music listener's voyage into the music of the 1960s, having been deemed 'culturally, historically, or artistically

---

[34]Marina72, 'Dear Christine: A Tribute in Art, Poetry, and Prose', *Homepage of Tara Hanks*, May 2020, https://tarahanks.com/2020/05/13/dear-christine-a-tribute-in-art-poetry-and-prose/.
[35]Marina72, 'Dear Christine'.
[36]Bob Stanley, *Yeah Yeah Yeah: The Story of Modern Pop* (London: Faber and Faber, 2013), 210.
[37]The late 1950s and early 1960s saw the rise of the girl group within pop music. Influential producer Phi Spector had created a 'wall of sound' that featured The Crystals and The Ronettes and utilized the voice of Darlene Love on the tracks issued by the studio. At the same time the songwriters based in the Brill building produced a considerable number of songs that were recorded by several New York-based girl groups including The Shirelles, The Cookies, The Chiffons and the Shangri-las. Finally, based in Detroit under the guidance of Berry Gordy, the Motown record label would produce all-girl groups including The Supremes, The Vandellas, The Marvelettes, and The Velvelettes that would influence the British invasion of America during the 1960; Stanley, *Yeah Yeah Yeah*, 211.

significant' by the Library of Congress in 2020 and chosen for preservation in the National Recording Registry.[38] Springfield's musical and cultural credentials to fulfil Woolley's demand for a Profumo-era singer to perform *Scandal*'s theme song were unquestionable.

Springfield and the Pet Shop Boys collaborated for the second time on 'Nothing Has Been Proved', following their duet 'What Have I Done to Deserve This?' in 1987, which peaked at No. 2 in both the UK and the US. She also had commercial success in 1989 with the Pet Shop Boys' dance-inspired song 'In Private'. When Springfield died in 1999, the music press and recording industry had already hailed her as an iconic figure from the 1960s.

Her late-1980s revival seemed to alleviate the bitterness associated with the public relations disasters that had plagued her for the previous twenty years. Dusty rose phoenix-like from the ashes of bygone pop celebrity. The scandal that enveloped Dusty was in its own way a parallel of the Profumo affair, which in its own more prosaic way made her the logical choice to sing the theme song for *Scandal*.

Thanks to the triumph and implied assumption of 'Nothing Has Been Proved', Dusty was able to rebuild herself as a 'commercially acceptable survivor'.[39] The media focused on Springfield's 1960s identity, including her instantly recognizable hair and make-up and her love of soul music, particularly her promotion of the Motown sound in the UK. According to Ann Randall, Dusty made the decision to remain steadfastly impartial to stop journalists from asking about her first-hand experiences of 'drugs, alcohol, and lesbian sex'.[40]

Due to her complexity and sensitivity, only a select few people were able to access this inner sanctuary. Even now, more than twenty years after her passing, the mystery of Springfield's private life still perplexes and intrigues both the media and her fans. Her return to the pop charts and introduction to a new generation of music fans was entirely due to the Pet Shop Boys. Tennant, a lifelong admirer of her voice, was the driving force behind the revival of a singer whose popular stardom had collapsed as a result (partly) of prejudice against her sexuality. All three of her collaborative chart successes serve as descriptors of her loss of popularity and challenge the treatment of her by the British press. Commencing with the very fittingly-named 'What Have I Done to Deserve This?', Dusty addresses the undeserved attention given to her personal lifestyle. The two also aptly-named tracks from the *Scandal* recordings further state her case, declaring 'Nothing Has Been Proved', whilst 'In Private' can be read as a request for respectful observance of her private life. As one of the composers of these three ballads,

---

[38] Library of Congress, *National Recording Registry Class Produces Ultimate 'Stay at Home' Playlist*, 25 March 2020, https://www.loc.gov/item/prn-20-023/?loclr=twloc.
[39] Ann J. Randall, *Dusty! Queen of the Post Mods* (Oxford: Oxford University Press, 2009), 13.
[40] Randall, *Dusty!*, 13.

for Tennant – who was constantly questioned about his sexuality as much as the band's musical ability – these songs clearly advocate understanding and tolerance of the LGBTQIA+ community.

Protest and historical songs

To situate 'Nothing Has Been Proved', we need to contextualize the historical interpretation of the song. Many songs that entered the music charts or became popular outside the typical subject matter of boy-meets-girl/love-oriented context can be found if we look at popular music that has been created since the end of the Second World War. Building upon the socialist and politically left-leaning folk songs of Arlo Guthrie and Pete Seeger specifically aimed at an American audience, folk singer and labour activist Ewan McColl (b. Henry James Miller) picked up their mantle and challenged the status quo within the UK. MacColl wrote ballads praising both Ho Chi Minh and Joseph Stalin, as well as covering contentious topics like the way of life of the Traveller community and the prejudice against the Roma people. He also spoke out against criminal injustices. In 'The Ballad of Tim Evans', he protests against the hanging of Tim Evans, convicted in 1950 of killing his wife and daughter before serial killer John Christie was found guilty of killing several women at 10 Rillington Place in 1953.[41] On an Oak Tree in Russell Square the plaque dedicated to MacColl recognizes him for his 'strength and singleness of purpose' in the struggle 'for Peace and Socialism'.[42] Importantly, Guthrie, Seeger and MacColl laid the foundation for future musicians to deliver messages that challenged conformity and addressed controversial subject matter.

Within the commercially successful popular music arena, Bob Dylan is the best-known advocate of the folk protest song. Dylan's early work fulfilled the expectations of folk performers with his use of traditional instrumentation together with an honest authenticity as a platform for social and political criticism.[43] The merger of rock 'n' roll with the liberal, left-leaning sense of social duty of 1930s folk music, achieved in the 1960s by Dylan and others, went against conventional political beliefs. *Rolling*

---

[41] See Ludovic Kennedy's book *10 Rillington Place* for an extensive account of Christie and the circumstances surrounding the wrongful conviction of Timothy Evans for killing his wife Beryl and his daughter Geraldine in Notting Hill in January 1950. Ludovic Kennedy, *10 Rillington Place* (London: HarperCollins, 1995).

[42] Friends and relatives meet by the tree twice a year to celebrate his birth on 25 January and remember him after his passing on 22 October. These groups, which frequently feature his wife Peggy Seeger, sing popular songs by MacColl at these events. 'Tree, Ewan MacColl – memorial tree', *Friends of Russell Square*, https://www.friendsofrussellsquare.org/sample-page/__trashed/.

[43] John Street, *Rebel Rock: The Politics of Popular Music* (Oxford: Blackwell, 1986), 143.

Stone magazine presents Dylan as poet, singer, songwriter, custodian and gatekeeper for the beat generation.[44] Dylan's song lyrics present a communication that merits deeper study 'to the extent that the personal is political and the popular is political'.[45] Lindberg et al. argue that his words move in time with the music, adding emotional weight to analogies that are used to compare and reinforce our impressions: his songs 'reveal truths about the stories we love and the reality we live in'.[46] The protest and socially conscious songs 'Blowin' in the Wind' and 'The Times They Are A-Changing' both confirm what we already know and lead us to seek out things that we haven't looked for.

Nonetheless, it is Barry McGuire's rendition of P. F. Sloan's 1964 song 'Eve of Destruction' that is the most well-known 1960s song that 'chronicles different dysfunctions in American society'.[47] Sloan addresses several happening issues, including the use of young men not even old enough to vote to fight the war in Southeast Asia and the expansion of nuclear weapons. Moreover, the song directly compares the threat of communism – 'think of all the hate there is in Red China' – with that of those opposed to the Civil Rights movement: 'Then take a look around to Selma, Alabama.' Underlying these themes, Sloan emphasized that worldwide catastrophe would occur unless humanity becomes aware of it and takes action to avert it.[48] The song's noteworthiness arises from its position as the first protest song to attain extensive popular chart success, peaking at No. 1 on the US Billboard chart and No. 3 on the UK singles chart.

The 1970s and early 1980s continued to see a range of controversial subjects receiving musical attention from a range of artists. These included miscarriages of justice (Dylan's 'Hurricane'), social commentary (the Specials' 'Ghost Town' and the Jam's 'Town Called Malice') and biographical history (U2's 'Pride', Peter Gabriel's 'Biko' and the Special AKA's 'Free Nelson Mandela'). 'Nothing Has Been Proved' is an amalgamation of these three styles and offers its listener a pop lyric representation of the Profumo affair, its actors, the suicide of Stephen Ward and a cultural commentary on 1960s Britain.

---

[44]Jonathan Cott, *Bob Dylan: The Essential Interviews* (New York: Simon & Schuster, 2017), xvi.

[45]Paul D. Fischer, 'Challenging Music as Expression in the United States', in Martin Cloonan and Reebee Garafalo (eds), *Policing Pop* (Philadelphia: Temple University Press, 2003), 222.

[46]Ulf Lindberg, Gestur Guðmundsson, Morten Michelsen and Hans Weisethaunet, *Rock Criticism from the Beginning: Amusers, Bruisers, & Cool-Headed Cruisers* (New York: Peter Lang, 2011); Bernard Gendron, *Between Montmartre and the Mudd Club* (Chicago: University of Chicago Press, 2002), 170.

[47]R. Serge Denisoff and Mark H. Levine, 'The Popular Protest Song: The Case of "Eve of Destruction"', *Public Opinion Quarterly* 35, no. 1 (1971): 119.

[48]Denisoff and Levine, 'The Popular Protest Song', 117–22.

History doesn't repeat itself, but it often rhymes

Let us consider the application of 'Nothing Has Been Proved' as a musical text for use by the historian. The Profumo controversy is specifically referred to as 'British politician sex' by Joel in the seventh verse of 'We Didn't Start the Fire'. Joel's remark is expanded upon by the Pet Shop Boys, who address the tensions of such epistemological uncertainty while providing a labyrinthine account of scandal, enigmatic crimes and suicide with the lyrics, 'It may be false, it may be true / But Nothing Has Been Proved.' This claim enables us to understand this sequence of historical events from a different angle to how it was presented at the time. The song uses the key players in the Profumo case, referring to them only by their first names, to present a timeline of the important events that occurred between April and August 1963. John Lawton remarks that 1963 was a year 'in which Britain began to shrug off one way of life and adopt another' through the 'loud' emergence of the Beatles and the 'physical' implications of the Profumo saga.[49] 'Nothing Has Been Proved' contains two lyrical references to the release of the Beatles' number one album *Please Please Me*. In contrast to Joel's laundry-list which contains numerous cultural references, these two separate lines are the only pop cultural allusions in 'Nothing Has Been Proved'. The lines in question pay homage to the first Beatles album, which was released on 22 March 1963, reinforcing the teenage phenomenon of Beatlemania. Early in May 1963, the album topped the album chart, where it remained for a record-breaking thirty weeks. Tennant maintains a connection with the Beatles with the adaptation of the opening lyrics of the track 'Please Please Me', so that 'Last night I said these words to my girl' becomes 'Last night he wrote these words to his friend.' Tennant had learnt to play guitar to songbooks of Beatles songs.[50]

Tennant and Lowe provide a now famous musical depiction of how a personal ministerial lapse and resignation turned into a serious crisis for the government. They make the case that the widely acknowledged themes of moral depravity, dishonesty, ineptitude and security risk cover more extensive flaws in executive function and the complacency of the upper class. Applying a programme of cover-up and scapegoating, the government's flaws intensified as the crisis deepened, leading to ruthless exposure and scathing condemnation within the media, the legal system and both Houses of Parliament. Additionally, 'Nothing Has Been Proved' plays a significant role in shifting the focus of the Profumo controversy away from Profumo

---

[49]John Lawton, *Unholy Joy: 50 Years On – A Short History of the Profumo Affair* (London: Grove Press, 2013), 1.
[50]Will Hodgkinson, 'Soundtrack of my life: Neil Tennant', *Guardian*, 12 November 2006, https://www.theguardian.com/music/2006/nov/12/popandrock6.

and onto Stephen Ward, who serves as the scapegoat for the failings of Macmillan's government in the turbulent political climate of 1963.

The well-documented history of the Profumo affair has been, and continues to be, the subject of academic and popular commentaries. However, it is helpful to have a basic understanding of the main storyline in order to see that 'Nothing Has Been Proved' is a text that stimulates historical investigation. As a guest of Ward, Christine Keeler first met John Profumo, the then Minister for War in Macmillan's cabinet, in July 1961 at Spring Cottage, Cliveden, the home of Viscount Astor.[51] At the same time that Keeler had a brief sexual relationship with Profumo, she was also meeting Yevgeny Ivanov, a Russian naval attaché known to MI5. Ivanov was also a confidant of Ward. With closed ranks and a sincere admission by Profumo to his party hierarchy at the time, the entire incident could have been kept out of the public eye. Profumo's transgression had occurred countless times in previous administrations, and similar indiscretions would frequently make tabloid news for subsequent governments. However, Keeler had previously had complicated relationships with two West Indians in 1962, Johnny Edgecombe and Aloysius 'Lucky' Gordon, both of whom had criminal records in the United Kingdom, resulting in the trial of Edgecombe. In that trial, Keeler had committed perjury and in 1963 the rumour machine was set in motion to expose the whole sordid affair.

When commenting on the 'rumour upon rumour involving a member of the government front bench' in March 1963, Labour MP Colonel George Wigg purposefully invoked parliamentary privilege and asked for the creation of a Select Committee of Inquiry so that the minister in question could be 'freed from the imputations and innuendoes'.[52] With a decaying government dropping rapidly in the opinion polls and the opposition parties confident of the authenticity of the information being fed to them regarding a possible Profumo–Keeler–Ivanov triangle, an opportunity existed for Labour and others to attack Macmillan and his government.[53] Moreover,

---

[51] The affair lasted less than one month and concluded with the infamous letter from Profumo to Keeler, a significant piece of evidence that the press obtained and published in their tirade against Profumo prior to his resignation.

[52] George Wigg, Journalists Imprisonment, Hansard, HC Deb 21, March 1963, vol 674, 726, https://api.parliament.uk/historic-hansard/commons/1963/mar/21/journalists-imprisonment#S 5CV0674P0_19630321_HOC_512.

[53] Following a party on 23 December 1962, George Wigg had been informed of Keeler's indiscretions. Keeler met former MP John Lewis during the event, which she attended with Paul Mann. She told Mann and Lewis, two men Richard Davenport-Hines had characterized as being less than reliable at preserving secrets, about her experiences, including lengthy conversations about Ward, Edgecombe and most importantly Profumo. Lewis had also harboured animosity for Ward since the separation and divorce from his wife Joy in 1954. Profumo's response to Wigg's criticism of the living circumstances of the British army stationed on the Rhine and the poorly equipped troops in Kuwait further cemented Wigg's reputation as a man who 'nurses his grievances'. Richard Davenport-Hines, *An English Affair: Sex, Class and Power in the Age of Profumo* (London: Harper Press, 2013), 105, 205.

they were supported by a constant stream of sensational front-page stories from the mainstream media that kept all of the main protagonists in this matter in the public eye. Profumo would then deny in the House of Commons any connection with Keeler.

This brings the story up to the starting point of 'Nothing Has Been Proved'. All the contentious events that contributed to the Profumo scandal's fame had already occurred. The lyrics begin 'Mandy's in the papers 'cause she tried to go to Spain', referring to Rice-Davies' arrest on 23 April 1963.[54] They conclude with 'The funeral's very quiet because all his friends have fled', which refers to 9 August 1963, the day on which the coroner's jury found that Ward had committed suicide and also the day of Ward's funeral at Mortlake Cemetery, which was attended by only six mourners. Kenneth Tynan left 100 white roses as a floral tribute and a note with the simple inscription 'To Stephen Ward, Victim of Hypocrisy'. In between these opening and closing lines, we are taken through the investigation, arrest, trial and final letter written by Ward prior to his drug overdose.

On 5 June, Profumo delivered his resignation letter as Minister for War and applied for the office of steward of the Chiltern Hundreds to give up his House of Commons seat. Tennant observes the reaction to this decision lyrically as 'In the house a resignation / Guilty faces, everyone.'[55] More damaging than Profumo's errors was that they seemed to reveal a society and ruling class in decline. Articles proposing or defending such opinions, largely argued in the 'quality' press, reflected, or at least helped to form, the views of the Conservative Party's 'backbone' at Westminster and within constituency organizations across the country. *The Times*' Sir William J. Haley challenged this viewpoint. Haley, a former director general of the British Broadcasting Corporation, had joined the *Times* as editor in 1952, a post long regarded as the most important and influential in British journalism. The following week Haley's viewpoint on the matter was clear in his editorial entitled 'It is a moral issue'.[56] Haley delivered an attack on the declining moral standards of the country following eleven years of Conservative government. He thundered, 'Everyone has been so busy assuring the public that the affair is not one of morals, that it is time to assert that it is. Morals have been discounted too long.'[57]

---

[54] Appointed by Sir Joseph Simpson, Commissioner of the Metropolitan Police, Chief Inspector Samuel Herbert and Detective Sergeant John Burrows led the police investigation into Stephen Ward's sexual activities and influences. Herbert and Burrows targeted Rice-Davies in their pursuit of Ward. Rice-Davies' arrest, remand at Holloway and subsequent trial which delayed her trip to Spain relates to her relationship with Peter Rachman, who had died the previous November, and was for motoring and insurance offences. Rice-Davies recalled that Herbert and Burrows had threatened her with further arrest if she did not cooperate with them.
[55] Dusty Springfield, 'Nothing Has Been Proved', Parlophone, 1989.
[56] William Haley, 'It *is* a moral issue', *The Times*, 11 June 1963, 139.
[57] Haley, 'It *is* a moral issue', 139.

In any case, the song is fundamentally accurate, albeit inevitably condensed and unclear, but sufficient to pique interest in further research into the specifics of the events it describes. The characters are recognizable and genuine even though they only have first names. Ward was treated unfairly by politicians, falsely accused by the police, abandoned by wealthy patients and friends, betrayed by girlfriends, despised by the legal system and reviled by puritanical upholders of traditional morals. Ward's public humiliation in the Denning Report in the summer of 1963, concluding that he had lived off the immoral earnings of Keeler and Rice-Davies, left Lord Denning to wage a lifelong defence against any suggestion of Ward's potential innocence. The scandal sparked a media frenzy, which rocked the administration and contributed to one of the scandal's key players committing suicide. According to the song's theme, nothing had been proven. Tennant is essentially criticizing the lustful, puritanical impulses that lead to such horrific events over matters that should be kept private and individual, and, in reality, a matter of personal choice.

Conclusion

In 1989 Billy Joel and Dusty Springfield with the help of the Pet Shop Boys delivered two songs that presented two differing representations of post-war history. 'We Didn't Start the Fire' essentially covers the first forty years of Billy Joel's life and provides an audio-historical and cultural portrait of significant occasions and figures as they were encountered by the baby boomer generation. These unrelated memories of Joel were presented as a list, with the Cold War serving as the only known historical fact to connect them. This listing captures the mood of the date the song and album *Storm Front* were released. With the subsequent lowering of tension between the United States and the Soviet bloc following the fall of communism in the later months of 1989, the track appears relevant to post-war American history and its use by academics as a source of historical reference and pedogeological topics for students in the 1990s is understandable. However, the randomness and disconnection of the people and events mentioned brings with it a problem for future generations of students and academics. Their understanding of these entities as references points for the period 1949–89 diminishes with time, and the song does not carry the same impact as it did in the immediate aftermath of its release. Indeed, during his 2022 tour, Joel admitted to his audiences that he had not recorded anything new in close to thirty years, so they were going to hear 'the same shit you heard last time'.[58] Nonetheless, 'We Didn't Start the Fire' has now become part of the obligatory encore crowd pleaser.

---

[58] Giselle Au-Nhien Nguyen, 'Billy Joel review – Seasoned showman delivers timeless classics and signature dead-pan banter', *Guardian*, 11 December 2022, https://www.theguardian.com/music/2022/dec/11/billy-joel-review-seasoned-showman-delivers-timeless-classics-and-signature-dead-pan-banter.

The song 'Nothing Has Been Proved' continues a long tradition of songs that take on challenging or uncomfortable issues and provide an accurate portrayal of such subjects that endures. The Profumo affair has endured in 1960s media conceptualizations, in academic studies of British politics, culture and society, and in popular culture. The general population, the mainstream entertainment media and researchers are all still fascinated by it. The majority of those connected to the controversy have spoken out about what happened; in the case of Keeler, her memoirs of the event changed with each new edition. Concerted efforts were made to prevent the story from being told on both the big and small screens. The 1963 film *The Christine Keeler Story* failed to receive BFB classification and was only shown outside the United Kingdom, but prominent politicians and members of the aristocratic upper class continued to try to stymie any production.

The story of Keeler, Profumo and Ward eventually appeared on the big screen in 1989 with the release of *Scandal*, and in 2019 the six-hour docudrama series *The Trial of Christine Keeler* appeared on BBC television.[59] Presented in a sympathetically feminist manner, the story was beamed into the living rooms of the great British public; for many of them it was the first time they had been allowed to see a televised interpretation of the scandal and of the lives of the key players in this saga. Moreover, the deaths in the twenty-first century of first Profumo, then Rice-Davies and finally Keeler have also given the media a regular opportunity to revisit the summer of 1963 and to continue to question the handling and policy of the whole affair by past and present governments.

Indeed, even though sixty years have passed since the tumultuous summer of 1963, the Profumo scandal remains high in popular cultural recollections of the Swinging Sixties. Academic and public debate continues to centre on Profumo's dishonesty, the credulity of his parliamentary colleagues, their potential involvement and complicity in the scandal, and, most importantly, the class repercussions of a botched cover-up. Additionally, two contentious issues remain that continue to ignite public, academic and legal interest in the scandal. First is the failure to have Ward's guilty conviction quashed. After the release of *Stephen Ward Was Innocent, OK: The Case for Overturning his Conviction*, Geoffrey Robertson QC, the book's author, presented the Ward family's argument for a judicial review of Ward's case in 2017 by the Criminal Case Review Commission (CCRC). The CCRC's decision not to recommend a review of the osteopath's 1963 conviction was, it said, due to the failure to locate an original transcript of the judge's summing up. The secondly contentious issue that keeps the Profumo affair alive is that many official government documents on the scandal remain closed to the public, even though all the major parties concerned are no

---

[59]Additionally, the story has been transposed onto the London stage. *A Letter of Resignation* by Hugh Whitemore was first performed in 1997, and *Stephen Ward*, a musical by Andrew Lloyd Webber, debuted in the West End in December 2013.

longer alive. Originally scheduled to be released in January 2064, following intervention from the Advisory Council on National Records, the release date for this material has now been brought forward to January 2048. Amongst the outstanding issues relating to the crisis of 1963 are questions about espionage, sex, power and class, which may potentially be resolved at some point in the future.

The parameters of popular songs and their representation of historical events are as relevant today as they were when Guthrie, Seeger and MacColl were alive. Individuals and social groups can link the lyrical content to its momentarily activated social meanings through clever articulation of the subject matter's limits. This is a world in which the historian can use the past to understand where pop politics operate. Social gestures, as indicated by the intelligent use of sound and style, welcome the researcher who determines the direction, relevance and validity in which the listener participates when interpreting the song and its message.

Bibliography

Aldgate, Anthony and Jeffrey Richards. *Best of British: Cinema and Society from 1930 to the Present*. London: I.B. Tauris, 2002.

Blanchard, Tasmin. 'The photo that launched a thousand poses: photographing Christine Keeler'. *Observer*, 10 February 2002, https://www.theguardian.com/theobserver/2002/feb/10/features.magazine57.

Chatham43. *Profumo Affair Dr Stephen Ward statement 22/03/63*, 28 July 2009, https://www.youtube.com/watch?v=6dcIxHW7_yE.

Cott, Jonathan. *Bob Dylan: The Essential Interviews*. New York: Simon & Schuster, 2017.

Davenport-Hines, Richard. *An English Affair: Sex, Class and Power in the Age of Profumo*. London: Harper Press, 2013.

Denisoff, R. Serge and Mark H. Levine. 'The Popular Protest Song: The Case of "Eve of Destruction"'. *Public Opinion Quarterly* 35, no. 1 (1971): 117–22.

Ettinger, Steven. *Torah 24/7: A Timely Guide for the Modern Spirit*. Jerusalem and New York: Devorah Publishing, 2003.

Farmer, Richard. 'The Profumo affair in popular culture: *The Keeler Affair* (1963) and "the commercial exploitation of a public scandal"'. *Contemporary British History* 31, no. 3 (2016): 452–70.

Fischer, Paul D. 'Challenging Music as Expression in the United States'. In Martin Cloonan and Reebee Garafalo (eds), *Policing Pop*, 221–38. Philadelphia: Temple University Press, 2003.

Forbes, Alex. *Songlab: A Songwriting Playbook for Teens*. Ashland, OR: AudioGO/Blackstone, 2013.

Fox, James. 'Poor Stephen'. *London Review of Books* 9, no. 14 (1987), https://www.lrb.co.uk/the-paper/v09/n14.

Gendron, Bernard. *Between Montmartre and the Mudd Club*. Chicago: University of Chicago Press, 2002.

Haley, William. 'It *is* a moral issue'. *The Times*, 11 June 1963.

Hodgkinson, Will. 'Soundtrack of my life: Neil Tennant'. *Guardian*, 12 November 2006, https://www.theguardian.com/music/2006/nov/12/popandrock6.
Kennedy, Ludovic. *10 Rillington Place*. London: HarperCollins, 1995.
Kennedy, Ludovic. *The Trial of Stephen Ward*. London: Victor Gollancz, 1964.
Larkin, Philip. *High Windows*. London: Faber and Faber, 1974.
Lawton, John. *Unholy Joy: 50 Years On – A Short History of the Profumo Affair*. London: Grove Press, 2013.
Library of Congress. *National Recording Registry Class Produces Ultimate 'Stay at Home' Playlist*, 25 March 2020, https://www.loc.gov/item/prn-20-023/?loclr=twloc.
Lindberg, Ulf, Gestur Guðmundsson, Morten Michelsen and Hans Weisethaunet. *Rock Criticism from the Beginning: Amusers, Bruisers, & Cool-Headed Cruisers*. New York: Peter Lang, 2011.
Luck, Richard. 'Christine Keeler, Harvey Weinstein, and a very scandalous film'. *New European*, 4 May 2019, https://www.theneweuropean.co.uk/brexit-news-profumo-affair-movie-remake-story-behind-original-45176/.
Marina72. 'Dear Christine: A Tribute in Art, Poetry, and Prose'. *Homepage of Tara Hanks*, May 2020, https://tarahanks.com/2020/05/13/dear-christine-a-tribute-in-art-poetry-and-prose/.
Nguyen, Giselle Au-Nhien. 'Billy Joel review – Seasoned showman delivers timeless classics and signature dead-pan banter'. *Guardian*, 11 December 2022, https://www.theguardian.com/music/2022/dec/11/billy-joel-review-seasoned-showman-delivers-timeless-classics-and-signature-dead-pan-banter.
Perren, Alisa. 'Sex, Lies and Marketing: Miramax and the Development of the Quality Indie Blockbuster'. *Film Quarterly* 55, no. 2 (2001): 30–9.
Petridis, Alexis. 'Pet Shop Boys: "The acoustic guitar should be banned"'. *Guardian*, 24 January 2020, https://www.theguardian.com/music/2020/jan/24/pet-shop-boys-the-acoustic-guitar-should-be-banned.
Petrie, Duncan J. *Creativity and Constraint in the British Film Industry*. New York: Palgrave Macmillan, 1991.
Randall, Ann J. *Dusty! Queen of the Post Mods*. Oxford: Oxford University Press, 2009.
Robinson, Lucy. 'How hard is it to remember Bananarama? The perennial forgetting of girls in music'. *Popular Music History* 12, no. 2 (2020): 152–73.
Snapes, Laura. 'The 100 greatest UK No 1s: No 1, Pet Shop Boys – West End Girls'. *Guardian*, 5 June 2020, https://www.theguardian.com/music/2020/jun/05/the-100-greatest-uk-no-1s-no-1-pet-shop-boys-west-end-girls.
Stanley, Bob. *Yeah Yeah Yeah: The Story of Modern Pop*. London: Faber and Faber, 2013.
Street, John. *Rebel Rock: The Politics of Popular Music*. Oxford: Blackwell, 1986.
Tennant, Neil. 'My Favourite Portrait', *Face to Face* (The Gallery Supporters' Magazine) 19 (2006), https://www.npg.org.uk/support/individual/face-to-face/my-favourite-portrait/my-favourite-portrait-by-neil-tennant.
Thatcher, Margaret. 'Speech to Conservative Party conference', 9 October 1987, www.margaretthatcher.org/speeches/displaydocument.asp?docid=106941.
Valentine, Penny and Vicki Wickham. *Dancing with Demons: The Authorised Biography of Dusty Springfield*. New York: St Martin's Press, 2014.
'When gay became a four-letter word'. *BBC*, 20 January 2000, http://news.bbc.co.uk/1/hi/scotland/611704.stm.

Wickham, Phil and Erinna Mettler. *Back to the Future: The Fall and Rise of the British Film Industry in the 1980s*. London: BFI, 2005.
Wood, Amy Louise. '"Somebody do Something!": Lynching Photographs, Historical Memory, and the Possibility of Sympathetic Spectatorship'. *European Journal of American Studies* 14, no. 4 (2019), https://doi.org/10.4000/ejas.15512.

CHAPTER EIGHT

Go West, Young Band

Torsten Kathke

Introduction

The Pet Shop Boys' 1993 cover of 'Go West', a song originally released by the Village People in 1979, connected three utopian images which were on the face incongruous, but here easily combined into a zeitgeisty whole. The Village People, a group created by producers Jacques Morali and Henri Belolo to specifically appeal to the gay subculture that had become increasingly visible in the 1970s, had appropriated the phrase 'Go West', a nineteenth-century slogan dating to the colonization of the US West.[1] The trope, usually cited as 'Go West, young man!' in their telling was directed primarily at gay men escaping the suffocating oppression of their sexuality in small-town America. 'Go West' featured lyrics like 'together we will leave someday' and 'together we will start life new', thinly veiled references to the opportunities presented by immersing oneself in the LGBTQ communities of West Coast cities such as San Francisco or Los Angeles; the former home to the Castro district, which was, in the 1970s, 'At the Center of the Gay Universe' as an essay in photographer-writer Hal Fischer's *The Gay Seventies* has it; the latter allowing for the unincorporated territory of West Hollywood to congeal into a hot spot of gay urbanism after white flight had seen

---

[1] Thomas Fuller, '"Go West, Young Man!" – An Elusive Slogan', *Indiana Magazine of History* 100, no. 3 (2004): 231–42; Alex Midgley, '"Macho Types Wanted": The Village People, Homophobia, and Representation in 1970s', *Australasian Journal of American Studies* 33, no. 1 (2014): 106–7.

the well-to-do white middle class abandon downtowns across the United States.[2]

The Pet Shop Boys' version of the song carries within it both of these origins and puts them in communication with a third 'West' – that of the promise of Western-style democracy and capitalism for formerly Soviet countries after the end of the Cold War. As it came along at a time that MTV and similar music video channels were still mostly playing music videos (MTV's reality TV show *The Real World* premiered in 1992, and at the time of the single's release in 1993 had become a veritable phenomenon, but it was still an oddity in MTV's line-up, which was dominated by music), the song's abstract visuals were a major factor in its success and need to be taken into account to sufficiently contextualize it in the media landscape of the era.

'Go West' featured retro futuristic computer-generated imagery similar to the movies *Metropolis* and *Tron*, as well as animated red stars and marching groups of men in white halter tops waving red flags among intercuts of imagery evoking the stark socialist realism of 1930s through 1950s Soviet propaganda.[3] The chorus and chord progressions are reminiscent of the Soviet national anthem. Rather than redeclaring victory for the West in the just-concluded Cold War, the Pet Shop Boys' version of the song, I argue, uses the established cliché of American 'Manifest Destiny' and the *frontier* of nineteenth-century historian Frederick Jackson Turner as well as the original context of the 1970s song in order to construct, in its music and visual accompaniment, a comprehensive utopia suffused with camp irony. While gesturing toward an escape from history (*pace* Fukuyama), however, this utopia cannot help but reconstruct its contradictions, especially the violence inherent in the West's legacy of capitalist conquest and the imagery of a marching army.[4]

---

[2]Troy Peters and Griff Williams, *Hal Fischer: The Gay Seventies* (Cheltenham: Gallery 16, 2019); 'The Birth of Gay Urbanism in 1970s West Hollywood', KCET, 26 February 2016, https://www.kcet.org/shows/lost-la/is-l-a-losing-its-outrageous-past-the-birth-of-gay-urbanism-in-1970s-west-hollywood. Note that 'gay' will be employed in the following to specifically refer to homosexuality in the given historic context, as many of the references in the media discussed address a male gay subculture prevalent in the 1970s and early 1980s before the AIDS epidemic.

[3]For the defining aspects and societal uses of the style, see Catriona Moore et al., 'Social Realism', in *Routledge Encyclopedia of Modernism* (London: Routledge, 2016), https://doi.org/10.4324/9781135000356-REMO25-1.

[4]Patricia Nelson Limerick, *The Legacy of Conquest: The Unbroken Past of the American West* (New York: Norton, 1987).

FIGURE 8.1 *Tennant and Lowe's costumes for 'Go West' (1993) – a distinct change from their previously dour, understated sartorial presentation. Getty Images, Steve Pyke/Contributor.*

West

Manifest Destiny

To make sense of the various layers of imagery and interpretation that undergird 'Go West', it is necessary to map the phrase and its usage to its origin in the nineteenth-century United States. This will enable us to then see in which ways the Pet Shop Boys' use of the tune links not only to a 1970s disco hit tailored to the gay community, but to a perplexing number of associations that the 'West' has and had in US society, which in turn the

Village People's songwriters had themselves relied on and translated for their purposes.⁵

Though the idea of west as the direction in which progress is assumed dates back further and found its most pertinent expression in Irish philosopher Bishop Berkeley's 1728 poem 'Verses on the Prospect of Planting Arts and Learning in America' in which the stanza 'Westward the course of empire takes its way' appears, the phrase 'Go West' first saw widespread use during the phase of massive westward expansion of the United States during the nineteenth century.⁶ It is generally cited as 'Go West, young man', a phrase typically attributed to New York newspaper editor, one time Congressman and lifelong expansionist booster Horace Greeley. Greeley, a factotum of mid-nineteenth century US politics, had been instrumental in getting William Henry Harrison elected to his very short presidency in 1840, and had then founded the penny paper *New York Tribune* on 10 April 1841, only a week after Harrison's untimely death on 4 April.⁷ The *Oxford Dictionary of Quotations* attributes the phrase both to Greeley ('Go West, young man, and grow up with the country') and to John B. L. Soule ('Go West, young man, go West!'). Neither 'origin' appears to be factual.⁸

Greeley's memoir *Recollections of a Busy Life*, first published in 1868, does not contain the full citation, but it features the phrase 'Going West' in quotation marks, indicating that Greeley considered it something of a standing expression by that time.⁹ 'Go West' had featured in newspaper advertisements at least as far back as the 1850s, and by the 1870s 'Go West, young man' could be found in speeches, memoirs, newspaper articles and all

---

⁵The song was written by Village People producers and project founders Jacques Morali and Henri Belolo as well as then-lead singer Victor Willis for the group's eponymous 1979 album *Go West*. It was released originally as the second single from the album in June 1979, after the more successful 'In the Navy', which had come out three months prior.

⁶For an in-depth study of the highly influential afterlife of that one line of poetry, see Elizabeth Kiszonas, 'Westward Empire: George Berkeley's "Verses on the Prospect of Planting of Arts" in American Art and Cultural History' (PhD diss.: University of Arkansas, 2019), https://scholarworks.uark.edu/etd/3432.

⁷While, to the morbid amusement of generations of bored students, historians long accepted Harrison's cause of death as pneumonia, contracted after he had given an interminably long inaugural speech a month earlier in cold weather and not wearing an overcoat, a more recent re-examination attributes it to typhoid fever, presumably from the White House's contaminated water supply. Jane McHugh and Philip A. Mackowiak, 'Death in the White House: President William Henry Harrison's Atypical Pneumonia', *Clinical Infectious Diseases* 59, no. 7 (2014): 990–5, https://doi.org/10.1093/cid/ciu470.

⁸*The Oxford Dictionary of Quotations* (Oxford: Oxford University Press, 1999), 351, 544; '"Go West, Young Man . . ." History's Newsstand Blog', *History's Newsstand Blog | Old Newspapers Original & Authentic* (blog), 20 December 2010, http://blog.rarenewspapers.com/?p=3575; 'Fact or Myth: Did Horace Greeley Really Say "Go West Young Man"?', *GenealogyBank Blog* (blog), 10 December 2012, https://blog.genealogybank.com/fact-or-myth-did-horace-greeley-really-say-go-west-young-man.html.

⁹Horace Greeley, *Recollections of a Busy Life* (New York: J. B. Ford and Company, 1868), 55.

kind of other printed matter – often attributed to Greeley.[10] Since one of Greeley's editorials features the rest of the full quotation about Washington, DC not being 'a nice place to live in' usually given as the source of the phrase, as well as similar sentiments (though not the phrase itself), it is likely that, as 'going West' as a practice became popular for many Americans in the years following the first Homestead Act's passage, and Greeley was a known advocate for expansion, the amorphous 'Go West' that likely originated numerous times in different contexts (after all, it is simply a verb and a cardinal direction combined) became erroneously mapped onto him and one specific editorial. As checking old newspapers would have been very difficult in an age before readily accessible databases, the myth outran the reality.[11]

Greeley served as the natural conduit for 'Go West', having been involved deeply with promoting the settler colonialist idea of the United States's 'Manifest Destiny' to spread from the Atlantic to the Pacific. Attaching him to the idea was therefore logical, and in a way entirely appropriate, even if the exact phrasing of 'Go West, young man' was not his. At least Greeley had used the short version of the phrase when recommending to R. L. Sanderson, a *New York Tribune* correspondent, who wrote to him for career advice in 1871, 'Of course, I say to all who are in want of work, Go West!'[12] One year later, Greeley was dead, though not without fitting in an unsuccessful presidential run beforehand. 'Go West', however, took on a life of its own.

Conquests

The recommendation and the concept were always connected to American democratic ideals. These dated back to the United States imagined as a

---

[10] *The New York Herald* in 1855 featured, for example, an advertisement reading 'Wanted – to go West, a young man of good address and considerable business experience, desires a situation as a salesman [. . .]'. The *Eaton Democrat* reported on a 'supposed murderer' in the same year, claiming he had 'made arrangements to go West'. 'Wanted', *New York Herald*, 5 May 1855 (Washington, DC: Library of Congress, Chronicling America); 'Arrest of a Supposed Murderer', *Eaton Democrat*, 31 May 1855 (Washington, DC: Library of Congress, Chronicling America). Among the many quotations of the phrase were, e.g., John Hanson Beadle, *The Undeveloped West: Or, Five Years in the Territories* (n.p.p.: National Publishing Company, 1873), 34; *Proceedings of the First Annual Convention of the Brotherhood of Locomotive Firemen and Enginemen, Hornellsville, New York, December 1874* (1874), 5; Judson Elliott Walker, *Campaigns of General Custer in the North-West, and the Final Surrender of Sitting Bull* (New York: Jenkins & Thomas, 1881), 105; Maine Dept of Agriculture, *Agriculture of Maine. Annual Report of the Commissioner of Agriculture* (1884), 137–8.
[11] 'Fact or Myth'.
[12] Horace Greeley, 'Horace Greeley to R. L. Sanderson', Autograph letter signed, 2 pages + docket, 15 November 1871 (New York: Gilder Lehrman Institute of American History), https://www.gilderlehrman.org/node/2226.

utopia of free landholders, an idea prominently featured in the thought of Thomas Jefferson, who hoped for the country to be constituted of yeoman farmers not working for anyone but themselves. Yeomanry required land. Only those who could wrest enough from a parcel that was theirs qualified, in the Jeffersonian sense, as free.[13] Jefferson himself set aside his strict constructionist view of the US Constitution, and his conviction that the federal government should do as little as possible, leaving self-governance mostly at the state and local levels, in order to complete the Louisiana Purchase during his first presidential term in 1803. The controversial purchase of a territory half again the then-United States' size opened up huge swaths of land to settlement.[14]

It is in this connection with the West as a place whose abundance would make freedom and self-rule possible that we find a most conspicuous contradiction: the very taking of land from Indigenous Americans fundamentally enabled participatory democracy for those who could profit from the land: mostly white Americans, both native-born as well as immigrant. While there had been a patchwork of laws that made settlement in the moving 'West' (the Midwest had once been less mid, more West) legal, profitable or both before that time, it was the first Homestead Act in 1862 that opened the floodgates. The Civil War left many veterans out of a job and out of the means to make a living comfortably in the East. The West, soon subject to large numbers of settlers thanks to the building of the Transcontinental Railroad and its various branches and competitors, also became subject to growing mythologization in a dawning age of mass media.[15]

Yet the airy arcadia that the Village People harmonized about more than a century after Greeley's passing relied on the massive and organized displacement of myriad peoples from their homelands by what has been referred to, in an extension of sociologist Robert Blauner's term describing US race relations, as 'internal colonialism' within the United States. To

---

[13]It went without saying that Jefferson's idealized republic of yeoman farmers included many more unfree subjects – enslaved people and women not eligible to participate in deliberative democracy's institutions foremost – than free farmers.

[14]The literature on Jefferson is vast and, befitting Jefferson himself, contradictory. There is, however, general agreement that Jefferson fretted about the constitutionality and propriety of the Louisiana Purchase. On the Louisiana Purchase in the context of American Empire, see, e.g., Walter Nugent, *Habits of Empire* (New York: Knopf Doubleday Publishing Group, 2008), 41–72, esp. 65–6.

[15]The key policies enabling the westward expansion of the United States in the second half of the nineteenth century were the Homestead Acts, the first of which was passed in 1862. While all in all about 1.6 million people filed for claims until 1934, with about 40% of these succeeding, Black Americans were severely under-represented. Congress passed the Southern Homestead Act in 1866 explicitly to increase their numbers, but with the bureaucracy staffed mostly by (often corrupt) white Southerners, by 1870 only about 4,000 Black people had claimed homesteads. Keri Leigh Merritt, *Masterless Men* (Cambridge: Cambridge University Press, 2017), 329; Warren Hoffnagle, 'The Southern Homestead Act: Its Origins and Operation', *The Historian* 32, no. 4 (1970): 628.

Blauner, 'racism has generally accompanied colonialism'.[16] Viewed this way, going West also creates a racial tension within the mass wealth creation event that the Homestead Acts would become. While hundreds of thousands could and did make claims, only a minuscule number among them were African Americans, making the acts a lopsided government redistribution programme overwhelmingly favouring whites for three generations.[17] Since the West of the Village People's 'Go West' was mapped pretty closely onto California, a state that had been annexed by the United States in an unprovoked war of expansion in the first place, it also contained another displacement (or, alternatively severing of connections to their former homeland), that of Mexicans in what became the Southwestern United States. All over the region, some held on to only part of their land and their power, while many lost both. Even if they could hold on to their property, their choices were to assimilate into an alien, often hostile nation in which they were considered ethnic and cultural inferiors, or to physically remove themselves from it.[18]

The West carries within it – to amend essential New Western historian Patricia Nelson Limerick's portentous phrase – a threefold 'legacy of conquest': one of Indigenous lands and peoples, one of the formerly Hispanic Southwest, and one of the European conquest of Africa that included the transatlantic slave trade, which ultimately precipitated the American Civil War. The fact that the question of Black American citizenship was not solved once and for all in a Jeffersonian affirmative after the war, and that instead the post-Civil War Reconstruction period ended in the repression of those freed after the abolition of slavery in the Southern Jim Crow system for the better part of another century, affected the West as well. In a very real sense, the Civil War never ended there, giving way to, in Richard Maxwell Brown's phrase, the 'Western Civil War of Incorporation' or, as Elliott West has it with somewhat different temporal framing, 'Greater Reconstruction'.[19] The legacy of the American West, a mythical and real place of longing as much as a true geography of want and violence, remains embedded in the phrase 'Go West'. This is despite the fact that the meaning the lyricists who employed it in a minor disco anthem in the late 1970s had in mind harked back to only a small part of Western mythology.

---

[16] Robert Blauner, 'Internal Colonialism and Ghetto Revolt', *Social Problems* 16, no. 4 (1969): 396, https://doi.org/10.2307/799949; cf. also Dorceta Taylor, 'Internal Colonialism: Native American Communities in the West', in Dorceta Taylor, *Toxic Communities* (New York: New York University Press, 2014), 47–68, https://doi.org/10.18574/nyu/9781479805150.003.0008.
[17] Merritt, *Masterless Men*, 38.
[18] Cf. Torsten Kathke, *Wires That Bind: Nation, Region, and Technology in the Southwestern United States, 1854–1920* (Bielefeld: transcript, 2017), 209, 222.
[19] Richard Maxwell Brown, *No Duty to Retreat: Violence and Values in American History and Society* (Norman: University of Oklahoma Press, 1994), 44, *passim*; Elliott West, *The Last Indian War: The Nez Perce Story* (Oxford: Oxford University Press, 2011), xx–xxiii.

Village

Macho men

When disco music producers Henri Belolo and Jacques Morali sent out a casting call for 'macho types with mustache' in 1975, the implication that what they were looking for was men who represented the San Francisco-born gay 'Castro Clone' masculinity ideal was clear, though only to some of the band's eventual target group.[20] Belolo, a DJ turned music promoter turned producer, had left his native Morocco first for Paris in 1960 and then for New York City in 1973. He met Morali, who had begun his career in a record shop in Orly airport and since also moved to the United States, early in 1975, and the two put together a group made up of three Black female singers, the Ritchie Family. They cast it to perform the 1940s hit 'Brazil', inspired by Morali's having seen a movie starring Carmen Miranda featuring the song.[21] The group immediately landed a top 20 hit. Looking to build on that success, Morali and Belolo looked for a male counterpart act to the all-woman vocal group.

After a chance run-in on the streets of New York with a man in Native American dress, they followed him to his place of work, a bar in which he bartended and danced. Drinking beer and taking in the scene, they noticed a man dressed as a cowboy watching the dancer. Belolo claims both of them 'had the same idea. We said, "My God, look at those characters." So we started to fantasize about what were the characters of America.'[22] The conception of a group around singer, songwriter and performer Victor Willis followed, as well as an advert calling for 'macho types' to complete the group.[23] They called the project the Village People after New York City's Greenwich Village, home to much of the city's gay subculture, including the

---

[20] Known variously also as the 'Christopher Street Clone', 'Homosexual Clone' or 'Gay Clone'. Christelle Klein-Scholz, 'From the "Homosexual Clone" to the "AIDS Clone": The Impact of AIDS on the Body of the Gay Male', *E-Rea. Revue Électronique d'études Sur Le Monde Anglophone* 12, no. 1 (2014), https://doi.org/10.4000/erea.4153. For a concise definition of the aesthetic, see Les K. Wright cited in David Higgs, *Queer Sites: Gay Urban Histories Since 1600* (London: Routledge, 2002), 183. Cf. also Jack Halberstam, *Female Masculinity* (Durham, NC: Duke University Press, 2019).

[21] In Belolo's telling: 'Henri Belolo | DJHistory.Com', 1 January 2010, https://web.archive.org/web/20100101135406/http://djhistory.com/interviews/henri-belolo. If the story is not apocryphal, the likeliest candidate is Busby Berkeley's *The Gang's All Here*, which features Miranda performing the song. *The Gang's All Here* (Twentieth Century Fox, 1943). As the accounts given by Belolo at different times and those by others in various interviews differ slightly, the true origin story of the Village People is as polymorphous as the band's membership over the decades.

[22] Jeff Pearlman, '"Y.M.C.A." (An Oral History)', *SPIN* (June 2008), 75.

[23] There are at least two different versions of the casting advertisement relayed. The one calling for 'macho types' mentioned above, and one reading 'Macho Types Wanted: Must Dance and Have a Moustache' in 'The Village People', *Rolling Stone* 289 (19 April 1979).

Stonewall Inn, the riot in front of which in 1969 had become a focal point of the burgeoning gay liberation movement.

While the increasing de-stigmatization of homosexuality over the previous four decades has made Morali's and Belolo's wink-wink, nudge-nudge references much more widely understandable as related to the urban gay scene of the 1970s, the mass appeal of the Village People lay in their clever use of visual and lyrical *double entendres*. At the height of the disco era this enabled the group to skirt censorship and blackballing by radio stations while producing danceable club hits for a queer audience, but with enormous mainstream appeal. Their first hit, 'San Francisco (You've Got Me)' already played on similar themes as 'Go West'. A recognizably standard disco song that easily gave away that it had been released on Casablanca Records, the same label as Donna Summer, its lyrics drew inspiration from the titular city's gay culture with lines like 'Dress the way you please and put your mind at ease / It's a city known for its freedom' or 'Baby baby feel fast and free / Baby baby let's do hot night / Come on baby let's you and me swing.' The song finishes with a plea to the 'baby' repeatedly called on to 'Show me, show me the way' to the magical place that was the 'City by the Bay, y'all'.[24]

The B-side of the single was the song 'Fire Island', paying tribute to yet another LGBTQ haven ('Fire isla-and – fire, fire island – it's a funky weekend – funky – a funky funky weeke-end / You never know just who you meet, maybe someone out of your wildest fantasies, yeah'). This marked the beginning of a run of what could be termed 'haven songs' that picked out queer utopian – or at least heterotopian – spaces and stretched the bounds of the double in *double entendre* to communicate a kinship between the group and the gay community: 'Y.M.C.A.' celebrates an institution in which young men can meet other young men ('hang out with all the boys'), 'In the Navy', the first single from the *Go West* album, likewise described a primarily homosocial space.

Arcadia

But where the preceding songs sang about specific shelters – circumscribed places or institutions one had to gain access to – from a homophobic, heteronormative mainstream culture, 'Go West' painted on a much larger canvas. It could avail itself of a rich American literary tradition of Edenic places ripe for settlement, from the first promotional literature produced by British adventurers and explorers about the 'virgin lands' of the American continent, to the road-tripping taking-control-of-one's-life-and-the-country contained in Beat poet Jack Kerouac's ode to US automotive mobility, *On the Road*, via Walt Whitman's muscular stanzas of self- and land-possession.[25]

---

[24] Village People, 'San Francisco (You've Got Me)', Telefunken, 1977.
[25] Cf. Connell O'Donovan, 'Go West', http://www.connellodonovan.com/gowest.html.

Whether on purpose or not, these aspects are even more foregrounded in the additional lyrics provided by Neil Tennant in the Pet Shop Boys' extension of the song to the computer-controlled dance beats of 1990s club culture. 'Where the air is free' may not mean anything specific, as Tennant himself recognized, but it does produce a mood of openness and possibility not yet fully realized in the original song.[26]

The 'West' the song referenced also had always had a queer component, long before the gay community of the Castro formed in California's foremost former gold rush town. Removed from the societal constraints of Eastern life both in its urban centres and small-town communities, the US West offered a space of experimentation and self-fulfilment that was not limited to American Dreams of economic abundance. Lacking a large number of women, the West was also a much more inherently male space than the rest of the country. As Western historian Peter Boag has fruitfully shown, this made possible a multitude of non-heteronormative interpretations of sexuality, companionship and family.[27] These meanings, too, are contained in the Foucauldian dispositive of the 'American West' and naturally make it a much queerer space that very easily fit both versions of the songs than the strictly cis-heteronormative interpretations that course through much of the well-known literary and filmic representations of the American West.

The fact that the Western movie and its companion in the American imaginary, the Western TV show, became staples at times in which media representations tended to emphasize conservatism and continuity of traditional masculinity (the 1900s and the 1950s respectively) obscures this much more varied and vibrant cultural and literary history of the West.[28]

---

[26]'Absolutely Pet Shop Boys Unofficial Web Site – Interviews – Very – Go West', 27 August 2012, https://web.archive.org/web/20120827184236/http://www.petshopboys.net/html/interviews/very012.shtml.

[27]Peter Boag, *Re-Dressing America's Frontier Past* (Oakland, CA: University of California Press, 2012). See also Chris Packard, *Queer Cowboys: And Other Erotic Male Friendships in Nineteenth-Century American Literature* (Cham: Springer, 2016). Indigeneity in its relation to queerness in the North American West has also received scholarly attention: Lisa Tatonetti, 'The Indigenous Erotics of Riding Bareback, or, the West Has Always Been Queer', *Western American Literature* 53, no. 1 (2018): 1–10. The literature on the American West in general is expansive and works on queerness within its confines and in relation to the East have proliferated in the decades since the New Western History first became conceptualized. For example, Susan Bernardin, *The Routledge Companion to Gender and the American West* (London: Routledge, 2022); Geoffrey W. Bateman, 'Queer Wests: An Introduction', *Western American Literature* 51, no. 2 (2016): 129–41; Kim Emery, 'Steers, Queers, and Manifest Destiny: Representing the Lesbian Subject in Turn-of-the-Century Texas', *Journal of the History of Sexuality* 5, no. 1 (1994): 26–57; Andrew C. Isenberg, 'The Code of the West: Sexuality, Homosociality, and Wyatt Earp', *Western Historical Quarterly* 40, no. 2 (2009): 139–57.

[28]Brigitte Georgi-Findlay, 'Family Crises on the Frontiers: Nation, Gender, and Belonging in US Television Westerns', in Eva-Sabine Zehelein, Andrea Carosso and Aida Rosende-Pérez (eds), *Family in Crisis? Crossing Borders, Crossing Narratives* (Bielefeld: transcript, 2020), 145–54, https://doi.org/10.1515/9783839450611-012.

Cover

They wouldn't normally do this kind of thing

The Pet Shop Boys were not known for recording cover versions of songs. Until 'Go West' came out in 1993, they had only ever done seven (eight if one counts the double bill of 'Where the Streets Have No Name / I Can't Take My Eyes Off You' twice) covers that were eventually released, three of which appeared on their 1988 EP *Introspective*, the others constituting singles B-sides. All but the mash-up of 'Where the Streets Have No Name' were produced in the years of 1988 and 1989 and are included in the 'Further Listening' extended re-release of *Introspective*.[29] Before 'Go West', only 'Always on My Mind' and 'Where the Streets Have No Name' had been released as singles.[30]

'Go West' was the album-closer for 1993's *Very*, though a short untitled hidden track beginning with the words 'I believe in ecstasy' and sung by Chris Lowe, rather than the familiar lead voice of Neil Tennant, served as a coda to the record. Such tracks were a popular feature on 1990s compact discs, and like most, this one, too, was not marked on the album in any way. The Pet Shop Boys originally performed 'Go West' at a concert accompanying an exhibition artist and filmmaker Derek Jarman held for AIDS charities at the Manchester City Art Gallery in May 1992. Jarman had directed several Pet Shop Boys music videos, 'It's a Sin' and 'Always on My Mind' among them. The benefit show took place at the Haçienda night club and coincided with the venue's ten-year-anniversary celebrations. Starting off with 'West End Girls' and 'Rent', the set list contained ten songs, culminating in 'Domino Dancing' and finally, 'Go West'.[31] The group repeated their performance a month later at a benefit concert for the then-new Lifebeat non-profit organization dedicated to safe sex in the music industry at the Roseland Ballroom on Manhattan's 239 West 52nd Street.

The years 1991 and 1992 marked a shift within the music industry towards increased recognition of the existence of queer performers as well as the subject of the AIDS epidemic after Queen's iconic lead singer Freddie Mercury had died of the disease in November 1991. But music was still, as

---

[29]The EP featured three – 'Always on My Mind', 'I'm Not Scared' and 'It's Alright' – whereas 'Losing My Mind' had been recorded as a demo version for Liza Minnelli's album *Results*, produced by the Pet Shop Boys, and released as a B-side on the 'Jealousy' single. 'What Keeps Mankind Alive', written by Kurt Weill and Bertolt Brecht for their *Threepenny Opera*, was track 3 on disc 2 of the 'Can You Forgive Her?' single. 'Introspective', PetShopBoys.co.uk, https://www.petshopboys.co.uk/product/album/introspective; 'Can You Forgive Her?', PetShopBoys.co.uk, https://www.petshopboys.co.uk/product/single/can-you-forgive-her.

[30]'Cover Versions by Pet Shop Boys | SecondHandSongs', https://secondhandsongs.com/artist/153/covers?sort=date#covers.

[31]'FAC 51 The Hacienda | Pet Shop Boys PSB51', https://factoryrecords.org/cerysmatic/fac51psb51.php.

Lifebeat founder and music manager Bob Caviano put it, 'a man-dominated and chauvinistic business'. This had led to a lack of response to the crisis 'because of homophobia, sexism and racism'. Caviano had trouble getting some artists to perform at the benefit, for fear that they would be thought of as gay or HIV-infected by association. Still, in addition to Tennant and Lowe, the New York show featured hip hop group Salt-N-Pepa, who adjusted their breakout hit 'Let's Talk About Sex' to 'Let's Talk About AIDS', for an accompanying public service single release.[32]

While the Pet Shop Boys had first planned to cover the Beatles' 'The Fool on the Hill', according to Tennant, Lowe one morning entered London's Nomis Studios where they rehearsed, 'and said "I've looked through my records and decided we'll do this song called 'Go West'"'. As Lowe relates, Tennant at first was firmly against it, but let himself be convinced when Lowe 'point[ed] out that it was the same chord change as Pachelbel's Canon'.[33]

The pace back east

The Statue of Liberty is red and shiny, sitting in a sea of red, sending out rings of white radio waves. A red-hatted sailor in a white halter top crashes the cymbals. The Pet Shop Boys' 'Go West' starts off with a new musical intro not present in the Village People song, one availing itself, as established, of the chord progressions of Pachelbel's Canon, which in turn are the same as in the Soviet national anthem.[34] While the Pet Shop Boys frequently included references to Russian and Soviet history and culture in their work, beginning with Lenin's railway route back to Russia 'from Lake Geneva to the Finland Station' referenced in the lyrics to their first top 10 hit, 'West End Girls', 'Go West' as one of their most enduring songs, with its musical similarity to the Soviet national anthem and its video overtly connecting Russia and the United States, is by far the most obvious example.[35]

---

[32]'History: 1992', PetShopBoys.co.uk, https://www.petshopboys.co.uk/history/1992; Sheila Rule, 'At Roseland, a Benefit Concert for AIDS', *New York Times*, 8 June 1992, https://www.nytimes.com/1992/06/08/news/at-roseland-a-benefit-concert-for-aids.html.

[33]'Absolutely Pet Shop Boys Unofficial Web Site – Interviews – Very – Go West'. Tennant's telling in the interview also makes it seem likely that he acquiesced to Lowe's idea because Lowe, after his initial presentation of the song to Tennant, had started down a path he was unlikely to abandon either way.

[34]Although this appears not to have been the original intention, by the time the song was released the Pet Shop Boys themselves recognized the parallels. As Lowe recalls, 'It does sound surprisingly like the former Soviet anthem, we have subsequently discovered. It's remarkably similar.' They leaned into the similarity for the video production. 'Absolutely Pet Shop Boys Unofficial Web Site – Interviews – Very – Go West'.

[35]'Go West – Pet Shop Boys & Pachelbel – Pet Shop Boys Community', https://www.petshopboys-forum.com/viewtopic.php?t=19145. On various Russian and/or Soviet influences in the works of the band, see Wayne Studer, 'PSB Songs with "Russian Connections"',

But the video to 'Go West', directed by prolific music video director Howard Greenhalgh, who had already managed the similarly computer-generated 'Can You Forgive Her' and would go on to direct multiple more Pet Shop Boys videos, does not content itself with only visually drawing the two former rival superpowers closer together.[36] While its palette relies on red as a striking accent color, the Pet Shop Boys themselves are dressed in blue and yellow, donning their half-globe-shaped hats, while a troop of stylized sailors wears white shirts with red accents.[37] Red, the one colour represented in both the US and Soviet flags, connects the symbols of both: the Statue of Liberty and the five-pointed red star associated with communism and the Red Army. A 3D model of a red star variously floats and turns but is most often seen attached to a cityscape of white skyscrapers on which the lower-case word 'east' demonstratively rotates. The red Statue of Liberty soon doubles and flanks the upward march of a red-bereted army up a white stairwell into the sky, toward a golden gate (no doubt referencing once again San Francisco) in the shape of a 'W' with an exaggerated middle spike.

At one minute and fifteen seconds, one of the sailors can be seen running at the camera with a red flag. This is, on the one hand, an image out of Soviet propaganda, but it also recalls the famed '1984' Apple commercial for their first Macintosh computer that aired during the 1984 Superbowl. In it, a woman dressed in a white shirt and red pants runs at the camera holding a large hammer that she ultimately throws into a 'Big Brother'-like projection screen, exploding the indoctrination video playing on it. As the company repeatedly advertised its computers as tools of self-actualization and democratization, this interpretation overlaps with the move away from communism, toward individualism and capitalism.[38] Fourteen seconds later, the computer-generated Statue of Liberty has turned into backing singer

---

Commentary: Interpretation and Analysis of Every Song by Pet Shop Boys, http://www.geowayne.com/newDesign/lists/russian.htm. The line 'to the Finland Station' does double duty, not only denoting the terminus of Lenin's train ride to St Petersburg, but also the title of historian Edmund Wilson's influential book on revolutionary thought and the origins of socialism, *To the Finland Station: A Study in the Writing and Acting of History*. Tennant, who graduated with a degree in history from the Polytechnic of North London (today part of London Metropolitan University) in 1975, likely was aware of the book, which had been republished with a new introduction in 1971. Edmund Wilson, *To the Finland Station: A Study in the Acting and Writing of History* (New York: Farrar, Straus and Giroux, 2019).

[36]'Howard Greenhalgh', IMDb, https://www.imdb.com/name/nm0339037/.
[37]As the YouTube comments under the video on the official Pet Shop Boys channel attest, this has lately been interpreted by some as tacit support of the Ukrainian cause even before the Russian invasion. *Pet Shop Boys: Go West*, 2009, https://www.youtube.com/watch?v=LNBjMRvOB5M. The costumes were designed by director and costume designer David Fielding who also worked with the Pet Shop Boys on 'My October Symphony'. David Fielding, 'David Fielding | Director | Designer | Theatre | Opera', http://www.davidfielding.co.uk/.
[38]*1984 Apple's Macintosh Commercial (HD)*, 2012, https://www.youtube.com/watch?v=VtvjbmoDx-I.

Sylvia Mason-James wearing a red dress, holding the statue's signature torch and wearing a crown with starlike spikes. Whether explicit and on purpose, or implicit (by the coincidence of the backing singer's race), the visual of a Black woman embodying the Statue of Liberty reaches back to one of the original meanings of the statue, which was suggested by French abolitionist Edouard de Laboulaye in part as a symbol for the abolition of slavery, as well as to a persistent rumour that the statue itself was based upon a Black model.[39]

The real-life visuals of the Pet Shop Boys on Moscow's Red Square, which begin in the instant that the phrase 'the pace back east' is sung, sit somewhat disconnectedly in between the computer-generated parts of the video. Presenting the Pet Shop Boys in their futuristic blue and yellow costumes, they show, among other things, a relief of Lenin pointing left, a gesture which the band emulate. As the video makes use of stylized computerized maps, on which left indicates going 'West', this once again supports the direction the song is advocating.

The Pet Shop Boys' 'Go West' expanded on the ideas contained in the original song, in part by loosely riffing on the lyrics and in part by inserting a new mid-section that made some of the allusions more concrete. Where the Village People's West implies a promised land, the Pet Shop Boys name it: 'There where the air is free / We'll be (We'll be) what we want to be / Now if we make a stand / We'll find (We'll find) our promised land.' Tennant attributes some of the changes to simply playing fast and loose with the original lyrics, something that can be seen throughout the song, which sometimes substitutes phrases from the Village People's original with somewhat more nonsensical ones. For example, 'Busy pace back East / (The hustling) Rustling of the feet' is replaced by 'And the pace back East / (The hustling) Rustling just to feed.'

Yet one might also interpret this interchange between male voices as more overtly homosexual in nature than what the Village People put forward in the 1970s. Where the line in the Village People version is '(I want you) / Happy and carefree / (So that's why) I have no protest / (When you say) You want to go West', the Pet Shop Boys change it to a much more direct '(I want you) How could I disagree? / (So that's why) I make no protest / (When you say) You will do the rest.' Not only is the lyrical 'I' in the 1970s song content with seeing someone else 'happy and carefree', while in the 1993 version it cannot disagree with someone unambiguously wanting it, the edit from 'You want to go West' to 'You will do the rest' further implies a level of a trusting relationship in which two men go West together.

---

[39]'Sylvia Mason-James', IMDb, https://www.imdb.com/name/nm1126721/; Rebecca M. Joseph, Brooke Rosenblatt and Carolyn Kinebrew, 'Black Statue of Liberty – Summary Report – Statue of Liberty National Monument (US National Park Service)', https://www.nps.gov/stli/learn/historyculture/black-statue-of-liberty.htm.

In contrast to the inherent homoeroticism of the interplay between Tennant's voice and the all-male choir on the Pet Shop Boys' track, the original reads much more like its album companion 'In the Navy': a boosterist advertisement directed at an interchangeable object which is really every listener of the song. While the gulf between the two versions is not exceedingly vast – the original still contains the certainly suggestive line '(Together) Your hand in my hand / (Together) We will make the plan' – it is noticeable. Critics at the time likewise did notice. Caroline Sullivan, writing in the *Guardian* even declared that it made 'the Village People original seem flagrantly heterosexual'.[40]

In the video this is further enhanced by the visual of multiple clones of Chris Lowe mouthing the response phrases, which were performed by 'a lusty-voiced, 16-strong male choir'.[41] The choir, which Tennant referred to as 'a big choir of butch men', was a group of Broadway performers recorded by composer and arranger Richard Niles. Its sound resembled the Alexandrov Ensemble (known better as the Red Army Choir), which had attained some popularity in the West because they had collaborated with Finnish comedy rockers Leningrad Cowboys, including on a 1992 cover of the Beatles' 'Back in the U.S.S.R.' and a thoroughly campy live performance of the same band's 'Happy Together' during their 'Total Balalaika Show' concert on Helsinki's Senaatintori in June 1993, three months before the release of 'Go West'.[42]

The Leningrad Cowboys may have been an inspiration for the general ethos of the Pet Shop Boys' 'Go West', as they ironically connected, in their name and demeanor, and by virtue of their origin in Finland, East and West. The male Broadway choir on 'Go West' reproduced the pensive harmonies of the Alexandrov Ensemble so well that one industry publication even called them 'a Cossack choir'.[43] In connection with this, there is a second dualism in 'going West.' While, in addition to its two already established meanings – the forceful conquest of the North American West and the West as a queer arcadia – it can be interpreted as the formerly Soviet states turning towards

---

[40] Caroline Sullivan, 'Rock/Pop: Heavy Petting', *Guardian*, 24 September 1993.

[41] Jonathan Bernstein, 'Spins', *SPIN* (November 1993), 130. See also 'Absolutely Pet Shop Boys Unofficial Web Site – Interviews – Very – Go West'.

[42] In it, Leningrad Cowboys lead singer Sakke Järvenpää puts his arm around the uniformed Red Army Choir soloist as he intones 'so happy together'. It is an image that can be read so strikingly gay that it forcefully demonstrates the change in political tone since then, highlighting the homophobic and repressive politics of present-day Russia. *Total Balalaika Show* (Provisual, Sputnik, 1994).

[43] 'New Releases: Singles', *Music & Media* 10, no. 39 (25 September 1993): 16. In addition, according to Ian Balfour, 'The Pet Shop Boys' aural and video versions of the Village People's "Go West" song reconfigure the decidedly 70s song – post-Stonewall – to feature a large collection of background vocalists who resemble nothing more nor less than A Gay Men's Chorus, a social formation that postdates the heyday of the Village People.' Ian Balfour, 'Queen Theory: Notes on the Pet Shop Boys', in *Queen Theory: Notes on the Pet Shop Boys* (Durham, NC: Duke University Press, 2002), 368, https://doi.org/10.1515/9780822383376-014.

freedom and (somewhat more problematically) the Western-style capitalism of the 1990s. Yet, there is also another possible meaning, which was not lost on some listeners in countries formerly under the thrall of the Soviet Union: that Russia's path West would lead them to conquer Eastern Europe.[44]

Tennant–Lowe '93

The Pet Shop Boys had toured North America for the first time in 1991, experiencing the post-Cold War United States.[45] This may well have affected their choice of the song, and the visuals of its presentation. *Very*'s orange Lego-block packaging design, a version of which is also present in the album's third single, 'I Wouldn't Normally Do This Kind of Thing', is absent from both 'Can You Forgive Her', the first single released, which opts for imagery from the computer-graphics-supported music video in which the Pet Shop Boys wear their iconic 'traffic cone' hats, and 'Go West', the second single released. 'Go West' charts its own course design-wise, with most versions of the single going for a white background on which one or more round images in red, white and blue are arranged which clearly take their look from US presidential campaign buttons.

The most common design, used on CD singles, simply has one circle in the middle, with a red flattened upside-down U-shaped banderole in which the white capital letters 'Pet Shop Boys' are arranged forming the top and a blue U reading 'Tennant Lowe' the bottom. In a small gap between the two Us, blue stars are placed, while the middle of the circle is filled out by the heads of the two Pet Shop Boys wearing the mushroom-like 'dunce' hats they sport in the video in blue.[46] A blue 'Go' sits above a red 'West' in the lower half of the circle. Other designs featured on 7" singles used four different circles, and 12" pressings sported nine. All picked up the reds and blues of the US campaign-button theme, some showing US flags, some only either Tennant or Lowe, and some the names of the remixes contained on the discs.[47]

---

[44] As Tennant explained, '[P]eople thought that we had done a song that was based on the Soviet national anthem, and these Hungarian fans wrote to us and said, "I hear this song and I am frightened", because they thought it was suggesting that the Russians should invade Eastern Europe again, because they would go west. Maybe that's why the Russians like it.' 'Absolutely Pet Shop Boys Unofficial Web Site – Interviews – Very – Go West'.

[45] For an in-depth account of their tour, see Chris Heath, *Pet Shop Boys versus America* (London: Random House, 2020). The book was first published in 1993.

[46] Balfour, 'Queen Theory', 368.

[47] Images of the various international versions of the single can be found on the Discogs website. With a few exceptions, mostly for promotional releases, they all look very similar. The CD single described above is the one I own, duly purchased when it came out. As CDs had in the early 90s just overtaken cassettes as the dominant medium for music consumption, it would have been the most widely seen design. *Pet Shop Boys – Go West*, 1993, https://www.discogs.com/master/30702-Pet-Shop-Boys-Go-West.

The similarity to campaign buttons made variously through the 1960s and 1970s, including ones used by John F. Kennedy, Lyndon Johnson, Gerald Ford, George McGovern and others, is striking. Among the much more varied designs of actual US election campaign buttons which feature various logotypes and green, yellow, black, orange or even gold colours, the red, white and blue was unmistakably American, and matched the American flag printed on the CDs themselves.[48] The American-ness of the release emphasized that the 'West' alluded to was definitely the West of US national myth. The evocation of the Pacific Ocean by using library sound footage of seagulls at the start of the track tied that West clearly to California, a place that the *Overland Monthly* had, already in 1883, called 'America, only more so'.[49] (In the video, images of Lowe cloned several times and floating through the air on a surfboard, as well as on stylized beach balls, which also line the stairway to the golden 'W' further emphasizing the Californian connection.)

In 1993, the Pet Shop Boys had remade a Village People song about escaping an oppressive East for California, and updated it with then-cutting-edge computer graphics, the bravado of their electronic production, and a gusto for bratty, whimsical sci-fi visuals nodding to both American cityscapes and Soviet Brutalism, combined into one 'East'. They had made 'Go West' their own, interpreting its sincere aspiration through a still-hopeful irony. The song, founded on an uninterrogated vision of imperial settler colonialism still coursing through much of US popular and political culture, was re-envisioned as a much more overtly gay love song which at the same time sought to connect two formerly separated and warring hemispheres. The Pet Shop Boys' efforts could easily have deconstructed the song beyond repair, leaving it as a sad, unfulfilled and always problematic testimony to the exclusiveness of the American Dream. Instead, they rebuilt it, changed it, and, while not detracting from all the inborn issues of its expansionist framing, ultimately turned it back onto itself to again become what it had always been – only more so.

---

[48]See, for example, these buttons from the Harvard Kennedy School collection: *Kennedy for President*, 1960 (Cambridge, MA: Harvard Kennedy School Library & Knowledge Services PB_0615); *McGovern for President in '72*, 1972 (Cambridge, MA: Harvard Kennedy School Library & Knowledge Services PB_0826); *'Let Us Continue …' Johnson–Humphrey*, n.d., (Cambridge, MA: Harvard Kennedy School Library & Knowledge Services PB_1607); *Confident Peace Prosperity Ford–Dole in '76*, 1976 (Cambridge, MA: Harvard Kennedy School Library & Knowledge Services PB_0391).

[49]The unnamed author writes that 'All this is merely America, "only more so".' In yet another case of mistaken origins when it comes to slogans about the American West, the quote has often been attributed to author and environmentalist Wallace Stegner, who employed it in a 1967 article. 'Current Comment', *Overland Monthly and Out West Magazine* 2, no. 12 (December 1883): 658; 'California: The Experimental Society', *Chronicle of Higher Education*, 29 May 2010, https://www.chronicle.com/blognetwork/edgeofthewest/california-the-experimental-society; Tim McCormick, '"America … Only More so" (California) Famous Line from This 1967 Article by Wallace Stegner https://T.Co/Pg0QUw7nXw', *Twitter*, 25 October 2015, https://twitter.com/tmccormick/status/658374441764679680.

Coda

The past isn't even past, that's how long it lasts

On 10 February 2023, almost thirty years after the release of the longingly campy and contradictorily optimistic 'Go West' in 1993, the Pet Shop Boys released 'Living in the Past'. Dubbed a 'home demo', the sparsely orchestrated piece was presented as a video made up of heavily stylized black-and-white footage of Vladimir Putin unveiling a statue of Stalin in Volgograd on 2 February, walking the corridors of power and being sworn in for yet another presidential term. The video was intercut with images of protests in Russia and marching soldiers in camouflage fatigues. Inspired by the February ceremony, the song was hastily produced within just a week, clearly indicating that it was meant as an explicit entry in an ongoing public debate.

Ostensibly sung from Putin's perspective, but with the trademark Pet Shop Boys ironic detachment that here reads more like sarcastic disdain than anything else, Tennant intones, 'The West is effete / And they're begging for more / I'll get it all back / The old status quo', before promising that 'I remember how it was / And I won't let it go' and, riffing on William Faulkner's famous line, refrains 'The past isn't even past / That's how long it lasts.'[50]

While the Village People's version of 'Go West' ended in a confident exclamation point, a directive to find sanctuary, the Pet Shop Boys' cover rubbed out that punctuation in order to pencil in a tentative question mark. It's a song seemingly aware of the discourse surrounding Francis Fukuyama's 'end of history', and cautiously hopeful that it will materialize, even as the gay utopia of a carefree California life had crumbled under the weight of homophobic pushback (the murder of the first out gay politician in the United States, Harvey Milk, in 1978, after the original song would have been recorded but before its release, already puncturing the fantasy) and the AIDS epidemic.

Picking up on Faulkner's insight about the past never being dead, 'Living in the Past' communicates across decades of not only world history but also the personal history of Tennant and Lowe's oeuvre. It speaks especially to 'Go West' as the song that most clearly connects to the convulsions surrounding the end of the Soviet Union, now that the rise of Russia's oligarchic autocracy, in its nascent state when the single was released, is in full view. The punctuation mark with 'Living in the Past' is a full-stop, though one with a blinking cursor behind it, ready to be turned into an

---

[50] 'Living in the Past', *PetShopBoys.co.uk*, https://www.petshopboys.co.uk/pet-texts/2023-02-10/living-in-the-past; *Pet Shop Boys – Living in the Past (Home Demo)*, 2023, https://www.youtube.com/watch?v=bH-JzfkAvD8.

ellipsis.[51] As sly commentators on current events and as students of a history of the present, the Pet Shop Boys have reached back to one of their greatest successes and come full circle, arriving once more at an intellectual locus of symbolic potential and wistful memory, their own personal Finland Station.

Bibliography

1984 Apple's Macintosh Commercial (HD), 2012. https://www.youtube.com/watch?v=VtvjbmoDx-I.

'Absolutely Pet Shop Boys Unofficial Web Site – Interviews – Very – Go West', 27 August 2012, https://web.archive.org/web/20120827184236/http://www.petshopboys.net/html/interviews/very012.shtml.

Agriculture, Maine Dept of. *Agriculture of Maine. Annual Report of the Commissioner of Agriculture*, 1884.

Balfour, Ian. 'Queen Theory: Notes on the Pet Shop Boys'. In *Queen Theory: Notes on the Pet Shop Boys*, 357–71. Durham, NC: Duke University Press, 2002, https://doi.org/10.1515/9780822383376-014.

Bateman, Geoffrey W. 'Queer Wests: An Introduction'. *Western American Literature* 51, no. 2 (2016): 129–41.

Beadle, John Hanson. *The Undeveloped West: Or, Five Years in the Territories*. n.p.p.: National Publishing Company, 1873.

Bernardin, Susan. *The Routledge Companion to Gender and the American West*. London: Routledge, 2022.

Bernstein, Jonathan. 'Spins'. *SPIN*, November 1993.

Blauner, Robert. 'Internal Colonialism and Ghetto Revolt'. *Social Problems* 16, no. 4 (1969): 393–408, https://doi.org/10.2307/799949.

Boag, Peter. *Re-Dressing America's Frontier Past*. Oakland: University of California Press, 2012.

Brown, Richard Maxwell. *No Duty to Retreat: Violence and Values in American History and Society*. Norman: University of Oklahoma Press, 1994.

Chronicle of Higher Education. 'California: The Experimental Society', 29 May 2010, https://www.chronicle.com/blognetwork/edgeofthewest/california-the-experimental-society.

Confident Peace Prosperity Ford–Dole in '76. 1976. Cambridge, MA: Harvard Kennedy School Library & Knowledge Services PB_0391.

'Cover Versions by Pet Shop Boys | SecondHandSongs', https://secondhandsongs.com/artist/153/covers?sort=date#covers.

'Current Comment'. *Overland Monthly and Out West Magazine* 2, no. 12 (December 1883): 657–8.

Eaton Democrat. 'Arrest of a Supposed Murderer', 31 May 1855. Washington, DC: Library of Congress, Chronicling America.

Emery, Kim. 'Steers, Queers, and Manifest Destiny: Representing the Lesbian Subject in Turn-of-the-Century Texas'. *Journal of the History of Sexuality* 5, no. 1 (1994): 26–57.

---

[51]The latter being, as Ian Balfour has argued, 'one of the most characteristic structures in the work of the Pet Shop Boys'. Balfour, 'Queen Theory', 362.

'FAC 51 The Hacienda | Pet Shop Boys PSB51', https://factoryrecords.org/cerysmatic/fac51psb51.php.
Fielding, David. 'David Fielding | Director | Designer | Theatre | Opera', http://www.davidfielding.co.uk/.
Fuller, Thomas. '"Go West, Young Man!" – An Elusive Slogan'. *Indiana Magazine of History* 100, no. 3 (2004): 231–42.
The Gang's All Here. Twentieth Century Fox, 1943.
GenealogyBank Blog. 'Fact or Myth: Did Horace Greeley Really Say "Go West, Young Man"?' 10 December 2012, https://blog.genealogybank.com/fact-or-myth-did-horace-greeley-really-say-go-west-young-man.html.
Georgi-Findlay, Brigitte. 'Family Crises on the Frontiers: Nation, Gender, and Belonging in US Television Westerns'. In Eva-Sabine Zehelein, Andrea Carosso and Aida Rosende-Pérez (eds), *Family in Crisis? Crossing Borders, Crossing Narratives*, 145–54. Bielefeld: transcript, 2020, https://doi.org/10.1515/9783839450611-012.
'Go West – Pet Shop Boys & Pachelbel – Pet Shop Boys Community', https://www.petshopboys-forum.com/viewtopic.php?t=19145.
Greeley, Horace. *Recollections of a Busy Life*. New York: J.B. Ford and Company, 1868.
Greeley, Horace. Autograph letter signed, 2 pages + docket. 'Horace Greeley to R. L. Sanderson'. Autograph letter signed, 2 pages + docket, 15 November 1871. New York: Gilder Lehrman Institute of American History, https://www.gilderlehrman.org/node/2226.
Halberstam, Jack. *Female Masculinity*. Durham, NC: Duke University Press, 2019.
Heath, Chris. *Pet Shop Boys versus America*. London: Random House UK, 2020.
'Henri Belolo | DJHistory.Com'. 1 January 2010, https://web.archive.org/web/20100101135406/http://djhistory.com/interviews/henri-belolo.
Higgs, David. *Queer Sites: Gay Urban Histories Since 1600*. London: Routledge, 2002.
History's Newsstand Blog | Old Newspapers Original & Authentic. '"Go West, Young Man . . ."'. 20 December 2010, http://blog.rarenewspapers.com/?p=3575.
Hoffnagle, Warren. 'The Southern Homestead Act: Its Origins and Operation'. *The Historian* 32, no. 4 (1970): 612–29.
IMDb. 'Howard Greenhalgh', https://www.imdb.com/name/nm0339037/.
IMDb. 'Sylvia Mason-James', https://www.imdb.com/name/nm1126721/.
Isenberg, Andrew C. 'The Code of the West: Sexuality, Homosociality, and Wyatt Earp'. *Western Historical Quarterly* 40, no. 2 (2009): 139–57.
Joseph, Rebecca M., Brooke Rosenblatt and Carolyn Kinebrew. 'Black Statue of Liberty – Summary Report – Statue of Liberty National Monument (US National Park Service)', https://www.nps.gov/stli/learn/historyculture/black-statue-of-liberty.htm.
Kathke, Torsten. *Wires That Bind: Nation, Region, and Technology in the Southwestern United States, 1854–1920*. Bielefeld: transcript Verlag, 2017.
KCET. 'The Birth of Gay Urbanism in 1970s West Hollywood'. 26 February 2016, https://www.kcet.org/shows/lost-la/is-l-a-losing-its-outrageous-past-the-birth-of-gay-urbanism-in-1970s-west-hollywood.
Kennedy for President. 1960. Cambridge, MA: Harvard Kennedy School Library & Knowledge Services PB_0615.

Kiszonas, Elizabeth. 'Westward Empire: George Berkeley's "Verses on the Prospect of Planting of Arts" in American Art and Cultural History'. PhD dissertation, University of Arkansas, 2019, https://scholarworks.uark.edu/etd/3432.

Klein-Scholz, Christelle. 'From the "Homosexual Clone" to the "AIDS Clone": The Impact of AIDS on the Body of the Gay Male'. *E-Rea. Revue Électronique d'études Sur Le Monde Anglophone* 12, no. 1 (15 December 2014), https://doi.org/10.4000/erea.4153.

'Let Us Continue . . .'. *Johnson–Humphrey*. n.d. Cambridge, MA: Harvard Kennedy School Library & Knowledge Services PB_1607.

'Living in the Past', https://www.petshopboys.co.uk/pet-texts/2023-02-10/living-in-the-past.

McCormick, Tim. '"America . . . Only More so" (California) Famous Line from This 1967 Article by Wallace Stegner Https://T.Co/Pg0QUw7nXw'. *Twitter*, 25 October 2015, https://twitter.com/tmccormick/status/658374441764679680.

McGovern for President in '72. 1972. Cambridge, MA: Harvard Kennedy School Library & Knowledge Services PB_0826.

McHugh, Jane and Philip A. Mackowiak. 'Death in the White House: President William Henry Harrison's Atypical Pneumonia'. *Clinical Infectious Diseases* 59, no. 7 (1 October 2014): 990–5, https://doi.org/10.1093/cid/ciu470.

Merritt, Keri Leigh. *Masterless Men*. Cambridge: Cambridge University Press, 2017.

Midgley, Alex. '"Macho Types Wanted": The Village People, Homophobia, and Representation in 1970s'. *Australasian Journal of American Studies* 33, no. 1 (2014): 104–19.

Moore, Catriona, Eldon Pei, Irena Vladimirsky and Phoebe Scott. 'Social Realism'. In *Routledge Encyclopedia of Modernism*. London: Routledge, 2016, https://doi.org/10.4324/9781135000356-REMO25-1.

Nelson Limerick, Patricia. *The Legacy of Conquest: The Unbroken Past of the American West*. New York: Norton, 1987.

'New Releases: Singles'. *Music & Media* 10, no. 39 (25 September 1993): 16.

New York Herald. 'Wanted', 5 May 1855. Washington, DC: Library of Congress, Chronicling America.

Nugent, Walter. *Habits of Empire*. New York: Knopf Doubleday Publishing Group, 2008.

O'Donovan, Connell. 'Go West', http://www.connellodonovan.com/gowest.html.

The Oxford Dictionary of Quotations. Oxford: Oxford University Press, 1999.

Packard, C. *Queer Cowboys: And Other Erotic Male Friendships in Nineteenth-Century American Literature*. Cham: Springer, 2016.

Pearlman, Jeff. '"Y.M.C.A." (An Oral History)'. *SPIN*, June 2008.

'Pet Shop Boys. 'History: 1992', https://www.petshopboys.co.uk/history/1992.

Pet Shop Boys – Go West. 1993, https://www.discogs.com/master/30702-Pet-Shop-Boys-Go-West.

Pet Shop Boys – Living in the Past (Home Demo). 2023, https://www.youtube.com/watch?v=bH-JzfkAvD8.

Pet Shop Boys. 'Can You Forgive Her?' https://www.petshopboys.co.uk/product/single/can-you-forgive-her.

Pet Shop Boys: Go West. 2009, https://www.youtube.com/watch?v=LNBjMRvOB5M.

Pet Shop Boys. 'Introspective', https://www.petshopboys.co.uk/product/album/introspective.

Peters, Troy and Griff Williams. *Hal Fischer: The Gay Seventies*. Cheltenham: Gallery 16, 2019.
Proceedings of the First Annual Convention of the Brotherhood of Locomotive Firemen and Enginemen, Hornellsville, New York, December 1874. 1874.
Rule, Sheila. 'At Roseland, a Benefit Concert for AIDS'. *New York Times*, 8 June 1992, https://www.nytimes.com/1992/06/08/news/at-roseland-a-benefit-concert-for-aids.html.
Studer, Wayne. 'PSB Songs with "Russian Connections"'. *Commentary: Interpretation and Analysis of Every Song by Pet Shop Boys*, http://www.geowayne.com/newDesign/lists/russian.htm.
Sullivan, Caroline. 'Rock/Pop: Heavy Petting'. *Guardian*, 24 September 1993.
Tatonetti, Lisa. 'The Indigenous Erotics of Riding Bareback, or, the West Has Always Been Queer'. *Western American Literature* 53, no. 1 (2018): 1–10.
Taylor, Dorceta. 'Internal Colonialism: Native American Communities in the West'. In Dorceta Taylor, *Toxic Communities: Environmental Racism, Industrial Pollution, and Residential Mobility*, 47–68. New York: New York University Press, 2014, https://doi.org/10.18574/nyu/9781479805150.003.0008.
Total Balalaika Show. Provisual, Sputnik, 1994.
Village People. 'San Francisco (You've Got Me)'. 1977.
'The Village People'. *Rolling Stone* 289, 19 April 1979.
Walker, Judson Elliott. *Campaigns of General Custer in the North-West, and the Final Surrender of Sitting Bull*. New York: Jenkins & Thomas, 1881.
West, Elliott. *The Last Indian War: The Nez Perce Story*. Oxford: Oxford University Press, 2011.
Wilson, Edmund. *To the Finland Station: A Study in the Acting and Writing of History*. New York: Farrar, Straus and Giroux, 2019.

PART FOUR

We're the Pet Shop Boys: Metanarrativity and Manifestations

CHAPTER NINE

It's a Sin

Religious Imagery and Queer Identities in *It Couldn't Happen Here*

Lisa-Marie Pöhland

Introduction

It Couldn't Happen Here (1999), directed by Jack Bond and starring Neil Tennant and Chris Lowe, relies heavily on the use of religious and especially Christian imagery. A blind pastor, nuns that turn out to be exotic dancers, and a crucifix that is raised with a crane are just the most striking examples. Accentuated by the Pet Shop Boys' music – a duo with a complicated and delicate history in engaging with queer topics – the connection between religious and queer motives in the film's images, its dialogue and its music is almost inescapable. The purpose of this chapter is to explore this connection further and in more detail. The question of whether queer people appear deviant or as the 'Other' to a straight, cis majority will be of central focus in the following analysis since this is a problem highlighted by queer religious studies as well as queer film studies. I argue that by presenting every character as caricature – tacky, morally questionable and generally peculiar – the movie makes a point of not presenting queer character in that way. With every character appearing odd, eventually no character does when compared to the others. Still, a sentiment of not belonging or not fitting in with the other characters of the film is expressed through the two main characters, Chris and Neil.

The central question of this chapter is how the film portrays Christian motifs with respect to queerness. For this purpose, the chapter first examines queer theological studies as a theoretical background to base the analysis on. In order to do justice to these key issues, I cannot avoid classifying certain motives and their social contexts. What follows is an in-depth analysis of the film's imagery, dialogue and song lyrics, as well as the context in which they appear, in order to conclude the synergy of style and meaning in this film. I will use film analysis techniques such as composition, cinematography and metaphor and character analysis. Finally, a concluding discussion will outline the relationship between religion and sexual identity. *It Couldn't Happen Here* is a surrealistic, experimental film. The key storyline is a journey the protagonists embark on to escape from their old lives similar to the song that lends its name to the film. The film offers a critique of a community in which white, straight and cis personae oppress and exclude minorities, particularly queer and gender non-conforming people, and teach this ideology to children from an early age. Thus, the film expresses the struggles of growing up queer under the influence of religious fundamentalism and also works as social criticism. I also argue that those characters who might be in a position of superiority in this context are demonstrating hypocrisy which aligns with queer biblical interpretations that give special importance to those who are oppressed by the authorities.

'As you did to the least of these who are members of my family, you did to me': religious symbols and queer lenses

Queer biblical and queer theological studies have existed since the late 1990s.[1] Scholars of these studies argue that the 'subversive intentions of queer theory'[2] and the perspectives born out of these approaches hold high potential, especially for religious studies. Nevertheless, some scholars such as Annika Thiem and Johannes N. Vorster criticize the authority that is still attributed to biblical texts by rereading and reclaiming them despite their weaponization against minorities.[3] First being developed at the intersection of activism and theory, queer studies take into account the imbrication of various identities, religious and sexual identities being only one example.[4]

---

[1] Claudia Schippert. 'Implications of Queer Theory for the Study of Religion and Gender: Entering the Third Decade', *Religion and Gender* 1, no. 1 (2011): 67.
[2] Schippert, 'Implications of Queer Theory', 67.
[3] Annika Thiem, 'The Art of Queer Rejections: The Everyday Life of Biblical Discourse', *Neotestamentica* 48, no. 1 (2014): 34; Johannes N. Vorster, 'The Queering of the Biblical Discourse', *Scriptura* 111, no. 2 (2012): 608–9.
[4] Schippert, 'Implications of Queer Theory', 67–8.

Through their subversive character, queer studies shed new light on the study of religion. As the work in this field progresses, there has been a shift away from merely identifying queer religious practices or practitioners, with recent works allowing much more room for queer theoretical critique.[5]

In conservative readings, the divine embodies hegemonic masculinity.[6] This understanding is also being challenged by queer theological and queer biblical scholars such as Robert E. Shore-Goss and Claudia Schippert. One claim brought forward by queer theological studies is that the notion of a queer Jesus holds just as much truth as heteronormative interpretations. Shore-Goss summarizes,

> Queer constructions of Jesus in biblical interpretation and popular media are accused of being blasphemous fictions, while the same charge can be levied against the constructions of heteronormative and cisgender Christian churches who marginalize and stigmatize LGBTI people.[7]

Shore-Goss goes on to claim that the rejection of any alternative ideas about the hermeneutics of Jesus is a means of maintaining hegemony and justifying the lifestyles of the privileged. He further states, 'White, Western, conservative Christians who claim Jesus as white, male, cis and heterosexual, weaponize a Jesus who is socially constructed to oppress and exclude LGBTQIA+ people and other minorities.'[8] By using these interpretations, queer people are placed in the position of the Other, the deviant or the evil. What is thus also questioned by works of queer theology is the problematic legitimization of power structures, hence because of their 'enduring influence in the public sphere and contemporary culture, the Bible has the potential to justify violence against minoritized groups'.[9] It is even argued that the secularity that some Western states claim is heavily influenced by Christianity, much to the detriment of non-white, non-heterosexual, non-Christian minorities.[10]

A prominent example of minorities such as LGBTQIA+ people being portrayed as deviant by the majority is the use of the AIDS crisis for propaganda purposes in the 1980s. The eponymous song of the Pet Shop Boy's film *It Couldn't Happen Here* (1987) itself is an allegory of this very problem. Not only was the epidemic framed as a 'gay disease', but in a

---

[5]Schippert, 'Implications of Queer Theory', 70.
[6]Will Moore, 'A Godly Man and a Manly God: Resolving the Tension of Divine Masculinities in the Bible', *Journal for Interdisciplinary Biblical Studies* 2, no. 2 (2021): 71.
[7]Robert E. Shore-Goss, 'Queering Jesus: LGBTQI Dangerous Remembering and Imaginative Resistance', *Journal for Interdisciplinary Biblical Studies* 2, no. 2. (2021): 47.
[8]Shore-Goss, 'Queering Jesus', 47.
[9]Chris Greenough, 'Editorial: Queer Theory and the Bible', *Journal for Interdisciplinary Biblical Studies* 2, no. 2 (2021): 2.
[10]Schippert, 'Implications of Queer Theory', 73–4; Thiem, 'Art of Queer Rejections', 35.

religious context it was often presented as God's punishment.[11] Framing the disease in this way was another means to the end of further justifying the exclusion and oppression of sexual and racial minorities. In Britain, this was spearheaded by the Conservative government of Margaret Thatcher. The attitude of the government towards AIDS ranged from dismissive – 'good Christian people [...] will not get AIDS', according to the junior Health Minister, Edwina Currie, in February 1987[12] – to seeing it as a means of getting rid of an undesirable population. 'I do not agree with homosexuality,' Tory Member of Parliament Peter Bruinvels stated boldly. 'I think Clause 28 will help outlaw it and the rest will be done by AIDS, with a substantial number of homosexuals dying of AIDS. I think that's probably the best way.'[13]

This was a prevailing idea of the time, with one infamous tabloid headline of the period reading '"I'd shoot my son if he had AIDS", says vicar.'[14] Even when other high-risk groups such as haemophiliacs were recognized, these were mainly portrayed as innocent victims by the media in contrast to homosexual men, who suffered from the disease because of immoral behaviour.[15] While in the 1960s some 'aspects of British culture had been liberalised and decriminalised',[16] homosexuality remained stigmatized.

These minorities suffer religious abuse, not only at the hands of the state, the press and the Church, but also in some cases in their private spaces, which is at the very least damaging and potentially traumatizing.[17] This also means that growing up queer in a religious community, with religious education or under religious fundamentalism, often requires an effort to negotiate both identities or to conceal one.[18] Both strategies not only threaten an individual's mental health but also their social networks.[19] In

---

[11] Ahoura Afshar, 'The Anti-Gay Rights Movement in the United States: The Framing of Religion', *Essex Human Rights Review* 3, no. 1 (2006): 75.
[12] Matt Cook, 'AIDS, Mass Observation, and the Fate of the Permissive Turn', *Journal of the History of Sexuality* 26, no. 2 (2017): 244–5.
[13] Darryl W. Bullock, *Pride, Pop and Politics: Music, Theatre and LGBT Activism, 1970–2021* (London: Omnibus, 2022), 272. For more on Clause 28, otherwise known as Section 28, see Bodie A. Ashton, 'He Dreamed of Machines: Queer Heritage and the Pet Shop Boys' "Turing Test"', in this volume.
[14] Martin Pendergast, 'HIV in Britain 1982–1990?: The Christian Reaction', *New Blackfriars* 71, no. 840 (1990): 347.
[15] Adam Burgess, 'The Development of Risk Politics in the UK: Thatcher's "Remarkable" but Forgotten "Don't Die of Ignorance" AIDS Campaign', *Health, Risk & Society* 19, no. 5–6 (2017): 6.
[16] Burgess, 'The Development of Risk Politics', 7.
[17] Shore-Goss, 'Queering Jesus', 48.
[18] Ruard R. Ganzevoort, Mark Van der Laan and Erik Olsman, 'Growing Up Gay and Religious. Conflict, Dialogue, and Religious Identity Strategies', *Mental Health, Religion & Culture* 14, no.3 (2011): 209.
[19] Ganzevoort, van der Laan and Olsman, 'Growing Up Gay and Religious', 220.

sum, being queer within a religious community requires identity strategies, but even if a queer person does not consider themself religious, they are oftentimes still pushed into a subordinate position of the deviant due to the remaining influence of religion on the public.

The suppression of minorities through physical, emotional or spiritual violence contrasts with interpretations of Jesus' ministry as queer readings of scriptures as well as queer analysis of religious communities point out.[20] The almost sanitized and whitewashed image presented by a heteronormative Christianity erases the importance of minorities in the biblical story, which is after all a story of resistance in which 'Jesus is remembered and imagined as "one of us"',[21] hence the existence of a black Jesus, a Hispanic one, or even a lesbian Christa (i.e., a feminine form of Christ) in some religious communities. Not only do these theories and interpretations put forward that Jesus stood in solidarity with minorities and the oppressed, but they also state that he was one of them. After all, he was crucified for his religious and political beliefs, statements and behaviours. Jesus' actions themselves can be seen as subversive, since his ministry challenged those who held political and religious power.[22]

In several passages, the Bible offers 'a hermeneutic principle of the Christ as present in the "least" or those excluded; it reflects a principle of solidarity that marginalized and abjected groups use in their counter-constructions of Jesus'.[23] When the marginalized and excluded read the story of Jesus through the lens of their own experience, they can encounter a closeness to Jesus' resistance that more privileged readers may not feel to the same extent. In other words, a Christianity that disregards or even excludes minorities and their understandings of scripture is criticized and even accused of hypocrisy.

Similar to queer biblical studies are the practices of queer film studies. Through an analysis of symbols, dialogues, characters, camera angles or film music, a film can be re-evaluated and reinterpreted. By examining cultural products through a queer lens, theorists intend to 'problematize the production of dominant and normative categories of sexuality'.[24] Similar to how queer theory is applied in theological studies, queer film theories assume that through a change of perspective, queer motives, characters and experiences can be found in many films throughout history, although they were only implied in many cases, also referred to as queer-coding.[25] This is based on the realization that many viewers do not simply decide on the

---

[20]Greenough, 'Queer Theory and the Bible', 2.
[21]Shore-Goss, 'Queering Jesus', 49.
[22]Shore-Goss, 'Queering Jesus', 50–1.
[23]Shore-Goss, 'Queering Jesus', 50.
[24]Schippert, 'Implications of Queer Theory', 67.
[25]Shore-Goss, 'Queering Jesus', 55; Koeun Kim, 'Queer-coded Villains (And Why You Should Care)', *Dialogues@ RU* (2007): 158; Vito Russo Russo, *The Celluloid Closet* (New York: Harper & Row, 1981), 36.

sexual identity of a character based on the sexual activity exhibited on screen.[26] Other indicators are at play, such as stereotypes (e.g., homosexual men as 'sissies'), the depiction of certain experiences (e.g., the loss of social bonds), mannerisms (e.g., the limp wrist) and behaviours (e.g., application of identity strategies).[27] Those indicators are not always sexually motivated but linked to queerness nevertheless. Only if films are viewed exclusively through a conservative, straight lens, production laws as well as ostracism from society lead to a seeming absence of queer people and motives from cinema.

Non-conformability to gendered norms is considered an indicator of a queer subtext as well.[28] Another aspect closely connected to the question of gender is the handling of stereotypes in films.[29] While subversion of gendered norms is anticipated, the focus of criticism is especially on the implications of those depictions. Criticisms include the subversion of gender norms as the only implication of queerness, its primary attribution to the villains of films, its use to make queer people appear deviant or its use as a punchline.[30] In a film, this can be realized, for example, through the characters' clothing or mannerisms.

Filmic depiction exhibits ideological tendencies and dynamics and relations between groups as well.[31] Since 'Britain's churches and the faith they represent remain deeply embedded within culture and society',[32] and considering my former elucidations on conservative Christianity's stance on queerness, it can be assumed that a queer analysis of the religious symbols in a British film from 1988 could reveal conflicts between religious beliefs and queerness. Another aspect that substantiates this presumption is the AIDS crisis, which has been utilized for anti-LGBTQIA+ propaganda, especially by churches at the time.

---

[26]Kim, 'Queer-coded Villains', 157.
[27]Greenough, 'Queer Theory and the Bible', 1; Richard Dyer, *The Matter of Images: Essays on Representations* (London: Routledge, 1993), 1; Alexander Doty and Ben Gove, 'Queer Representation in the Mass Media', in Andy Medhurst and Sally Munt (eds), *Lesbian and Gay Studies – A Critical Introduction* (London and Washington, DC: Cassell, 1997), 87; Kim, 'Queer-coded Villains', 161.
[28]Greenough, 'Queer Theory and the Bible', 1.
[29]Kim, 'Queer-coded Villains', 161; Doty and Gove, 'Queer Representation', 87; Dyer, *The Matter of Images*, 1.
[30]Kim, 'Queer-coded Villains', 157–61; Tricia Jenkins, '"Potential Lesbians at Two O'Clock": The Heterosexualization of Lesbianism in the Recent Teen Film', *Journal of Popular Culture* 38, no. 3 (2005): 493; Armağan Gökçearslan, 'The Effect of Cartoon Movies on Children's Gender Development', *Procedia – Social and Behavioral Sciences* 2, no. 2 (2010): 5206.
[31]Dyer, *The Matter of Images*, 1; Ricarda Drüeke, Elisabeth Klaus and Anita Moser, 'Mediale und künstlerische Bild-Diskurse zu Flucht und Migration', in Manfred Oberlechner, Christine W. Trültzsch-Wijnen and Patrick Duval (eds), *Migration Bildet* (Baden-Baden: Nomos Verlagsgesellschaft, 2007), 315–16.
[32]Daniel Gover, 'Christian Interest Groups in A Religiously Changing United Kingdom: Issues, Strategies, Influence', *Politics and Religion* 15, no. 3 (2022): 462.

A queer journey and a journey of queerness

In *It Couldn't Happen Here* the aforementioned subversion of (gendered) stereotypes can be found aplenty, for example in a scene in which Chris is disguised as a female fortune teller[33] or when Chris and Neil buy a car advertised as the 'Honeymoon special'[34] covered in pink, fluffy ribbons and decorated with flowers. However, to define a feasible frame, I will only present scenes that fit both a queer theoretical context and can be read with reference to Queer Theological Studies in the following analysis. These indicators have been established by queer film studies before and include the playing with the aforementioned stereotypes.

Both members of the Pet Shop Boys portray characters with their real names. Though the film is a work of fiction, there are parallels to the Pet Shop Boys' real lives, such as Neil Tennant's upbringing at a Catholic school that he also processes in the songs 'It's a Sin' and 'This Must Be the Place I Waited Years to Leave'.[35] When mentioned in this chapter, first names are thus used to refer to the fictional characters rather than the actual Pet Shop Boys members, even though the film is inspired by their experiences. Because of the surrealistic style of *It Couldn't Happen Here*, the film is disjointed in terms of chronology and spatial aspects. For this reason, the following analysis is not chronological, but logical. Also, Neil sometimes mentions scenes from the film as if they happened to him in the past, even though Chris is seen in the scene. However, both men appear on screen together. Therefore, they are analysed as separate characters. In addition, some actors impersonate several different characters. Sometimes these characters, although different in appearance and mannerisms, even have the same name. Each scene is then analysed individually and in the context of the film.

Despite the seemingly random concatenation of scenes and characters, *It Couldn't Happen Here* could be summarized as being about escaping an old life. Chris, as an example, is first seen packing a huge trunk before leaving a boarding house,[36] and Neil is heard in several voiceovers, writing postcards to his mother he presumably left some time ago.[37] That both men are constantly travelling during the film is another indicator of this assumption. First, Chris is running away on foot[38] and Neil is shown riding a bike at night and until the next day.[39] Later, they purchase a car by which they travel,[40] and almost at the end of the film, they get on a train[41] and are

---

[33] *It Couldn't Happen Here*, directed by Jack Bond (Parlophone Records, 1988), DVD, 00:14:48.
[34] *It Couldn't Happen Here*, 00:25:55.
[35] Pet Shop Boys, 'This Must Be the Place I Waited Years to Leave', Parlophone, 1990.
[36] *It Couldn't Happen Here*, 00:05:18.
[37] *It Couldn't Happen Here*, 00:04:46.
[38] *It Couldn't Happen Here*, 00:09:45.
[39] *It Couldn't Happen Here*, 00:00:46.
[40] *It Couldn't Happen Here*, 00:25:49.
[41] *It Couldn't Happen Here*, 00:01:06.

picked up by a limousine at the station.[42] The titular song supports the notion of a journey with the aim of leaving something behind. The bittersweet lyrics ('We've found ourselves back where we started from. / I may be wrong, I thought we said / It couldn't happen here') carry with them the promise of a new lease on life and, at the same time, a disappointing outcome.[43] The journey is a queer motif on itself and a reappearing trope in queer depictions. This is not the only time the Pet Shop Boys use this motif in such a way. In their song 'Being Boring' (1990) the act of leaving an unaccepting place had already been thematized.[44] By leaving behind the place and people who cannot understand, accept or even tolerate queer identities, freedom is attained by the LGBTQIA+ people who otherwise cannot live as their authentic self or suffer discrimination if they attempt to. At the same time, 'It Couldn't Happen Here' as well as 'Being Boring' are shaped by the experiences of the AIDS crisis of the time. Consequently, there is a threat that the people embarking on the journey cannot escape through a change of locations.

The blind leading the blind?

In addition to the journey that is central to the film, some scenes can be interpreted as flashbacks in which Neil and Chris are children. They are part of a group of boys who are led by a man whose clothes and cross-necklace indicate that he is a priest. These possible flashback scenes occur seemingly parallel to the plot of the adults Neil and Chris since at 00:11:19, Neil is located at the same beach as the priest. The presence of the children at the same time as the adults is one example of the disjointed chronology of the film, which appears as a stream of consciousness. The disjointedness in combination with the reorientation towards childhood implies a fragmented sense of self linked to the identity strategies applied by the characters when they had to negotiate their religious upbringing and their intrinsic identities. When Neil sees the priest, he recites the lines of 'It's a Sin' in a voiceover, expressing the traumatic experience of being demonized for his identity from a young age on. He states, 'When I look back upon my life, it's always with a sense of shame. I've always been the one to blame.' As the group of boys comes into frame, he continues, 'For everything I long to do, no matter when or where, or who has one thing in common too. It's a sin.'[45]

The priest is presumably in charge of this group and is leading them somewhere, as the boys follow in a line behind him. It is striking that the priest is supposedly blind in these scenes. It cannot be confirmed whether his

---

[42] *It Couldn't Happen Here*, 01:09:44.
[43] *It Couldn't Happen Here*, 00:13:03.
[44] Pet Shop Boys, 'Being Boring', Parlophone, 1990.
[45] *It Couldn't Happen Here*, 00:11:48.

blindness is real, feigned or metaphorical. In the Bible, there are instances in which eyesight is relevant and also used as a metaphor. With the boys following him around, there is an analogy between the priest and Matthew 15.14 – 'Let them alone: they are blind leaders'[46] – in which the blindness of the priest is to be seen as metaphorical. Furthermore, when the priest reappears later and hitches a ride with the adult Neil and Chris[47] he is apparently able to see. Nevertheless, he is the same priest as before and this is made apparent by his catchphrase 'I smell youth'[48] he had already used while searching for the boys, the words from a sermon he spoke before, and because Neil and Chris think they might recognize him. Maybe, however, they simply remember *a* priest from their childhood and they link their negative experiences to this man. His proximity and similar behaviour then indicate that all priests are alike. The priest then tells them that he 'used to be blind',[49] which changed after he started to eat carrots, though he still cannot see during the day. In the hitchhiker scene, he is mainly presented as a lunatic. A lot of what he says does not make any sense and additionally, he is a murderer now, who had killed four people including a nun.[50] Thus, it is impossible to judge the verisimilitude of his words. After he gets out of the car at night, he immediately pretends to be blind again.[51] A question of the flashback scene is thus whether he is actually blind or pretending to be blind, or if his blindness is to be seen metaphorically. Having said that, he promptly loses the boys at an amusement park. While the priest is absorbed in his sermon, the boys get distracted by a laughing clown.[52] Though possibly the priest cannot see the attractions around him, he surely hears the clown but ignores him.

However, his alleged blindness does not stop the priest from having a look through a View-Master-type mutoscope through which a film is shown.[53] The film is a skit in which two men, embodied by Tennant and Lowe, make approaches on a woman dressed like a maid. While doing so, they touch her, kiss her and lift her skirt. The maid seems excited by it and acts responsive to both men. The priest comments on the scene with the words 'This machine isn't working,'[54] which could be interpreted in several ways. On the one hand, it could mean that it does not work for him as he is blind and cannot see the skit or because he identifies as a man of God and does not find it enjoyable. This is a metaphor, equating the machine with a

---

[46]Matthew 15.14 (KJV).
[47]*It Couldn't Happen Here*, 00:28:47.
[48]*It Couldn't Happen Here*, 00:29:00.
[49]*It Couldn't Happen Here*, 00:30:16.
[50]*It Couldn't Happen Here*, 00:28:10.
[51]*It Couldn't Happen Here*, 00:35:16.
[52]*It Couldn't Happen Here*, 00:13:36.
[53]*It Couldn't Happen Here*, 00:15:35.
[54]*It Couldn't Happen Here*, 00:16:54.

way of life and indicating that a lifestyle that does not work for some people is completely acceptable and enjoyable to others. On the other hand, it is a depiction of the formerly mentioned hypocrisy[55] of a priest that has been shown preaching to a group of children about a God-fearing life,[56] but who does not completely abjure profligate, earthly joys. Subsequently, he denies his action by claiming that the machine was not working anyway.

This critique is taken even further when the priest is searching for the boys who are running away from him in the amusement park. They pass by several attractions which again can be seen as symbols of earthly but sinful joys. This is underpinned by the song 'It's a Sin' playing in the background. During the chase, the priest ends up on a Ferris wheel.[57] In one of its cabins, there is a lightly clad, overweight woman who eats from a huge plate with her bare hands.[58] In other cabins, two drunk men bawl loudly,[59] two mud-covered women fight,[60] and a man dressed as a vampire kisses the neck of a woman.[61] In the last cabin, a naked man injects himself with a substance.[62] Regardless of whether these behaviours are subjectively considered offensive or sinful, the amusement park at night is not an appropriate place for the boys who stand at the Ferris wheel and watch the cabins go by. In this scene, the priest is just another person among the people in the cabins, while he shouts for the boys and calls them heathens.

At the pinnacle of the night, the boys arrive at a theatre. On stage there is a group of nuns, whose erotic dance and poses juxtapose their costumes.[63] At the sight of the stage, the boys utter 'Father forgive me' in unison.[64] Eventually, the priest also arrives at the theatre. However, before he finds the boys, he is walking around the seats and even on stage during the performance for a while.[65] Regardless of whether he is actually blind or not – in other words, whether he is actually unable to recognize what is happening around him or if he just pretends not to see it – he is ascribed a series of behaviours (including, at best, negligence) at odds with his position of pastoral care within the Church. All he cares about is finding Neil and Chris and starts preaching again after he does.[66] All of it, from the chase to the sermon, to the re-encounter as adults is an extended metaphor for systematic abuse that is not recognized by the Church. The priest is blind to the abuse the boys suffer

---

[55] Shore-Goss, 'Queering Jesus', 47–8; Greenough, 'Queer Theory and the Bible', 2.
[56] *It Couldn't Happen Here*, 00:11:18.
[57] *It Couldn't Happen Here*, 00:17:01.
[58] *It Couldn't Happen Here*, 00:17:16.
[59] *It Couldn't Happen Here*, 00:17:24.
[60] *It Couldn't Happen Here*, 00:17:29.
[61] *It Couldn't Happen Here*, 00:17:41.
[62] *It Couldn't Happen Here*, 00:17:44.
[63] *It Couldn't Happen Here*, 00:18:10.
[64] *It Couldn't Happen Here*, 00:18:16.
[65] *It Couldn't Happen Here*, 00:19:21.
[66] *It Couldn't Happen Here*, 00:20:48.

from him. In the few minutes of the film when they run from him, they are exposed to a world which provides joys and temptations, oftentimes age-inappropriate ones. The scenes show no regard of their childhood innocence and so does the priest, who presumably oversees the children but does not stop them from encountering the scene at the Ferris wheel or the nun on stage. At the same time, the priest is always behind them telling them that all of it is a sin. In other words, the boys are without guidance completely. Not only are they without guidance, but the one supposed to guide them, in fact places them in a position in which their mental wellbeing is threatened because of the rejection they experience from a young age onwards. He further fuels the rhetoric that wants to push queer people into a subordinate position and justifies public and domestic discrimination against them.

In connection to the occurrences at the mutoscope and the claim that carrots cured his blindness, the priest's obliviousness of the nuns on stage could also be an indicator of his own suppressed homosexual tendencies. This is another explanation for why the mutoscope is not working for him – because the skit is a display of approaches between a woman and the men. Furthermore, the carrots – a distinctively phallic vegetable – he supposedly ate are symbolic as well. After he no longer fights his desires, his life changes completely. He is then able to 'see' the truth. This in consequence prompts him to disregard his own teachings. Eventually, he turns into a person his old self would condemn as a sinner.

Interestingly, the priest only seems to care about Neil and Chris, as the other boys in the group also disappear, but are never found or mentioned again. From a queer analytic perspective, this is an expression of criticism of a Church in which a potentially queer child is a problem child. The song 'It's a Sin', which plays throughout the chase, also describes the experience of growing up with the feeling that everything desired is wrong and sinful. The lyrics are the most prominent and obvious expression of this traumatizing experience and its consequences in the film. In the song, the feeling of being deviant in a society that views a queer identity as wrong or shameful is described. It is tinged with criticism of a religious practice that makes people believe from an early age that their identity, and therefore their whole life, is sinful.[67] At some point during their religious upbringing the young boys discover their sexual identity and have to come to terms with the realization that it is them who their community rejects as deviant. They have to come to terms with the realization that their desires are viewed as sinful and that they cannot be themselves with their family or friends. They find themselves exactly in the situation that is ultimately harmful to many children growing up under religious fundamentalism and find themselves in a situation in which they have to negotiate their identity or conceal one in order to not endanger social bonds or even their physical wellbeing. There is also a

---

[67]Shore-Goss, 'Queering Jesus', 47–8.

parallel with the autobiographic experiences of Neil Tennant at the Catholic school he processes in 'This Must Be the Place I Waited Years to Leave'. Lyrics such as 'Living a law just short of delusion, when we fall in love there's confusion'[68] confirm this notion. The line 'I dreamt I was back in uniform'[69] indicates a similar flashback to the one in the film.

After the priest finds them at the theatre, he leads Neil and Chris to a pier at which a giant wooden cross is lifted from the sea by a crane. While he is standing there, he continues his sermon while the blind person's cane catches fire.[70] This scene includes a medium close-up of him, shot from a slightly below-eye-level angle. With a thunderstorm raging and dockworkers in the background over which the priest seems to tower while he shouts and describes circles with his fiery cane, he appears demonic and overpowering. He is taller than the boys, he seems stronger, and with the cane he has an item that can be used as a weapon and thus the power to abuse them. Eventually, as children, the boys have no chance to escape him. This reflects the image of him that Neil and Chris remember from their childhood: an evil hypocrite who was scolding them for what they did wrong in the eyes of the Church.

Members of the family – analysing family bonds

The scenes in which the priest is leading the group of boys bear testimony to the fact that they had received a religious upbringing. In Chris's case, it also shows that religion is still a part of his adult life. His room in a boarding house has a cross on the wall.[71] Whether he is observant at this point remains unclear, but the owner of the boarding house, who seems rather matronly in the following scenes, *is* a Christian and includes the tenants in her practices as the breakfast scene shows.

In the dining room, next to Chris, there is a vicar, a family of three and a man called Dredge.[72] Dredge wears big fake ears, is constantly joking, laughing loudly, and uses tacky prank props on other guests who are annoyed by him, especially Chris. Nevertheless, Dredge seems confident as he never shies away from continuing his obnoxious behaviour even when other people are visibly annoyed. Since Chris is sitting, and he is standing, Dredge is positioned higher than Chris in almost every frame. This is symbolic of the way Dredge is looking down on Chris and at the same time how he is able to foreground himself because Chris does not speak up. Chris

---

[68]Pet Shop Boys, 'This Must Be the Place I Waited Years to Leave'.
[69]Pet Shop Boys, 'This Must Be the Place I Waited Years to Leave'.
[70]*It Couldn't Happen Here*, 00:21:53.
[71]*It Couldn't Happen Here*, 00:05:18.
[72]*It Couldn't Happen Here*, 00:06:28.

looks down the whole time and keeps quiet. Not only does Chris avoid eye contact, but he also has his back turned to the other guests. Apart from signalling his distance from them, this also serves a functional reason purpose as the array of tables allows everyone a good view of the landlady and her altar-like arrangement. She enters at 00:07:21 and places a comically large plate of eggs and bacon in front of Chris. Like all side characters in this film, the landlady is performed in an exaggerated and caricature-like fashion. She talks loudly and in an unnatural manner, and, just like her house, she looks extremely tacky and her mannerisms are overstated. Right after entering, she moves to the altar and turns on an illuminated picture of the Last Supper, which starts playing tinny organ music. She subsequently instructs everyone to rise. Even while standing, Chris does not raise his eyes and Dredge does not stop his flat joking. The landlady theatrically speaks an intercessory prayer during which she vigorously tells Dredge to 'Shut up.'[73] When the prayer is over, she again focuses her attention on Chris.

Although there is no indication that the landlady is his real mother, she acts motherly towards Chris. She calls him 'Chrissy darling',[74] wants to make sure he eats plenty and tells him how much she will miss him while hugging him. Chris certainly is her favourite guest, as she pays no attention at all to the vicar, is annoyed by Dredge, and rants about the upbringing of the family's child.[75] During her scolding of the child, the focus of the camera is on Chris, in a momentary eye-level shot, who remains expressionless, while the landlady rants in the background. He then gets up while organ music starts playing again. The landlady and Dredge both look at him, smile and laugh.[76] Next, he throws his breakfast at the landlady who is in shock and asks, 'Chrissy darling, what have I done to deserve this?'[77] After details of his religious upbringing are known, it is plausible that Chris kept his emotions in but is not particularly fond of the landlady's treatment.

Though the characters in this scene are not those of a traditional family, the behaviour of the landlady towards Chris allows their relationship to be classified as a familiar one. The whole scene as well as the setting can be described as exaggerated. It is colourful and tacky, like the decoration that is playing the organ music. The one exception to this is Chris himself, who is wearing a simple outfit including a black beanie and a black leather jacket and who does not speak at all – almost as if he does not want to attract attention. This can be considered as the coping mechanism of someone who presumes their identity will be rejected by the people around them.[78] It is

---

[73] *It Couldn't Happen Here*, 00:07:54.
[74] *It Couldn't Happen Here*, 00:08:12.
[75] *It Couldn't Happen Here*, 00:08:50.
[76] *It Couldn't Happen Here*, 00:09:20.
[77] *It Couldn't Happen Here*, 00:09:27.
[78] Ganzevoort, van der Laan and Olsman, 'Growing Up Gay and Religious', 209; Shore-Goss, 'Queering Jesus', 48.

furthermore a reversal of the stereotypical depictions of queer men in films at the time, who are themselves the colourful characters, act flamboyantly and so attract a lot of attention. In a way, the surrounding scene is visually even more queer-coded than Chris. By the subversion of that depiction the film makes a point: that this very lobsided stereotypical depiction of queerness does not fit every queer person. In this case it does not fit Chris. Very appropriately, just as the stereotypes do not represent the fictitious Chris, neither do they match the real-life Chris Lowe: the 'understated' Pet Shop Boys member, shying away from the attention garnered by his counterpart, and reflected in his style and also the Pet Shop Boys' stage performances.

Additionally, Chris's quietness, lack of eye contact and his position within the picture allow both the landlady and Dredge to look down on him, carrying with it the implication of superiority. However, since there is no suggestion that these characters are *actually* superior to Chris, be this in terms of morality or in terms of power, this most likely signals a superiority the characters ascribe to *themselves*, but also again the way they foreground themselves because of Chris's stoicism. Dredge and the landlady appear entitled in comparison, as they do not keep their beliefs, personalities or opinions to themselves, no matter if they are asked for them or not. In contrast to Chris, Dredge is loud and annoying to those around him. However, he does not seem to care and appears disproportionately self-confident. The scene highlights the difference between someone who was told frequently that their identity is unacceptable or sinful and someone who was not. There might be other reasons as well, but apparently, by keeping quiet and acting as she wishes him to (for example, by taking part in the prayer or keeping the cross on his wall), Chris won the landlady's favour. At the same time, he was visibly annoyed and uncomfortable. Eventually, his pent-up frustration gets released in a situation that unleashes turmoil around him. He then runs away, with the song 'It Couldn't Happen Here' playing,[79] leaving everything behind including his trunk. This is the beginning of his journey in the film, as he leaves behind surroundings that do him no good. Even though the landlady is most likely genuinely unaware what she has done 'to deserve this', knowing about Chris's upbringing it is reasonable to assume that he continued to suffer in these overwhelming, overbearing surroundings. To be unaware of his needs and boundaries, or to disregard them, makes the landlady appear even more entitled and overbearing.

Later in the film, Neil calls his mother from a phone box. The song from which the landlady quotes earlier – 'What Have I Done to Deserve This?' – depicts the dialogue between them. This is only one parallel between the landlady and Neil's mother. Neil's relationship with his mother is comparable

---

[79] *It Couldn't Happen Here*, 00:10:12.

to the relationship between Chris and the boarding-house landlady in some points. Fittingly, both women are portrayed by Barbara Windsor. In the past, Neil might have tried to put on a mask to win his mother's favour by fitting her idea of a good child. He sings 'I bought you drinks. I brought you flowers / I read you books and talked for hours'[80] and 'You always wanted me to be something I wasn't.'[81] During the phone call, no religious symbolism as such is featured. However, it can be put in a queer religious context and is relevant to an understanding of Neil's character. Furthermore, because of the surrealistic style of the film, it can also be considered a partner to the breakfast scene at the boarding house. Lastly, it was most likely both or one of his parents who consigned Neil to the care of the Church.

Despite the song 'What Have I Done to Deserve This?' also fitting the context of lovers, it can be interpreted differently in the context of the film. It describes the troubled relationship between an estranged son and his mother, who both address reproaches to each other. Keeping in mind that Neil received a religious upbringing, his mother might not have been especially delighted by the idea of having a gay son. The troubled mother–son relationship becomes apparent too when his mother sings the lines 'You went away, it should make me feel better'[82] and 'You always wanted too much.'[83] These lines reveal that she is not able to accept who he is and would prefer him to leave. He on the other hand does not understand what he did wrong to deserve his mother's rejection of him and his identity. At least, he did everything to please her as elaborated before. While Neil asks why he deserves this treatment, his mother asks, 'How am I gonna get through?'[84], an ambiguous line depending on the situation. On the one hand, she does not know how to 'get through' to her son, whose actions, feelings and identity she does not understand. On the other hand, she might be asking how she can go on with her life now that she knows about his sexual identity and that they have abandoned each other. When Neil hangs up in frustration, his head starts bleeding and the phone box starts spinning[85] – a visual expression of the emotional impact of the conversation.

While they are on the phone, Chris dances to the song 'What Have I Done to Deserve This?' in the sunset.[86] Dancing to the phone call between Neil and his mother means that there is a relatedness to the situation that evokes Chris's empathy. He might have had comparable experiences and thus, the call evokes his feelings which he expresses through dance. Furthermore, since he dances in front of a sunset, only his silhouette is visible and his face

---

[80] *It Couldn't Happen Here*, 00:59:05.
[81] *It Couldn't Happen Here*, 00:59:49.
[82] *It Couldn't Happen Here*, 00:59:33.
[83] *It Couldn't Happen Here*, 00:59:50.
[84] *It Couldn't Happen Here*, 00:01:10.
[85] *It Couldn't Happen Here*, 01:01:54.
[86] *It Couldn't Happen Here*, 01:00:20.

is unrecognizable. He could be replaced by any person, implying that this experience is similar to that of many queer children growing up in a conservative environment. Another indicator of the interchangeability of Neil and Chris's experiences is the already noted fact that Neil writes to his mother about scenes in which Chris is seen as if they are anecdotes from their family.

When the comic and the hostile go hand-in-hand – hypocrisy in other characters

When Neil is shopping for the postcards he is writing to his mother during the film, several supposedly humoristic but obscene cards, accentuating the breasts of women, are visible in a medium close-up.[87] In a voiceover, Neil comments, 'Comic postcards. Ever since I was a child, the comic and the hostile seemed to go hand-in-hand.'[88] On the one hand, this is a remark about the misogynistic postcard motifs, but it also depicts the experience of someone who grew up gay in a heterosexist society. First of all, the postcards are playing into a frivolous type of humour most likely enjoyed by older, heterosexual men. As a child, Neil would thus be expected to grow into finding these depictions humorous as well, but he did not. Secondly, gay men, and queer people in general, are oftentimes the butt of the joke applying the same sense of humour. Thus, Neil considers this type of humour hostile.

The person selling the postcards is called Dredge and is played by Gareth Hunt, just like Dredge from the boarding house. However, this Dredge – name and actor notwithstanding – is characterized in a completely different way and shows different mannerisms as well; like the landlady and Neil's mother, Dredge and Dredge are familiar but different.[89] Furthermore, he is displaying hypocrisy when deciding what is appropriate and what is not. Without paying much attention to Neil, he deluges the characters (and thus the audience) in a flood of words. He complains about the 'hooligans' and 'bike gangs' who in his eyes are swarming the beach in increasing numbers nowadays.[90] He also complains about politicians who are the worst in his opinion and that 'your decent English holiday-maker, they all go to Spain'.[91] At the same time, he exhibits morally questionable behaviour towards women. Besides the aforementioned postcards he is selling, he watches two naked women at the beach through binoculars,[92] and when the wind lifts the

---

[87] *It Couldn't Happen Here*, 00:02:36.
[88] *It Couldn't Happen Here*, 00:02:42.
[89] *It Couldn't Happen Here*, 00:10:59.
[90] *It Couldn't Happen Here*, 00:03:13.
[91] *It Couldn't Happen Here*, 00:03:22.
[92] *It Couldn't Happen Here*, 00:03:07.

skirt of a woman during his monologue, he watches, visibly affected.[93] In the background, 'Suburbia' is playing, a song that juxtaposes the presumed calm and sheltered suburbia with hooliganism.

Generally, Dredge the vendor complains about the moral decay of the society surrounding him, while not reflecting on his own reprehensible behaviour at all. Similar to the blind priest, he only pays attention to what he identifies as a problem while he considers himself morally superior. In general, the whole scene is a display of subjective moral superiority which is also a link to queer theological studies that criticize a straight, white, conservative Christianity which claims a superior position by the exclusion and even suppression of others.

Still healed, so far? Depicting queerness in a religious context

By applying a queer theological studies lens to the analysis of *It Couldn't Happen Here*, the viewer can immediately identify the characters that embody the discipline's central critique of white, conservative Christianity, namely that it ensures its supremacy by actively and selectively marginalizing certain minorities as 'deviant'.[94] It is clear that Dredge the vendor and the blind priest are not in any meaningful way morally superior to those they shame. Dredge is a voyeur and the priest turns out to be a lunatic, a murderer and almost certainly a paedophile. At the same time, he is either metaphorically or literally blind to sinful behaviours around him or within his own identity. The Gospel of Matthew's appeal to equity – 'And why beholdest thou the mote that is in thy brother's eye, but considerest not the beam that is in thine own eye?'[95] – appears to be fitting to describe both the priest and Dredge. Certainly, both characters should be considered hypocrites.

Another critique is focused on the abuse that makes children believe their identities are wrong and sinful, which can be a traumatic experience, requires identity strategies, and often leads to psychological and social consequences.[96] In the film, this is visualized by adding flashback scenes about Neil and Chris's religious upbringing. The consequences are expressed in the troubled relationship between Neil and his mother, in Chris's behaviour at the boarding house, and most saliently in the song 'It's a Sin'. To truly be himself, Neil had to leave his mother, who is not able to accept him as he is. To avoid

---

[93] *It Couldn't Happen Here*, 00:03:03.
[94] Shore-Goss, 'Queering Jesus', 47; Greenough, 'Queer Theory and the Bible', 2.
[95] Matthew 7.3 (KJV).
[96] Shore-Goss, 'Queering Jesus', 48; Ganzevoort, van der Laan and Olsman, 'Queer Theory and the Bible', 209–20.

ostracism at the boarding house, Chris keeps quiet and acts in a way that pleases the landlady. In 'It's a Sin' the internalized feeling of shame they are still struggling with as adults is described.

While the side characters are caricatures, and sometimes even portrayed by the same actors, there is a dichotomy between recurring characters. Even the priest, who supposedly is the same man he was in the flashback scenes, changes drastically from the man who raised the boys to the lunatic they encounter later. Nevertheless, all of the side-characters analysed in this chapter (the mother/landlady, both Dredges and the priest) are either conservatives, religious or at least take part in religious practices. Since all of these characters are exaggerated caricatures, I argue that the film presents every character as deviant to such an extent that, subsequently, there is no depiction of queer people as deviant or the Other to a straight, cis majority. If anything, Chris and Neil appear the most ordinary and reasonable of all the characters featured. This is a subversion of stereotypical film depictions of the time, in which queer people are depicted a little bit louder, a little bit more flamboyant or generally as the Other to a straight majority surrounding them. However, it does not change the fact that the minor characters mentioned in this analysis consider themselves either morally superior or at least the 'norm'. They seem confident and entitled in their actions and beliefs. However, they are also shown to assess their own action and the people around them inaccurately. Most of them lack basic self-awareness, such as the landlady, who believes she did nothing to provoke Chris's blaze of anger. However, contrary to what she might think, she did not provide a safe and familiar surrounding for Chris. Rather, she disregarded his needs and boundaries. Especially in the observation of religious beliefs and practices, it becomes apparent that some characters are not as righteous or pious as they first seem. The most salient example is the blind priest. But even if there are no certain conclusions about the religious background of some of the characters, their trust in their own ethos is presented as very dubious.

The critique of conservative Christianity found in *It Couldn't Happen Here* includes conflicts between religious beliefs and the identity of the main characters. Starting with the religious upbringing of Chris and Neil, the reflection on the consequences that this experience has had on their adult life and how it impacts their social bonds, and even the overall journey they had to undergo in search of a place where they could be themselves, is a representation and a reflection of the struggle of growing up queer under religious fundamentalism. This is what makes this type of journey a core motif in many queer narratives. Furthermore, minor characters who might be expected to act morally superior in a conservative understanding, or who are at least part of a majority, exhibit hypocritical opinions. Most of them lack self-awareness and almost all of them cause discomfort to the protagonists. This is supposed to highlight the unjust framing by conservative society and Christianity in which they present themselves superior to those who are deviant in their eyes. It shows how one interpretation of scripture which is utilized to uphold hegemony and justify the lifestyle of the privileged is at the same time harming those who are assigned special importance by different interpretations of the same scripture. Lastly, the film depicts the conflict that arises from growing up queer under the influence of religious fundamentalism and extensively criticizes certain religious practices. It highlights the shame some people still feel until adulthood and emphasizes the troubles that can result from such a background. Ultimately, *It Couldn't Happen Here* is a film about a journey the protagonists undertake to deal with these very troubles.

Bibliography

Afshar, Ahoura, 'The Anti-Gay Rights Movement in the United States: The Framing of Religion'. *Essex Human Rights Review* 3, no. 1 (2006): 64–79.

Buckland, Warren. 'Film semiotics'. In *A Companion to Film Theory*, 84–104. Oxford: Blackwell, 1995.

Burgess, Adam. 'The Development of Risk Politics in the UK: Thatcher's "Remarkable" but Forgotten "Don't Die of Ignorance" AIDS Campaign'. *Health, Risk & Society* 19, no. 5–6 (2017): 227–45.

Doty, Alexander and Ben Gove. 'Queer Representation in the Mass Media'. In Andy Medhurst and Sally Munt (eds), *Lesbian and Gay Studies: A Critical Introduction*, 84–9. London: Cassell, 1997.

Drüecke, Ricarda, Elisabeth Klaus and Anita Moser. 'Mediale Und Künstlerische Bild-Diskurse Zu Flucht Und Migration'. In Manfred Oberlechner, Trültzsch-Wijnen Christine W. and Patrick Duval (eds), *Migration Bildet*, 315–36. Baden- Baden: Nomos, 2017.

Dyer, Richard. *The Matter of Images: Essays on Representation*. London: Routledge, 1993.

Ganzevoort, Ruard R., Mark van der Laan and Erik Olsman. 'Growing up Gay and Religious: Conflict, Dialogue, and Religious Identity Strategies'. *Mental Health, Religion & Culture* 14, no. 3 (2011): 209–22.

Gökçearslan, Armağan. 'The Effect of Cartoon Movies on Children's Gender Development'. *Procedia – Social and Behavioral Sciences* 2, no. 2 (2010): 5202–7, https://doi.org/10.1016/j.sbspro.2010.03.846.

Gover, Daniel. 'Christian Interest Groups in a Religiously Changing United Kingdom: Issues, Strategies, Influence'. *Politics and Religion* 15, no. 3 (2022): 462–84, https://doi.org/10.1017/s1755048321000274.

Greenough, Chris. 'Editorial: Queer Theory and the Bible'. *Journal for Interdisciplinary Biblical Studies* 2, no. 2 (2021): 1–4.

Jenkins, Tricia. '"Potential Lesbians at Two O'clock": The Heterosexualization of Lesbianism in the Recent Teen Film'. *Journal of Popular Culture* 38, no. 3 (2005): 491–504, https://doi.org/10.1111/j.0022-3840.2005.00125.x.

Kim, Koeun. 'Queer-coded Villains (And Why You Should Care)'. *Dialogues@ RU* (2007): 156–65.

Moore, Will. 'A Godly Man and a Manly God: Resolving the Tension of Divine Masculinities in the Bible'. *Journal for Interdisciplinary Biblical Studies* 2, no. 2 (2021): 71–94.

Pendergast, Martin. 'HIV in Britain 1982–1990: The Christian Reaction'. *New Blackfriars* 71, no. 840 (1990): 347–54.

Russo, Vito. *The Celluloid Closet*. New York: Harper & Row, 1981.

Schippert, Claudia. 'Implications of Queer Theory for the Study of Religion and Gender: Entering the Third Decade'. *Religion and Gender* 1, no. 1 (2011): 66, https://doi.org/10.18352/rg.8.

Shore-Goss, Robert E. 'Queering Jesus: LGBTQI Dangerous Remembering and Imaginative Resistance'. *Journal for Interdisciplinary Biblical Studies* 2, no. 2. (2021): 47–70.

Tennant, Neil and Chris Lowe. *It Couldn't Happen Here*. Directed by Jack Bond. United Kingdom: Parlophone Records, 1988.

Thiem, Annika. 'The Art of Queer Rejections: The Everyday Life of Biblical Discourse'. *Neotestamentica* 48, no. 1 (2014): 33–56.

Vorster, Johannes N. 'The Queering of Biblical Discourse'. *Scriptura* 111, no. 1 (2012), https://doi.org/10.7833/111-1-39.

Wallach Scott, Joan. *Gender and the Politics of History*. New York: Columbia University Press, 1988.

CHAPTER TEN

What Have I Done to Deserve This?

Personal, Professional and Political Representations in *Smash Hits* during the 'Imperial Phase' (1986–8)

Lexi Webster

Introduction

Neil Tennant coined the phrase 'imperial phase' with reference only to the run of success the duo had between the release of 'It's a Sin' and 'Heart' from their second studio album, *Actually*.[1] The phrase's meaning has since been codified by its (re)use, referring to an artist's simultaneous commercial and creative peak. Whilst I recognize Tennant's perspective, this chapter reconsiders Pet Shop Boys' imperial phase through the lens of an expanded understanding of the concept. I draw from Tom Ewing's essay for *Pitchfork*, in which he expands upon a tripartite conceptualization of an *imperial phase* as comprising 'command, permission, and self-definition'.[2] In so doing, I include in my understanding of

---

[1] Chris Heath, 'Pet Shop Boys 1987–1988', *Actually remastered* (booklet) (Parlophone, 2001).
[2] Tom Ewing, 'Imperial', *Pitchfork*, 28 May 2010, https://pitchfork.com/features/poptimist/7811-poptimist-29/.

Pet Shop Boys' imperial phase the year prior to *Actually*'s release, which saw the second release of 'West End Girls' reach number 1 in the UK and the USA, and the release of their first studio album (*Please*). The year 1986 was also the first in which Tennant fully committed to a career in music, having quit his position as Assistant Editor of *Smash Hits* magazine in 1985. As such, I contextualize my extended understanding of Pet Shop Boys' imperial phase as comprising the years 1986 through 1988 with explicit relation to this chapter's examination of their representation in *Smash Hits* magazine during that time. I contend that it is specifically *Smash Hits* magazine that enabled Pet Shop Boys' capacity for command, permission and self-definition during an imperial phase of discursive representation in pop culture journalism. This chapter therefore examines how this phase defined Pet Shop Boys as a successful exercise in constructing a career and character typified by a contrarian and ambivalent personal, professional and political positioning vis-à-vis social class, celebrity and Thatcherite neoliberalism.

Ambivalence, the imperial phase and *Smash Hits* magazine

Arguing the role of ambivalence and contrarianism in Pet Shop Boys' personae and work is not a unique thesis in and of itself. Indeed, my examination of the duo's constructed personae draws from existing work that engages with the same notions. For example, Maus explicitly tackles the ubiquity of ambivalence – or 'setting out an opposition, along with an unclear or undecidable relation between the terms of the opposition' – in Pet Shop Boys' music.[3] Specifically, Maus argues the duo's purposeful construction of contrast and conflict in their songs' lyrical text worlds and their musical composition, and in the political-professional positioning of the duo as role models of an alternative masculinity and of a queered authenticity. This reading of purposeful ambivalence brings to bear the role of Ewing's notion of *self-definition* in the making of an artist's imperial phase.[4] However, self-definition alone is not enough to determine the temporality of an imperial phase. More recently, Hills and Wodtke have also explored the role of contrast and conflict in the Pet Shop Boys' career, highlighting practices aligned with *permission* and *command*.[5] For example,

---

[3] Fred E. Maus, 'Glamour and evasion: the fabulous ambivalence of the Pet Shop Boys', *Popular Music* 20, no.3 (2001): 386, doi: 10.1017/S0261143001001568.

[4] Ewing, 'Imperial'.

[5] Matt Hills, 'When the Pet Shop Boys were "imperial": Fans' self-ageing and the neoliberal life course of "successful" text-ageing', *Journal of Fandom Studies* 7, no. 2 (2019): 151–67, doi: 10.1386/jfs.7.2.151_1; Larissa Wodtke, 'The irony and the ecstasy: The queer aging of Pet Shop Boys and LCD Soundsystem in Electronic Dance Music', *Dancecult: Journal of Electronic Dance Music Culture* 11, no.1 (2019): 30–52, doi: 10.12801/1947-5403.2019.11.01.03.

Hills examines competing understandings – between fans and artists – of the Pet Shop Boys' imperial phase of commercial *and creative* success borne from the duality between fans' aging and the aging of artistic outputs-as-texts.[6] Wodtke also considers the role of age, focusing on how Tennant's age gives the duo a 'belated, knowing position', enabling them to construct 'a queer [and ironic] tension between notions of immediate authenticity and the distance of age' in a genre that privileges youth.[7] The excitement and goodwill from a committed fanbase, wherein success is not merely counted in chart positioning but in creative output, evokes the *permission* of Ewing's conceptualization of an imperial phase. Indeed, this success, enabling an artist not only to take a knowing position in a genre but to purposefully construct ironic tension from the conflict between this knowing success and the genre's expectations is tantamount to *command*.[8] Ewing specifically cites Tennant's radio interview, in which the latter explicitly states that he 'felt at the time [of releasing *Actually*] we had the secret of contemporary pop music'.[9] These understandings from extant literature indicate that duality – in the form of purposeful ambivalence, contrast and/or contrarianism – directly underpins the Pet Shop Boys' career and character in their command of a genre, their permission from interested audiences and the self-definition of their artistic identity. This chapter contributes to an understanding of how contrarianism, conflict and ambivalence are manifested in the representation of the duo *beyond* song and in discourses of pop culture journalism. However, here I focus on how command, permission and self-definition coincide in one temporal span – what I refer to as the *imperial phase of their discursive representation*.

Smash Hits magazine in the years 1986 through 1988 represents a unique discursive environment within which to study the manifestation of Pet Shop Boys' command, permission and self-definition. The knowledge of pop music that Tennant alludes to having as they entered their imperial phase can in no small part be attributed to his time at *Smash Hits*, where he worked as a journalist, news editor and – ultimately – assistant editor of the magazine.[10] The duo's *command* of pop music in time for the successes of the single 'West End Girls' – which reached number 1 in the UK and the USA in 1986 – and the release of their second studio album – in 1987 – might arguably be deeply embedded in the simultaneous contrast and complementarity between the roles of pop culture journalist and popstar that had manifested in Tennant's career before 1986. This professional positioning may also have contributed to the *permission* the Pet Shop Boys were granted and to have enabled the conditions for their controlled *self-*

---

[6]Hills, 'When the Pet Shop Boys were "imperial"', *passim*.
[7]Wodtke, 'The irony and the ecstasy', 30.
[8]Ewing, 'Imperial'.
[9]Ewing, 'Imperial'; Heath, 'Pet Shop Boys 1987–1988'.
[10]Heath, 'Pet Shop Boys 1987–1988'.

definition during the height of their commercial success. That is, the potentially nepotistic relationship contracted between Tennant and *Smash Hits* following his tenure at the magazine could account for heightened interest and goodwill shown to the Pet Shop Boys by the publication and enabled the duo to control – whether implicitly or explicitly – their representations therein. Indeed, the (relative) decline of success the duo experienced after 1988 may well also be connected to the natural dilution of this relationship over time. The ever-changing rules and fast-paced nature of pop music – especially in the 1980s – may have rendered Tennant's command of pop music passé without the insider knowledge that comes with being an assistant editor for one of the UK's major pop culture publications. Similarly, the further Tennant (and Pet Shop Boys) drifted towards pop stardom and away from music journalism, the less the permission of interest and goodwill may have been extended by *Smash Hits* and, by extension, the more constrained the possibilities may have become for the duo's control over their self-definition in the publication. I argue, then, that issues of *Smash Hits* published in 1986, 1987 and 1988 represent an *imperial phase*. This imperial phase relates specifically to Pet Shop Boys' discursive representation in pop culture journalism beyond song, in which they establish, by themselves and along with others, both a career and character that encapsulate a career and character of contrarianism, contradiction and ambivalence.

Methods: data, discourse and critique

The data relied on in this study were sourced from the seventy-nine issues of *Smash Hits* magazine published throughout 1986, 1987 and 1988. Using optical character recognition, all mentions of Pet Shop Boys, Neil Tennant and/or Chris Lowe were identified across a digitized collection of published issues. Each piece within which there was a mention of the duo (or either of the two as individuals) was extracted in its entirety to form the final dataset, which comprised 410 contributions and included – *inter alia* – artist interviews, album and single reviews, fan letters, posters and puzzles. The dataset included both self-representations and representations of the duo by others. The duo's self-representations offer explicit insight into the strategies they used to construct their own personal and professional identities. How they are represented by others offers insight into both their success and the 'interest, excitement, and goodwill towards [their] work'.[11] I therefore argue that the inclusion of both self- and other representations is an ideal mechanism for identifying how (far) Pet Shop Boys' *self-definition* and *command* during their imperial phase are granted *permission* from others in the pop music industry, including journalists and fellow pop stars. This

---

[11] Ewing, 'Imperial'.

chapter focuses primarily on data gleaned from interviews with the duo, though the analysis is supplemented by other contributions in the dataset.

I examine the data using a socio-cognitive approach to critical discourse studies.[12] In so doing, I refer to these representations as comprising discourse(s) – or, 'ways of being in the world' – that reflect how individuals and communities understand and construct their own social position in relation to others.[13] I contend that this approach is particularly appropriate for analysing how Pet Shop Boys are positioned – by themselves and others – during an imperial phase of pop culture representation. It is therefore also important to note that these discourses are manifested in texts (of any mode), constrained by processes of those texts' production and distribution, and embedded in wider political-economic structures.[14] As such, I refer specifically to the role *Smash Hits* plays in selecting, editing and, ultimately, platforming the representations of Pet Shop Boys by themselves and by others. I also rely on understandings of the political economy of celebrity and Thatcherite neoliberalism in 1980s Britain to offer potential explanations for both text and discursive practices.

In performing this socio-cognitive analysis, I focus primarily on three key features of discursive representation: (1) representations of *identity*; (2) representations of *activity*; and (3) strategies for legitimizing such representations.[15] I also refer explicitly to the discursive practices (e.g., processes relating to *Smash Hit*'s distribution, production and consumption) and social factors (e.g., the political economies of celebrity, pop music and [inter]national contexts) that afford, constrain or otherwise influence these representations.[16] The ultimate goal of any approach to critical discourse studies is *critique*, or to mount a challenge to social inequalities as they are manifested in ideology and discourse. This chapter does exactly that, arguing that representations of the Pet Shop Boys in *Smash Hits* magazine comprise both (re)productions of and resistance to social inequalities inherent in the political economies of celebrity, social class and (pop) culture at the height of their success. I contend that the ways in which Pet Shop Boys simultaneously reproduce and resist dominant social power relations in their imperial phase of pop culture representation reflects a discursively constructed career and character typified by ambivalence, contrarianism and contradiction.

---

[12] Teun A. Van Dijk, 'Critical discourse studies: A sociocognitive approach', in Ruth Wodak and Michael Meyer (eds), *Methods for Critical Discourse Analysis* (London: SAGE, 2009), 62–85.
[13] James Paul Gee, *Social Linguistics and Literacies: Ideology in Discourses*, 4th edn (London: Routledge, 2012), 152; Susan T. Fiske and Shelley E. Taylor, *Social Cognition*, 2nd edn (New York: McGraw-Hill, 1991).
[14] Norman Fairclough, *Critical Discourse Studies* (London: Longman, 1995).
[15] Majid KhosraviNik, 'Actor-descriptions, action attributions, and argumentation: Towards a systematization of CDA analytical categories in the representation of social groups', *Critical Discourse Studies* 7, no.1 (2010): 55- 72, doi: 10.1080/17405900903453948.
[16] Veronika Koller, 'How to analyse collective identity in discourse: Textual and contextual parameters', *Critical Approaches to Discourse Analysis Across Disciplines* 5, no. 2 (2012): 19–38.

'*I* still go to the launderette': social class and personal circumstances

Unsurprisingly, personal representations of Tennant and Lowe come primarily in the form of self-representations during interviews, comprising stories and histories of their youth, family and current circumstances. Of course, the journalistic discourse surrounding the interviews also constructs personal representations from the perspective of the interviewer and, while these representations are far less substantial, they do supplement the duo's self-representations. I argue that personal representations of the Pet Shop Boys in *Smash Hits* magazine reflect purposeful contrasts between the pair. In this section, I focus on the contrasts constructed in relation to the Tennant and Lowe's *implied* differential positioning in relation to their social class.

The framing of both Tennant's and Lowe's identity is highlighted with both implicit and explicit reference to their socio-economic status. Tennant explicitly identifies himself as '[coming] from an ordinary middle-class family' and being 'a bit upset' when he was called 'poshie' by his grammar school classmates.[17] On the other hand, Lowe's social class positioning is only ever implicitly constructed. In fact, Lowe explicitly engages in *class dis-identification*, wherein he invokes the rhetoric of class politics to distinguish 'working class people' from 'posh people' (rather than *middle class*, for instance) and to distinguish the concept of 'posh' from the concept of being 'snooty'.[18] Both Tennant and Lowe share a disavowal of 'poshness', with Tennant citing personal experience of the denigration that Lowe refers to more generally. However, Lowe's explicit self-positioning as *not being posh*, in combination with his framing of direct opposition between so-called 'posh' and 'working class' people, constructs an implicit self-positioning of himself within the latter social category. The contrasts created in these self-representations reflect not only an apparent difference in their self-positioning within social categories of class, but also a difference in their approaches to identity. That is, Tennant offers more explicit strategies of personal identification, whereas Lowe favours implicit and abstract narratives to align himself with ways of being in the world.

Contrasts between the pair's class positioning are also made implicitly with reference to their starkly different taste in living arrangements. For example, in 1986 Tennant described Lowe's flat as 'not a very nice [one]', explaining that 'it overlooks a building site' and implying – by mentioning

---

[17] 'Personal File: Neil Tennant – Pet Shop Boys', *Smash Hits*, 15–28 January 1986.
[18] Aaron Reeves, Emily Gilbert and Daniel Holman, 'Class dis-identification, cultural stereotypes, and music preferences: Experimental evidence from the UK', *Poetics* 50 (2015): 44–61, doi: 10.1016/j.poetic.2015.01.002; Chris Heath, 'Pet Shop Boys: What does it take to make these men happy?', *Smash Hits*, 26 February–11 March 1986, 45.
[19] Heath, 'Pet Shop Boys: What does it take to make these men happy?', 45.

only these items and nothing else – that it contains only 'amazing '60s foam rubber chairs [...] a futon, a black and white television and a record player'.[19] In the same interview, Lowe described Tennant's studio flat in Chelsea – the location is explicitly named in parentheses, assumedly by the author of the piece, following Lowe's naming of the road only – as having 'a really good view', that 'the best thing about it is that he's got a water heater and central heating', and that there are 'horribly uncomfortable chairs', which he explains is because the flat is rented.[20] In later interviews, Tennant called Lowe's flat 'depressing' and 'vile'.[21] Lowe agreed with Tennant's assessment of his flat as vile and adds comments on his own curtains as 'disgusting', giving the reasoning once again that this is because the flat is rented.[22] The contrast constructed between Tennant's flat, with its nice view and mod cons of central heating, and Lowe's hovel at the beginning of their careers in pop stardom reasserts their differential class positioning. By the time this 1987 interview, though, each had bought or was in the process of buying his own flat, and there is a surprising revelation that Lowe's new flat is more expensive than Tennant's. However, this does not impinge on Lowe's implied working-class credentials, with him insisting '*I* still go to the launderette' when Tennant gushes about his new washing machine.[23] The emphasis on the first-person pronoun *I*, in combination with the adverb *still*, reinforces the difference between the class-connoting activities the pair engage in currently and have engaged in historically. I argue that these contrasts are purposeful in their representation of Lowe and Tennant's class identities, constructing the pair as foils for one another. Indeed, there also appears to be a consensual reification of this differential positioning of the pair by various journalists and authors of pieces in *Smash Hits* magazine, who variably refer to Tennant and his activities as 'a snoot', 'snooty' or 'swank' throughout the years studied in this chapter.

The evocation by the Pet Shop Boys of the cultural politics of class reflects an awareness of 'how the social value of the self is assessed' in the context of UK pop music.[24] That is, the duo's *self-definition* as positioned within – or beyond, as Lowe claims – a given social class also reflects a *command* of the context within which they are embedded.[25] The two construct their identities in relation to the cultural politics of class in 1980s Britain, reflecting as a duo an ambivalent position that both decries social class distinctions between *posh* and *not* whilst simultaneously reifying practices of *snootiness*

---

[20]Heath, 'Pet Shop Boys: What does it take to make these men happy?', 45
[21]Tom Hibbert, 'And a rather good LP it is, too!', *Smash Hits*, 9 September–22 September 1987, 47; Vici McDonald, 'The Pet Shop Boys: Tips for modern living', *Smash Hits*, 12–25 August 1987, 16.
[22]McDonald, 'The Pet Shop Boys: Tips for modern living', 17.
[23]McDonald, 'The Pet Shop Boys: Tips for modern living', 16.
[24]Reeves, Gilbert, and Holman, 'Class dis-identification', 46.
[25]Ewing, 'Imperial'.

and *swank*. Indeed, the reification of this positioning by *Smash Hits* is also representative of the *permission* granted by the publication to contribute to this knowing self-identification. At a time of rising class tensions under Thatcher's premiership and the simultaneous rise of celebrity power, these personal representations serve to both reproduce and resist social inequities of the time.[26]

'We don't want to be pathetic pop stars': celebrity and professional positioning

As with personal representations of class identity, professional representations of the Pet Shop Boys reflect a tension for the duo within the political economy of celebrity. However, unlike the primarily self-focused representations of the personal, these representations of professional positioning within celebrity and pop culture are multidirectional. That is, tensions and in/consistencies are constructed within and between the Pet Shop Boys' self-representations, their representations of others in the world of celebrity, and others' representations of them. I argue in this section that the Pet Shop Boys construct an ambivalent and contrarian positioning to the identity and activities associated with fame and celebrity status. Moreover, though, I argue that this position is also consensually taken up by others in their representation of the Pet Shop Boys. I focus here, then, on both the professional positioning of the duo vis-à-vis the political economy of celebrity *and* the social positioning of the pair in relation to others in the fame game.

The pair rely on an ironic ambivalence to position themselves simultaneously within and beyond the identity of celebrity and pop stardom. On the one hand, Tennant repeatedly constructs an explicit opposition between the pair and other pop stars. In 1987, Tennant explained that '[they] won't speak to any of the press, because [they] don't want to be pathetic pop stars who've always got their cheesy faces everywhere'.[27] Similarly, in 1988, he positioned himself and Chris as 'normal' in opposition to 'all these pop stars being mad all the time'.[28] On the other hand, however, the pair also consistently highlighted their fame and success. For example, in the same 1987 interview, the pair highlighted how they had been made – and refused

---

[26]Simon Frith and Jon Savage, 'Pearls and Swine: The intellectuals and the mass media', in Steve Redhead, Derek Wynne and Justin O'Connor (eds), *The Clubcultures Reader: Readings in Popular Cultural Studies* (Oxford: Blackwell, 1998), 7–17; Tania Lewis, 'Branding, celebritization and the lifestyle expert', *Cultural Studies* 24, no. 4 (2010): 580–98, doi: 10.1080/09502386.2010.488406. For more on Thatcherism and the Pet Shop Boys' relationship to Conservative neoliberalism, see both Jonathan Dean's and Stephanie Polsky's chapters in this volume.
[27]McDonald, 'The Pet Shop Boys: Tips for modern living', 15
[28]Sylvia Patterson, 'Pet Shop Boys: A demented duo', *Smash Hits*, 7–20 September 1998, 38.

– offers to include their music in soft drinks commercials and movies by major Hollywood directors for one reason or another.[29] Similarly in 1988, they jokingly referred to using the fact that 'Madonna's a big fan' to impress people.[30] This notion of growing fame and success is reflected in *Smash Hits*' representations of the pair. The two go from 'quite famous' in 1986, to Tennant being an 'actually [...] famous pop star' in 1987, and the pair being 'rich and famous' in 1988.[31] The braggadocio the pair engage in around their own fame and the representation of this fame by *Smash Hits* as a publication arguably reflect *command* and *permission*, respectively. However, by assuming an identity of simultaneous stardom and normalcy, there is constructed a purposeful ironic tension in the pair's professional positioning.

The two also critique others for their actions in the name of celebrity. On the more trivial end of the spectrum, they make subtle and not-so-subtle jabs at others' self-indulgence in their fame. For example, Lowe ridicules Boy George for decorating his house with pictures of himself and Tennant immediately explains that his own gold discs 'all sit in the cupboard under the kitchen sink!'[32] A distinction is drawn between the self-indulgence of Boy George and the success of the Pet Shop Boys, constructing a contrast in Tennant's perception of the two's *command* of pop stardom, whilst maintaining a discourse of normalcy for the duo. Similarly, Five Star were the group of 'mad [...] children' with equally mad 'lifestyles' that were mentioned before Tennant's explicit description of himself and Lowe as 'so normal'.[33] Again, there is a distinction drawn between the outcomes of celebrity, where Five Star represent those driven to lifestyles of excess and the Pet Shop Boys those who retain their pre-celebrity identity as 'normal' people. Whilst these distinctions appear inconsequential, the explicit opposition between the Pet Shop Boys and other artists has also led to more serious ramifications, with the power of celebrity being used both explicitly and implicitly in discursive combat. One example is when Jonathan King – disgraced record producer famed for producing the 1965 classic 'Everyone's Gone to the Moon', discovering the band Genesis, and multiple counts of indecent assault for which he was convicted in 2001 – argued that Pet Shop Boys' 'It's A Sin' was so similar to Cat Stevens' 'Wild World' that he recorded his own version of the latter, 'carefully ripping off the arrangement of "It's A Sin" to make the verses sound as similar as possible' and demonstrate the

---

[29]McDonald, 'The Pet Shop Boys: Tips for modern living'.
[30]Suzan Colon, 'What would you say to a dead cockroach?', *Smash Hits*, 10–23 February 1988, 12.
[31]'Bitz', *Smash Hits*, 23 April–6 May 1986, 4–9; Heath, 'Pet Shop Boys: What does it take to make these men happy?', *passim*; '"Quite Good" Pop Book Shock!', *Smash Hits*, 19 October–1 November 1988, 36.
[32]McDonald, 'The Pet Shop Boys: Tips for modern living', 16.
[33]Patterson, 'Pet Shop Boys: A demented duo', 38.

two songs' similarity.[34] King had form for outlandish criticisms, particularly of BBC outputs, and of being sued in response.[35] The Pet Shop Boys implicitly invoked the functions and features of pop stardom – namely, copyright law surrounding their artistic outputs as musicians – to sue King. In response, King explicitly invoked the power of celebrity, and was quoted as stating that 'if [the case ever goes to court] I'm sure I could find 30 or 40 major celebrities to say they think the songs are similar'.[36] Note that he mentioned 'major celebrities' and not 'musicians' or 'artists'. This is arguably the madness and self-indulgence of celebrity to which the Pet Shop Boys construct their *self-definition* of being in direct opposition. Indeed, all of King's apparent showbiz capital did not, inevitably, lend itself to success in this legal squabble. Ultimately, he settled with the Pet Shop Boys out of court.

On a more extreme level, Tennant blames the power of celebrity on some of society's ills. For example, when asked his opinion on nuclear disarmament, he states that '[he thinks] Sylvester Stallone is more responsible for [the US bombing of Libya] than Ronald Reagan because he's created a climate in America that makes people think in those terms'.[37] Implicitly invoking the role of hegemony in generating and maintaining dominant ways of thinking, Tennant directly critiques the highly influential power of celebrity capital, which he indicates can have in/direct impacts as far-reaching as geopolitics and warfare.[38] In so doing, Tennant engages in an ideological resistance to the political economy of celebrity. This appears to be in direct contradiction to the duo's engagement with the more positive outcomes of celebrity, including commercial success and social recognition. However, the apparent ambivalence in Pet Shop Boys' representation of their own and others' celebrity is arguably representative of their conceptual distinction between celebrity as a *feature* of pop stardom – or, an identity – and celebrity as a *function* of the same – or, an activity. In other words, it is not fame that is the problem, but what is done with it. Indeed, this 'detached and ambivalent approach' to celebrity continues in the digital age of the twenty-first century in relation to their use – or not – of social media.[39] These themes are also reflected in recent musical outputs, namely the *Agenda* EP, which includes tracks like 'On Social Media' and 'What Are We Going to Do About the Rich?' I therefore argue that their ambivalent professional positioning in relation to celebrity constitutes a carefully crafted reproduction and resistance of celebrity and the capital that comes with it.

---

[34]'How the stars voted', *Smash Hits*, 16–29 December 1987, 7.
[35]Janet Street-Porter, 'Editor-At-Large: He lured boys. He's a bully. Now he bleats', *Independent*, 3 April 2005.
[36]'How the stars voted', 7.
[37]'Bitz', 31.
[38]Antonio Gramsci, *Selections from the Prison Notebooks*, trans./eds. Quintin Hoare and Geoffrey Nowell-Smith (London: Lawrence & Wishart, 1971).
[39]Nick Levine, 'Why Pet Shop Boys are still the cleverest men in pop', *BBC Culture*, 21 January 2020.

'I hate the whole idea of the City': Thatcherite neoliberalism and political commentary

In addition to vilifying the potential influence of celebrity capital, Tennant (and, to a lesser – or at least less frequent – extent, Lowe) is not at all shy in extending his acerbic commentary to other political matters, including how the monarchy 'holds Britain back' and how Thatcherite neoliberalism has led only to rampant consumerism and the decimation of nationalized industries.[40] These criticisms appear to be motivated by the negative impact of wealth inequality on political and social life. As such, the representations of others in Pet Shop Boys' political commentary reflect an apparent contradiction in their perception of wealth. As with the power that comes with celebrity, there are tensions constructed in the Pet Shop Boys' views of wealth inequality and their own wealth as a consequence of their commercial success.

As with the self-indulgence of celebrity, Tennant critiques the accumulation of money in excess. For example, when imagining being stuck in a lift with Princess Diana, he explains how he 'could have a chat with [her] about whether she deserves the ludicrous amount of money she gets' before they would 'decide she doesn't'.[41] In the very same interview, he ironically imagines a future wherein 'The Pet Shop Boys will carry on', but that Tennant and Lowe will not perform, only 'make the records [...] and make *lots* of money'.[42] A year later, Tennant explained how he missed his work in the *Smash Hits* office before pop stardom, including 'the trying to get paid more money'.[43] In the same year, the pair explained that their planned tour was cancelled because of its cost, with Lowe elaborating that '[he didn't] mind breaking even' but that it would be a 'waste of money' to lose 'thousands of pounds on this tour which [he] wasn't even enjoying'.[44] The contrasts between Diana's and the duo's accumulation of wealth are predicated on both explicit and implicit references to *moral desert*, or the notion that 'someone [...] deserves something [...] in virtue of [their possession of some feature]'.[45] In this case, the feature that warrants the moral desert of wealth accumulation appears to be engagement in hard work, or a work ethic. That is, there is constructed a distinction between those who *work* for their wealth (i.e., Tennant and Lowe) and those who do not (i.e. Princess Diana).

---

[40]'Should we scrap the royal family?', *Smash Hits*, 16–29 July 1986, 48; Hibbert, 'And a rather good LP it is, too!', 46.
[41]'Personal File: Neil Tennant – Pet Shop Boys', 14.
[42]'Personal File: Neil Tennant – Pet Shop Boys', 14.
[43]Heath, 'Pet Shop Boys 1987–1988', 31.
[44]McDonald, 'The Pet Shop Boys: Tips for modern living', 15.
[45]Fred Feldman and Brad Skow, 'Desert', in Edward N. Zalta (ed.), *The Stanford Encyclopedia of Philosophy* (Winter 2020 Edition), https://plato.stanford.edu/archives/win2020/entries/desert/.

This enables Tennant and Lowe to enjoy, and oftentimes flaunt, their success and concomitant wealth as deserved outcomes of their artistic endeavours. In doing so, the pair resist socio-historical legacies pertaining to the deserving and undeserving poor, reframing these discourses to highlight the role of desert, and lack thereof, in wealth accumulation as a critique of elite structures of inherited, undeserved, wealth.

In their *self-definition* as being deserving of wealth through work, Tennant and Lowe again position themselves in alignment with the average person. This is both reinforced and challenged by their critique of 1980s Thatcherite neoliberalism, including its associated individualism, wealth inequalities and restricted government spending on national infrastructure. This critique is never more explicit than in the duo's discussion with Tim Hibbert of the ideas and stories underpinning each of the songs on the *Actually* album.[46] In this interview, Tennant (who provides a far more substantial contribution than his counterpart on most matters political) uses social positioning vis-à-vis others to construe a critique of Thatcher's Britain. For example, he explains that the song 'Shopping' is 'about the nationalized industries being sold off' and that he sings from the perspective of 'the people in the City'.[47] Indeed, he explicitly positions himself *against* 'these vile, non-productive yuppie Sloane Ranger types' – an insult that is also levelled at Princess Diana in the earlier 1986 interview.[48] In his description of 'It Couldn't Happen Here', Tennant positions himself against the paradigmatic 'people' of Britain, who have lost their collective spirit of 'helping each other' since the Second World War.[49] Finally, he aligns himself with 'everyone' in detailing the focus of 'King's Cross' on waiting, including 'waiting for things to get better' and 'waiting in the dole office'.[50] Again, these differential positionings of the pair in relation to social groups variably comprising the self and the other is reflective of their awareness of the cultural politics of class in 1980s Britain. Indeed, Tennant's reference to Margaret Thatcher as the 'Most Very Horrible Thing' in 1987 and putting her son, Mark, in the same category in 1986 also indicate an awareness of articulating party-political positions in audience-friendly formats.[51] The *self-definition* of Tennant – and, by extension, the Pet Shop Boys – as distinctly anti-Thatcher and anti-Thatcherism arguably demonstrates his *command* of pop stardom, pop journalism and (pop) politics.

The political positioning of the Pet Shop Boys is an extension of their personal positioning in relation to class consciousness and their professional positioning as critical of (the misuse of) celebrity capital. That is, their

---

[46]Hibbert, 'And a rather good LP it is, too!', 46.
[47]Hibbert, 'And a rather good LP it is, too!', 46.
[48]Hibbert, 'And a rather good LP it is, too!'; 'Personal File: Neil Tennant – Pet Shop Boys'.
[49]Hibbert, 'And a rather good LP it is, too!', 46.
[50]Hibbert, 'And a rather good LP it is, too!', 47.
[51]'How the stars voted', 65; 'Pop Stars – they speak!!', *Smash Hits*, 16–19 December-1986, 48–51.

political commentary reflects an ideological resistance to the enforced cultural politics of class, the potentially damaging influence of excess capital in all forms and the neoliberal political-economic context of state-enabled inequality. However, their focus on the deservedness of pay through work and the contextualization of worth through social productivity – which they use to position themselves against both royalty and City 'yuppies' – also serve to reproduce the neoliberal principles that underpinned Thatcherism.[52] As such, they again construct an ambivalence – whether knowingly or not – towards the political-economic structures that defined 1980s Britain.

Conclusion: 'the secret is not to wear whatever you're meant to wear'

The ambivalent, contradictory and contrarian position taken up by the Pet Shop Boys, and consented to by others in their discursive representation of them, can best be encapsulated by a quote from Chris Lowe in 1988: 'The secret is not to wear whatever you're meant to wear [...] Be non-conformist.'[53] Whilst Lowe was talking about fashion and not wearing dinner jackets to awards ceremonies, this phrase – in his own words – 'just about sums [them] up'.[54] That is, the imperial phase of the pair's discursive representation in *Smash Hits* is typified by contradiction, contrarianism and ambivalence personally, professionally and politically.

I contend that Pet Shop Boys' self-definition, command and permission during this imperial phase extended much further than the local context of pop music. Their self-definition as *people* – rather than as artists – deserving of the fame and fortune that follows commercial success is reliant on positioning themselves (1) in alignment with the ordinary person who deserves reward for honest work; and (2) in direct opposition to non-productive members of society, including royalty and City types. Their knowledge of the contexts within which their character and career are embedded – including the enforced cultural politics of social class, the negative potential of celebrity power and the sweeping political-economic inequalities of Thatcherite neoliberalism – demonstrates a command of the growing role that (pop) culture has played in influencing personal and political experiences of the time. Finally, their ongoing creative and commercial success throughout this time established the permission required to articulate their self-definition and command within the pop music industry (and beyond). This imperial phase of representation in *Smash Hits*

---

[52]Bob Jessop et al., 'Authoritarian populism, two nations, and Thatcherism', *New Left Review* 147 (1984): 32–60.
[53]'The BPI Awards', *Smash Hits*, 24 February–8 March 1988, 41.
[54]'The BPI Awards', 41.

magazine saw the pair simultaneously (re)produce and resist hegemonic discourses of celebrity, class consciousness and Thatcherite neoliberalism. By taking this ambivalent and contrarian approach, I contend that the Pet Shop Boys purposefully (re)constructed an alternative '[way] of being' in the world of celebrity and pop culture in 1980s Britain.[55]

Bibliography

'Bitz'. *Smash Hits*, 23April–6 May 1986, 4–9.
'The BPI Awards'. *Smash Hits*, 24 February–8 March 1988, 38–41.
Colon, Suzan. 'What would you say to a dead cockroach?' *Smash Hits*, 10–23 February 1988, 12–13.
Ewing, Tom. 'Imperial'. *Pitchfork*, 28 May 2010, https://pitchfork.com/features/poptimist/7811-poptimist-29/.
Fairclough, Norman. *Critical Discourse Analysis*. London: Longman, 1995.
Feldman, Fred and Brad Skow. 'Desert'. In Edward N. Zalta (ed.), *The Stanford Encyclopedia of Philosophy*, https://plato.stanford.edu/archives/win2020/entries/desert/.
Fiske, Susan T. and Shelley E. Taylor. *Social Cognition*, 2nd edn. New York: McGraw-Hill, 1991.
Frith, Simon and Jon Savage. 'Pearls and swine: Intellectuals and the mass media'. In Steve Redhead, Derek Wynne and Justin O'Connor (eds), *The Clubcultures Reader: Readings in Popular Cultural Studies*, 7–17. Oxford: Blackwell, 1998.
Gee, James P. *Social Linguistics and Literacies: Ideology in Discourses*, 4th edn. Abingdon: Routledge, 2012.
Gramsci, Antonio. *Selections from the Prison Notebooks*. Translated by Quintin Hoare and Geoffrey Nowell Smith. London: Lawrence and Wishart, 1971.
'Great pop tiffs of our time: Pt 103'. *Smash Hits*, 16–29 December 1987, 7.
Heath, Chris. 'Pet Shop Boys: What does it take to make these men happy?'. *Smash Hits*, 26 February–11 March 1986, 43–5.
Heath, Chris. 'Neil Tennant: Smash Hits Editor for a day!?'. *Smash Hits*, 25 February–10 March 1987, 30–1.
Heath, Chris. *'Pet Shop Boys 1987–1988'*, *Actually remastered* (booklet). Parlophone.
Hibbert, Tom. 'And a rather good LP it is, too!'. *Smash Hits*, 9–22 September 1987, 46–7.
Hills, Matt. 'When the Pet Shop Boys were "imperial": Fans' self-ageing and the neoliberal life course of "successful" text-ageing'. *Journal of Fandom Studies* 7, no. 2 (2019): 151–67, doi: 10.1386/jfs.7.2.151_1.
'How the stars voted'. *Smash Hits*, 16–29 December 1987, 64–6.
Jessop, Bob, Kevin Bonnet, Simon Bromley and Tom Ling. 'Authoritarian populism, two nations, and Thatcherism'. *New Left Review* 1, no. 147 (1984): 32–60, https://www.proquest.com/scholarly-journals/authoritarian-populism-two-nations-thatcherism/docview/1301904733/se-2.

---

[55]Gee, *Social Linguistics and Literacies*, 152.

KhosraviNik, Majid. 'Actor-descriptions, action attributions, and argumentation: Towards a systematization of CDA analytical categories in the representation of social groups'. *Critical Discourse Studies* 7, no. 1 (2010): 55–72, doi: 10.1080/17405900903453948.

Koller, Veronika. 'How to analyse collective identity in discourse: Textual and contextual parameters'. *Critical Approaches to Discourse Analysis Across Disciplines* 5, no. 2 (2012): 19–38, http://cadaad.net/2012_volume_5_issue_2/79-66.

Levine, Nick. 'Why Pet Shop Boys are still the cleverest men in pop'. *BBC Culture*, 21 January 2020, https://www.bbc.com/culture/article/20200121-why-pet-shop-boys-are-still-the-cleverest-men-in-pop.

Lewis, Tania. 'Branding, celebritization, and the lifestyle expert'. *Celebrity Studies* 24, no. 4 (2010): 580–98, doi: 10.1080/09502386.2010.488406.

Maus, Fred E. 'Glamour and evasion: The fabulous ambivalence of the Pet Shop Boys'. *Popular Music* 20, no. 3 (2001): 379–93, doi: 10.1017/S0261143001001568.

McDonald, Vici. 'The Pet Shop Boys: Tips for Modern Living'. *Smash Hits*, 12–25 August 1987, 14–16.

Patterson, Sylvia. 'Pet Shop Boys: A demented duo'. *Smash Hits*, 7–20 September 1988, 38–40.

'Personal File: Neil Tennant – Pet Shop Boys'. *Smash Hits*, 15–28 January 1986, 14.

'Pop Stars – They speak!!'. *Smash Hits*, 17–30 December 1986, 48–51.

'"Quite Good" Pop Book Shock!'. *Smash Hits*, 19 October–1 November 1988, 36.

Reeves, Aaron, Emily Gilbert and Daniel Holman. 'Class dis-identification, cultural stereotypes, and music preferences: Experimental evidence from the UK'. *Poetics* 50 (2015): 44–61, doi: 10.1016/j.poetic.2015.01.002.

'Should we scrap the royal family?'. *Smash Hits*, 16–29 July 1986, 46–8.

Street-Porter, Janet. 'Editor-At-Large: He lured boys. He's a bully. Now he bleats'. *Independent*, 3 April 2005, https://www.independent.co.uk/voices/columnists/janet-street-porter/editoratlarge-he-lured-boys-he-s-a-bully-now-he-bleats-530894.html.

van Dijk, Teun A. 'Critical discourse studies: A sociocognitive approach'. In Ruth Wodak and Michael Meyer (eds), *Methods for Critical Discourse Analysis*, 62–85. London: SAGE, 2015.

Wodtke, Larissa. 'The irony and the ecstasy: The queer aging of Pet Shop Boys and LCD Soundsystem in Electronic Dance Music'. *Dancecult: Journal of Electronic Dance Music Culture*, 11, no. 1 (2019): 30–52, doi: 10.12801/1947-5403.2019.11.01.03.

CHAPTER ELEVEN

You've Been Around but You Don't Look Too Rough

Dreamworld: The Greatest Hits Live and the Pet Shop Boys as Legacy Artists

A. S. Waysdorf

Introduction

The Pet Shop Boys, and their fandom, have largely presented themselves in sort of an anti-nostalgia fashion, conspicuously keeping up with trends in pop and dance and regularly releasing new music in line with them.[1] Thus, it is somewhat surprising that the tour accompanying the release of 2020's *Hotspot* was billed as *Dreamworld: The Greatest Hits Live*. After substantial Covid-19 delays, the tour finally kicked off in 2022, visiting the UK and Europe and including a high-profile (and broadcast on the BBC) Glastonbury set. With an accompanying Spotify playlist to highlight these 'most iconic hits, as well as some of their most loved single releases', it seems that the focus of the Pet Shop Boys at this stage is not the new, Berlin-influenced dance music of their twentieth studio album, but their legacy.

---

[1] Matt Hills, 'When the Pet Shop Boys Were "Imperial": Fans' Self-Ageing and the Neoliberal Life Course of "Successful" Text-Ageing', *Journal of Fandom Studies* 7, no. 2 (2019): 151–67, doi: 10.1386/jfs.7.2.151_1.

Bottomley argues that reissues, of which Greatest Hits albums are a part, have a narrativizing and legitimizing function in popular music.[2] They serve to establish what is considered important out of pop's past – a way to reconsider what might have been missed by the mainstream, or further enforce what is already considered important with new packaging and storytelling. Reissuing creates value by stating that this music is worth remembering and gives it new context through contemporary paratexts, rendering it visible to both long-term and potential fans of an artist. As older popular music starts to become part of a 'cultural heritage' framework[3] and young fans become increasingly interested in music of the past,[4] there is a significant opportunity for artists like the Pet Shop Boys to establish themselves as 'legends' – a group that transcends their era and continues to have relevance into the next decades.

This chapter argues that the *Dreamworld* tour is the Pet Shop Boys' way of narrativizing and establishing their legacy into the 2020s, but in a way that is, effectively, still under the band's (presumed) control (compared to a physical release). Establishing a Greatest Hits in this fashion narrativizes the Pet Shop Boys as important, but still existing, artists in pop music's history, showcasing their present vitality but also their long-spanning collection of memorable songs. This presentation does include those who have continually seen themselves as Pet Shop Boys fans,[5] but more crucially addresses potential and latent or lapsed fans, for whom the Greatest Hits are a reminder of the role the band has played in popular music throughout the decades. In doing so, the Pet Shop Boys seek to use this *Greatest Hits* tour to confirm their legacy – and that they are still living up to it.

---

[2]Andrew J. Bottomley, 'Play It Again: Rock Music Reissues and the Production of the Past for the Present', *Popular Music and Society* 39, no. 2 (2016): 151–74, doi: 10.1080/03007766.2015.1036539.

[3]Andy Bennett '"Heritage Rock": Rock Music, Representation and Heritage Discourse', *Poetics* 37, no. 5–6 (2009): 474–89, doi: 10.1016/j.poetic.2009.09.006; Andy Bennett and Susanne Janssen, 'Popular Music, Cultural Memory, and Heritage', *Popular Music and Society* 39, no. 1 (2016): 1–7, doi: 10.1080/03007766.2015.1061332; Arno van der Hoeven, 'Narratives of Popular Music Heritage and Cultural Identity: The Affordances and Constraints of Popular Music Memories', *European Journal of Cultural Studies* 21 no. 2 (2018): 207–22, doi: 10.1177/1367549415609328; Les Roberts, 'Talkin' 'Bout My Generation: Popular Music and the Culture of Heritage', *International Journal of Heritage Studies* 20, no. 3 (2012): 262–80, doi: 10.1080/13527258.2012.740497.

[4]Andy Bennett, '"Things They Do Look Awful Cool": Ageing Rock Icons and Contemporary Youth Audiences', *Leisure/Loisir* 32, no. 2 (2008): 259–78, doi: 10.1080/14927713.2008.9651410; Bennett, '"Heritage Rock"'; Jean Hogarty, *Popular Music and Retro Culture in the Digital Era* (New York and London: Routledge, 2017).

[5]Fred E. Maus, 'Glamour and Evasion: The Fabulous Ambivalence of the Pet Shop Boys', *Popular Music* 20, no 3 (2001): 379–93, doi: 10.1017/s0261143001001568; Hills, 'When The Pet Shop Boys'.

FIGURE 11.1 *The Pet Shop Boys' 2022–3* Dreamworld: The Greatest Hits *tour.*

This used to be the future: music heritage and reissues

For all popular music is associated with youth, recent years have shown the importance of history, heritage and legacy, for both performers and fans. Fans, rather than losing interest in music as they age, are increasingly shown to maintain their fandom over their lifetimes,[6] considering it an important pillar of their self-identity. Older musicians are regularly found on the touring circuit, from acknowledged 'legends' like the Rolling Stones or Elton John, whose concerts are reliably high grossers,[7] to 'retro' festivals such as the Butlin's Big Weekenders in the UK, Denmark's Vi Elsker Heroes or Belgium's W Festival featuring more one-off favourites. Songs from decades ago resurface as TikTok hits and soundtracks to popular media, bringing them into public consciousness and chart success, like Kate Bush's 1985 hit 'Running Up That Hill' becoming a bigger worldwide hit in 2022 than it was

---

[6]Tonya Anderson, 'Still Kissing Their Posters Goodnight: Female Fandom and the Politics of Popular Music', *Participations: Journal of Audience & Reception Studies* 9, no. 2 (2012): 239–64; Simone Driessen, 'Larger than life: exploring the transcultural fan practices of the Dutch Backstreet Boys fandom', *Participations: Journal of Audience and Reception Studies* 12, no. 2 (2015): 180–96.
[7]Karen Gwee, 'They've Raked in Millions', *NME*, 3 July 2019, https://www.nme.com/news/music/highest-grossing-world-tours-2019-far-2523268.

when it was first released after being featured in the fourth season of the hit Netflix show *Stranger Things*.[8] Older popular music is not simply replaced by new hits – rather, it continues to have relevance and meaning for listeners, both ones that heard it when it was new and ones who are discovering it now.

Indeed, we frequently understand popular music in terms of heritage and legacy.[9] Those who grew up with this music are no longer young – rather, they are now of an age that they start to look back, remember and commemorate what shaped them. Popular music, particularly rock, is seen to have played a substantial role in the cultural life of the late twentieth century and the people who lived through it, seen 'not merely as something particular to their youth, but rather as a key element in their collective cultural awareness and a major contributor to their generational identity'.[10] To this end, there has been a considerable 'heritagisation' of rock music, with exhibitions and other sorts of retrospectives now fairly common,[11] such as the *David Bowie Is . . .* exhibition developed by the V&A Museum, which toured museums worldwide in the 2010s; the opening of museums like Seattle's Experience Music Project or Nashville's National Museum of African American Music;[12] important places like landmarks from ABBA's career in Stockholm or the Beatles' Liverpool history incorporated into tourism routes;[13] and other such ways for popular music to be memorialized and recognized as having a lasting impact on culture. This operates not only at a grassroots, fan-driven level,[14] but increasingly as part of 'official' heritage networks[15] sponsored by regions and governments and thus now part of more traditional cultural heritage networks. The Beatles sit alongside Jane Austen as worthy of being remembered into the future.

Bennett[16] credits this largely to rock discourses that have highlighted the perceived quality of rock music – its artistry and authenticity – that separate it from disposable popular culture and thus makes it worthy of

---

[8]Mark Savage, 'Running Up That Hill Was the UK's Song of the Summer', *BBC News*, 5 September 2022, https://www.bbc.com/news/entertainment-arts-62799443.
[9]Bennett '"Heritage Rock"'; Bennett and Janssen, 'Popular Music, Cultural Memory'; van der Hoeven, 'Narratives of Popular Music Heritage'; Roberts, 'Talkin' 'Bout My Generation'.
[10]Bennet, '"Heritage Rock"', 478.
[11]Marion Leonard, 'Constructing Histories through Material Culture: Popular Music, Museums and Collecting', *Popular Music History* 2, no. 2 (2007): 147–67, doi: 10.1558/pomh.v2i2.147.
[12]Sarah Baker, Lauren Istvandity and Raphaël Nowak, 'The Sound of Music Heritage: Curating Popular Music in Music Museums and Exhibitions', *International Journal of Heritage Studies* 22, no 1 (2016): 70–81, doi: 10.1080/13527258.2015.1095784.
[13]Leonieke Bolderman, *Contemporary Music Tourism: A Theory of Musical Topophilia* (London: Routledge, 2020).
[14]Sarah Baker, 'Do-It-Yourself Institutions of Popular Music Heritage: The Preservation of Music's Material Past in Community Archives, Museums and Halls of Fame', *Archives and Records* 37, no. 2 (2016): 170–87, doi: 10.1080/23257962.2015.1106933.
[15]Roberts, 'Talkin' 'Bout My Generation'.
[16]Andy Bennett, '"Things They Do Look Awful Cool"'; Bennett, '"Heritage Rock"'.

commemoration and cultural memory. However, as discourses around popular music have changed, calling into question the supposed superiority of rock compared to other forms,[17] so too has what popular music gets thought about in terms of heritage and legacy. For example, the closing ceremonies of the London 2012 Olympics featured not only the rock bands that defined the baby-boomer generation, but George Michael, the Spice Girls, and indeed, the Pet Shop Boys, as part of its 'A Symphony of British Music' programme. At the same time, there is a considerable industry around discussing, reconsidering and historizing popular music,[18] seeing it as something that not only has a legacy, but a legacy that should be learned and appreciated by newer generations. It is expected that audiences, particularly fan or enthusiast audiences, have some familiarity with popular music's past.

On some level, this can be credited to the accessibility of older music.[19] Recorded popular music does not go away – it continues to not only have a presence in popular culture, but to be generally listenable. Songs are encountered on the radio and in other media and can usually be found in stores and streaming services. They sound much the same as they did when they were first released, particularly if they've been through a recent remaster,[20] and cyclical trends of rediscovery and reuse have kept at least some feeling relevant.[21] It is still possible for a fan of the Pet Shop Boys from the 1980s to keep listening to the music they fell in love with in the 2020s. It is also possible for someone to discover the band in the 2020s and become a fan.

This is not to say that all older music is equally accessible – or visible. Rather, it must be *made* visible. With more than seventy years of recorded popular music to select from, and more being released and marketed every day, visibility becomes one of the main obstacles for continued listening. One of the music industry's main strategies for visibility is to resurface older material through reissuing it. A reissue is when previously released recordings are released again, often (although not always) with a promise of an update – remastered sound to suit new technology, unreleased demo or live recordings, new packaging and paratexts. This new/old work can be in the same format as it was originally, such as an anniversary edition of a beloved album, or recontextualized, such as a compilation highlighting a genre or

---

[17] Miles Parks Grier, 'Said the Hooker to the Thief', *Journal of Popular Music Studies* 25, no. 1 (2013): 31–55; Kate Grover, 'Rock Trolls and Recovery', *Journal of Popular Music Studies* 34, no. 1 (2022): 29–34, doi: 10.1525/jpms.2022.34.1.29.
[18] Bennett, '"Things They Do Look Awful Cool"'; Andy Bennett and Sarah Baker, 'Classic Albums: The Re-Presentation of the Rock Album on British Television', in Ian Inglis (ed.), *Popular Music and Television in Britain* (London: Routledge, 2010), 41–54; Leanne Weston, '(Re)Writing Music History: Television, Memory, and Nostalgia in The People's History of Pop', *Velvet Light Trap* 88 (2021): 59–70.
[19] Hogarty, *Retro Culture*.
[20] Bottomley, 'Play It Again'.
[21] Hogarty, *Retro Culture*.

music scene. Bottomley analyses reissues as a cultural and industrial practice, noting that they are 'social and historical texts that often re-emerge and are rendered culturally significant at particular times and for particular reasons'.[22] Reissues are done for a reason, and usually with some sort of argument in mind about the relevance and value of what is being reissued. Whether it serves to further canonize a work already considered important (such as Bottomley's example of the fortieth anniversary reissue of the Beach Boys' *Pet Sounds*) or to introduce an obscure or out-of-print archival favourite to a wider audience (Bottomley uses Gary Wilson's *You Think You Know Me* as an example here), the reissue's goal is to argue that this music should be listened to and appreciated by contemporary audiences.

To that end, it is usually surrounded by paratexts to make that point, highlighting the characteristics of the work that make it valuable and what the particular reissue has done to enhance it. Presentation matters deeply. When a work is reissued, 'promotional stickers create expectations; artwork and packaging convey status; liner notes direct listener attention and (re) write history to bolster artistic integrity'.[23] Audiences must be addressed by the way in which the reissue is presented. For fans that know this music, why should it be acquired again? For potential new listeners, why should it be picked up in the first place? The paratextual framing of a reissue establishes what about this music is important and places it in the historical context that has been built up around it since, situating it in the artist's history as well as within popular music more generally. A reissue is therefore an act of narrativization.

Reissues are a thriving segment of the music industry, even in the streaming era, but that doesn't mean all reissues are thought of in the same way. Bottomley dismisses most 'greatest hits' compilations, which he acknowledges as reissues, as budget repackaging without the care put into more quality reissues, 'the epitome of a copyright holder exploiting its intellectual property for sheer profit maximization'.[24] Indeed, greatest hits compilations have a bad reputation among fans – as music critic Amanda Petrusich notes, they 'can feel like a cheat',[25] providing a way to simply get to the familiar without the context of the album surrounding them. Real fans don't need a Greatest Hits – they already have access to these songs and should prefer to hear them in their intended place, with the wrinkles and curiosities of the artist's career intact. However, the Greatest Hits concept has undoubtedly been successful throughout pop music history, with several of the bestselling albums of all time being Greatest Hits collections, such as *Their Greatest Hits* by the

---

[22]Bottomley, 'Play It Again', 152.
[23]Bottomley, 'Play It Again', 170.
[24]Bottomley, 'Play It Again', 158.
[25]Amanda Petrusich, 'Long Live the Greatest-Hits Album', *New Yorker*, 4 December 2020, https://www.newyorker.com/culture/culture-desk/long-live-the-greatest-hits-album.

Eagles, which currently holds the title of best-selling album of all time in the US and third worldwide, and the Beatles' *1*, which was the bestselling album of the 2000s.[26] What makes Greatest Hits albums suspicious for fans is what makes them so appealing to the general public, in that they provide a convenient way to hear all the popular songs of an artist at once, without having to explore the back catalogue or learn anything more about them. For much of pop music history, they were also easy moneymakers: cheap to produce, needing little to no involvement from the artist, and an easy sell to consumers. This gave Greatest Hits albums another kind of negative connotation, that of low-effort cash grabs for record labels,[27] as easily disposable as they are to pick up. While certainly valuable monetarily, for more devoted listeners, their value was minimal.

In recent years, though, even the monetary value of Greatest Hits albums has declined.[28] Music streaming has taken over the specific function of a cheap collection of commercial hits, in that it is now even easier and less costly for a listener to find the popular hits of an artist. While more elaborate – and costly – retrospectives still have their place, the classic Greatest Hits is not the staple it once was, replaced by playlists or even just the 'Popular' listing on Spotify.

However, the idea of the Greatest Hits remains. As the commercial need for them has faded, the role that they can play in introducing and narrativizing an artist's career has come to the fore.[29] Bottomley, while dismissive of Greatest Hits albums in general, does note that 'the mere act of issuing a "greatest hits" collection could be viewed as an attempt to legitimate and canonize an artist (i.e. one must have multiple "hits" worth propagating)'.[30] While lacking the presentation and deeper storytelling of a 'quality' retrospective, the succinctness of a Greatest Hits has its own sort of narrativizing power. In stating that there is a Greatest Hits, and presenting a collection as such, a claim is made that this artist is important enough that this is necessary. After all, with only one or two hits, a separate framing isn't necessary.

---

[26]Stephen Thomas Erlewine, 'Why the Death of Greatest Hits Albums and Reissues Is Worth Mourning', *Pitchfork*, 2 May 2016, https://pitchfork.com/features/article/9887-why-the-death-of-greatest-hits-albums-and-reissues-is-worth-mourning/; Matthew Perpetua, 'Everything Hits: Spoon Releases An Old School Greatest Hits Album Into A Digital Age', *NPR*, 24 July 2019, https://www.npr.org/2019/07/24/744642060/spoon-releases-an-old-school-greatest-hits-album-into-a-digital-age; 'Top-Selling Albums of the Decade', Reuters, 9 December 2009, https://www.reuters.com/news/picture/top-selling-albums-of-the-decade-idUSRTXRNFA.
[27]Erlewine, 'Why the Death of Greatest Hits Albums and Reissues Is Worth Mourning'; Robert Plummer, 'Is the Greatest Hits Album Dead?' *BBC News*, 2 February 2018, https://www.bbc.com/news/business-42701623; Perpetua, 'Everything Hits'.
[28]Perpetua, 'Everything Hits'.
[29]Perpetua, 'Everything Hits'; Petrusich, 'Long Live'.
[30]Bottomley, 'Play it Again', 158.

It must also be said that playlists, while not a physical reissue, serves much of the same purpose as certain kinds of reissues. Eriksson situates Spotify playlists in particular as a 'container technology' for music, holding it in place and facilitating its movement.[31] A playlist in this context is a collection of songs arranged in a certain way, given a certain title, and promoted to listeners – a package to make consumption easier. When a song is sorted into a playlist it is thus given meaning. These function in much the same way as musical compilations from prior eras of containers, although they can be changed at much more frequent intervals due to the lack of physical media that must be altered and redistributed. With playlists as Spotify's preferred music delivery system,[32] there is considerable narrativizing potential in the form. Like other kinds of reissues, they recontextualize music from its original place, making the listener think about them in a new way. The way the container is labelled goes a long way to determine the song's meaning. The move to a more virtual container shows that this kind of reissue logic can work outside of a specific reissue – labelling a collection of songs serves much of the same purpose.

It is here that we can situate the *Dreamworld* tour. While not a Greatest Hits album in the traditional sense, it still uses that container as a label, both on the tour itself and on the accompanying playlist and promotions. There is a statement being made with this tour that the Pet Shop Boys are worth thinking about in terms of a legacy – and that all fans, whether they have been following the group for decades, have fallen off with their fandom, or are only now learning about the group, can be addressed through it. At this stage, at this time, the Pet Shop Boys are establishing a legacy.

They called us the Pop Kids: curating the Greatest Hits

The Introduction to the *Dreamworld* tour programme describes the tour in the following way:

> *Dreamworld* offers audiences a chance to experience the soundtrack of their lives in a live environment, but it becomes clear during rehearsals that this is also an opportunity for Neil and Chris to revisit and refine their back catalogue. In *Dreamworld*, songs with monolithic status can still be interrogated and modified.[33]

---

[31] Maria Eriksson, 'The Editorial Playlist as Container Technology: On Spotify and the Logistical Role of Digital Music Packages', *Journal of Cultural Economy* 13, no. 4 (2020): 415–27, doi:10.1080/17530350.2019.1708780.
[32] Eriksson, 'The Editorial Playlist'.
[33] Peter Robinson, *Dreamworld: The Greatest Hits Live Tour Programme* (2022), 3.

There are two elements in this description that set out the (intended) meanings of this tour. On the one hand, it is a looking back – a 'soundtrack of their lives' for listeners, a remembrance of the importance of the Pet Shop Boys in general and the personal importance for the fans attending. At the same time, it is positioned as explicitly not simply an exercise in nostalgia, but a revisiting with the potential for something new to come of it. This is a Greatest Hits as active decision-making, with clear direction from the band, rather than an after-the-fact cash grab from a label or other outside force.

This sense of control over the Greatest Hits concept is central to the tour programme. The programme features interviews with the Pet Shop Boys themselves, their touring band, creative director, video content creator, lighting designers, music producer, musical director, costume designer/stylist and stage director (and short questionnaires with the crew) – a documentation of the process behind the tour as well as its conceptualization. The overall sense is one of deliberate choices. In the programme's interview with the Pet Shop Boys themselves, when asked what constitutes a great hit, they respond:

Neil: It's a very technical thing. It has to be very popular . . .
Chris: . . . with us!
Neil: For instance, we live in a universe in which 'Dreamland' was a massive international hit.
Chris: That literally is a dreamworld. But to us, if it sounds like a hit, it was a hit.
Neil: We can't fit all our hits into just one show. When we first put together the setlist it was far too long.[34]

What constitutes a Greatest Hit here, then, is not only the chart performance of a song – something out of the band's control, even if they are rather proud of their success – but the way it feels to them and the way it can be fitted into a tour setlist. While the term assumes certain songs, the band leave themselves open for incorporation of later work (such as new single 'Dreamland') and thus a further narrativization of their career. It is also stressed that they have too many hits for the ideal length of a concert – that they are a band with a long history of success, a legacy, and they are the ones determining exactly how it is done.

This control over the idea of the Greatest Hits means that *Dreamworld* can be specifically used to present an overview of their career in a way that other hits compilations might not be. A tour needs to be listened to in order, rather than cherrypicked, which means that how and where songs are presented becomes deeply important to their contextualization. While it is constrained by the container label – there has to be space for 'West End Girls' and 'Always On My Mind' – the structure of a tour setlist raises new

---

[34]Robinson, *Dreamworld*, 8.

possibilities for contextualization. It is not just the 80s compilation regulars that get the status of 'hits' here. Prominent placement for slightly later songs like 'Can You Forgive Her?' and 'New York City Boy' highlight them as the fan favourites they are. Songs are showcased by style rather than period, such as *Hotspot*'s 'Monkey Business' positioning with other dance-oriented tracks at the midpoint. 'Being Boring', which famously failed to climb higher than number 10 on the UK charts, marking the end of the 'imperial phase', serves as the night's closer, displaying the esteem and prominence it has since gained in the group's back catalogue. This is a Greatest Hits that emphasizes the breadth and longevity of their career and how these songs have been received over the decades, not only how they were received in the moment.

There is even a sense of novelty to the process, as communicated by the band and the important figures on the tour. While the Pet Shop Boys do have previous greatest hits albums, Chris notes that 'they're not called *Greatest Hits* though, are they?'[35] The act of curating a Greatest Hits is positioned as a novelty for the band, something they haven't really done on a conscious level before, despite existing hits collections. These previous collections are used by Neil in the interview to periodize the group – *Discography*, from 1991, as a document of their 'imperial phase' as a 'singles band', *PopArt* to close out their 'albumy, conceptual' 90s period, and *Ultimate*, from 2010, dismissed somewhat as a Christmas release, but also a close-out of the 'producers' phase of the 2000s and something that allows them to leave their label Parlophone and move into a new 'electronic duo' phase (although they would release 2012's *Elysium* with Parlophone).[36] Thus the *Dreamworld* tour is also positioned as something new for the group to do, but still in the tradition of their previous collections – a look towards the future in closing out a particular era for the group, a deliberate choice to tour in this fashion.

This idea of the *Greatest Hits* tour as something contemporary, rather than nostalgic, is maintained in the interviews with the other creative principals of the tour. Creative director Tom Scutt posits the 'big idea' of the tour's design as 'sewing together the past, the present, and the future' of the Pet Shop Boys, and stresses how he wants to 'produce something that feels like a new piece of art, but also envelops their whole back catalogue and acknowledges the weight of their legacy'. Video content creator Luke Halls states that, in making video for the tour, 'Even though this is a greatest hits show and you want to remind people of the great cultural references they've generated, you don't want to detract from their current music and who Neil and Chris are now.'[37] History and legacy are inherent to the concept of a *Greatest Hits* tour, but *Dreamworld* is extensively positioned in the

---

[35]Robinson, *Dreamworld*, 8.
[36]It is also worth noting that the duo's most recent compilation, *Smash*, which at the time of writing has not yet been released, is also published through Parlophone.
[37]Robinson, *Dreamworld*, 24.

programme as not just about legacy. The way the tour is conceptualized, from the band itself to those charged with executing the group's vision, is about the present relevance of the group as much as it is about remembering what they have accomplished.

That this is the stated vision for the *Greatest Hits* tour is perhaps unsurprising. As Hills discusses, contemporary Pet Shop Boys fandom is, at least in part, based on a certain negotiation, even denial, of the aging of the group and their work. Hills' discussion of later-period Pet Shop boys fandom builds on Neil Tennant's famous coining of the 'imperial phase' to refer to the period of greatest success for the group, exploring how this phrase is invoked by fans as a way to negotiate the band's aging. While it can be used as a form of looking back, recalling successes past, it is also used to discuss current and even future music – that the imperial phase 'could be reactivated and restored at any time thanks to the skilfulness of Tennant/Lowe',[38] with new music that is just as compelling and contemporary as any of the hits of the past. To be a fan of the Pet Shop Boys, or at least one that posts on the Pet Shop Boys forum and has an interest in paratexts around the band, one must embrace the group as a contemporary concern rather than something from a former time.

Aging is thus complicated for the Pet Shop Boys and their fans, unwilling to fully embrace the nostalgia of other 80s and 90s hitmakers but also unwilling to give up the memory of the Pet Shop Boys being relevant to the wider culture. This is a tension throughout the choices made by the Pet Shop Boys in the 2020s. The US leg of the *Dreamworld* tour was done as a co-headlining act with New Order (under the name of the *Unity Tour*). The year 2022, one focused on touring, had little output of new music, but featured the release of a collaboration single with Soft Cell. Both these moves seemingly position the group closer to the nostalgia market. However, 2022 also featured an official remix of a track from the popular German house duo Claptone, showing a continuing connection to the contemporary dance scene. Hills refers to these competing discourses as a desire for a neoliberal 'successful aging', aging without succumbing to decline or reactionary nostalgia. This discourse is repeated in the tour programme, which, after all, is something that probably only dedicated fans of the group would be interested enough in to purchase and read. It is therefore necessary to discuss doing a *Greatest Hits* tour as something other than an exercise in nostalgia and indicate to fans that just because this is happening doesn't mean that the band is going to turn to exclusively looking towards the past. Rather, doing a *Greatest Hits* tour, and organizing the Greatest Hits in a band-directed fashion, can be presented as a statement about the band's present and an investment in its future.

---

[38] Hills, 'When The Pet Shop Boys', 257.

I still quite like some of your early stuff: the *Greatest Hits* audience

Yet, it is still a *Greatest Hits* tour. As discussed above, the concept of the Greatest Hits is not designed for the kind of fans that read concert programmes. It is a format designed for the more casual listener, those who want to pick up a collection – or attend a show – featuring all the songs they already know from elsewhere, without too many digressions. In doing a *Greatest Hits* tour, the Pet Shop Boys are therefore not catering to their most hardcore fans. Rather, this can be seen as an appeal to legacy, positioning the group as one that should be recalled and remembered by more than just the hardcore. This is a different tack from how Baym[39] and others sees musicians with strong fanbases operating in the contemporary age, where they make direct appeals to devoted and/or long-term fans for support and financing. Instead, with this kind of branding, the Pet Shop Boys are focusing on latent and newer fans, positioning this tour as an entry point and a solidification of 'legacy' status.

Most discussions of long-term fandom focus on fandom that has endured, at more or less the same intensity, throughout the fan's life.[40] However, in the spirit of Sandvoss and Kearns' discussion of 'ordinary fandom'[41] and Hills'[42] idea of 'momentary fandom', in discussing fandom over the life course it is also useful to discuss the contours and potential of latent fandom – fandom that lies dormant and is then reactivated. Just as a 'momentary fan' does not participate in the seemingly endless overflow and extensions that make up twenty-first-century fandom but focuses their fandom in the moment that they are watching, a latent fan might not follow an artist past their own youth or an artist's fashionability, but can find themselves remembering and reconnecting with their fandom at a later date. This is, perhaps, not the most admirable kind of fandom for researchers, but undoubtedly a kind of fandom that exists as older media becomes more easily accessible and referenced. It is latent in that it is not part of the fan's day-to-day life or identity, for the most part, but is then triggered and reactivated by some kind of event that brings this latency to the fore.

---

[39]Nancy Baym, *Playing to the Crowd: Musicians, Audiences, and the Intimate Work of Connection* (New York: NYU Press, 2018).
[40]Anderson, 'Still Kissing'; Bennett, '"Heritage Rock"'; Driessen, 'Larger than Life'; C. Lee Harrington and Denise D. Bielby, 'A Life Course Perspective on Fandom', *International Journal of Cultural Studies* 13, no. 5 (2010): 429–50.
[41]Cornel Sandvoss and Laura Kearns, 'From Interpretive Communities to Interpretative Fairs: Ordinary Fandom, Textual Selection and Digital Media', in Linda Duits, Koos Zwan, and Stijn Reijnders (eds), *The Ashgate Research Companion to Fan Cultures* (London: Routledge, 2014), 91–106.
[42]Matt Hills, 'When Television Doesn't Overflow "Beyond the Box": The Invisibility of "Momentary" Fandom', *Critical Studies in Television: The International Journal of Television Studies* 5, no. 1 (2010): 97–110, doi: 10.7227/cst.5.1.10.

An example of this kind of event could be a prominent *Greatest Hits* tour and accompanying publicity, something that brings a prior favourite back to the attention of the latent fan. In addition to their regular tour, the Pet Shop Boys brought the *Dreamworld* tour to various festivals, as they have done in the past, including a televised slot at Glastonbury, closing out the weekend at the Other Stage. This kind of visibility for the show seems to encourage a reactivation of latent fans, a reminder of the hits and songs they've had and an encouragement to reconnect with them, as can be seen in this Twitter thread reacting to the Glastonbury set (see Figure 11.2).

While the Twitter posters recognize that the Pet Shop Boys are a great band that they have fond memories of, neither of them indicates a 'hardcore' fandom. Rather, they are reminded of how much they appreciate the band by watching the performance and discussing it with others who are at a similar level of fandom. With this reminder, they might also be interested in escalating their fandom by actually seeing the tour in person.

A *Greatest Hits* format lends itself to this kind of popular attention. While the Pet Shop Boys have played Glastonbury before, and tour regularly, the concentrated focus on 'the hits' here encourages both accessibility and

FIGURE 11.2 *Twitter thread reacting to the Glastonbury set in the* Dreamworld *tour.*

appreciation of the role they have played in pop history. There is no distraction from what has been understood for years as important and no obstacles to appreciation for those who haven't been following the ins and outs of their entire career. This is summed up well by the *Guardian* review of the Pet Shop Boys' set:

> Much has been made of the advanced age of some of this year's Glastonbury stage headliners, as if this represented some kind of lack of imagination on behalf of the bookers. But that limited mindset discounts the massive contributions that these venerable artists have made to pop history, not to mention the continued pertinence of the most vital among them. Arguably – and I would argue it to the death – that is Pet Shop Boys, who draw one of the vastest (and most euphoric) crowds on the Other stage all weekend for a victory lap of their greatest hits, most of which still bite fiercely hard today.[43]

The reviewer refers to their set – 'the best [Glastonbury] set I've ever seen' – as a 'victory lap' for the group, suggesting that doing a tour like this, with this kind of prominence, cements the band as legacy and legendary artists. A triumphant *Greatest Hits* tour successfully confirms the band as part of the growing field of popular music heritage.

Of course, this only works because the Pet Shop Boys seem relevant and interesting, and not just to latent and enduring fans. The reviewer of the Glastonbury set mentions her age – thirty-three, which means she was too young to remember the 'imperial phase' (which encompassed the mid- to late 1980s), and claims that 'I didn't really grow up hearing their songs.' As Bennett[44] and Hogarty[45] stress, it is important to note that the fandom of legacy artists is not confined to those that were there for their first flush of success, but that there is an often-considerable fanbase of younger fans. Hogarty argues that a combination of technological accessibility and cultural shifts means that a significant amount of younger music listeners are fans of older music, willing to go outside of their generational cohort. Popular music is no longer the exclusive terrain of youth and thus a site of intergenerational conflict, but 'the site of intergenerational sharing in terms of musical tastes, memories, and nostalgia'.[46] Parents share music with their children, and children find their own interests in older music on streaming services and record shop remasters. Rather than being seen as an obsolete relic of the past, older popular music is seen as vital and worth listening to, particularly

---

[43] Laura Snapes, 'Pet Shop Boys reviewed', *Guardian*, 27 June 2023, https://www.theguardian.com/music/live/2022/jun/26/sunday-at-glastonbury-the-build-to-kendrick-lamar-lorde-and-pet-shop-boys.
[44] Bennett, 'Things They Do'.
[45] Hogarty, *Retro Culture*.
[46] Hogarty, *Retro Culture*, 8–9.

if a music fan wishes to be knowledgeable or cultured. It is this mindset, as much as the nostalgic desires of older fans, that keeps reissues relevant and artists from previous decades embarking on successful tours and headlining major festivals. There is a wide pool of potential fans for older artists, in addition to the enduring and latent fans.

Hogarty sees this as inherently negative – a sign that 'that the contemporary structure of feeling is more about the past than it is about the present',[47] that young people no longer dream of the future and instead find themselves trapped in the ghosts of the past, unable to build a culture for themselves, finding only 'inauthentic' pastiches of previous forms and vapid commercial presentations. However, it must be asked why popular music must be without a history to be valid – that it must perpetually be youth-focused, with relevance only for what is newest. This is somewhat unreasonable to expect after over seventy years of what could generally be considered pop music as we know it, especially with so much of it preserved. Rather, as popular music matures, it can be expected that those who care about the form will seek to pass what mattered onto the next generation, while the next generation seeks their own meaning in the form's past. As with other art forms, there is an expectation that to be serious about your interest you need to have knowledge of what came before. Therefore, the young popular music fan, as Bennett discusses, is given a way into music of previous generations through a 'ready-made canon of music – a series of past-masters whose music is to be taken "seriously" and regarded as the best of its kind'[48] – a sense of heritage and legacy, as discussed above.

This does not mean that the canon is immutable. Bennett stresses rock music's perceived differences from pop, particularly rock music of the 1960s and 1970s, as what made it suited for a certain kind of heritage discourse, one 'grounded in a rock–pop distinction (propped up by the music journalism of the day) that regarded rock as art while dismissing chart-orientated "pop" music as commercially derived ephemera'[49]. However, as Grier[50] and Grover[51] discuss, this perceived superiority has been greatly called into question by contemporary music critics (and their readers), with rock's supposed 'authenticity' critiqued as its own kind of studied performance and the general nature of its canon critiqued as dismissive of any tastes other than that of the straight, white men who continually make and perpetuate them. With this critique of rock's inherent superiority as a form there has been a reconsideration of pop as a genre, moving from seeing it entirely as lowest common-denominator ephemera to its own sound with its own qualities and strengths.

---

[47]Hogarty, *Retro Culture*, 35.
[48]Bennett, 'Things They Do', 266.
[49]Bennett, 'Things They Do', 266.
[50]Grier, 'Said the Hooker'.
[51]Grover, 'Rock Trolls'.

The Pet Shop Boys fit well into the current critical zeitgeist. They have never been shy about their dislike of traditional rock aesthetics and attitudes, proudly 'inauthentic' and 'artificial' in their tastes, their music and their live presentation.[52] They have also been proudly commercial, pleased to be a group with big hits and notable successes, a stance that has passed on to their fans.[53] These stances put them outside of the traditional rock canon, and thus the heritage and legacy-making practices that have been built around it. However, while revelling in artifice and artificiality, the Pet Shop Boys have, as Butler discusses, 'moved beyond rock's values to construct an authenticity of [their] own'.[54] While eschewing the stances of rock, they still, in some ways, fit into the kind of 'authentic' work that a music critic would appreciate – written by the band, with a clear artistic vision, an uncompromising commitment to the work they want to produce, and with an element of quality to the music and lyrics that are not often found in their genre. Maus makes the claim that 'there are many reasons to think of the Pet Shop Boys' songs as artistic, and as serious in purpose. They combine carefully crafted music, full of thoughtful, imaginative touches, with subtle, psychologically astute lyrics.'[55] In looking for alternatives to a chauvinistic rock-based canon, the Pet Shop Boys stand out.

In this environment, it thus makes sense for the Pet Shop Boys to make themselves, and their back catalogue, visible in an easily understood way. This is also where the specific choices made in the setlist come into play – highlighting established fan favourites and particular styles reinforces this idea of the Pet Shop Boys as an artistic, authentic pop group to a broader audience, at a time when pop music itself is going through a reappreciation. It showcases the breadth of the group's history and the quality they've upheld throughout. Additionally, it (re)informs audiences that they not only have hits, but they have songs that could have, in an environment that appreciated what they were doing, been hits as well, songs that are just as valid and interesting as the familiar singles. As discussed, this is *Greatest Hits* with a particular narrative about the expanse and long-term appreciation of their entire career. The format reminds the public, and particularly latent and potential fans, that there is a significant body of work worth remembering – or learning.

At the same time, doing it as a tour, instead of another collection, positions the band as vibrant now, instead of only on recordings from decades ago. By showcasing their current energy and vitality, a case is made that latent fans should remember their work while potential fans can see the group as one with both a suitable legacy and contemporary relevance. Enduring fans have

---

[52]Maus, 'Glamour and Evasion'; Mark Butler, 'Taking It Seriously: Intertextuality and Authenticity in Two Covers by the Pet Shop Boys', *Popular Music* 22, no. 1 (2003): 1–19, doi: 10.1017/s0261143003003015.
[53]Maus, 'Glamour and Evasion'.
[54]Butler, 'Taking it Seriously', 14.
[55]Maus, 'Glamour and Evasion', 381.

both a new tour to watch and the enjoyment of seeing the band return to a certain level of prominence – while not perhaps the 'imperial era' of chart dominance, at least a certain level of respect and legacy/legendary status for the group.

Conclusion

What this chapter argues is that the Pet Shop Boys' positioning as we head into the 2020s is that of a legacy, legendary artist – a group that not only has a past selection of hits to draw on, but a continued relevance to the present. This is done through the particular logic of the *Dreamworld: The Greatest Hits Live* tour. The container label[56] of the *Greatest Hits* suggests that not only are there multiple hits to remember,[57] but that they can be encountered in an accessible, easy-to-understand way. The necessities for appreciating the group are given in this one tour and/or playlist, making it appealing not only to enduring fans who have loved the band throughout its existence, but lapsed fans who might not have put thought into the group in a while, as well as potential fans coming in now. The format works to narrativize the band in a way that is seen to be in their control. As popular music increasingly starts to think of itself in terms of legacy and heritage, reminding the audience of the Pet Shop Boys' success is a way to lay claim to that kind of status. As the music canon shifts from an exclusively rock-oriented focus, there is space for the Pet Shop Boys, and bands like them, to claim their place.

Doing this iteration of their *Greatest Hits* as a tour also presents the band as in control of this legacy – that what the *Greatest Hits* are and how they will be presented is designed by the band, under their control, and not part of a label-mandated cash grab or even simple pandering to nostalgia. It is treated by the band as an exercise in remembering as well as a look towards the future, seeing how their past can be recontextualized for future work. Performing live rather than releasing another compilation also showcases that the group are now, at the moment, capable of living up to their *Greatest Hits*, delivering them with energy and vitality. This can also be seen as a new phase for the Pet Shop Boys – as admired legends.

Bibliography

Anderson, Tonya. 'Still Kissing Their Posters Goodnight: Female Fandom and the Politics of Popular Music.' *Participations: Journal of Audience & Reception Studies* 9, no. 2 (2012): 239–64.

---

[56] Eriksson, 'The Editorial Playlist'.
[57] Bottomley, 'Play It Again'.

Baker, Sarah. 'Do-It-Yourself Institutions of Popular Music Heritage: The Preservation of Music's Material Past in Community Archives, Museums and Halls of Fame.' *Archives and Records* 37, no. 2 (2016): 170–87, doi:10.1080/23257962.2015.1106933.

Baker, Sarah, Lauren Istvandity and Raphaël Nowak. 'The Sound of Music Heritage: Curating Popular Music in Music Museums and Exhibitions.' *International Journal of Heritage Studies* 22, no. 1 (2016): 70–81, doi:10.1080/13527258.2015.1095784.

Baym, Nancy. *Playing to the Crowd: Musicians, Audiences, and the Intimate Work of Connection*. New York: NYU Press, 2018.

Bennett, Andy. '"Things They Do Look Awful Cool": Ageing Rock Icons and Contemporary Youth Audiences.' *Leisure/Loisir* 32, no. 2 (2008): 259–78, doi:10.1080/14927713.2008.9651410.

Bennett, Andy. '"Heritage Rock": Rock Music, Representation and Heritage Discourse.' *Poetics* 37, no. 5–6 (2009): 474–89, doi:10.1016/j.poetic.2009.09.006.

Bennet, Andy and Sarah Baker. 'Classic Albums: The Re-Presentation of the Rock Album on British Television.' In Ian Inglis (ed.), *Popular Music and Television in Britain*, 41–54. London: Routledge, 2010.

Bennett, Andy and Susanne Janssen. 'Popular Music, Cultural Memory, and Heritage.' *Popular Music and Society* 39, no. 1 (2016): 1–7, doi:10.1080/03007766.2015.1061332.

Bolderman, Leonieke. *Contemporary Music Tourism: A Theory of Musical Topophilia*. London: Routledge, 2020.

Bottomley, Andrew J. 'Play It Again: Rock Music Reissues and the Production of the Past for the Present.' *Popular Music and Society* 39, no. 2 (2016): 151–74, doi:10.1080/03007766.2015.1036539.

Butler, Mark. 'Taking It Seriously: Intertextuality and Authenticity in Two Covers by the Pet Shop Boys.' *Popular Music* 22, no. 1 (2003): 1–19, doi:10.1017/s0261143003003015.

Driessen, Simone. 'Larger than life: exploring the transcultural fan practices of the Dutch Backstreet Boys fandom.' *Participations Journal of Audience and Reception Studies* 12, no. 2 (2015): 180–96.

Eriksson, Maria. 'The Editorial Playlist as Container Technology: On Spotify and the Logistical Role of Digital Music Packages.' *Journal of Cultural Economy* 13, no. 4 (2020): 415–27, doi:10.1080/17530350.2019.1708780.

Erlewine, Stephen Thomas. 'Why the Death of Greatest Hits Albums and Reissues Is Worth Mourning.' *Pitchfork*, 2 May 2016, https://pitchfork.com/features/article/9887-why-the-death-of-greatest-hits-albums-and-reissues-is-worth-mourning/.

Grier, Miles Parks. 'Said the Hooker to the Thief.' *Journal of Popular Music Studies* 25, no. 1 (2013): 31–55, https://doi.org/10.1111/jpms.12013.

Grover, Kate. 'Rock Trolls and Recovery.' *Journal of Popular Music Studies* 34, no. 1 (2022): 29–34, doi:10.1525/jpms.2022.34.1.29.

Gwee, Karen. 2019. 'They've Raked in Millions.' *NME*, 3 July 2019, https://www.nme.com/news/music/highest-grossing-world-tours-2019-far-2523268.

Harrington, C. Lee and Denise D. Bielby. 'A Life Course Perspective on Fandom.' *International Journal of Cultural Studies* 13, no. 5 (2010): 429–50, https://doi.org/10.1177/1367877910372702.

Hills, Matt. 'When Television Doesn't Overflow "Beyond the Box": The Invisibility of "Momentary" Fandom.' *Critical Studies in Television: The International Journal of Television Studies* 5, no. 1 (2010): 97–110, doi:10.7227/cst.5.1.10.

Hills, Matt. 'When the Pet Shop Boys Were "Imperial": Fans' Self-Ageing and the Neoliberal Life Course of "Successful" Text-Ageing.' *Journal of Fandom Studies* 7, no. 2 (2019): 151–67, doi:10.1386/jfs.7.2.151_1.

Hoeven, Arno van der. 'Narratives of Popular Music Heritage and Cultural Identity: The Affordances and Constraints of Popular Music Memories.' *European Journal of Cultural Studies* 21, no. 2 (2018): 207–22, doi:10.1177/1367549415609328.

Hogarty, Jean. *Popular Music and Retro Culture in the Digital Era*. New York and London: Routledge, 2017.

Leonard, Marion. 'Constructing Histories through Material Culture: Popular Music, Museums and Collecting.' *Popular Music History* 2, no. 2 (2007): 147–67, doi:10.1558/pomh.v2i2.147.

Maus, Fred E. 'Glamour and Evasion: The Fabulous Ambivalence of the Pet Shop Boys.' *Popular Music* 20, no. 3 (2001): 379–93, doi:10.1017/s0261143001001568.

Perpetua, Matthew. 'Everything Hits: Spoon Releases An Old School Greatest Hits Album Into A Digital Age.' *NPR*, 24 July 2019, https://www.npr.org/2019/07/24/744642060/spoon-releases-an-old-school-greatest-hits-album-into-a-digital-age.

Petrusich, Amanda. 'Long Live the Greatest-Hits Album.' *New Yorker*, 4 December 2020, https://www.newyorker.com/culture/culture-desk/long-live-the-greatest-hits-album.

Plummer, Robert. 'Is the Greatest Hits Album Dead?' *BBC News*, 2 February 2018, https://www.bbc.com/news/business-42701623.

Reuters. 'Top-Selling Albums of the Decade.' 9 December 2009, https://www.reuters.com/news/picture/top-selling-albums-of-the-decade-idUSRTXRNFA

Roberts, Les. 'Talkin' 'Bout My Generation: Popular Music and the Culture of Heritage.' *International Journal of Heritage Studies* 20, no. 3 (2012): 262–80, doi:10.1080/13527258.2012.740497.

Robinson, Peter. *Dreamworld: The Greatest Hits Live Tour Programme*. 2022.

Sandvoss, Cornel and Laura Kearns. 'From Interpretive Communities to Interpretative Fairs: Ordinary Fandom, Textual Selection and Digital Media.' In Linda Duits, Koos Zwan, and Stijn Reijnders (eds), *The Ashgate Research Companion to Fan Cultures*, 91–106. London: Routledge, 2014.

Savage, Mark. 'Running Up That Hill Was the UK's Song of the Summer.' *BBC News*, 5 September 2022, https://www.bbc.com/news/entertainment-arts-62799443.

Snapes, Laura. 'Pet Shop Boys reviewed.' *Guardian*, 27 June 2023, https://www.theguardian.com/music/live/2022/jun/26/sunday-at-glastonbury-the-build-to-kendrick-lamar-lorde-and-pet-shop-boys.

Weston, Leanne. '(Re)Writing Music History: Television, Memory, and Nostalgia in The People's History of Pop.' *Velvet Light Trap* 88 (2021): 59–70.

CHAPTER TWELVE

It's (Not) Obvious

Queerness and Queer Identities Pre- and Post-*Bilingual*

Bodie A. Ashton and Carolin Isabel Steiner

The Pet Shop Boys' long careers in music mean that the timeline of their productions lends itself to periodization. The most well-known of these periodizations is known as the 'imperial phase' – that moment, between 1986 and 1988, when Neil Tennant and Chris Lowe 'felt [. . .] that we had the secret of contemporary pop music, that we knew what was required', and consequently were at the height of their critical and commercial acclaim.[1] Another milestone that offered differentiation of different artistic periods concerns the Pet Shop Boys' record label. In 1984, Tennant and Lowe first recorded 'West End Girls' and 'One More Chance' with the legendary American producer Bobby Orlando, who signed them with Bobcat Records in the United States. This collaboration resulted in a minor club hit but little success, so Orlando was dropped in favour of Stephen Hague and the duo signed with Parlophone in 1985. The result was not only the international phenomenon of a now-rerecorded 'West End Girls', but indeed a recording legacy that covered eleven studio albums, four remix albums,

---

[1] Neil Tennant, interview with Chris Heath, 'Pet Shop Boys 1987–1988', *Pet Shop Boys Actually/Further Listening 1987–1988* liner notes (2018), i. For an analysis of the role of the music press in the founding and maintenance of the 'imperial phase', see also Lexi Webster, 'What Have I Done to Deserve This? Personal, Professional and Political Representations in *Smash Hits* during the Imperial Phase', in this volume.

seven compilations, three EPs and over fifty million records sold.[2] In 2013, however, and coinciding with the release of *Electric*, the Pet Shop Boys left Parlophone and founded their own label, x2, which has since produced (as of the time of writing) *Electric*, *Super* (2016), the *Agenda* EP and the *Inner Sanctum* live album (2019) and *Hotspot* (2020). Thus put, we could easily divide the Pet Shop Boys' run into three distinct eras: the short Bobby O. establishment year, the three-decade-long association with Parlophone, and the now decade-long self-publishing period.

It is, however, also possible to read the Pet Shop Boys in periodizations that have little to do with marketing or commercial success. Indeed, while it is commonplace to examine the Pet Shop Boys through the lens of queerness, and to recognize them as an established and influential gay group, in self-defining terms at least this was not always the case. Until the 1990s, neither Tennant nor Lowe would comment on their sexuality. However, in light of mounting pressure in the music press and from some segments of the gay community, in 1994 Tennant publicly came out. Though this was hardly a shock to industry insiders, nor to most of the Pet Shop Boys' fans ('In truth, you'd have to have been fairly thick not to have noticed,' *Classic Pop* declared in a 2018 retrospective),[3] it marked a significant turning point in how the Pet Shop Boys presented their music.

In this chapter, we argue that Tennant's coming-out, though the reluctant outcome of years'-long coercion, acted as a watershed moment. Where previously most Pet Shop Boys hits were sexually ambiguous, from *Bilingual* (1996) onwards, Tennant and Lowe increasingly engaged with queerness and gay sex in an open, explicit fashion. In this way, we propose a three-phased approach to the Pet Shop Boys' discography: the first decade (1984–94), in which the Pet Shop Boys' works were extensively queer-coded but not outright queer; an interregnum (1994–5), coinciding with Tennant's coming-out, in which Tennant and Lowe focused on their immediate legacy (and, arguably, the perceived consequences of the coming-out); and the post-coming-out era (1996–present), bookended by *Bilingual*, in which Tennant determined to embrace his public homosexuality. Through these lenses, we argue that we can approach how Tennant and Lowe conceive of the 'gay self' in both a private and public eye – and, consequently, we can begin to understand what Tennant and Lowe imagine a queer existence to be, how this has changed over time, and what circumstances have served to shape it.

---

[2] Jamie Crossan, 'Pet Shop Boys part with Parlophone and announce release of new album', *NME*, 14 March 2013, https://www.nme.com/news/music/pet-shop-boys-15-1262150.
[3] Ian Wade, 'Top 40 Pet Shop Boys Singles: #20: Liberation', *Classic Pop Presents Pet Shop Boys* (2018), 92.

Everyone knows when they look at us: early Pet Shop Boys (1984–94)

It is, of course, impossible to undo the past. Neil Tennant's declaration of his sexuality occurred three decades ago, meaning that his public gay persona is older than at least one of this volume's contributors. Consequently, it is difficult to remove the Pet Shop Boys' corpus from this now-known fact, just as it is also difficult not to read this back into the past.[4] In many ways, this is understandable; Neil Tennant would explain in 1994 that much of the group's oeuvre came from his own personal experience – not an uncommon position for a musician, but one that inexorably ties that experience, and thus the oeuvre, to his homosexuality. At the same time, the *ex post facto* retrospectives often seek to declare as self-evident facts that, at the time, were anything but.

Take 'It's a Sin' (1987), for example. One of the group's most iconic songs, it stands as a heartfelt and bittersweet testimony to the inner crisis of a young man growing up gay, in which 'the romance of homosexual longing is weighed up against the shame of homosexual wrongdoing'.[5] Engaging with 'It's a Sin' in 2023 is to take into account not only the original recording, but also nearly three and a half decades of live performance, not to mention the award-winning Russell T. Davies-helmed Channel 4 drama of the same name, the sequin-spangled live performance of the song by gay icons Sir Elton John and Years & Years' Olly Alexander at the 2021 Brit Awards, and that duo's cover being released as a single in the same year. From this vantage point, 'It's a Sin' cannot *possibly* be anything other than a gay anthem (as, indeed, it is), nor – surely – could any listener miss its glaringly obvious subtext. Yet, at the time of its release, this context *did* escape some listeners. The Salvation Army considered the song a heartening reflection of the fact that people still took the concept of 'sin' seriously.[6] In Tennant's native Newcastle, a local parish priest 'delivered a sermon on it, and reflected on how the Church changed from the promise of a ghastly hell to the message of love'.[7] The Catholic Agency for Overseas Development (CAFOD) appeared to be so taken by the song that it asked Neil

---

[4]In one of the early writing sessions for this chapter, one of us was forced to remind the other to 'remove your queer glasses' when listening to the lyrics – not, as it turns out, an easy undertaking!
[5]Paul Burston, 'Honestly', *Attitude* 1, no. 4 (1994): 68.
[6]Arwa Haider, 'It's a Sin – Pure pop provocation from the Pet Shop Boys', *Financial Times*, 11 October 2021, https://ig.ft.com/life-of-a-song/its-a-sin.html.
[7]Neil Tennant, cited in Andrew Sullivan [The Daily Dish], 'For Hard-Core Petheads: The Tennant Interview in Full', *The Atlantic*, 5 June 2009, https://www.theatlantic.com/daily-dish/archive/2009/06/for-hard-core-petheads-the-tennant-interview-in-full/200905/. 'Positive Role Model' was originally recorded for the soundtrack of the Pet Shop Boys' stage play *Closer to Heaven* in 2001, though it was performed by Tennant and Lowe at some concerts in 2000. Their own version of it, with substantially changed lyrics, was released as the B-side to the German issue of the single 'London' (2002), before appearing worldwide on their third remix album, *Disco 3* (2003).

Tennant to appear in an advertisement alongside Cardinal Basil Hume, who was President of the Catholic Bishops' Conference of England and Wales. Needless to say, Tennant did not take CAFOD up on the offer.[8]

In many ways, Tennant has argued in the past, 'It's a Sin' is an exemplar for the listener interpreting a song in ways not supported by the evidence at hand; quite aside from the Catholic Church's misplaced enthusiasm for it, it was originally intended to be 'kind of big and funny and camp', rather than deep and meaningful and cross-generationally enduring, and by Tennant's own estimation took him 'about fifteen minutes' to write.[9] Tennant has always acknowledged that fans will 'read things into' his songs, even if those things were absent from his intentions at the time of writing and recording.[10] Such was also true when, in 2009, he was interviewed by Andrew Sullivan, who asked whether the title of the song 'Positive Role Model' (2001/2003) included 'a double entendre' referring to the narrator's HIV+ status. Tennant responded, 'No. I mean, yes you are crazy, it doesn't.'[11] Nevertheless, and without explicit refutation in the song itself, Sullivan's interpretation is conceivable and plausible, even though it had not actually crossed the songwriter's mind in the process of writing the work itself.

Thus, we must take it with a grain of salt when Kristof Magnusson argues of 'Being Boring' (1990), 'With "We were never being boring", only the sexually liberated gays of the late seventies and early eighties could have been meant, who were fertile ground for the [AIDS] virus.'[12] This is not to say that Magnusson was wrong to read the song as such; Tennant *did* write 'Being Boring' as a lament for the lost generation of queer youth in the face of the HIV/AIDS pandemic. Nor was this an unlikely interpretation for Magnusson, himself a queer teenager at the time, to take to heart.[13] But it was not the *only* interpretation possible, given the subject matter, the lyrics and even the video accompanying the release of the single (kissing men and homoerotic imagery notwithstanding).

None of this precludes the Pet Shop Boys from having written and produced queer songs prior to Tennant's coming out in 1994 – to make that argument would be patently absurd. However, where that queerness appears within the pre-1994 corpus, it is certainly not *queerly explicit* – that is to say, it is not engaged in a way that brooks no doubt that the song should be listened to with an LGBTQIA+ context in mind. Instead, these songs often

---

[8]'History (1987)', *PetShopBoys.co.uk*, https://www.petshopboys.co.uk/history/1987; Stephen I. Gregson, 'Narrative, Spectacle, Performance: A Dramaturgical Investigation into the Relationship between an Aesthetic Event and the Social World in Rock and Pop Culture' (PhD diss., Pennsylvania State University, 2005), 66.
[9]Neil Tennant, interview with Chris Heath, 'Pet Shop Boys 1987–1988', *Pet Shop Boys Actually/ Further Listening 1987–1988* liner notes (2018), 7.
[10]Burston, 'Honestly', 64.
[11]Neil Tennant, cited in Sullivan, 'For Hard-Core Petheads'.
[12]Kristof Magnusson, *Pet Shop Boys* (Cologne: Kiepenhauer und Witsch, 2021), 34.
[13]Magnusson, *Pet Shop Boys*, 33.

appear as *queer-coded* outputs. A term most often applied to cinema, queer-coding refers to the portrayal of characters and circumstances in ways that are meant to be implicitly received as outside a hetero- and cis-normative baseline, without acknowledging in as many words that the character is indeed queer.[14] This coding is often achieved through the use of visual cues, social behaviours and the vocabulary associated – often via stereotypes – with queer sexuality. Jeffery Masten argues, for example, that Horatio's description of Hamlet as 'sweet' was a clear nod by William Shakespeare to contemporaneous audiences to an implied homoromanticism between the two friends.[15] Similarly, Richard Dyer has noted that F. W. Murnau's legendary adaptation of Bram Stoker's *Dracula* in the 1922 film *Nosferatu* (1922) is one that is 'eminently readable as gay' because of its conscious hinting at common homosexual tropes of its era: the vampire Orlok is gaunt, with limp wrists, a mincing gait and his face powdered white but accentuated by lipstick. 'When Orloc [sic.] goes down on [the protagonist Thomas] as he sleeps,' Dyer concludes wryly, 'he is not just making do with male "blood".'[16]

In other words, queer-coding ensures that an image – be it a person, a relationship, a setting – is to be understood as queer only if the viewer (or, in this case, the listener) possesses the key to decipher that code. Queer code, when wielded by the queer community itself, is well-nigh indecipherable to the outside observer, as indeed most inside practices of subcommunities are. The LGBTQIA+ subculture is awash with examples of this coding, up to and including generating its own form of signalling (such as the famous 'hanky code' in the United States) or its own language (such as Polari, which was prevalent in Britain as a means 'to criticise others without them knowing').[17]

---

[14] Vito Russo, *The Celluloid Closet: Homosexuality in the Movies* (New York: Harper Row, 1995), 59.

[15] Jeffery Masten, *Queer Philologies: Sex, Language, and Affect in Shakespeare's Time* (Philadelphia: University of Pennsylvania Press, 2016), 70–1; cf. Haley Hulan, 'Bury Your Gays: History, Usage, and Context', *McNair Scholars Journal* 21, no. 1 (2017): 18–19.

[16] Richard Dyer, 'Less and More than Women and Men: Lesbian and Gay Cinema in Weimar Germany', *New German Critique* 51 (1990): 23. Molly Harrabin also points to the connection between Orlok's queer-coding and perceived 'Jewishness' as a signal to contemporary audiences of his 'Otherness', a result of both anti-Semitic and homophobic tropes. Molly Harrabin, 'Racially Profiled? "Jewish" Vampires in Friedrich Wilhelm Murnau's *Nosferatu* (1922)', *Studies in European Cinema* (2023), doi: 10.1080/17411548.2023.2224702.

[17] For the 'hanky code', the defining work remains the photographic exhibition *Gay Semiotics*, developed by Hal Fischer in San Francisco in 1977. This is discussed in retrospect in Hal Fischer and Julia Bryan-Wilson, 'Gay Semiotics Revisited', *Aperture* 218 (2015): 32–9. Polari is discussed in depth in its own 'biography': Paul Baker, *Fabulosa! The Story of Polari, Britain's Secret Gay Language* (London: Reaktion, 2020); cf. David Wilkinson, 'Ever Fallen in Love (with Someone You Shouldn't Have?): Punk, Politics, and Same-Sex Passion', *Key Words: A Journal of Cultural Materialism* 13 (2015): 69. A twenty-first-century example is the adoption of Swedish furniture chain IKEA's stuffed shark toy, *Blåhaj*, as a symbol of the international transgender community, much to the bemusement and bewilderment of straight and cisgender journalists. Alice Gibbs, 'How the IKEA Shark Became a Trans Icon', *Newsweek*, 23 October 2022, https://www.newsweek.com/how-ikea-shark-became-trans-icon-1753400.

With this in mind, and especially considering the circumstances in which the Pet Shop Boys burst onto the international music scene, it is in retrospect perhaps unsurprising that Tennant and Lowe resort to code rather than to outright gay lyricism. Certainly, as *Please* entered the charts on both sides of the Atlantic in 1986, it brought with it a slew of hits: 'West End Girls', 'Suburbia', 'Opportunities (Let's Make Lots of Money)' and the bittersweet 'Love Comes Quickly'. Yet, engaged with on the basis of their lyrics, none of these songs unequivocally raised a (rainbow) flag, much less nailed the colours to the wall. Indeed, while 'Love Comes Quickly' alternated between the nearly ecstatic words of falling uncontrollably and unexpectedly in love and the heart-wrenching musical accompaniment suggesting sorrow and pain, it could just as easily describe *any* relationship. Even Tennant is unsure of the genesis of the song:

> The whole song was about how you can suddenly fall in love with someone and you can't help it. I was writing something gorgeously romantic, but I don't think it was about my life. Unless, now I think about it, it was about a friend falling in love, going through the traumatic start of a relationship, always rushing off and bursting into tears [. . .] When you fall in love with someone, it's totally disruptive. You're having a comfortable life, and suddenly everything's just turned upside down. All your priorities change. But the song is also saying that, after it's happened, you suddenly realise you hadn't really been alive at all.[18]

It is tempting to read in the tone of the song a sort of haunting quality, well in keeping with the experiences of a young man in the midst of the HIV/AIDS crisis and the bitter revanchism of the Thatcherite establishment, discovering with a mixture of excitable wonder and depressed existential dread the stigmatized pull of gay romance. Perhaps, that young man *does* exist between the verses and mournful, pulsating synth notes. If so, however, he is only there as a hint, an echo, and one of whom Neil Tennant himself seems (or at least professes to be) unaware. Something similar can be said of the Boys' celebrations of dating ('Tonight is Forever') and casual sex ('I Want a Lover'). Again, there is potentially more than just *moral* ambiguity at play when Tennant announces 'I don't want another drink or fight / I want a lover. / I don't care whether it's wrong or right / I want a lover tonight.'[19] But, insofar as the listener may guess that the person who will share the narrator's cab (and his bed, 'just as soon as we get home') is another man, nothing in the song itself suggests this (with the possible exception of the chorus refrain of 'tonight', achieved by overdubbing Tennant's voice in a slightly lower timbre, which *may*, at a stretch, suggest his lover joining him in song).

---

[18]Neil Tennant, interview with Chris Heath, 'Pet Shop Boys 1984–1986', *Pet Shop Boys Please/ Further Listening 1984–1986* liner notes (2018), 12–13.
[19]Pet Shop Boys, 'I Want a Lover', Parlophone, 1986.

Instead, it is our familiarity with Tennant, our knowledge of his sexuality as an immutable fact read into a song recorded eight years *before* that knowledge was made public, that plants this suggestion. Instead, of all of the *Please* songs, only one may plausibly be considered to sail close to the wind of explicit queer declaration. The album's penultimate track, 'Later Tonight', points in poetic mournfulness to an object of unrequited desire: 'That boy never cast a look in your direction / Never tried to hook for your affection.' In spite of the seeming ambivalence of the object of his affections, the narrator remains enchanted: 'He is the head boy of a school of thought / That plays in your intentions, night and day.'[20]

Here, unlike in 'Love Comes Quickly', Tennant is clear as to the inspiration for the song's 'head boy': 'It was about three of us staring out the window from the *Smash Hits* office at a cute boy walking down Carnaby Street.'[21] Yet again, however, the lyrics are couched in ambiguity; the person pining for this beautiful, 'tall and proud' man is not 'I', but 'you', offering a degree of uncertainty – could the addressee be a heterosexual woman? This, coupled with the track's slow, melancholy pacing and its placement at the tail end of the record, effectively buried its implications; as Tennant lamented to Chris Heath, 'This is the most gay song we've ever written, practically, and no one noticed at the time.'[22]

Tennant and Lowe returned to the recording studio in 1987 for *Actually*, an album that cemented their reputation for sly lyrical flourishes and (rightly or wrongly) irony. Once more, these characteristics can be seen in their flirtation with queer themes that rarely emerged from a fog of subcultural deniability. Most of the album's roster deals with themes of relationships and sex, but they remained open to interpretation. 'It's a Sin' has already been discussed at length here, but further examples abound. 'What Have I Done to Deserve This?', their first collaboration with Dusty Springfield, occupies a curious and yet, arguably, emblematic place on the album's back cover. On the one hand, the song is an exploration of the transactional nature of modern love, typified by Tennant's opening two lines: 'You always wanted a lover / I only wanted a job.'[23] In this, it engages with the commodification of romance that is later expanded upon in the same album, most presciently in 'Rent'. The dialogue between Tennant and Springfield suggests that it is *their* relationship being described through fast-talking and slow-walking people, poured drinks and crushed flowers. Springfield, however, had just returned to the recording studio, with her previously successful career of the 1960s and 1970s having been undermined by (among other things) the scandal of her same-sex

---

[20] Pet Shop Boys, 'Later Tonight', Parlophone, 1986.
[21] Neil Tennant, interview with Chris Heath, 'Pet Shop Boys 1984–1986', *Pet Shop Boys Please/ Further Listening 1984–1986* liner notes (2018), 21.
[22] Neil Tennant, interview with Chris Heath, 'Pet Shop Boys 1984–1986', *Pet Shop Boys Please/ Further Listening 1984–1986* liner notes (2018), 21.
[23] Pet Shop Boys and Dusty Springfield, 'What Have I Done to Deserve This?', Parlophone, 1987.

romantic life. The dialogue being undertaken, therefore, likely only carries the *veneer* of heterosexuality, while hinting at something rather less normative. This subversion of gender and sexual normativities is continued in 'Rent' while still maintaining a veneer of heterosexuality, where Tennant describes the song's narrator as existing in a submissive relationship, in which the narrator benefits materially from the trappings of affection. Tennant sings of being dressed up and bought things – objectifications not expected of a male partner – while the declaration 'I'm your puppet' is slightly modified by Tennant's normally crystal-clear diction, which here teasingly half-renders 'puppet' as 'poppet', a diminutive term of endearment more commonly applied to a woman.[24] (Tennant later stated that he wrote the song from the perspective of a 'a female prostitute [or] a kept woman [. . .] in America. I vaguely thought of one of the Kennedys for some reason.')[25]

The pattern continues throughout the album. 'It Couldn't Happen Here', the first of the Pet Shop Boys' songs dedicated to a community ravaged by AIDS, skirts around making this connection plain to a listener not immediately aware that the people 'in six-inch heels / quoting magazines' were the characters Tennant often saw in London's gay clubs nearly a decade and a half earlier.[26] 'Heart', a surprise number 1 hit that topped the chart for three weeks, succeeded in Tennant's estimation precisely because it was 'a completely straightforward love song with a wacky video', without subtext of any kind.[27] 'I Want to Wake Up', another lamenting unrequited love through the guise of a messy love triangle (or quadrangle) that may or may not be bisexual in nature ('It's mad to be in love with someone else / When you're in love with he / She's in love with me / But you know as well as I do I can never think of anyone else but you'), obfuscates the possible queerness of the relationship at the heart of the song through imperfect grammar and a hazy picture of the affairs being discussed.[28]

How the Pet Shop Boys intended to engage with questions of sexuality was laid down in the foundations of their first two albums. Not long after *Actually*'s success, and at the height of the 'imperial phase', Tennant and Lowe performed at *Before the Act*, a benefit on behalf of the gay community and in opposition to the Conservative government's Section 28 reforms outlawing LGBTQIA+ education in schools. Moreover, their collaboration with Dusty Springfield would not be their last conspicuous work with a queer community icon. To this extent, as Tennant would later explain in 1994, 'I do think that we have

---

[24]Pet Shop Boys, 'Rent', Parlophone, 1987.
[25]Neil Tennant, interview with Chris Heath, 'Pet Shop Boys 1987–1988', *Pet Shop Boys Actually/Further Listening 1987–1988* liner notes (2018), 10.
[26]Neil Tennant, cited in Sullivan, 'For Hard-Core Petheads'.
[27]The video's most famous drawcard was that it starred Ian McKellen as a vampire. Neil Tennant, interview with Chris Heath, 'Pet Shop Boys 1987–1988', *Pet Shop Boys Actually/Further Listening 1987–1988* liner notes (2018), 20.
[28]Pet Shop Boys, 'I Want to Wake Up', Parlophone, 1987.

contributed [...] rather a lot to what you might call "gay culture".'[29] If this engagement with queerness was unequivocal, however, it stood in sharp contrast to the Pet Shop Boys' musical output which, in spite of its queer trappings, defied easy and clear-cut classification. Symbolic of this was the next album, *Introspective* (1988), which boldly appeared with a rainbow cover that was not, according to Tennant, intended to reflect the Pride flag. This is representative of the peculiar place held by the album in the group's discography. Two songs, 'I Want a Dog' and 'Domino Dancing', are direct references to Chris Lowe's long-time friend and (in some quarters) rumoured lover, Peter Andreas; ostensibly, the first song resulted from Andreas' regret that he wanted a small dog because his flat was too small to accommodate a larger one, while 'Domino Dancing' had its origins in Andreas beating Tennant and Lowe at dominos while they were in Antigua, and celebrating each victory with a dance.[30] In the former, the narrator finds resolution by rejecting the idea of getting a cat, something that would fit nicely with his lived reality, and instead opts for a chihuahua – quite possibly the most feminine-coded breed of dog one could acquire short of a cat. The latter song, while on the surface about a heterosexual romance, came with a music video following two admirers pursuing a beautiful woman, only to end up in a shirtless, sweaty fight in the street first, before wrestling in the shallow water on the beach. This, too, was the closing shot of the video – the public drew their conclusions.

Indeed, the closest Tennant and Lowe came to speaking openly about queerness in this period came not from a track on this so-called 'imperial album', but from the B-side to the single 'It's Alright', the funereal and sweet 'Your Funny Uncle'. Like much of the Pet Shop Boys' supporting catalogue, 'Your Funny Uncle' encapsulates much of what is quintessential about the group: mournful optimism and hopeful sadness, interspersed with poetry and the Book of Revelations. Written about the funeral of a friend of Tennant's, who had died of AIDS, its timing given the then-current health crisis was likely indicative for fans, as was the titular 'funny uncle', recalling the by-then outdated slang term 'funny fellow' to refer to a gay man.[31]

Likewise, 1990's *Behaviour*, in spite of its more sentimental, heartfelt and, ironically, introspective orientation, steered clear of more than oblique positions on its creators' sexuality. While 'So Hard', the album's lead single, detailed the disintegration of a relationship rocked by mutual infidelity (and

---

[29]Burston, 'Honestly', 66.
[30]Neil Tennant, interview with Jon Savage, *Pet Shop Boys Alternative* liner notes (1995), 13; Neil Tennant, interview with Chris Heath, 'Pet Shop Boys 1988–1989', *Pet Shop Boys Introspective/Further Listening 1988–1989* liner notes (2018), 9.
[31]This play on words is unlikely to have been deliberate. Tennant recalled meeting his friend's uncle, 'who had been in the army all of his life and suddenly found himself at the funeral of his evidently gay nephew who'd died of Aids. I think it must have been quite a difficult situation for him, but he was really nice.' Neil Tennant, interview with Chris Heath, 'Pet Shop Boys 1988–1989', *Pet Shop Boys Introspective/Further Listening 1988–1989* liner notes (2018), 28.

with its title and the line 'We make it so hard for ourselves' acting as a double entendre), the two-track medley of 'Nervously' and 'The End of the World' began with the possibility that Neil Tennant's narrator and his potential love interest might *both* be the 'nervous boy' of the lyrics. 'The End of the World' repeats the refrain 'It's just a boy, or a girl / It's not the end of the world' – at once both a cautious reprimand for those in the press who had speculated at length at this point and offering faint endorsement for the loved ones of queer youth that their romantic partners did not necessitate 'teenage destruction', regardless of their gender. Ironically, the B-side for 'So Hard' declared confidently, 'Everyone knows when they look at us / Of course they do, it must be obvious,' and yet *Behaviour* – the haunting queer requiem of 'Being Boring' notwithstanding – further muddied the waters.[32]

Tennant and Lowe's last studio outing in this first, pre-coming-out phase was *Very*, along with its rare, limited-release companion album, *Relentless* (1993). Brimming with high-energy dance and disco-inspired electronic tracks, it is not infrequently referred to as the Pet Shop Boys' 'coming-out' album.[33] In style, there is something to this. The muted visuals and vocals of *Behaviour* are gone; instead, Tennant and Lowe appear in the singles videos in front of flamboyant computer-generated landscapes and wearing a variety of garish jumpsuits: pink, black and white in 'I Wouldn't Normally Do This Kind of Thing'; blue and yellow (with a vast array of athletic, white tank-topped men) in 'Go West'; bright orange in 'Can You Forgive Her?' Here, too, are far more playful allusions: 'Can You Forgive Her?' imagines a closeted gay man facing his (female) partner after she twigs to his hidden sexuality, his 'youthful follies and changing teams', while the very title of 'Liberation' and its celebration of unrestrained love invokes the contemporaneous gay liberation movement. Even here, however, the disaster of AIDS is ever-present, represented by the surreal 'Dreaming of the Queen', as well as the Chris Lowe-helmed hidden track, two minutes after the end of 'Go West'. Usually referred to as 'Postscript', though it has no official title, the short song acts as a eulogy for Peter Andreas, who at the time of the album's release was terminally ill.

Once again, though, the album's reputation as 'the gay album' relies extensively on the listener's familiarity with queer-coding. 'Can You Forgive Her?', for example, is on the face of it about a failing relationship between a man and a woman. Our recognition of the man's sexuality comes from implicit clues within the lyrics: that he prefers disco to rock music; that he 'changed teams'; that at school he was 'easily led / behind the cricket pavilion and the bicycle shed', suggesting that he attended an independent, likely

---

[32]Pet Shop Boys, 'It Must Be Obvious', Parlophone, 1990.
[33]Rik Flynn, 'Making Pet Shop Boys: Very', *Classic Pop*, 5 July 2021, https://www.classicpopmag.com/2021/07/pet-shop-boys-very/; David Bennun, 'Pet Shop Boys, Beyond the Hits: Dreaming of the Queen', *The Quietus*, 28 April 2021, https://thequietus.com/articles/29906-pet-shop-boys-best-of-b-sides-album-tracks-beyond-the-hits.

single-sex school, and that these were areas to be frequented exclusively by other boys. 'I Wouldn't Normally Do This Kind of Thing' documents a joyous change in the narrator's life and, while the nature of this change is left unspoken, it is dismissed by the people he knows as 'just a phase he's going through'. 'Go West' – its homoerotic video notwithstanding – was, of course, not written by Tennant and Lowe.[34]

It is, in fact, striking that *Very*, with its reputation as a formative gay record, continues to don a veil that, by now, is fraying at the edges, but nevertheless still covers its songs' meanings. This is not to say that there are not more explicit works from the same period. These fall into two categories. In the case of 'We Came from Outer Space' and 'One Thing Leads to Another', both were released on the limited-edition companion synthpop album, *Relentless*. This album holds a curious position in the Pet Shop Boys back catalogue, for the simple fact that it only went through one publication run, has never been reissued, and its songs have neither appeared on the Pet Shop Boys *Further Listening* collections, nor on B-side compilations, nor (as of the time of writing) on any streaming service. For the most part an instrumental track without singing, 'We Came from Outer Space' includes a recurring motif in which a distorted female voice asks, 'Do you know the difference between the two genders?', whereupon a male voice hesitantly responds, 'No?' – suggesting, naturally, that there *is* no difference in how the genders should be perceived, and therefore in whom one can love. More explicitly, the closing track – 'One Thing Leads to Another' – provides a narration of the song's protagonist's life rewinding from his moment of death. Prior to the car accident that ends his life, we discover that the protagonist has found a lover: 'She's a man / but when you get down to it / She says sure you can / You wanna make love to her.'[35]

Also, more than suggestive were the B-sides to 'Yesterday, When I Was Mad'. One, 'If Love Were All', is a cover of a composition originally by the legendary gay playwright Noël Coward, in which Tennant laments, 'I think if only somebody splendid really needed me / Someone affectionate and dear. / Cares would be ended if I knew that he / Wanted to have me near.'[36] A second B-side, 'Some Speculation', has Tennant, uncharacteristically in falsetto, singing once more about unfaithfulness while taking aim at the media for constantly questioning his sex life. The lines 'Going away with someone new / Yesterday I went there too' do, however, suggest a love triangle that at least hints at a queer liaison.[37] Finally, and most boldly, 'Euroboy' – a high powered dance/trance track helmed by Chris Lowe – shares its name with a gay soft

---

[34]Cf. Adrian Daub, 'The End of the West', and Torsten Kathke, 'Go West, Young Band!', in this volume, for a closer analysis of 'Go West'.
[35]Pet Shop Boys, 'One Thing Leads to Another', Parlophone, 1993.
[36]Pet Shop Boys, 'If Love Were All', Parlophone, 1993.
[37]Pet Shop Boys, 'Some Speculation', Parlophone, 1993.

porn magazine, while the sparse lyrics are largely comprised of 'You want a lover / You want a new lover' and 'You was my lover man.'[38]

Overall, the pre-1994 oeuvre of the Pet Shop Boys contains significant queer code. Outright declarations of queerness, however, are conspicuous by their absence. It seems not to be coincidental that, on the occasions when Tennant and Lowe abandoned pretence and deniability and revelled in unfiltered queer content, they did so either through the medium of a B-side to a single (such as 'Your Funny Uncle' or 'Euroboy') or via *Relentless*, an album designed to have a limited audience. These were records for the in-group, the truest and most dedicated fans, not the casual listener. To hear Chris Lowe declare 'You was my lover man', or Neil Tennant wax lyrical about a carefree existence if an 'affectionate and dear' man would have him, was a deep cut, an open secret, a rare instance of an uncoded message sent in the clear but only for those most receptive to it.

This is not to say that the Pet Shop Boys' pre-1994 discography is an exercise in denial. Far from it: gay and queer allusions abound, and these helped to cement the group as a staple of gay club culture in Britain and Europe (and, to a lesser extent, the United States) throughout the second half of the 1980s and the first half of the 1990s. As journalist Paul Burston explains in his 1994 interview with Tennant for *Attitude*, there has always been a queer reading of Pet Shop Boys lyrics, though some of these readings are closer to the surface than others. Burston's first experience listening to the Pet Shop Boys came during an evening at the legendary LGBTQIA+ nightclub Heaven in Charing Cross in 1986. '[I was] watching a boy in a tight white vest dancing to *Opportunities*', he recalls:

> He wasn't being ironic. Neither, at the time, were the Boys. I've always thought that there was something vaguely sexual about that song. In the video, Neil, dressed like a proper toff, hangs around a garage, trying to solicit a response from a very sullen Chris Lowe: 'I've got the brains, you've got the looks, let's make lots of money.' Basically, it's a song about pulling a fast one, and there's always been more than one way of interpreting that.[39]

The question of identity depends on who I'm meant to be: the *Attitude* interview (1994)

The circumstances of Neil Tennant's public coming out are, in many ways, as understated as much of the Pet Shop Boys' discography. In 1994, Tennant sat

---

[38]Pet Shop Boys, 'Euroboy', Parlophone, 1993. According to Chris Lowe, he was not familiar with the magazine at the time – a claim of questionable veracity. Cf. Chris Lowe, interview with Jon Savage, *Pet Shop Boys Alternative* liner notes (1995), 27.
[39]Burston, 'Honestly', 68.

for an interview with *Attitude*, the United Kingdom's leading gay magazine. Briefed beforehand that 'Neil Tennant has Something To Tell Me', and warned to 'please respect his feelings and please, *please* be gentle with him', Paul Burston was surprised to find that nearly the first half of the interview passed before anyone – including, for that matter, himself – raised the issue of Tennant's sexuality. Eventually, amid discussions of the recording of 'Absolutely Fabulous' or Kylie Minogue's latest album, Burston asked what he termed a 'very long, elaborate question' about the group's relationship with the gay community and the gay press. At length, Tennant replied:

> I could spend several pages discussing the notion of 'gay culture', but for the sake of argument, I would just say that we have contributed a lot. And the simple reason for this is that I have written songs from my own point of view [. . .] What I'm actually saying is, I am gay, and I have written songs from that point of view.[40]

Tennant concluded this line of questioning with 'a glass of mineral water' and the curt segue: 'Well, what's your next question?'[41]

Though the acknowledgement may appear at first glance anticlimactic, it represented something of a policy shift. Previously, Tennant and Lowe had insisted that they had no need to discuss their sex lives in the press, arguing that there was a need to separate the private and public arenas. This had led to no small degree of criticism from some quarters; as has already been noted elsewhere in this volume, the lack of an explicit statement of queerness led many American audiences to feel alienated by the Pet Shop Boys while, closer to home, Jimmy Somerville of the Communards and Bronski Beat heavily criticized Tennant and Lowe along similar lines.[42] Under these circumstances, and after years of innuendo, Tennant evidently felt that it was no longer tenable, nor productive, to avoid declaring what many of his fans and listeners had presumed for the best part of a decade.

Why *had* he avoided this issue? To some extent, we can perhaps read in this the characteristic Pet Shop Boys obstinance and oppositional stance. When Jimmy Somerville took to the national press in 1986 to criticize Tennant and Lowe because 'they still won't publicly admit they're gay', he took the extraordinary step of doing so in the pages of the *Sun*, a tabloid that heretofore had earned an unenviable reputation for sensationalism and sleaze. The *Sun*, after all, had been in the vanguard of demonizing the British gay community as AIDS tore through it, labelling it a 'gay blood plague' in

---

[40]Burston, 'Honestly', 64–6.
[41]Burston, 'Honestly', 66.
[42]Burston, 'Honestly', 64; Olivia Laing, 'Lyrical: Neil Tennant', *Fantastic Man* 34 (2021–2), https://www.fantasticman.com/features/neil-tennant; Mark Lindores, 'West End Boys', *Classic Pop Presents Pet Shop Boys* (2018), 15; Jan-Niklas Jäger, *Factually: Pet Shop Boys in Theorie und Praxis* (Mainz: Ventil, 2019), 97.

1983 before, in 1986, running an infamous headline in which a Humberside vicar declared, 'I'd shoot my son if he had AIDS.'[43] But Somerville's deal with 'the enemy' was not Tennant's chief bone to pick. Instead, he found the opinion 'arrogant of him, actually'. He continued:

> He obviously thought that he had a right to talk about us in that way, and that his views on the subject were more important than our own views. His view is that the entire point of being a pop star is to be a positive role model. I reject any notion of being a positive role model to anyone. I personally find that an arrogant way to think of oneself.[44]

To be clear, Tennant has never suggested that the Pet Shop Boys' music should not be tied to queer identification. When Andrew Sullivan interviewed him in 2009 and expressed that the Boys' discography is 'music that has made me feel less lonely as a human being and as a gay person', Tennant replied, 'I know this sounds corny but that's actually one of the reasons we write it.'[45] But, he explained, there was a difference between what Somerville was attempting to do with Bronski Beat, and what Neil Tennant was trying to do with the Pet Shop Boys. 'Jimmy Somerville was, in effect, a politician using the medium of pop music to put his message across. The Pet Shop Boys came along to make fabulous records. We didn't come along to be politicians.'[46]

A further reason to sidestep the issue was Tennant's fear that the group would be pigeon-holed. He had always sought to 'make my lyrics generally applicable', to straight and queer audiences alike: by coming out, he feared that he would cease being a pop star, and would instead become 'gay pop star Neil Tennant'.[47] This would silo the Pet Shop Boys away, shepherd them into an enforced identity in which their broad appeal would be fettered away. This, he felt, was antithetical not only to the ambitions of the Pet Shop Boys as musicians, but also to the wellbeing of queer people as a whole, whose identities would be narrowed to that which was imperfectly described as 'gay culture'. 'They use it to marginalise you,' he told Ian Harrison many years later, recalling that, when his friend and musical collaborator Dusty Springfield died,

---

[43]Russell T. Davies, 'I looked away for years. Finally, I have put Aids at the centre of a drama', *Observer*, 3 January 2021, https://www.theguardian.com/tv-and-radio/2021/jan/03/russell-t-davies-i-looked-away-for-years-finally-i-have-put-aids-at-the-centre-of-a-drama.
[44]Burston, 'Honestly', 64.
[45]Neil Tennant, cited in Sullivan, 'For Hard-Core Petheads'.
[46]Burston, 'Honestly', 66.
[47]Ian Harrison, '"We Prefer Not to Be Fake . . ." Neil Tennant of the Pet Shop Boys Interviewed', *MOJO* (2013), https://www.mojo4music.com/articles/stories/we-prefer-not-to-be-fake-pet-shop-boys-interviewed/.

I did some interviews at the request of her management and the first person said to me, 'Why was she such a gay icon?' and I said, 'To call her a gay icon is simply to marginalise her, it's to say, "She's only of interest to gay people", and you have this stereotyped idea of what gay people like' [. . .] [I]t annoys me because there's a lot of sort of ghettoising that goes on with it. Because you know, gay people like Oasis as well, believe it or not.[48]

Did you see me coming? Was I that obvious? *Bilingual* and after (1996–present)

Tennant's fears of 'ghettoising' seemed in some ways to be realized by the time the next studio album, *Bilingual*, was recorded in 1996. When the album was due for release in the United States, the Pet Shop Boys signed with Atlantic Records, only to find to their surprise (and Tennant's resentment) that the marketing would not be coordinated through the label's regular marketing section, but through a separate and distinct 'gay marketing department'.[49] In and of itself, Tennant had no objection to acknowledging a gay audience, nor the existence of a group of marketers focusing on queer music-lovers, but, he noted, 'I think they think, "that's it"' – the Pet Shop Boys were now gay and gay only, thus realizing his concern that his name would always be preceded by the rider 'gay pop star'.[50]

But the album itself, on the other hand, seemed to ignore Tennant's own worries; whereas his *Attitude* interview in 1994 had been reluctant and cautious, the product at least in part of coercion and submitting to external pressures, *Bilingual* was nothing if not exuberantly queer, in a way that no previous record – not even the supposed 'gay album' *Very* – had even come close to. While the opening medley of 'Discoteca' and 'Single' played in familiar queer-coded territory, the rap-and-disco-inspired 'Metamorphosis' had Tennant narrating not to give in to 'a long-term suppression of an adolescent urge', resulting in answers to his questions about 'the big S-E-X'. His likening of himself as 'once a caterpillar, now a butterfly' allowed little room for interpretation, only reinforced by Chris Lowe's more gruffly and masculine-intoned line 'It's all about love, it's a metamorphosis' in alternating chorus lines.[51] The following song, 'Electricity', has Tennant inhabit the

---

[48]Harrison, '"We Prefer Not to Be Fake"'.
[49]Neil Tennant, interview with Guy Raz, 'All Things Considered', *NPR*, 9 September 2012, https://www.npr.org/2012/09/09/160750906/pet-shop-boys-leave-west-end-to-explore-elysium.
[50]Harrison, '"We Prefer Not to Be Fake"'.
[51]Pet Shop Boys, 'Metamorphosis', Parlophone, 1996.

flamboyant persona of a drag queen, inspired by the New York and Las Vegas disco legend Monti Rock III – better known through his 1970s guise as the face of the outrageous Disco Tex and His Sex-O-Lettes.[52] Any lingering doubts are dispelled by the time Tennant and Lowe turn to 'Se a Vida É (That's the Way Life Is)', the fifth track on the album, in which Tennant implores the listener, 'You've got to throw those skeletons out of your closet / And come outside.'[53] Hardly less clear was the single 'A Red Letter Day', a swelling, heartening reminder of the importance of love and the desire for security that comes from it: 'But for all of those who don't fit in / Who follow their instincts and are told they sin / This is a prayer for a different way' recalls the Pet Shop Boys' much earlier parable of queer life, 1987's 'It's a Sin' (as well as *Very*'s 'To Speak is a Sin', which according to Tennant is set in a gay bar), while cementing the fact that the behaviour condemned as 'sin' – that is, homosexuality – is no less than a natural and instinctual drive.[54] As if to dispel the last vestiges of the aforementioned closeted skeletons, Tennant and Lowe also made a bold design choice for one of the singles: while 'Before' was released on CD featuring portraits of the two musicians on the sleeve, the cover for the 12" vinyl displayed a close-up shot of a flaccid penis framed by blue-tinted pubic hair.

Bilingual is a turning point in the Pet Shop Boys' development as artists. Prior to its publication in 1996, the principal means by which Tennant and Lowe communicated queer messages was through queer-coding, with some being more veiled than others. *Bilingual*, on the other hand, marked the first moment that Tennant self-consciously took to the recording studio with the aim of declaring his sexuality explicitly through his music. From this point onwards, the Pet Shop Boys' output would increasingly tie itself to such unequivocal identifications with queerness. When, in 1999, they released *Nightlife*, the album included not only several playful engagements with the *Nosferatu*-like tropes of vampirism that Dyer identifies as 'eminently gay', but also a duet with Kylie Minogue in which Tennant's narrator is explicitly identified as gay, while the video for the hit single 'New York City Boy' is a pastiche of gay staples, including drag, go-go-dancing sailors and the legendary Studio 54 nightclub.[55] *Release* (2002), musically a more restrained album more in the mould of *Behaviour*, pushed the boundaries even further. In 'The Night I Fell in Love', Tennant and Lowe approached the issue of homophobia in music, and in particular the homophobic lyrics of rapper Eminem. The song sees a male teenage fan invited to Eminem's room after a concert, where they sleep together until, in the morning, the boy realizes he is late for school. Meanwhile, other contemporary recordings celebrate sexy

---

[52]Pet Shop Boys, 'Electricity', Parlophone, 1996.
[53]Pet Shop Boys, 'Se a Vida É (That's the Way Life Is)', Parlophone, 1996.
[54]Pet Shop Boys, 'A Red Letter Day', Parlophone, 1996.
[55]Pet Shop Boys, 'Vampires', Parlophone, 1999; Pet Shop Boys and Kylie Minogue, 'In Denial', Parlophone, 1999.

(and explicitly male) northerners and, in at least two instances, gay affairs with married men.[56]

The shifting weight that Tennant and Lowe place on the explicit expression of queerness in their oeuvre is further illustrated by the release of their 2008 record *Yes*. The record bears close sonic ties to 1988's *Introspective*, in that it – much like its earlier companion – makes extensive use of fusion sounds, while overall being dominated by a distinctively upbeat pop-feel. While *Introspective* borrows from Latin American soundscapes (such as on 'Domino Dancing'), *Yes* combines, for instance, country folk with the Pet Shop Boys' distinctive pop synths on the song 'Beautiful People'. The acoustic guitar opening on 'Did You See Me Coming?' as well as the guitar on 'Building a Wall' are also tiebacks to their very early (and subsequently scrapped) work inspired by Pete Shelley's 'Homosapien'.[57] Clearly, *Yes* is a record well aware of its roots and one that does not shy away from playfully engaging with them. The album artwork, thus, might well be one of the most interesting aspects of the record: a checkmark, made up of eleven coloured blocks, each symbolizing one track on the record. Designed by Mark Farrow and inspired by Gerhard Richter, the record was released in several limited issues, all following the straight (pun intended) design language of colourful blocks, often overlayed over the faces of Tennant and Lowe.[58] Whereas the duo vehemently denied that *Introspective*'s colourful rainbow blocks were inspired by the Pride flag, *Yes*'s colour band seems to almost scream an affirmation of visual queerness: yes, check mark! It's queer!

The Pet Shop Boys are all too happy to pair songs and records together, sometimes over decades, and in this sense 2008's *Yes* feels distinctively like a sister record to 1988's *Introspective*. It positions itself not only as a companion, but also a corrective voice for the previously explicitly unspoken, not only a literal but also figurative check mark and a lyrical affirmation of an outward queerness, which *Introspective* kept, well, introspective. Ironically, one of the most poignant corrective pieces on *Yes* finds its companion not on *Introspective*, but on *Behaviour* (1990). While Tennant and Lowe's narrator on the B-side track 'It Must Be Obvious' still struggled with the anxiety of being clocked as queer in the face of a failing relationship, *Yes*'s 'Did You See Me Coming?' feels like a love letter not only to the narrator's love interest but

---

[56]Pet Shop Boys, 'Sexy Northerner', Parlophone, 2002. Both songs about extramarital affairs have close ties with the Pet Shop Boys' past: 'Try It (I'm in Love with a Married Man)' was written by Bobby Orlando and originally recorded by his concept group Oh Romeo in 1983, while 'In Private' was written by Tennant and Lowe for Dusty Springfield, and covered by the Pet Shop Boys in 2006 in collaboration with Elton John. Pet Shop Boys, 'Try It (I'm in Love with a Married Man)', Parlophone, 2003; Pet Shop Boys and Elton John, 'In Private', Parlophone, 2006.

[57]Cf. Neil Tennant, *One Hundred Lyrics and a Poem: 1979–2016* (London: Faber & Faber, 2018), xiii.

[58]Sleevage, 'Pet Shop Boys: Yes', *Sleevage* (2010), https://web.archive.org/web/20100103033759/http://sleevage.com/pet-shop-boys-yes/.

also his younger, anxious self. Being read as queer is no longer a source of fear; rather, it is carefully wrapped in the giddy anticipation of a new relationship beginning to emerge on the horizon.

In later discography, too, the connection to gay relationships is made explicit. The Pet Shop Boys' first album of the 2020s, *Hotspot*, opens with the narrator meeting a former lover – his 'will-o-the-wisp' – on the U1 underground train in Berlin, with the line 'I think, my, you may have changed / But you're such a handsome thing', demonstrating clearly that the object of his observation is a man. In the final track of the album, 'Wedding in Berlin', a dance beat is superimposed over Mendelssohn's 'Wedding March' and the bells of the St Matthias church in Berlin, as Tennant impishly sings, 'We're getting married / A lot of people do it / Don't matter if they're straight or gay.'

Conclusion

In a 2001 interview with the LGBTQIA+ magazine *The Advocate*, Neil Tennant was asked about his plans for a gay music festival, *Wotapalava*, which was slated to take place over July and August of that year. Tennant explained the meaning of the festival's name:

> The title reflects our attitude on sexuality, which at the end of the day is a lot of fuss about nothing. Because some people have sex with people of the same sex, an entire culture has been created, broadly speaking, out of oppression. Which in a rational world would not be an issue. We hope we are moving toward a world where [sexual orientation] is not an issue, because we hate the idea of a gay ghetto.[59]

It is a curious paradox: on the one hand, Tennant has always been critical of the idea of an overarching 'gay culture', and for many years resisted pressure to openly identify himself as part of it. On the other hand, having finally done so, he and bandmate Chris Lowe wasted little time in embracing a newer, freer means of openly grasping their queer roots – not only through such visibly gay albums as *Bilingual*, but also through headlining Pride in London, and attempting to organize the world's first explicitly LGBTQIA+ pop festival. Tennant, however, saw little contradiction; explaining the concept of *Wotapalava*, he pointed to the fact that the headlining acts had little in common in terms of their musical output or stage presence, save for the fact that 'they're gay or have gay members'.[60] In hindsight, it is perhaps more plausible to suggest that the eventual failure of *Wotapalava* was much

---

[59] Carole Pope, 'West End Boys', *The Advocate*, 17 July 2001, https://www.thefreelibrary.com/West+End+Boys.-a076577632.
[60] Pope, 'West End Boys'.

more the result of this, and less the result of the highly-publicized withdrawal of Sinéad O'Connor.

That being said, Tennant's stance on *Wotapalava*, while puzzling from a commercial perspective, seems in turn to be entirely in keeping with his long-standing personal attitude with reference to his own sexuality and the role that it plays in his life as a musician, performer and public figure. '[B]eing gay isn't a cultural choice, which means you've got to like Barbra Streisand records,' he concluded. 'You can be what you want to be.'[61] This, in essence, is the sort of undifferentiated, liberal future in which it 'don't matter if they're straight or gay' that he has been hoping for, both in his public persona and in the music that he and Lowe have been making since the 1980s. Of course, perfect equality has not been achieved, and is not close to being achieved; in that regard, while the Pet Shop Boys will undoubtedly continue to produce music that preaches that sexuality should not make a difference to how someone is treated, the fact that they *will* continue to do that is a tacit admission that, in the world as it is, it *does* make a difference. To wit, the Pet Shop Boys will keep on making gay anthems in the hope that one day they won't need to.

What Tennant has wanted is to be is a songwriter who can reach people. Often, this has reflected his own experience, and within that experience is his reality as a gay man who has lived through the AIDS crisis, Section 28, its repeal, the equalization of the age of consent and the legislation of marriage equality. From the outset, he has sought to resist having the Pet Shop Boys characterized as *only* being a group making music for gay men. To that extent, and especially owing to the stigmatization of gay people at the time that the Pet Shop Boys gained their foothold in the international music scene and entered their 'imperial phase', the Boys' identification with queerness was at once clear to those 'in the know' and obscured to those outside of queer society, who did not recognize the queer-coding that Tennant and Lowe expertly wielded across a number of albums and singles. That coding remains to this day a vital element of the Pet Shop Boys' music.

From 1996 and the release of *Bilingual*, however, it has been complemented by more explicit messaging. 1999's 'You Only Tell Me You Love Me When You're Drunk', a haunting, country and western-inspired requiem to a failing relationship, casts both our narrator and his mercurial partner as male – the narrator by dint of being sung by Tennant, the partner owing to his drunkenness and his characterization as being 'subtle, solemn, and silent as a monk'.[62] It is not so much that this song was not possible in the Pet Shop Boys' discography prior to 1996 and the precedent set by *Bilingual* – indeed, as we have noted, other explicitly gay songs such as 'If Love Were All' or 'Euroboy' were released years earlier – but that it was not possible *as a single*

---

[61]Pope, 'West End Boys'.
[62]Pet Shop Boys, 'You Only Tell Me You Love Me When You're Drunk', Parlophone, 1999.

before this point. Tennant's coming-out interview in *Attitude* was not entirely of his own volition, that much is clear. But it would be a mistake to cast him as a helpless victim of outside machinations. Having found himself in such a situation, Tennant, in conjunction with Lowe, launched a distinct phase of their career, leaving aside pretence and innuendo and, while holding firm to the principle that their music is about much more than who they may sleep with, they have also embraced their role as queer statesmen of European synthpop. We as listeners are not certain who, precisely, is watching the beautiful mod boy as he walks past the Carnaby Street office in 'Later Tonight'; thirty-three years later, in 'Will-o-the-Wisp', it is not only obvious but explicit that the person gazing longingly at the 'handsome thing' on an U-Bahn journey through the middle of Berlin is none other than Neil Tennant himself.

Bibliography

Baker, Paul. *Fabulosa! The Story of Polari, Britain's Secret Gay Language*. London: Reaktion, 2020.

Bennun, David. 'Pet Shop Boys, Beyond the Hits: Dreaming of the Queen.' *The Quietus*, 28 April 2021, https://thequietus.com/articles/29906-pet-shop-boys-best-of-b-sides-album-tracks-beyond-the-hits.

Burston, Paul. 'Honestly.' *Attitude* 1, no. 4 (1994).

Crossan, Jamie. 'Pet Shop Boys part with Parlophone and announce release of new album.' *NME*, 14 March 2013, https://www.nme.com/news/music/pet-shop-boys-15-1262150.

Davies, Russell T. 'I looked away for years. Finally, I have put Aids at the centre of a drama.' *Observer*, 3 January 2021, https://www.theguardian.com/tv-and-radio/2021/jan/03/russell-t-davies-i-looked-away-for-years-finally-i-have-put-aids-at-the-centre-of-a-drama.

Dyer, Richard. 'Less and More than Women and Men: Lesbian and Gay Cinema in Weimar Germany.' *New German Critique* 51 (1990): 5–60.

Fischer, Hal and Julia Bryan-Wilson. 'Gay Semiotics Revisited.' *Aperture* 218 (2015): 32–9.

Flynn, Rik. 'Making Pet Shop Boys: Very.' *Classic Pop*, 5 July 2021, https://www.classicpopmag.com/2021/07/pet-shop-boys-very/.

Gibbs, Alice. 'How the IKEA Shark Became a Trans Icon.' *Newsweek*, 23 October 2022, https://www.newsweek.com/how-ikea-shark-became-trans-icon-1753400.

Gregson, Stephen I. 'Narrative, Spectacle, Performance: A Dramaturgical Investigation into the Relationship between an Aesthetic Event and the Social World in Rock and Pop Culture.' PhD diss., Pennsylvania State University, 2005.

Haider, Arwa. 'It's a Sin – Pure pop provocation from the Pet Shop Boys.' *Financial Times*, 11 October 2021, https://ig.ft.com/life-of-a-song/its-a-sin.html.

Harrabin, Molly. 'Racially Profiled? "Jewish" Vampires in Friedrich Wilhelm Murnau's *Nosferatu* (1922).' *Studies in European Cinema* (2023), doi: 10.1080/17411548.2023.2224702.

Harrison, Ian. '"We Prefer Not to Be Fake . . ." Neil Tennant of the Pet Shop Boys Interviewed.' *MOJO* (2013), https://www.mojo4music.com/articles/stories/we-prefer-not-to-be-fake-pet-shop-boys-interviewed/.

Heath, Chris. 'Pet Shop Boys 1984–1986.' *Pet Shop Boys Please/Further Listening 1984–1986* liner notes (2018).
Heath, Chris. 'Pet Shop Boys 1987–1988.' *Pet Shop Boys Actually/Further Listening 1987–1988* liner notes (2018).
Heath, Chris. 'Pet Shop Boys 1988–1989.' *Pet Shop Boys Introspective/Further Listening 1988–1989* liner notes (2018).
'History (1987)', *PetShopBoys.co.uk*, https://www.petshopboys.co.uk/history/1987.
Hulan, Haley. 'Bury Your Gays: History, Usage, and Context.' *McNair Scholars Journal* 21, no. 1 (2017): 17–27.
Jäger, Jan-Niklas. *Factually: Pet Shop Boys in Theorie und Praxis*. Mainz: Ventil, 2019.
Laing, Olivia. 'Lyrical: Neil Tennant.' *Fantastic Man* 34 (2021–2), https://www.fantasticman.com/features/neil-tennant.
Lindores, Mark. 'West End Boys.' *Classic Pop Presents Pet Shop Boys* (2018).
Magnusson, Kristof. *Pet Shop Boys*. Cologne: Kiepenhauer und Witsch, 2021.
Masten, Jeffery. *Queer Philologies: Sex, Language, and Affect in Shakespeare's Time*. Philadelphia: University of Pennsylvania Press, 2016.
Pope, Carole. 'West End Boys.' *The Advocate*, 17 July 2001, https://www.thefreelibrary.com/West+End+Boys.-a076577632.
Raz, Guy. 'All Things Considered.' *NPR*, 9 September 2012, https://www.npr.org/2012/09/09/160750906/pet-shop-boys-leave-west-end-to-explore-elysium.
Russo, Vito. *The Celluloid Closet: Homosexuality in the Movies*. New York: Harper Row, 1995.
Savage, Jon. *Pet Shop Boys Alternative* liner notes (1995).
Sleevage. 'Pet Shop Boys: Yes', *Sleevage* (2010), https://web.archive.org/web/20100103033759/http://sleevage.com/pet-shop-boys-yes/.
Sullivan, Andrew [The Daily Dish]. 'For Hard-Core Petheads: The Tennant Interview in Full.' *The Atlantic*, 5 June 2009, https://www.theatlantic.com/daily-dish/archive/2009/06/for-hard-core-petheads-the-tennant-interview-in-full/200905/.
Tennant, Neil. *One Hundred Lyrics and a Poem: 1979–2016*. London: Faber & Faber, 2018.
Wade, Ian. 'Top 40 Pet Shop Boys Singles: #20: Liberation.' *Classic Pop Presents Pet Shop Boys* (2018).
Wilkinson, David. 'Ever Fallen in Love (with Someone You Shouldn't Have?): Punk, Politics, and Same-Sex Passion.' *Key Words: A Journal of Cultural Materialism* 13 (2015): 57–76.

INDEX

9/11 126–7;
   see also War on Terror

ABBA 228
'Absolutely Fabulous' 257
academia 82, 92, 101
Actually 5, 7, 12–13, 83, 85
   composition of 105
   as imperial album 209–11, 251–2
   queerness in 61
   and socioeconomic critique 103–4, 220
   themes of 251
advertising 216–17
Advocate, The 262
Afghanistan 123
Africa 106
Agenda EP 56–7, 89–90, 218, 246
AIDS, *see* HIV/AIDS
Akhmatova, Anna 134
Alexander, Olly 247
Alexandrov Ensemble (Red Army Choir) 179
'Alone Again (Naturally)' 45
'Always on My Mind' 175, 233
American Psycho 99
Andreas, Peter 253–4
antiziganism 155
Arendt, Hannah 70
Argentina 6
Asher, Jane 59
Atlantic Records 259
Attitude 39, 88, 256–7, 259, 263
Austen, Jane 228
Australia 6

Band Aid 55, 57
Bassey, Shirley 146
Battleship Potemkin 2, 31

BBC Proms 2, 58
Beach Boys, the 230
Beatles, the 148, 157, 176, 228, 231
'Beautiful People' 261
'Before' 63, 260
Before the Act 59–60, 63, 65, 252
Behaviour 55, 61, 92, 253–4, 259, 261
'Being Boring' 13, 254
   as end of imperial phase 234
   and HIV/AIDS 17, 27–8, 61, 77–8, 196, 249
   video 61
Belolo, Henri 165, 172–3
Benjamin, Walter 135
Berkeley, Bishop 168
Berlin 56, 262, 264
Bernstein, Leonard 60
'Best Gay Possible, The' 69
Big Bang 111–12
Bilingual 12–13, 24, 246
   composition of 42
   as 'gay album' 43, 62–3, 259–60, 262
   linguistics of 39, 42, 58, 86–8
   and neoliberalism 86
   as pivotal album 260, 263
bin Laden, Osama 70
Black Monday 113
Blair, Tony 45
   and neoliberalism 85–6
   repeals Section 28 62
   and the 'special relationship' with the United States 25, 56
Blake, George 149
blindness 197
Bliss, Panti 69
Bobcat Records 245
Bonaparte, Napoléon (Napoléon I) 128
Bonaparte, Napoléon François Joseph Charles (Napoléon II) 128

Bond, Jack 2, 189
Boothby, Robert 149
Bowie, David 102, 228
Boy George 2, 217
Brazil 6
Brexit 56–7, 79, 87
Briley, Jack 36
Britishness 4–5, 8, 30, 102, 106, 130
Bronski Beat 257–8
Brown, Gordon 67
Brown, Wendy 80, 82
Bruinvels, Peter 192
Brutalism 121
'Building a Wall' 261
Bush, George W., Jr. 24–5, 45, 56, 86
Bush, Kate 227–8
Butlin's Big Weekenders 227
Buzzcocks, The 123

Cameron, David 50, 58
'Can You Forgive Her?' 13, 22, 39
   and closeted relationships 254–5
   and disco/rock divide 41
   as greatest hit 234
   single cover design 180
   video 177, 254
'Can You Hear the Dawn Break?' 129
Cashman, Michael 59–60
Caton-James, Michael 150
celebrity culture 55–8, 77, 93, 216, 218, 220, 222, 258
Chile 6
Chris (film character) 189, 199, 204, 206
   childhood of 196–7, 200
   living arrangements 195, 200–1, 203, 205
   queer-coding of 201–2
   subverts gender roles 195
Christianity
   abuse within Church 198–9
   biblical references in PSB songs 24, 253
   centrality to British culture and society 194
   criticism of 196–8
   parody of 189
   and sin 247–8
Christie, John Reginald 155
Claptone 235

Clash, the 124
Clause 28, *see* Section 28
Clinton, Bill 85
Clockwork Orange, A 109
Closer to Heaven (theatre production) 2
Cobain, Kurt 124
Cold War 56, 83, 116, 123, 144, 160
   and the collapse of the Soviet Union 166
   and the 'end of history' 117, 182
Colombia 6
Communards, the 149, 257
community 38
   American West as exploratory forerunner for 174
   and belonging 43–4
   critique of 41–3, 45–7, 53, 262–3
   as homogenous entity 36–7
   relationship with 257
   utopianism of 165
contrarianism 210
Costello, Elvis 19
Covid-19 17
Coward, Noël 255
Crying Game, The 2, 145
Culture Club 99
Currie, Edwina 192

Dancing with the Stars 20
Davies, William 82–3, 85, 89
'Delusions of Grandeur' 86
Dench, Judi 59
Deng Xiaoping 95
Depeche Mode 4, 12
Derrida, Jacques 117, 120–1, 126
Diana, Princess of Wales 26–7, 62, 130, 219–20
'Dictator Decides, The' 24
'Did You See Me Coming?' 261–2
disco 171, 259
   backlash against 37–8, 41
   inspiration on *Very* and *Relentless* 254
   PSB's relationship to 3
   queerness inherent in 41, 47, 167
   and sex 116
   style 36–8, 173
Discography 23, 234
'Discoteca' 23–4, 86–8, 134, 259

Disco Tex and His Sex-O-Lettes 260
Discovery tour 6
'DJ Culture' 64–5
'Do They Know It's Christmas?' 55, 57
'Domino Dancing' 12
   homoerotic imagery in 253
   and loss 129
   performed at the Haçienda 175
'Don Juan' 13
'Dreaming of the Queen'
   and Anxiety 26, 129
   and HIV/AIDS 27, 62, 129–30, 254
'Dreamland' 56, 233
Dreamworld: The Greatest Hits Live
   tour 225–6, 232, 235, 237
   as self-positioning 234, 241
du Maurier, Daphne 129
Duran Duran 99
Dust 123, 129
Dylan, Bob 155–6

Eagles, the 231
Earth, Wind & Fire 145
Edgecombe, Johnny 158
'Ego Music' 19
Electric 86, 246
'Electricity' 259–60
Eliot, T. S. 131
Elysium 50, 234
Eminem 260
'End of the World, The' 254
Erasure 149
Ethiopia 57
'Euroboy' 255–6, 263
European Union 43, 56–7, 87, 123
Evans, Elizabeth 79
Evans, Timothy 155

Farrow, Mark 261
Fatboy Slim 49
'Fire Island' 173
Five Star 217
'Flamboyant' 78, 93
'Forgotten Child, The' 89
'Fool on the Hill, The' 176
Foucault, Michel 79, 81–2, 174
Frankie Goes to Hollywood 99
friend of Dorothy 36, 44;
   see also community; queerness

Fry, Stephen 59
Fukuyama, Francis 117, 166, 182
Fundamental 7, 13, 25, 56
   and queerness 44–5

Gabriel, Peter 156
Geldof, Bob 55, 57
Genesis 217
Ghostbox 118
'Give Stupidity a Chance' 57, 89
Glastonbury 225, 237–8
Global Financial Crisis (2008) 82, 86, 88–9
'Go West' 45
   California as target of 171
   as a critique of capitalism 166
   differences between Village People original and PSB cover 35, 41, 174, 178
   as gay anthem 165, 178–9
   and HIV/AIDS 28–9
   inspiration for 179
   performed at London Pride 63
   performed at Olympics 50
   performed by PSB in 1992 175
   single cover design of 180–1
   and Soviet imagery 29, 166, 176–7
   as a turning point in PSB discography 39
   and utopia 166, 173
   video 176–9, 254–5
Gove, Michael 57
Gramsci, Antonio 79–80, 82
greatest hits
   appeal to 'ordinary' and 'momentary' fans 236–7, 240
   definition of 233–4
   as legacy formation 226, 232–4, 238, 240
   negative connotations of 231
   and playlists 232
   as reissues 230
   as self-positioning 235
   success of 230–1
Gordon, Aloysius 'Lucky' 153, 158
Greeley, Horace 168–9
Guthrie, Arlo 155, 162

Hague, Stephen 4, 245
Hall, Stuart 79–80, 82
Hamlet 249
handkerchief code 249
'Happiness is an Option' 44
Harrison, William Henry 168
Harvey, David 80
hauntology 135
  as absence 127–8, 130
  definition of 116–18, 121
  motifs of 118–20, 125
  multidirectionality of 119
  post-punk as example of 125
'Heart' 209, 252
Heath, Chris 8, 18, 21, 25, 115
Heaven (nightclub) 256
'Hell' 70
Heseltine, Michael 110
hip hop 99
Hitler, Adolf 13, 70
HIV/AIDS 13, 22, 62, 115–16, 125–6, 134, 248, 263
  activism and fundraising 27, 46, 63, 68, 175
  as divine punishment 192
  as 'gay plague' 60, 130, 150, 191–2, 194, 257–8
  impact on gay communities 28, 61, 64–5, 71, 150, 182
  prevalence during Thatcher years 104–7, 122, 192, 250
Ho Chi Minh 155
Hodges, Andrew 65
Homestead Act 169–70
homophobia 60–1, 64–5, 69–70, 103, 105
  in music industry 176, 260
homosexuality, *see* queerness
Hong Kong 6
Hotspot 1, 7, 56, 225, 234, 246, 262
'How Can You Expect to Be Taken Seriously' 78
  and criticism of celebrity 19, 55; *see also* celebrity culture
Hudson, Rock 150
Hunt, Gareth 204
Hurtt, Phil 36

'I Get Along' 86
'I Only Want to Be With You' 154
'I Want a Dog' 253
'I Want a Lover' 250
'I Want to Wake Up' 252
'I Wouldn't Normally Do This Kind of Thing' 180, 254–5
'If Love Were All' 255, 263
'I'm With Stupid' 25, 45, 56
Imitation Game, The 65
immigration 45, 56–7, 78, 97, 107, 110
imperial phase 113, 235, 238, 241
  definition of 209–10
  and success 211
  and permission/command interplay 211–12, 215–17, 220
  and self-definition 211–13, 215, 217–18, 220–1
  as periodization 245
'In Denial' 44
'In Private' 154, 261
'In the Navy' 173
'Indefinite Leave to Remain' 45, 78
Inner Sanctum 246
'Integral' 25, 45, 56, 82, 86
intellectualism 20, 22, 30
intersectionality 6–7, 46, 130
Introspective 12, 61, 145, 253, 261
  cover recordings on 175
Iraq War 86;
  see also War on Terror
irony 21, 85, 133, 166, 211, 251
It Couldn't Happen Here (film) 2, 189–91
  journey motif in 195–6, 206–7
  as parallel narrative of Tennant's and Lowe's biographies 195
  as surrealist film 190
'It Couldn't Happen Here' (song) 61–2, 10, 191
  as critique of contemporary Britain 220
  depiction of London's gay clubs in 252
  and HIV/AIDS 252
  as queer parable 196
'It's a Sin' 103, 198
  accusations of plagiarism 217–18
  and Christianity 60, 195, 198
  as gay anthem 5, 247, 260
  and homophobia 61, 77–8, 196

and imperial phase 209
  performed at London Pride 63
  and shame 205–6
  video 175
  writing process for 248
'It's Alright' 25–6, 253
'It Must Be Obvious' 254, 261
Ivanov, Yevgeny 142, 158

'Jack the Lad' 64
Jackson, Michael 128
Jacobsen, Arne 152
Jam, the 156
Japan 6, 31
Jarman, Derek 46, 175
Jefferson, Thomas 170
Jim Crow 171
Joel, Billy 141–4, 148, 157, 160
John, Elton 12, 40, 45, 227, 247
Johnson, Boris 50

Keeler, Christine 142, 147, 149, 152, 160
  as feminist icon 153, 161
  relationships of 156
Kerouac, Jack 173
King, Jonathan 217–18
'King of Rome' 128–9
'King's Cross' 5, 105–6, 220
Kipling, Rudyard 129
Korg MS-10 125
Kraftwerk 4

Labour Party 31, 45, 86, 123–4
  support for LGBTQIA+ education 149–50
  during Profumo affair 158
Lady Gaga 146
Larkin, Philip 148–9
Las Vegas 260
'Last to Die' 23
'Later Tonight' 115, 251, 264
Lawrence, D. H. 148
Lawrence, T. E. 64
'Left to My Own Devices' 23
Lenin, Vladimir Ill'ych 132, 178
Leningrad Cowboys 179
Lennon, John 49
Less than Zero 99

'Liberation' 39, 254
Libya 218
Liverpool 97, 110
'Living in the Past' 70, 182
London (city) 90, 97–9
  pivot toward financialization 96
  shifting geographies of 99–100, 105, 111–12, 124
  and urban decay 104, 107–10, 112
'London' (song) 56, 86
Los Angeles 54, 99, 165
'Love Comes Quickly' 250
'Love etc.' 39, 45–6
'Love is a Bourgeois Construct' 30, 89
Lowe, Chris
  and class 214–15
  decides to cover 'Go West' 176
  defines 'hits' 233
  inspirations of 21–2
  interviewed and reported about in *Smash Hits* 212
  political leanings 51–2
  meets Neil Tennant 3
  opinions about touring 219
  passions and interests of 58, 64
  and sexuality 246, 253, 256–7
  sings 175, 254–5, 259
  stage presence and public persona 53–4, 87, 181, 202, 221, 263
'Luna Park' 23

McColl, Ewan 155, 162
McGuire, Barry 156
McKellen, Ian 59, 63
Macmillan, Dorothy 149
Macmillan, Harold 149–50, 158
Madness 49
Madonna 31, 217
Major, John 62, 130
Man From the Future, A 52, 65–8, 71
Manchester 97
Mandelson, Peter 86
Manifest Destiny 166, 169
masculinity 174, 191, 210
Mason-James, Sylvia 44, 178
MCMLXXXIX tour 6–7
Mercury, Freddie 175
'Metamorphosis' 13, 42–3, 62, 259
Michael, George 49, 229

Milk, Harvey 182
Minnelli, Liza 40, 53, 146
Minogue, Kylie 40, 44, 146, 257, 260
Miramax 151
misogyny 204–5
monarchy 8, 27, 219
'Monkey Business' 234
Morali, Jacques 165, 172–3
Most Incredible Thing, The 2
Murnau, F. W. 249
Musik 2
Mussler, Mark 36
Mussolini, Benito 70
My Beautiful Laundrette 2, 99
'My October Symphony' 132–4
My Robot Friend 19

National Portrait Gallery 152
Neil (film character) 189, 199, 206
  childhood of 196–7, 200
  family of 195, 202–5
neoliberalism 78, 92–3, 95–6, 116, 120, 210
  combative 82–5
  criticism of 219–20
  definitions of 79–81
  as hegemony 122–3
  importance of naming 82
  inequalities of 111–12, 130, 221–2
  normative 82, 85–8
  and Othering 98
  punitive 82, 88–91
  and Third Way politics 88
'Nervously' 254
Netflix 228
New Order 18, 84, 235
New York City 36, 98–9, 172, 260
'New York City Boy' 44, 234, 260
Newcastle 112, 247
'Night I Fell in Love, The' 260
Nightlife 13, 44, 260
Northern Ireland 54–5, 57
Nosferatu 249, 260
nostalgia 20, 40, 235, 238
'Nothing Has Been Proved' 65, 141–2, 154, 157
  lyrics of 159
  as protest song 155–6
  video 147

written by Tennant and Lowe for Dusty Springfield 144–5

O'Connor, Sinéad (Shuhada' Sadaqat) 63, 263
Oliver, Stephen 59
Olympic Games 49–50, 68, 229
'On Social Media' 56, 218
One Direction 49
'One More Chance' 4, 245
'One Thing Leads to Another' 255
'Opportunities (Let's Make Lots of Money)' 250
  and financialization 101–2
  as parody of neoliberal economics 82–3, 85
  queerness in 256
  as a single produced by Bobby O. 4, 103
Orchestral Manoeuvres in the Dark 4
Orlando, Bobby ('Bobby O.') 4, 103, 245–6
Orton, Joe 142, 152
othering 189

'Paninaro' 14, 54, 58
Parlophone 234, 245
Performance tour 23, 53
PETA 19
Philby, Kim 13, 64
Pitchfork 209
Playboy 53
Please 1, 4, 13, 103, 115, 210
  choice of title of 30
  composition of 101, 250
  queerness in 250
Please Please Me 142, 148, 157
Polari 249
pop 99
  connection to post-punk 125
  dismissal as 'disposeable' or 'low culture' 20, 228–9
  importance of 13, 21, 32, 93, 238–9
  PSB's relationship with 3–4, 13
  and politics 92–3
  and sex 61, 115
PopArt: The Hits 234
Pope, Alexander 23–4
'Positive Role Model' 248

post-punk 123–4, 131
'Postscript (I Believe in Ecstasy)' 39, 175, 254
Powell, Enoch 110
Pride festivals and parades 63, 68–9, 262
Profumo, John 65, 121
    addresses House of Commons about affair 147
    denies affair 159
    as enduring political scandal 141–2, 150, 156
    as example of perceived moral decline 159
    secrecy surrounding affair 161–2
    support for 151
Puerto Rico 6
punk 123–4
Pussy Riot 70
Putin, Vladimir 69–71, 182

queer biblical studies/queer theological studies 193, 195, 205
    origins of 190
queer film studies 193–4
queer-coding 41, 246, 259
    definition of 249
    in early PSB 250, 256
    as strategy of 'covert' identification 193
    in synth music 39
queerness 125–6, 246, 258
    and activism 52, 68, 71
    as alternative label to 'gay' 105
    inextricability from PSB music 247
    and joy 42–3, 52
    partial decriminalization of homosexuality in UK 62
    recognition of in music industry 175–6
    and religion 191, 194, 199
    and temporality 40
    tropes and stereotypes of 36–7, 194
    and visibility 261

racism 96–7, 110
    and Brixton/Toxteth riots 107–9
    and civil rights movement 156
    as a complementary component of colonialism 171
    and HIV/AIDS 106–7
    in music industry 176
    as a reaction to cultural diversity 130
    and white flight 165–6
Reagan, Ronald 95, 100, 113, 123, 218
'Red Letter Day, A' 42–3, 260
Release 86, 260
Relentless 254–6
'Rent' 29, 103
    fan interpretations of 7–8
    performed at the Haçienda 175
    and transactional relationships 104, 251
'Requiem in Denim and Leopardskin' 124–5
Rice-Davies, Mandy 142, 147, 159–60
Richter, Gerhard 46, 261
Ritchie Family, the 172
rock
    and authenticity 228, 239
    glam 124
    and neoliberalism 124
    PSB's relationship with 3, 53
    as a vehicle for protest music 155
Rock, Monti III 260
Rolling Stones, the 227
Rose, Axl 19
Rose, Felipe 36
Rough Trade 124
Russia
    'anti-gay propaganda laws' in 70
    Decembrist Revolt (1825) in 132
    espionage 142, 149
    and expansionism 180, 182
    fan base of PSB in 31
    February Revolution (1917) in 132
    homophobia in 69–70
    invasion of Ukraine 77
    October Revolution (1917) in 132
    PSB's relationship with 69–70, 115

St. Elmo's Fire 99
Salt-N-Pepa 176
Salvation Army 247
San Francisco 99, 165
'San Francisco (You've Got Me)' 173
Savage, Jon 13, 53
Scandal 2, 142, 144–5

controversy surrounding production of 150–1
Schröder, Gerhard 85
'Se a Vida É (That's the Way Life Is)' 62, 260
Section 28 4, 59–60, 65, 71, 103, 149, 252, 263
    comparisons with Putin's anti-gay propaganda laws 70
    intended to 'outlaw' homosexuality 192
Seeger, Pete 155, 162
September 11, terror attacks on, *see* 9/11
sex 29, 44, 61, 105, 115–16, 250
'Sexy Northerner' 261
Shakespeare, William 249
'Shameless' 55, 78, 93
Sheffield 97
Shelley, Pete 261
Sherman, Martin 59–60
'Shopping' 12, 79
    and neoliberalism 83–5, 87, 91–2, 220
    and Thatcherite betrayal 104
Shostakovich, Dmitri 132
'Silver Age' 134
'Single-Bilingual' 42–3, 79
    and neoliberalism 82, 87–8, 91–2
    queer-coding in 259
Sloane, P. F. 156
Smash Hits 3, 31, 211–17, 221–2
Smash: The Singles 1985–2020 1
'Sodom and Gomorrah Show, The' 23–4, 44
'So Hard' 253–4
Soft Cell 4, 40, 63, 149, 235
'Some Speculation' 255
Somerville, Jimmy 257–8
'Somewhere' 60, 63
Sondheim, Stephen 60, 63
Soule, John B. L. 168
Sovietism 120, 176–7
    as failure 133, 177
    as mourning a 'lost' future 131
    reappropriated by Putin 182
    as stylistic alternative to capitalism 123
Spandau Ballet 99
Special AKA, The 156
Specials, The 19, 156

Spice Girls 49, 229
Spotify 232
Springfield, Dusty 2, 40, 53, 65, 112–13, 141, 160
    and camp affect 147
    chosen by PSB for collaboration 146, 154
    as gay icon 142, 144, 150, 252, 258–9
    homophobia directed toward 154, 251–2
    inspired by 'West End Girls' 146
    popularity in the 1960s 145, 153–4, 251
    revival of career 142, 154
Springsteen, Bruce 23
Stalin, Joseph 18, 70, 155
Stallone, Sylvester 218
Stevens, Cat (Yusuf Islam) 217
Stewart, Patrick 59
Stoker, Bram 249
Stonewall Equality Show 63, 68
Stonewall Inn 173
Stranger Things 228
Streisand, Barbra 146, 263
Studer, Wayne 27
Studio 54 260
Styrene, Poly 124
'Suburbia' 64, 107, 205, 250
subversiveness 19
Suez Crisis 121
Sullivan, Andrew 248, 258
Summer, Donna 38, 173
Sun, The 257–8
'Sunday Bloody Sunday' 54
Super 90, 246
surveillance state 7, 25, 45, 56, 86, 107
'Survivors, The' 63

Tennant, Neil
    and art 152
    Catholic upbringing 60, 195, 200
    and class 214–15
    coins term 'imperial phase' 209; *see also* imperial phase
    comes out 62, 88, 150, 246–7, 256–7, 264
    contribution to 'gay culture' 39–40, 252–3
    entanglement in neoliberalism 92–3

fan interpretations of 248, 256
fan of Dusty Springfield 154
fears being marginalized 258–9
interest in queer history 64
interest in Russian history 31
interviewed and reported about in *Smash Hits* 212
invited to appear with Cardinal Hume 248
meets Chris Lowe 3
motivations and lyrical principles of 1–3, 29, 263
One Hundred Lyrics and a Poem, 1979–2016 1, 20, 32
political leanings 45, 51–2, 219, 258
opposes covering 'Go West' 176
and particularity regarding collaborative choices 145–6
and political economy 218
pre-PSB musical endeavours 123, 129; *see also* Dust
and public persona 215, 263
schooling 92
speculates about the future of PSB 219
speculation about sexuality 154–5, 254–5
and success 58
tenure at *Smash Hits* 210–11, 219, 251;
  see also Neil (film character)
Thatcher, Margaret
  and anti-immigration 97, 110
  centralizes British economy on London 111
  and economic neoliberalism 22, 83–4, 95, 113, 130, 210
  end of political career 123
  and globalization 96
  and homophobia 70, 149, 192, 250; *see also* Section 28
  named 'Most Very Horrible Thing' by Neil Tennant 220
  reacts against 1960s permissiveness in favour of conservatism 100, 130–1, 149
  and rhetoric of law and order 108
  rise to power of 122
  scepticism of 'society' 112

Thatcher, Mark 220
'This Must Be the Place I Waited Years to Leave' 92, 195, 200
'This Used to Be the Future' 133–5
TikTok 227
'To Speak is a Sin' 260
'To Step Aside' 42
'Tonight is Forever' 250
Top of the Pops 4
transnationalism 6
Trump, Donald J. 22, 24, 57, 69–70, 79, 89
'Try It (I'm in Love With a Married Man)' 261
Turing, Alan 71
  advocated for by PSB 51, 68
  inspiration for Neil Tennant 65
  issued an apology by Prime Minister Gordon Brown 67
  issued a posthumous Royal Pardon 19, 67
  public interest in 50
  and relationship with Christopher Morcom 66
  target of judicial injustice 64
  trial of 66–7
  understanding of sexuality 66, 70
  universal Machine of 65
Turner, Frederick Jackson 166
Turner, Tina 146
'Twenty-Something' 79, 90–1
Twitter 237

U2 57, 71
  accolades 54
  criticism of 18, 54–5
Ukraine 70, 77–8
Ultimate 234
United Kingdom, the 71
  and colonialism 96–7, 101
United States of America, the 115
  Civil War 170–1
  and colonialism 170–1
  and expansionism 167–9, 181
  homophobia in 69, 71, 165, 182
  ideals of democracy 169–70
  image of PSB in 53, 63–4
  PSB's relationship with 25, 69
  relative lack of success in 26
Unity tour 18, 32, 235

Very 31, 41
   composition of 39
   cover design of 180
   as 'gay album' 62, 254–5, 260
   as pivotal album 46
   style 254
Vi Elsker Heroes 227
Victoria & Albert Museum (V&A) 152, 228
View to a Kill, A 99
Village People 28, 35, 40, 46, 170–1, 179, 181
   composition of 36, 165, 172–3
   style 36–8, 47, 172
'Vocal' 86

W Festival 227
Wainwright, Rufus 40, 63
Wall Street 99
Wallis, Dave 130
War on Terror 7, 23
Ward, Stephen 65, 142, 149
   challenges 'baseless rumours' 147
   death of 145, 156, 159
   as focal point of Profumo affair 157–8
   humiliation of 160
   reevaluation of 160–1
Warren, Dianne 40
'Was It Worth It?' 6
'We All Feel Better in the Dark' 53
'We Came From Outer Space' 255
'We Didn't Start the Fire' 141, 148, 160
'We're the Pet Shop Boys' 19
'Wedding in Berlin' 262
Weinstein, Harvey 151
Weinstein, Robert ('Bob') 151
West, Fred 70
'West End Girls' 250
   as beginning of imperial phase 210–11
   as greatest hit 233
   influences on 18
   lockdown version (2020) 5
   and neoliberalism 83, 131–2
   performed at *Before the Act* 59
   performed at the Haçienda 176
   performed at Olympics 49–50

   rerecorded with Stephen Hague 100–1, 245
   and sex 100, 132
   as a single produced by Bobby O. 4, 100, 103, 245
   as a song about New York 98–9
   voted greatest UK number one 2
'What Are We Going To Do About The Rich?' 56, 82, 89, 218
'What Have I Done to Deserve This?' 41, 112–13, 142, 145
   comment on intrusive press 154
   inspired by Kennedys 252
   as a transactional relationship 202–3, 251
'Where the Streets Have No Name (I Can't Take My Eyes Off You)' 19, 55, 175
Whitman, Walt 173
Wigg, George 158
Wilde, Oscar 23, 64–5
'Will-o'-the-Wisp' 262, 264
Williams, Robbie 19
Willis, Alta Sherral ('Allee') 145
Willis, Victor 36, 172
Wilson, Gary 230
Wilson, Sandy 60
Winds of Change 121
Windsor, Barbara 203
'Winner' 50
Winter of Discontent 121–3
Wogan, Terry 4
Woolley, Stephen 144–5
Wotapalava festival 63, 262–3

X, *see* Twitter
x2 246

Years & Years 247
Yes 39, 45, 260
'Yesterday, When I Was Mad' 255
'Y.M.C.A.' 173
'You Only Tell Me You Love Me When You're Drunk' 30, 263
'Your Funny Uncle' 253, 256

Zamyatin, Yevgeny 56